*Number Twenty: The Centennial Series of
The Association of Former Students,
Texas A&M University*

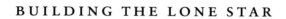

BUILDING THE LONE STAR

BUILDING THE
LONE STAR

*An Illustrated Guide
to Historic Sites*

By T. Lindsay Baker

TEXAS A&M UNIVERSITY PRESS
COLLEGE STATION

Library of Congress Cataloging-in-Publication Data

Baker, T. Lindsay.
  Building the Lone Star.

  Includes bibliographies and index.
    1. Historic sites—Texas—Guide-books. 2. Civil
engineering—Texas—History. 3. Infrastructure
(Economics)—Texas—History. 4. Texas—Description and
travel—1981-   —Guide-books. I. Title.
F387.B348 1986   917.64'0463   86-5860
ISBN 0-89096-289-8

Manufactured in the United States of America
First edition

TO MY FATHER
Garnell A. Baker

Contents

x

A Personal Introduction

This guide to historic engineering works in Texas is more than just a descriptive and historical listing of dams, bridges, waterworks, and highways. Over the past dozen years I have systematically visited, photographed, and documented scores of these sites in Texas, not to mention investigating engineering efforts outside the state. Readers may wonder why some structures appear and others do not. The simple reason is that I have chosen to share the places that I like best.

In selecting the sites, I believe I have chosen a representative sampling. Some of the projects are significant in themselves, like the Galveston Seawall or the High Bridge over the Pecos, but many others are little known and held only local importance when they were built. Today the significance of the latter type lies

The author being introduced to engineering at an early age. Photograph by Garnell A. Baker, ca. 1950, courtesy the photographer.

in their being preserved examples of engineering structures once common but now rare. At one time there were thousands of prefabricated iron truss spans like the East Navidad River Bridge and the Fort Griffin Iron Truss Bridge, but today their numbers are rapidly diminishing and they constitute a threatened historical resource.

I owe my awareness of historic engineering works to my father, a civil engineer. As I grew up in north-central Texas, he regularly exposed me to his impressions of a variety of engineering efforts. In travel he never failed to point out unusual or interesting features of construction projects, water systems, bridges, and railways.

My first remembrance of what I recognized as engineering originates in my early childhood. While I was very young, my parents discovered that I dearly loved to watch "choo choo trains." I must have been like thousands of other little boys, but since my dad worked for the Santa Fe Railway, he was more than pleased. While I was still quite small, my parents would bundle me up and take me in their maroon 1946 Ford down to the main line of the Gulf, Colorado and Santa Fe in Cleburne, my hometown, so that I could watch the regularly scheduled southbound freight at eight o'clock in the evening. This happened during the very last days of steam power, and I took great delight in watching the big black locomotives pull the freight cars across the East Willingham Street crossing. The old wooden motor-car sheds still stand beside that crossing, but the puffing locomotives are gone, long replaced by clean-looking diesels.

A couple of blocks south of the crossing where I watched the freight trains stands one of the structures that I have included in this book, the 1903 Trinity and Brazos Valley Railway Depot and Office Building. It is located across South Border Street from the much-modified 1880s Santa Fe passenger and freight station. The upper floor of the latter was removed in the 1940s, so I do not remember it in its glory, but as a child I wondered about what I thought was "the old depot" across the street. Built two and a half stories tall from red brick and white limestone, it always intrigued me. My first remembrance of this beautiful structure is of visions of steam escaping from pipes protruding from its walls. I was too little to understand that it was no longer a depot, that it had been converted to house a steam laundry. It looked like the stations in my picture books, and I liked it. The only

explanation that would satisfy my questions as to why the train didn't stop there was that the tracks leading to it had been taken up. As I grew older I continued to admire the fine old building, and I wondered what would happen to it after it fell vacant. It was a relief to me when Dan Leach bought it in the mid-1970s and began making efforts to preserve it.

As I grew up, I was fortunate that my parents enjoyed traveling. For as long as I can remember, each summer they took vacation trips either east or west. In addition to these lengthy pleasure trips, the family often drove from Cleburne across West Texas to visit my mother's parents in eastern New Mexico. This meant that we left the Eastern Cross Timbers in Johnson County and progressively crossed the Grand Prairie, Western Cross Timbers, Rolling Plains, and finally the High Plains. The geographical changes were dramatic and left a lasting impression. Along the way on such trips, my father *always* talked about the engineering efforts that we passed.

One of these projects, which is as fresh in my mind today as it was thirty-five years ago, is the 1937–38 Red Brick Road, which at the time was only about ten years old. Our drive westward from Cleburne toward New Mexico frequently took us through Parker and Palo Pinto counties toward Jacksboro, Lubbock, and beyond. This route included the brick-paved segment of U.S. 180 connecting Weatherford and Mineral Wells. We frequently stopped at a roadside park on the north side of the highway to take a short break, and I seemingly always walked over to look at the red bricks so neatly laid in rows to form the roadway. Since Cleburne had no brick streets, this is my first memory of brick pavement.

On another trip, this one only a weekend excursion, my parents took me to see the Alamo in San Antonio. On this trip we also visited the Chinese Sunken Gardens in Brackenridge Park. I remember the exotic plants that I had seen only in Tarzan movies, the swarms of mosquitoes, and the tall chimney that towered over the gardens. My child's mind conceived the idea that in the winter the gardens must somehow be covered with a removable roof and that the chimney served as a furnace that kept the inside warm during cold weather. This could not have been further from actual fact, for the chimney was part of the remains from the 1879 Alamo Portland and Roman Cement Works, the first site described in this book. Two decades would pass before I would understand the sequence of events that converted the cement factory into the botanical gardens I had visited as a child.

From an early age I remember my dad's story of his visit to the Cleburne Waterworks when he was a boy. He related to me vividly how he had taken an elevator down into the ground, where, by the light of incandescent bulbs, he could see the flowing water that was pumped to the surface. The story seemed like science fiction, but every time I walked by the old pumphouse, especially on warm summer evenings when all the lights were on, I would look through the open doorways and wonder if he could really have ridden an elevator down into the ground. Again time would pass before I knew the facts, and when the time came my father's story was confirmed. He had descended on an electric elevator to the base of the pumpwell beneath the building from which Cleburne's water supply was pumped.

While I was growing up, I took at least one trip annually to Galveston to visit with my Aunt Etelka and Uncle B. B. Williams. Since they had no children and my parents had only me, my aunt and uncle spoiled me royally when I went to the coast. Needless to say, I liked the treatment. As readers of this book will quickly learn, Galveston is a treasure trove of historic engineering works. I was exposed to many of these places as a boy, and I automatically assumed that they were just part of what I saw as the exotic way of life in the port city. Since my father worked for the Santa Fe, we always had passes that allowed us to ride the train from Cleburne to Galveston for free. I remember from my early trips to Galveston the combined anticipation and anxiety that I felt when I knew that Galveston Bay was coming and we would have to cross the 1909–12 Galveston Causeway. Looking from the passenger coach windows, it seemed almost as if there were no bridge beneath us as we crossed the bay. I always feared that there would be a derailment and we would all be killed and eaten by the fish.

My aunt and uncle lived on Avenue S, about eight blocks from the beach and the Galveston Seawall. Every morning of each visit, while it was cool, I walked there with one of the Gonzales children from next door. Even now I can remember the hot pavement beneath our bare feet on the way back. For years I never understood how the Galveston Seawall just behind the beach could protect the city from storms, but I slept well each night knowing that it was there. Once or twice my Uncle B. B. tried to explain to me the grade-raising project that accompanied the seawall's construction, but the concepts were too large for my small mind to comprehend. I simply couldn't believe what actually had taken place. Even today it is hard to imagine, as the 1903–11 Galveston Grade Raising is undoubtedly one of the engineering marvels of Texas.

Another attraction for me and the next-door Gonzales children was the nearest of several old coastal fortifications in Galveston. A huge, partially underground World War II artillery emplacement at Fort Crockett was within walking distance. When I first viewed it in the early 1950s, its guns already had been removed and it stood empty. We children took big sheets of corrugated cardboard to the top of the embankment and, carefully avoiding the clumps of prickly pears, "sledded" down the grassy slopes to the bottom. It was great fun. When the sun started getting hot, we would seek shelter in the open, south-facing mouth of the underground chambers, always taking care, since we had admonitions not to go there because of the danger of rattlesnakes. Until now my aunt didn't know that I disregarded her warnings and went inside.

The seawall, grade raising, and fortifications were not the only Galveston engineering works that intrigued me. One that remained an enigma to me for years was the Galveston Jetties. On each visit my aunt and uncle would drive to the extreme east end of the seawall near Fort San Jacinto so that we could watch the ships coming and going through the harbor entrance. Auntie and B. B. seemed to be disappointed when, on each visit, I enjoyed playing around the remains of an abandoned military machine gun emplacement at the end of the seawall. Every time we went there, my aunt and uncle pointed out the jetties, which were clearly visible, but I never could understand what they were or what they did. Their role in preventing sand from clogging the harbor entrance was beyond my comprehension. Years later I came to understand how the jetties operate and to admire the nineteenth-century engineers who dealt with the problems involved in making and keeping Galveston a deep-water port.

Another impression of my childhood visits to the coast was the taste of Galveston drinking water. When I first went there, the only water I had drunk regularly was either from the tap in Cleburne or from the windmill on our farm thirteen miles south at Blum in Hill County. Aunt Etelka explained that in Galveston "our water comes from Alta Loma on the mainland in a pipeline that goes under the bay," adding that "the pipes have been there a long time and leak some, so what you taste is probably seawater." The explanation was not particularly reassuring. Twenty years would pass before I started compiling my file on the Galveston Waterworks, and then I learned that she was not far from the truth. Even today Galveston receives its water supply from the mainland via an 1895 cast-iron influent main that passes beneath the bay.

I also have childhood memories of other engineering works that were closer to home. My first reminiscence of the Waco Suspension Bridge, sixty miles from Cleburne, is of riding across it in an automobile driven by my father. I had no idea at the time that it was a historic structure, other than because of my dad's recollection that his Model A had been "egged" by Waco teenagers as he was crossing it to return to Cleburne from a high-school football game in Waco. But I knew that if the bridge was in use when my dad was going to high school, it "had to be old"; I never dreamed that people had been crossing it since 1869. I have returned to the old suspension bridge frequently, sometimes to take pictures and conduct research but more often simply to enjoy its graceful beauty. I can't seem to stay away from it too long.

In 1965 I graduated from Cleburne High School and that summer started college at Texas Tech in Lubbock. This meant that I would be traveling back and forth the 320 miles between Lubbock and Cleburne pretty regularly. Soon I began stopping to take pictures of the old engineering works that I began noticing. These included water systems, bridges, railway depots, and oil fields. I did this simply because I enjoyed looking at the old relics of the past and thought that it would be worthwhile to record them on film so that I could better remember my visits. I was taking courses in history in Lubbock, and this academic study began allowing me to put the assorted old sites into a semblance of historical perspective. After four years at Texas Tech, I spent a year going to school in Austin. These were my first two semesters in graduate school, and I really had difficulty fitting myself into the routine of advanced study. Among my escapes was getting away to "root around" in the hinterland around Austin and San Antonio "to see what I could find." It was not long before I started finding engineering works.

On one of these trips to San Antonio, I learned that engineering goes back further in Texas history than I had ever imagined. Using Charles W. Ramsdell's guide to San Antonio, I "discovered" the acequias, the Spanish colonial irrigation ditches that for more than two centuries have served the Alamo City. I never imagined that such things could exist. A novice with four years of history survey courses under my belt, I was seeing things like the Espada Dam and Aqueduct, which had been providing irrigation water to small farmers for more than two centuries. None of my teachers had ever mentioned the existence of such things in Texas. In fact, none of them had ever mentioned any historic engineering works at all, other than those built by the Romans in Europe. As I stood in awe beside the two beautiful "Roman" arches that carry the Espada Aqueduct across the flowing water of Piedras Creek, I couldn't help but speculate, "If this is history, it's not like what I've been studying."

In the fall of 1970, I returned to Texas Tech, deciding to cast my lot for graduate study in history with my alma mater. As I completed my first semester, Seymour V. Connor, my major professor, asked me if I would be interested in going to work for a new research program that he and a civil engineer, Joseph E. Minor, were establishing. Called the History of Engineering Program, its purpose was to investigate historic engineering projects throughout the Southwest under contract to government agencies. Today the program is known as the Center for the History of Engineering. Professor Connor knew my interest in old engineering sites as well as in windmills. This combination of interests seemingly fitted me for the program's first contract, a project to identify and document historic water systems in the National Park Service's southwest region.

At the same time that I was hired, the program employed Steven R. Rae, a civil engineering student from Houston. From the outset Steve and I worked together like hand in glove. We identified hundreds of potentially significant historic water systems in six states, created files for each site, and placed pertinent historical and technical data into a computer for search and retrieval. We spent the better part of summer, 1971, visiting and documenting many of the sites we had identified. From the results of our combined library- and fieldwork, with guidance from professors Connor and Minor, we coauthored *Water for the Southwest* (1972).

The initial year at the History of Engineering Program whetted my growing appetite for discovering, visiting, and documenting old engineering projects.

Professor Cliff Keho at the remains of "Samson" windmills at the Post City Windmill Waterworks on the first field trip made by the author and Steven R. Rae for Texas Tech's History of Engineering Program. Photograph by the author, 1971.

On my own time I started ferreting out old mining districts, oil fields, water systems, and highways; carefully photographing their remains; and gathering copies of manuscript data, published reports, and interviews concerning them. While conducting fieldwork for Texas Tech, I started taking photographs of the sites with my own camera to have a personal photographic record of the places I had visited. In time I began assembling my own data files on the sites that I had enjoyed the most. My selection was purely personal and definitely subjective. The sites chosen, many of which appear in this book, are the ones that for one reason or another I personally had enjoyed and felt others might enjoy.

It is impossible to talk about all the engineering sites that I investigated while associated with Texas Tech between 1970 and 1979, but a few of them hold special memories for me. One of these is the 1908–1909 Post City Windmill Waterworks. This was the first historic engineering project that Steve Rae and I documented in the field after going to work for Texas Tech. One warm spring day in 1971, we drove to Post from Lubbock with Prof. Cliff Keho of the Tech civil engineering faculty. Together we chatted with the superintendent of the city water department and then headed up the steep road to the top of the Cap Rock Escarpment west of town. We turned right at the top, drove down a dirt road for a few hundred yards, and then set out on foot to locate the early twentieth-century reservoirs. There we carefully measured the structures, making copious descriptive notes. After photographing the reservoirs, we started back toward the car, when I stopped to look through some rubbish tips at the edge of the escarpment. There to the surprise of everyone I identified the remains of Samson windmills that had been used sixty years before to pump for the waterworks. Professor Keho, lifting up one of the windmill vanes for a photograph, came dangerously close to a rattlesnake bite from a critter curled up in the shade beneath. The encounter taught all of us a lesson in caution that we would thereafter use in the field.

Intermittently over the next nine years I was associated in one capacity or another with the History of Engineering Program, ending up as its manager. The interruptions to my work there came from travel overseas, teaching in Texas Tech's history department, and two years as a Fulbright lecturer in eastern Europe. In the course of this nine-year association, I visited hundreds of historic engineering works throughout the American Southwest, much of the time representing Texas Tech but often visiting the places on my own. During these years I successfully nominated numerous important sites, ranging from water treatment plants to bridges, from mining camps to windmills, to the National Register of Historic Places.

Balmorhea remains prominent in my memory from the first summer of fieldwork with Steve Rae in 1971. I still carry a strong impression of this small, spring-fed irrigation project in Trans-Pecos Texas. It is easy for me to conjure up a mental image of the narrow, rock-lined canal filled with ice-cold springwater that flows parallel to the highway through the dusty little town. This project secures most of its water from a series of springs and it converts the arid, desolate, windswept plain at the foot of the Davis Mountains into an oasis. The place is so beautiful that I return as often as I can.

Almost a decade ago the Texas Section of the American Society of Civil Engineers decided to select historic engineering projects in each of the geographical areas of the state for designation as ASCE state landmarks. Since I was familiar with sites throughout the state, I was asked to make recommendations for the various chapters to consider as "their" landmark. My suggestion for the El Paso chapter was the Franklin Canal, the first large-scale, Anglo-American irri-

gation effort in the El Paso Valley. Few engineering works have exerted more influence on the economic development of a region than has the Franklin Canal. Unfortunately, the project is an eyesore to most El Pasoans. South of downtown it is littered by very undistinguished collections of garbage and trash ranging from beer bottles to discarded tires. Because of its appearance, the El Paso ASCE chapter chose instead to mark downtown's monolithic, concrete Mills Building. Since the local people seem to ignore the historical significance of the Franklin Canal merely because it is unattractive, I hope its inclusion in this book will give it some of the recognition it deserves.

Among the numerous hydroelectric plants that I have visited over the years, the one that left the strongest impression was the Cuero Hydroelectric Plant. Constructed in 1896 and rebuilt several times, the facility ceased operating in 1965. Two local men purchased it from the utility company, keeping all its equipment intact. Wandering through the silent plant was like a visit to the 1920s, the decade in which most of the extant equipment was installed. Everything looked the way it must have sixty years ago; I walked around the big Allis-Chalmers generators, felt the cool, smooth marble at the control panels, and peered down into the pits to see the stilled turbines with the white water rushing around them.

Perhaps the eeriest of all the engineering projects that I have visited is the 1914–15 Humphrey Direct Action Pumping Plant on the Mexican border. The irrigation facility operated ineffectively for a short time before it was abandoned, and since that time it had stood empty in isolated ranch country beside the Rio Grande. It was a foggy morning in late July, 1975, when I met a ranch foreman at an unmarked gate a few miles below Del Rio. He had instructed me on the telephone the afternoon before, "Be at the gate at eight thirty sharp, and I'll meet you and take you to the pump house. Don't be late because I don't have time to waste." To be sure, I reached the gate a little early, and the foreman met me there at the promised eight thirty sharp. Clad in jeans, faded work shirt, work boots, and a tattered hat, he simply could not fathom why I wanted to take pictures of an old pumping station that had never worked.

We rode in his pickup down a ranch road that meandered through rough country until we came in sight of the old facility. There was no one around, and it was perfectly quiet with the last of the fog still hanging in the air. I went about my work of photographing the remains, but I felt I was being watched by the men who sixty years before had erected the buildings and installed the equipment. No place could be more ghostly than the big concrete buildings, vacant and unused for so many years, on the banks of the Rio Grande. The foreman waited patiently while I photographed the structures inside and out, and then he drove me back to the gate and locked it when I left.

Never having lived on the coast, lighthouses have appealed to me in studying Texas historic engineering works. The Gulf Coast boasts a number of fine nineteenth-century light stations, but the 1857 Aransas Pass Lighthouse remains the most prominent in my mind. Two Coast Guardsmen took me to St. Joseph Island in a launch in the summer of 1975. Had I not been in the company of the two uniformed servicemen, the old man who served as the caretaker for the private owners probably would never have permitted me to step from the boat onto the wooden dock. As it was, however, he gave me and the Coast Guardsmen the "Cook's tour" of the entire complex, even allowing us to climb to the top of the circular cast-iron staircase within the brick lighthouse tower. I remain impressed with the reclusive old watchman who lived in the station much like the lighthouse keepers of the past, leaving only once a week in his boat to go to town, buy groceries, and then return to the quiet of a lighthouse accessible only by sea.

Oil Springs, the birthplace of the Texas petroleum industry in 1866, is another place that I never tire of visiting. Since Oil Springs is located deep in the forest, it is very easy to get lost trying to reach the site. More than once I have become "turned around" in efforts to get to the old oil field from various directions. It was so muddy when I went there with local historian James McReynolds that the combined mud and water began seeping in at the bottom of the car doors. Another time I tried to reach Oil Springs via county and logging roads. I got so lost that I simply had to take the best possible course toward the afternoon sun over unmarked county and logging roads until I reached a paved highway and could find out where I was. Oil Springs, however, is extraordinary. Remarkably, the petroleum still oozes to the surface from the casings of some of the oldest oil wells in Texas. A local independent oil operator in the area affirmed to me that he was successfully pumping oil in commercial quantities from one well that he knew dated from the 1880s.

At least partially as a result of my efforts, a number of historic engineering works have been saved for posterity. My favorite among these is a very undistinguished little bridge built across the stream at the bottom of the Yellowhouse Canyon near Lubbock in 1913. When I moved to Lubbock in the mid-1960s, I noticed and photographed the little "bridge," which at that time was little more than a concrete culvert with old iron trusses tacked on as guardrails. I realized that there had to be more to the site than its appearance suggested, but I did little to pursue the story. Then in the early 1970s the City of Lubbock undertook the creation of a series of parks with small lakes scattered down the Yellowhouse Canyon. Though city officials first planned to scrap the culvert, they asked the History of Engineering Program to evaluate it and make recommendations concerning its disposition. In time we learned that the structure was probably the first engineered highway bridge in the entire county. The original construction plans were located in the files of the Austin Bridge Company of Dallas, the contractors for the project sixty years before. Together with civil engineers and my good friend William C. Griggs, we assembled a plan to restore the bridge to its original appearance and make it part of a footpath through the proposed park. The city accepted the recommendations, and in time its crews restored the attractive little Warren truss bridge to its present condition.

In 1979 I left the History of Engineering Program to become a curator at the Panhandle-Plains Historical Museum a hundred miles to the north, in Canyon. The change in employment, however, had no effect on my continued interest in Texas historic engineering works. I have since searched out "new" historic engineering projects, adding them to my files, while I have continued to revisit sites that I know to photograph them again and to record any changes that have taken place. In the course of time a few of my favorites have been lost, such as the 1906 Tin Top Suspension Bridge and the 1886 Calvert Ice, Water, and Electric Plant.

The preparation of this book prompted me to visit several historic engineering works that for one reason or another I had not documented before. Among these are some that I had taken for granted, such as the 1930–31 Copano Bay Causeway. I knew this structure not as a bridge but as the Copano Bay Causeway State Fishing Pier, where I have enjoyed saltwater fishing near Rockport. Another place that I had not documented was the site of the 1901 Lucas

Gusher, the discovery well for the Spindletop Oil Field. I had attempted to find the site of the well before but with no success. Finally I returned to the field in 1983 with David Hartman, the administrator of the Spindletop Museum, and he led me to the spot where the first great oil field west of the Mississippi was discovered.

For most of my life I have enjoyed the remarkable legacy of historic engineering works that past engineers have left for our benefit and pleasure. Back in 1969 I wondered whether the San Antonio acequias constituted legitimate "history," since none of my teachers had talked about such things; I only knew that I found them interesting. My enjoyment of this legacy has grown to the point that I simply cannot pass by a striking old bridge, railroad depot, or waterworks without stopping to look around and take a few photographs. For good or bad, I have now reached the compulsive stage.

The study of these old structures has given me a different perspective on the history of Texas. I now seek out the engineered structures in our built environment and try to understand their role in the society that created them. This study has given me a sincere appreciation for the efforts undertaken by Texans to solve problems with engineering answers. At times it has worked, and other times it hasn't. Some of the immediate fruits of these engineers' efforts are described and discussed in the pages that follow, but the larger fruits of their work may be seen in the development of Texas as we know it today.

Acknowledgments

In more than a dozen years of research on the Texas engineering heritage, hundreds of individuals have come to my aid both in the field and in libraries, archives, and museums. My first debt of gratitude, however, must go to my father, Garnell A. Baker, himself an engineer, for introducing me to these fascinating sites and structures. Had it not been for his enthusiasm, I never would have "caught the bug" for historic engineering projects. Without his insights, shared with me at an early age, undoubtedly my interest would never have been kindled and certainly this book would never have been written.

My active study of historic engineering sites began in late 1970, when I was employed as one of the first field researchers for the History of Engineering Program, now the Center for the History of Engineering, at Texas Tech University. My major professor, Seymour V. Connor, suggested that I apply for a position open in the new program to collaborate in a project with Steven R. Rae, a civil engineering student from Houston. I was chosen, and together the two of us prepared a study of historic water systems in the arid and semiarid Southwest. Steve had been selected by the cofounder of the program, Joseph E. Minor of the Civil Engineering Department. Thus I must thank professors Connor and Minor for believing that I could get the job done. In time I came to value these men both as scholarly advisers and as genuine friends. Their guidance proved to be invaluable.

In giving my thanks, one person at Texas Tech University stands out in my mind above all. Prof. George A. Whetstone of the Civil Engineering Department through the years has been my guide and adviser in interpreting the Texas engineering past. A prominent engineer and author, he has shared my enthusiasm for our legacy of historic engineering projects. He also has been both willing and able to interpret for me, a historian, the technical operation of systems that I probably would never have understood otherwise. After I completed the manuscript for this book, he generously consented to review the entire text with a critical eye, catching most of my glaring mistakes and misinterpretations.

During my association with the History of Engineering Program at Texas Tech during the decade of the 1970s, I worked with a number of people within the university who influenced my research on Texas historic engineering works. Among the faculty members whose shared expertise aided me were the already mentioned Seymour V. Connor, Joseph E. Minor, and George A. Whetstone as well as professors Ernst Kiesling, Jimmy Smith, Cliff Keho, Kishor Metha, James McDonald, and the late Dan Wells, all of the Civil Engineering Department. Among my colleagues at the History of Engineering Program were Steven R. Rae, William C. Griggs, John Moore, Wendell Bell, Lynn Joachim Bell, Don Abbe, Randall D. Henson, Murray Arrowsmith, James D. Carson, William L. Cummiford, Robert C. Williams, and Paul D. Hutchison.

As might be expected, librarians, archivists, and museum curators contributed heavily to the preparation of this study. Most prominently I must thank the staff of the Texas Tech University Library and the Southwest Collection at Texas Tech, where I conducted the bulk of my research in historic engineering journals and in standard Texas history source materials. Particularly helpful were Gloria Lyerla, Frank Temple, Roy Sylvan Dunn, and David Murrah. Likewise, I must give special thanks to Claire Kuehn and Lynne Guy, archivists and librarians at the Panhandle-Plains Historical Museum, Canyon, Texas.

Among the many other librarians, archivists, and curators who gave particular help to me on this project were David Gracy, Michael Dabrishus, and Donaly Brice, Texas State Library; Don Carlton, Barker Texas History Center, Austin; John W. Bullard and Cooper B. Waldsachs, Edward H. White II Museum of Flight Medicine, San Antonio; Ellen Kuniyuki Brown, Texas Collection, Baylor University; Tony Cundick, Kew Bridges Engines Trust and Water Supply Museum, Kew, London, England; W. Maury Darst, Galveston College; L. Tuffly Ellis, Texas State Historical Association; William C. Griggs, Harris County Heritage Society; David Hartman, Spindletop Museum, Beaumont; Mrs. Roland T. Jones, San Antonio Conservation Society; Sharmyn K. Lumdsen, Austin–Travis County Collection, Austin Public Library; Wyvonne Putnam, Navarro County Historical Society, Corsicana; James P. McGuire, Institute of Texan Cultures, San Antonio; Frank Mras, Port Isabel Lighthouse State Historic Site; Laura Geis Olafson, Galveston Historical Foundation; Penelope Graves Reddington, Ellis County Historical Museum and Gallery, Waxahachie; E. F. Smith, Gonzales County Historical Museum; and Joe White and Hyman Laufer, East Texas Oil Museum, Kilgore.

Individuals have been among the most helpful of all in my research into Texas' engineering heritage. Some of these people are the owners or custodians of specific engineering works; others are simply interested in their history and preservation. I would like to give special thanks to the following persons who directly contributed to my preparation of this book: Garnell A. Baker, Cleburne; J. C. Bouse, Jr., Port Bolivar; Lloyd Brown, Jefferson; Fred Burkett, Fort Worth; Clifton Caldwell, Albany; G. M. Canon, Denver, Colorado; Dick Coppedge, Cuero; Bill Droemer and Walter Droemer, Giddings; Jane Dunn, Corsicana; Steve Fildes, Lubbock; Ben Franklin, Kellyville; Donald E. Green, Edmond, Oklahoma; Harry E. Hammer, Missouri-Pacific Railroad, Saint Louis, Missouri; Verna Harris, Bluff Dale; Charles N. Jackson, Burlington Northern Railway, Amarillo; Alton Jones, Regency; Diana B. Kacmar, San Antonio; Dan Leach, Cleburne; J. F. Lynch, Southern Pacific Railroad, Houston; James McReynolds, Chireno; Jack B.

Moore, Abilene; Sam Pinson, Austin Bridge Company, Dallas; Ora Mae Rohan, Gulf Intracoastal Canal Association, Friendswood; J. H. Ryan, Alta Loma; Mardith K. Scheutz, San Antonio; Mrs. Vernon Schuder, Riverside; Cathey J. Simms, Dallas; Robert A. Steinbomer, Austin; and Billie Wolfe, Lubbock.

Because so many of the significant historic engineering works in Texas were built and are owned by municipalities, city officials and employees often have proved to be my most valuable informants on specific projects. I would like to thank particularly Hugh R. Anderson, San Antonio Water Board; Betty Baker, Planning Department, City of Austin; George Cheatham and Owen Holzheuser, Public Works Department, City of Galveston; Dan Clark and Dean Fountain, Parks and Recreation Department, City of Victoria; Ron Darner, Parks Department, City of San Antonio; John Haley, Water Department, City of Cleburne; John T. Hickerson, Raymond G. Clark, and Carroll C. Cason, El Paso Water Public Utilities Public Service Board; Glenn Johnson, mayor, Buffalo Gap; Pete Maddox, Water Department, City of Post; Clifton E. Moore, Electric Utilities Department, City of Austin; Hugh C. Norris, Wastewater Facilities, City of San Antonio; Ernest E. Scholl, Engineering Department, City of San Antonio; Calvin Spacek, city manager, City of Gonzales; Kerry Sweatt, city manager, Harold Green, assistant city manager, and Ray Jackson, Water and Sewer Department, all three of the City of Paris; and R. A. Thompson, Public Works Department, City of Houston.

County employees as well as employees of other government entities also have been more than generous with their assistance to me through the years. Among those of special note have been G. W. Altvater, executive director of the Port of Houston Authority; Janell Briggs, Engineering Department, Harris County; Joel L. Dyer, Galveston County Beach Park Board; and H. Lee Morgan, custodian of Lake Justiceburg. Similarly, several federal officials and employees deserve thanks for their assistance. I would like to mention especially Nicholas J. Blesser, Derek O. Hambly, and Douglas McChristian, all superintendents at the Fort Davis National Historic Site; Kenneth B. Bonham, Public Affairs Office, U.S. Army Corps of Engineers District, Galveston; Charles D. Turner, U.S. Air Force Range Control Officer, Port O'Connor; and W. C. Parker, commander, Port Aransas U.S. Coast Guard Station.

Completing the list of individuals who contributed valuable materials and information to this study are staff members of the Texas State Department of Highways and Public Transportation. These men were able to help me not only with highway-related sites, but also with data on other sites within their jurisdictions. Deserving particular thanks are B. E. Davis, Fort Worth; James R. Evans, Tyler; James M. Jones, Beswick Wray, and Ray Mimms, Corpus Christi; Orville G. Miller, Austin; Jack Skiles, Langtry; Dan Slak, Amarillo; Malcolm L. Steinberg, San Antonio; and Earl F. Wyatt, Yoakum.

In addition to contributing information and materials used in the preparation of this book, a number of people at my request reviewed individual site discussions from the manuscript. These were people who owned the sites or structures, who were familiar with their histories through their own personal research, or who knew about them because their companies or agencies were responsible for their construction or maintenance. Among the people who generously took their time to read through and correct textual material appearing in this book were Winston Atkins, San Jacinto Museum of History, LaPorte; Kenneth B. Bonham, U.S. Army Corps of Engineers District, Galveston; Janell Briggs, Engineering Department, Harris County; BMD John W. Brown, Port O'Connor U.S. Coast Guard Station; Bill Burk, Atchison, Topeka and Santa Fe Railway, Chicago, Illinois; G. M. Canon, Denver, Colorado; Paul H. Carlson, Texas Lutheran College, Seguin; W. Maury Darst, Galveston College; B. E. Davis, Texas Department of Highways and Public Transportation, Fort Worth; James R. Evans, Texas Department of Highways and Public Transportation, Tyler; Donald E. Green, Edmond, Oklahoma; David Hartman, Spindletop Museum; John T. Hickerson, El Paso Water Utilities Public Service Board; Roland S. Jary, Southwestern

Laboratories, Fort Worth; James M. Jones, Texas Department of Highways and Public Transportation, Corpus Christi; Dan Leach, Cleburne; Douglas C. McChristian, Fort Davis National Historic Site; H. J. McKenzie, Tyler; Orville C. Miller, Texas Department of Highways and Public Transportation, Austin; Clifton E. Moore, Electric Utility Department, City of Austin; Michael D. Moore, city manager, City of Cisco; Hugh C. Norris, Wastewater Facilities, City of San Antonio; Richard Ochs, Water Operations, U.S. Bureau of Reclamation, Amarillo; Laura Geis Olafson, Galveston Historical Foundation; J'Nell Pate, Tarrant County Junior College, Fort Worth; W. A. Potter, Texas Department of Highways and Public Transportation, Nederland; Dan Slak, Texas Department of Highways and Public Transportation, Amarillo; Curtis Smith, U.S. Bureau of Reclamation, El Paso; Gerald Smith, Engineering Department, City of Corpus Christi; Harlan J. Smith, director, McDonald Observatory; Elof H. Soderberg, general manager, Lower Colorado River Authority; Malcolm L. Steinberg, Texas Department of Highways and Public Transportation, San Antonio; Robert A. Steinbomer, Austin; Daniel A. Thornton, Eagle Lake; Royce Towns, commissioner, Precinct 3, Gonzales County; August A. Vaughn, Tulia; Donald R. Walker, Texas Tech University; Dallas Williams, Engineering Department, City of Fort Worth; and Earl F. Wyatt, Texas Department of Highways and Public Transportation, Yoakum.

Without the help of all these people and many others, this book certainly would not have appeared in its present form. Instead, it most likely would have gathered dust until my personal papers reached some archival repository only to be filed away and forgotten. I give my most sincere thanks to all the many people who made the study and its publication possible.

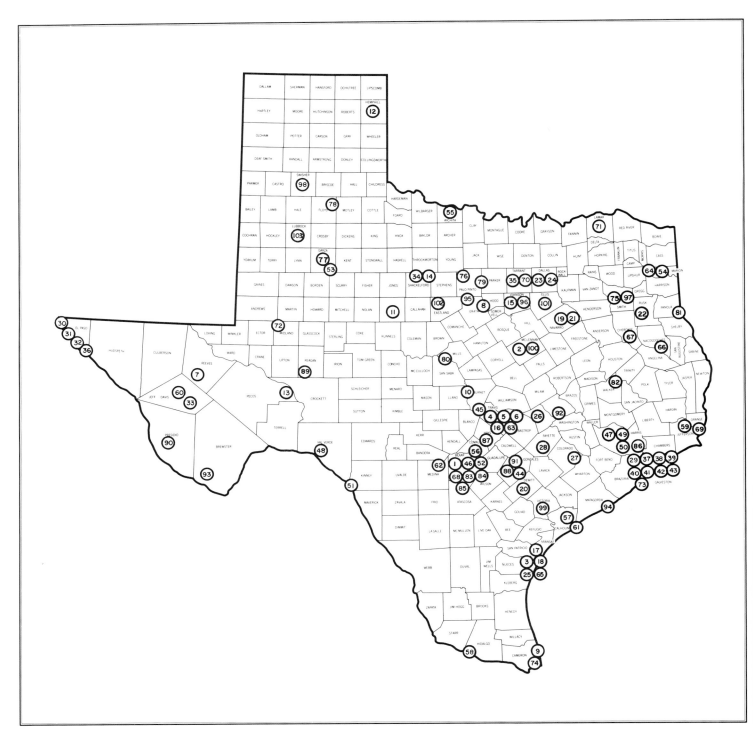

HISTORIC TEXAS ENGINEERING WORKS

BUILDING THE LONE STAR

The former Alamo Portland and Roman Cement Works with its smoke-stack and kilns. Photograph by the author, 1975.

1. Alamo Portland and Roman Cement Works

Established in 1880, the Alamo Portland and Roman Cement Works of San Antonio was the second portland cement works in the United States and the first such factory west of the Mississippi. Its remains today compose the justly famous Sunken Garden of Brackenridge Park and are visited by thousands of flower lovers each year. Most of these visitors never realize the significance in American industrial history of the present-day beauty spot.

In 1879 William Loyd, an Englishman who had had experience in cement manufacture in Britain, went on a hunting excursion on the northern outskirts of San Antonio. There he came upon the city-owned limestone quarries, which were part of the eighteenth-century grant of land from the viceroy of New Spain to the Villa de San Fernando, the original civil settlement at San Antonio. Here much of the stone for the Spanish colonial buildings in the town had been quarried, and the area remained an active quarry through most of the nineteenth century.

Loyd found in the area a blue argillaceous limestone, which he recognized as a possible "cement rock." The stone had the proper proportions of lime and clay to make true portland cement. The Englishman, at the suggestion of local businessmen, sent a specimen to George H. Kalteyer, a chemist who had been involved in experiments with cement rock for the German government. He analyzed the composition of the stone and indicated that it was indeed a natural cement rock. With this information in hand, Loyd and others began experimenting with ways to burn the stone to produce cement.

With the assistance of Kalteyer, Loyd and others organized the Alamo Portland and Roman Cement Company on January 15, 1880, with a capital stock of thirty-one hundred dollars. The city was forbidden by its charter to sell the quarries, so the fledgling company leased them for a five-year period, a lease agreement that would continue for years.

The original mill erected alongside the old quarries was a modest affair. Built of timber, it was equipped with a Blake jaw crusher, a pair of rollers, and a vertical French buhr grinding mill. A small side-valve steam engine with an iron-bound wooden flywheel provided the plant's only power. This initial facility had a capacity for only about ten barrels of cement daily, partly because its owners attempted to follow European practice in grinding burned lime and clay to a fineness that left only a 5 percent residue on a No. 50 cloth. All the product was bolted, and material rejected by the bolt was returned for more grinding. The building stood three stories tall, with the actual crushing and grinding conducted on the ground floor and the upper levels reserved for seasoning the ground cement. There it was spread on the floors six to nine inches deep for curing and then stored in large wooden bins. All fuel was hauled by wagon to the mill, which was three miles from the nearest railroad siding, and the finished product was then hauled to the city in heavy cloth bags.

With coke as fuel, burning at the Alamo Portland and Roman Cement Works consisted of placing limestone in alternate layers. This method required approximately a week for burning a kiln, with the production amounting to about 120 barrels of cement. The limestone after burning was hand sorted, with those portions that had clinkered being used for portland cement and the remainder being used in making a natural cement known as Roman cement.

During its first years of operation, the Alamo plant had a precarious commercial existence, supported in part by the sale of lime also burned in the kilns. The factory was near the county poorhouse, and its promoters were warned jestingly by their friends and associates that when they had finished their business they "wouldn't have far to go."

At first it was difficult for the Alamo firm to introduce its new product, because potential customers doubted its durability. To demonstrate its qualities, the company entered the business of constructing concrete sidewalks in various parts of the city. The newly laid walks were covered with wooden planks, ostensibly to protect their surfaces, but in reality the employees used this ploy to make secret inspections to determine the stability of their product.

The business of the cement company grew slowly, and in 1881 it expanded its plant and opened a new kiln. When sales finally reached a thousand barrels annually, enthusiasm took the place of anxiety. Company officers were able to see their firm as one of the largest cement producers in the country. The capital stock of the firm was increased to $10,000, and its name was changed to the Alamo Cement Company. In the 1880s the firm received $22.50 a ton for portland cement and $18.00 a ton for its Roman cement.

The business progressed, and in 1889 the facilities again were expanded. Soon thereafter a new rotary kiln was purchased and coal was substituted for coke as fuel. In 1901, after the discovery of the Spindletop Oil Field, petroleum replaced coal. By 1907 the demand for concrete had outstripped the capacity of the old cement works. The firm reorganized as the San Antonio Portland Cement Company and erected a new facility at its present location on Nacogdoches Road in the city.

The old cement works and quarries reverted to city administration at the lapse of the lease agreement. For about a decade the site stood vacant as an eyesore in what was becoming the increasingly beautiful Brackenridge Park. With the advent of a commission form of city government in San Antonio, Ray Lambert became the park commissioner in 1915, and he envisioned a greatly altered future for the old quarries and cement plant. Much of the remaining mill structure was pulled down, leaving the kilns and smokestack intact, and the area was proposed for a sunken flower garden. Lambert and park engineer W. S. Delery drew plans, solicited financial aid from local business leaders, and finally used city jail labor in 1917 to convert the former factory site into a garden area at a total expense of only seven thousand dollars. This complex included not only the gardens, complete with Japanese pagoda, but also a "Mexican village" in the kiln area of the former factory, where artisans made pottery and baskets for the tourist trade until the early 1940s.

Park Commissioner Lambert employed a young Japanese couple, Mr. and Mrs. Jingu, to manage the tearoom inside the pagoda, and for more than a quarter century they operated the meeting place in a genial and friendly manner. They successfully served as guides and hosts for thousands of San Antonio visitors who came to see the Japanese Sunken Garden. In July, 1942, during World War II, the lease for the tearoom was issued instead to a Chinese family, and the Jingus were forced from their employment of many years. The name was changed to the Chinese Sunken Garden. Today it is known as the Sunken Garden, and the Jingus are remembered only by older visitors to the park.

At the present time the old Alamo Portland and Roman Cement Works remains are preserved as part of the Sunken Garden complex. Its smokestack is one of the landmarks in Brackenridge Park, and its kilns are still visible at the base of the stack in a landscaped area. The site was marked by the City of San Antonio in 1944, and in 1977 it was placed on the National Register of Historic Places.

Location: The Alamo Portland and Roman Cement Works today is the most prominent portion of the Sunken Garden in Brackenridge Park, perhaps the most beautiful of all the San Antonio city parks. It is adjacent to the San Antonio Zoo and public recreational areas. Parking is available for visitors.

Suggested Reading:

Lesley, Robert W. *History of the Portland Cement Industry in the United States.* Chicago: International Trade Press, 1924.
"The Sunken Garden." Typescript. N.d., 2 lvs. Available at San Antonio Parks Department, Brackenridge Park, San Antonio, Tex.

2. *Amicable Building*

Even today the dominant feature of the Waco skyline is the steel-frame Amicable Building (1910–11), acclaimed in its day as the tallest building in the South. A writer in 1912 described the structure as "a gigantic sentinel on the main thoroughfare in the city . . . a building which has no equal south of Chicago." It was and is an impressive structure.

The idea of erecting such a building on the banks of the Brazos in Waco came from Artemus R. Roberts. Born in Missouri in 1864 and left fatherless at an

The Amicable Building as it now appears. Photograph by the author, 1975.

vide room for the open-air meal, downtown streets were roped off on three sides of the city block where the structure would rise. Tables were set up end-to-end on these streets, and seating was provided for visitors coming from all parts of the state. Hundreds of invited guests arrived in fancy dress to feast on delicacies and to drink to the health of Waco's "first born," the "first skyscraper in the Southwest."

The Amicable Building even today is remarkable. Erected on a steel framework, it stands twenty-two stories. Its height from sidewalk to rooftop is 246 feet and to the top of its flagpole, 303 feet. For many years it supported the broadcast tower of radio station WACO, which gave it a total height of 456 feet, 6 inches, but several years ago the steel tower was removed and replaced by another on the outskirts of the city. Builders used 3,720,000 pounds of steel and a total of 40,085,200 pounds of building materials in general in the construction of the pioneer skyscraper. It required 2,004 railway cars to haul all these materials to Waco.

The structure is one of the best-known architectural landmarks in the state. A story is told that dur-

early age, he suffered from a childhood disease that left him crippled. In 1877 he moved with his mother and sister to Alvarado, Texas, where he went to school.

He later entered the Sam Houston State Normal College in Huntsville, from which he graduated with honors. Roberts began his career as a schoolteacher, but he soon turned his attention to selling life insurance. A biographer notes that he perfected his abilities "not only in the field work, but also in the mathematical intricacies of insurance problems." Eminently successful, in 1909 he and others organized the Amicable Life Insurance Company of Waco with Roberts as its president. One of the provisions in the company charter allowed it to include its projected headquarters building as one million dollars of its assets.

The Amicable Building was constructed between 1910 and 1911. The insurance company celebrated the initiation of the project with a huge banquet, never surpassed in the annals of Waco history. To pro-

The steel water tank being raised for placement in the upper floors of the Amicable Building, March 23, 1911. Photograph courtesy American-Amicable Life Insurance Company, Waco, Texas.

5

Excavating the foundations for the Amicable Building on October 31, 1910. Photograph courtesy American-Amicable Life Insurance Company, Waco, Texas.

ing World War II an instructor at Randolph Field in San Antonio was briefing a group of air corps cadets about to take off on a flight to Dallas. He purportedly directed them, "Fly to the Amicable Building, . . . [and] then take a compass course nine degrees and you'll hit Dallas."

For many years the building was completely self-contained in its daily operations. Not only did it produce its own electricity, but it also had its own artesian well. The building even had its own shallow oil wells across the Bosque River for fueling its steam heating system. At one time the Amicable Building's electric-generation system was powerful enough to have been able to supply half the needs of the entire city of Waco.

The Amicable Building was long the commercial and financial heart of Waco. At one time or another almost every important city development or big business deal passed through its marble corridors to the offices of the dozens of attorneys, investors, or other professionals who once found it the most convenient place to transact their affairs. For decades it was known as "the nerve center of Central Texas."

On March 1, 1965, the Amicable Life Insurance Company merged with the American Life Insurance Company to form the American-Amicable Life Insurance Company. The firm retained its headquarters in the 1911 skyscraper, but changed its name to the Alico Building.

Location: The Amicable Building (now Alico Building) stands at 425 Austin Avenue in the downtown business district of Waco. It is only a short walk down Austin Avenue from the building past City Hall to another famous Waco historic engineering site, the 1869 Waco Suspension Bridge.

Suggested Reading:

Harrison, N. Hillary. "Sketches What Texans and Others Are Doing: Little Stories of Men, Women and Events." *The Texas Magazine* 6, no. 1 (May, 1912): 62–65.

"Waco, Texas—Buildings (Public)—Amicable," vertical file. Texas Collection, Baylor University, Waco, Tex.

3. *Aransas Pass Lighthouse*

Beginning service in 1857 and operating until 1952, the Aransas Pass Lighthouse is the second-oldest surviving lighthouse on the Texas coast. It was constructed by the Lighthouse Board of the U.S. Department of the Treasury, which at the time was responsible for navigational aids, and with the exception of the Civil War years was manned by federal employees for almost a century.

The U.S. government began aiding navigation on the Texas Gulf Coast in 1849 with the positioning of a light ship at Galveston, but other aids were soon added to assist mariners. Among these early efforts were small light towers placed at Point Bolivar and Pass Cavallo and brick lighthouses erected at Point Isabel and Brazos Santiago. In 1854 the Lighthouse Board erected three small screw-pile lighthouses on Galveston Bay, followed in 1857 by a long-needed light at Aransas Pass.

For several years the need for a navigational aid at Aransas Pass had been recognized. Congress, in fact, had authorized the erection of a light there as early as 1851. Consequently, Lt. H. S. Stellwagen was sent to the area to determine the best location for a light station. He recommended placing it at "the small island back of the pass," now known as Harbor Island, where it could serve as both a coastal guide and an aid to vessels crossing between St. Joseph Island and Mustang Island via the Aransas Pass to the protected waters behind the coastal islands. Stellwagen specifi-

cally noted that a light was needed in the area to provide vessels with a "landmark on a coast where there is so much sameness as to make it almost impossible to distinguish one place from another."

Lighthouse Board employees accordingly marked off a twenty-five-acre tract on the low island for the site of the new light. The location, standing only one to two feet above the surrounding water and covered with marsh grasses and black mangrove plants, must not have looked very appealing to the construction workers. Initial work began at the site in 1853, but was not completed until 1857.

The central feature of the complex was a brick tower sixty feet tall and bearing a fourth-order fixed Fresnel lens with lamp. From this location its light could be seen for thirteen miles. The tower was built from red brick provided under contract by a firm in Covington, New Jersey, for twenty dollars per thousand bricks. Octagonal in shape, it stands on a concrete foundation that in turn rests on a base of wooden cribbing and piles. The tower tapered toward the top, which was covered by a metal lantern housing the lens and light. A spiral cast-iron stairway led from the base of the tower to the lantern and provided its sole access from the ground. Its exterior was never painted. The tower was completed and the keeper first exhibited a light from it on July 15, 1857.

During the Civil War the Aransas Pass Lighthouse was used by soldiers from both sides as a vantage

Aransas Pass Light Station on Harbor Island as seen from the Lydia Ann Channel. Photograph by the author, 1975.

Aransas Pass Light Station showing, from left to right, the 1938 keeper's dwelling, the 1928 radio house, the 1916–19 double keepers' dwelling, and the 1857 lighthouse proper. Photograph by the author, 1975.

point for viewing local naval movements. Fearing that it might be used by Union spotters during an expected invasion of Texas, the state's Confederate commander ordered the beacon disabled. Thus, a few days before Christmas, 1862, rebel soldiers entered the tower with a large charge of black powder and blew several feet off the top.

After the close of the war, the Treasury Department Lighthouse Board made several fitful attempts to return the Aransas Pass Light to service, but substantial repair work did not start until February, 1867. At this time the top twenty feet of the brickwork was com-

pletely relaid, and a new metal lantern with fixed lens was installed. During this repair work the area experienced one of the most severe northers on record. The cold was so intense, according to one report, that fish, thrown ashore by the hundreds, froze on the banks, and all varieties of birds sought refuge in the tower and the workers' camp, perishing there in large numbers. Despite the weather problems, the lighthouse was repaired and relighted on the evening of July 15, 1867. It remained in service for the next eighty-five years, guiding shipping along the Texas Gulf Coast and through the pass.

Present-day watchman's hammock swung between the piers beneath the 1916–19 double keepers' dwelling. Shows the masonry base of the lighthouse tower in the background. Photograph by the author, 1975.

Detail of the brickwork and lantern at the top of the Aransas Pass Lighthouse. Photograph by the author, 1975.

The Aransas Pass Lighthouse has had an interesting range of auxiliary structures, most of them quarters for keepers and their assistants. By 1940 it housed four families and included, in addition to the lighthouse proper, a radio fog signal. At least twice the keepers' houses were destroyed by tropical storms, and on one of these occasions the keeper was favorably cited for keeping his light burning under perilous conditions. Today the auxiliary structures at the light station include a double dwelling made from hollow tile, erected between 1916 and 1919; a small frame residence for an assistant lighthouse keeper, con-

structed in 1933; the frame house built in 1938 for the principal lighthouse keeper; a frame radio house and concrete footings for the former radio mast, erected in 1928; the foundations for a 1922 oil storage building; footings for a double privy; and a wharf on the small bayou, which leads to the lighthouse complex from the Lydia Ann Channel. All of the buildings were erected on steel or wooden pilings or on high masonry foundations to place them above the high-water level during tropical storms, and they are connected with each other by elevated wooden walkways. Water at the light station since its founding has been provided by wooden cisterns that collect rainwater runoff from the roofs.

As the years passed and coastal currents continued to deposit sand in the area of the Aransas Pass, the channel between St. Joseph Island and Mustang Island gradually shifted southward away from the old lighthouse. By 1952 this change had altered navigation in the area to such an extent that the Aransas Pass Light no longer was effective as a guide for marine traffic passing between the two islands. Consequently, in that year the light station was abandoned. In 1955 the Coast Guard turned the station over to the General Services Administration, which in time sold it to private owners.

Location: The Aransas Pass Lighthouse is located on Harbor Island facing the Lydia Ann Channel behind St. Joseph Island, approximately one mile north of the town of Port Aransas. The only access to the light station is by water, and as private property it is not accessible to the public. A watchman protects it from intruders.

Suggested Reading:

Holland, Francis R., Jr. *The Aransas Pass Light Station: A History.* Corpus Christi, Tex.: privately printed, 1976.

4. Austin Artesian Well

One of the earliest major efforts at experimental well drilling conducted in the state, the Austin Artesian Well, still flows on the grounds of the Texas State Capitol. It is one of the least known of all the efforts underwritten by state government in water resource development.

In 1857 the Texas legislature passed an act calling

for the boring of an experimental artesian well on the grounds of the capitol in Austin. Johan Peterson, chosen as driller, began his work in April of that year in a spot at "the rear of the State House." Perhaps the legislators selected this location so they could observe their money being spent. After working for a year, Peterson reached a depth of three hundred feet using

Stone grotto and adjacent pool, which are fed by waters from the 1850s Austin Artesian Well, on the southeastern side of the state capitol grounds. Photograph by the author, 1975.

a horse-powered rig. His equipment was what today is termed a cable tool rig, one in which the horse produced the power to lift a heavy iron drill bit suspended from a cable to a prescribed level from which it automatically dropped to pound a hole in the ground.

Work on the well was suspended in April, 1858, until October of the same year, when Peterson resumed his project with new drilling equipment. This was a machine in which a steam engine replaced the horse as the motive power for repeatedly lifting the drill bit. By July 1, 1859, he had reached a depth of 471 feet, by July, 1861, a depth of almost 900 feet, and by early 1862, a depth of 1,160 feet. At this point Peterson's cable broke and he lost his drilling tools in the bottom of the well. Despite strenuous efforts to extract the bit, it never came free and remains at the bottom of the well. The demands on the state treasury during the Civil War years precluded any efforts to remove the broken tools and forced the suspension of further operations at the well site. The exact

date Peterson suspended his work on the well is not known, but we do know that on January 13, 1862, the legislature appropriated $465.88 as the "balance due Johan Peterson on boring [the] well in Capital [sic] Square."

At 323 feet, Johan Peterson had struck a vein of mineral water, which rose to within 40 feet of the surface. Although originally it did not flow at ground level, as he sank the well deeper, Peterson must have struck additional veins of water, for in time a small stream of mineral water did begin to flow at the surface. The state geologist in 1866 reported that the water was "clear and drank [sic] by many persons," some of whom chose it because of its purported healthful qualities and by others, "to be fashionable." Austin citizens were not the sole patrons of the well, however, as the geologist also noted that "cattle and horses are fond of the water, drinking it freely, although there is plenty of other water in the neighboring streams to which they have free access."

The Austin Artesian Well, in fact, became a popular retreat for outings by members of the Austin social elite. An official just after the Civil War recommended planting the area around the well with ornamental trees and shrubs to enhance its natural beauty. The popularity of the capitol grounds for promenades, however, was lessened during the days of Reconstruction by the catcalls and lascivious comments of Union army troops quartered in the area. The Texas secretary of state complained to the troops' superior officer in 1869 that "the soldiers Quartered in the Capitol Grounds on Yesterday evening used most obscene and insulting language within hearing of respectable Ladies passing through the Capitol Yard." He added that "many ladies in Austin would like to visit the Artesian Well morning and evening to drink the water, but are deterred from doing so" by the soldiers' verbal abuses.

The artesian well experiment was not forgotten. On November 25, 1871, the state legislature appropriated eleven thousand dollars to complete the drilling efforts. Two gentlemen named Millican and Steele began on March 20, 1872, to extract the lost drill bit, but all their efforts were to no avail. In the end they abandoned their attempt to continue the experiment.

The well remained unfinished on the capitol grounds even after the old statehouse burned in 1881. When the current capitol was erected between 1883 and 1888, it covered the old well, but its flow was conducted by a special pipe to a location on the southeast side of the grounds. There the water from the 1850s Austin Artesian Well continues to flow to the surface in a stone grotto seen by thousands of visitors annually.

Location: The Austin Artesian Well is actually located under the present state capitol in Austin, although its flow is carried to a small stone grotto on the southeastern side of the capitol grounds.

Suggested Reading:

Brown, Frank. "Annals of Travis County and of the City of Austin." Typescript and manuscript. University of Texas Archives, Austin, Tex.

Buckley, S. B. *A Preliminary Report of the Geological Survey of Texas.* Austin, Tex.: State Gazette, 1866.

Shumard, B. F. "State House Artesian Well at Austin." In *Texas Almanac for 1860,* pp. 161–62. Galveston, Tex.: Richardson & Co., n.d.

5. Austin Dam

Begun in 1890 and completed in 1893, the Austin Dam was acclaimed by its builders as the largest masonry dam in the world across a flowing stream. It stood for seven years until floodwaters in 1900 washed away its center section. Between 1911 and 1915 a second dam, this time of hollow concrete design, was built at the site, but it too was destroyed by successive floods in 1915, 1918, and 1935. The site today is occupied by the Tom Miller Dam, constructed between 1937 and 1939 by the Lower Colorado River Authority (LCRA).

At least as early as the 1880s Austin residents had discussed the construction of a dam across the Colorado River to impound water for both municipal supply and electricity generation. By the end of the decade a genuine movement had grown to promote the plan. In 1888 Mayor A. P. Wooldridge urged the initiation of such a project. In 1889 he was succeeded in office by Mayor John McDonald, who was elected on the issue of building a dam. Only a few months passed before final designs were prepared and a contract issued for construction.

Work began on the Austin Dam on November 5, 1890. The planned masonry structure was 1,275 feet long and an impressive 60 feet high. As work on the project progressed, the builders encountered difficulties stemming from poor foundation conditions and a lack of satisfactory procedures for drilling and grouting the rock. Once the footings were completed, the dam itself was built from rubble masonry faced with cut granite on both upstream and downstream faces. The entire crest of the dam served as its spillway. The main structure was completed and the final stone laid on May 2, 1893. Within a month water was flowing over the crest.

Lake McDonald, the reservoir created by the Austin Dam, became a very popular recreation area for local residents. Large boathouses were built around it, and small steam-powered excursion boats plied its waters. The best known of these was one called the *Ben Hur.* The reservoir, however, never lived up to the expectations of its creators. Although an adequate hydroelectric power station was installed at the east end of the dam, the supply of water was far less than

Construction on the foundations for the Austin Dam in 1891. Photograph courtesy Austin–Travis County Collection, Austin Public Library, Austin, Texas.

had been expected by the planners. Often there was insufficient flow to generate enough electricity for even the limited use planned for illuminating the streets, operating street railways, and supplying a small number of consumers. Compounding this problem was that of silting. The reservoir became filled with silt deposits amazingly quickly. In its first seven years, silt reduced the capacity of Lake McDonald from 49,300 acre feet to only 25,741 acre feet.

On April 7, 1900, however, the great dam across the Colorado River failed. The spectacular scene is probably best described in the words of an observer who witnessed it:

I was gazing intently at the great body of water as it swept gracefully over the crest of the dam, carrying with it acres of drift that parted as it went down the falls. The water over the crest was more than 10 ft. in depth, and was rising at the rate of 18 ins. an hour. The fall of the water was about 40 ft., and the roaring and surging that it produced can be better imagined than described. It was grand and awe-inspiring, and nothing in my opinion could in any measure compare with it, except the falls of Niagara.

While thus gazing with awe on a site such as I had never before witnessed, I noticed a sudden commotion of the waters near the center of the

View along the crest of the Austin Dam as it passes high water safely during the 1890s. In the foreground are the penstocks for the yet-to-be-constructed powerhouse. Photograph courtesy Austin–Travis County Collection, Austin Public Library, Austin, Texas.

The Austin Dam shortly after its destruction by floodwaters on April 7, 1900. Photograph courtesy Austin–Travis County Collection, Austin Public Library, Austin, Texas.

dam. For a moment the water where the commotion occured seemed to recede, but it was only for a moment. It then shot upward in a tremendous spout to a height of perhaps 50 ft. as if in gleeful fury, and I saw that the dam was giving way. The commotion spread toward the east end of the dam, and there was a trembling of the earth. The mighty waters roared and plunged with an indescribable fury, and the river, which a moment before had presented a scene of graceful grandeur as it curved over the dam, was turned into a seething maelstrom, so awful and so terrible that nothing save the pen of a Dante or a Byron could do it justice.

I was appalled and entranced. My feelings were such as I had never before and never again hope to experience. Suddenly above the dismal roar of the surging[,] raging waters came a cry, "The dam is breaking, the dam is breaking." The sound of the cry was so dismal as that of the maelstrom, and people shuddered and their blood seemed chilled, although the sun shone warmly from a cloudless sky. When the break occurred the distance from the crest of the wave as it rolled over the dam to the water below was about 40 ft. Imagine, then, if you can, a body of water 40 ft. in height and of great width and length suddenly released from confinement, and you will have a faint idea of the scene that I witnessed at the great dam across the Colorado River yesterday morning, a few minutes before 11 o'clock. It was a scene that beggars all description, and as the waters plunged and roared and seethed and foamed they seemed to laugh in utter scorn at the futile attempts of man to bridle them.

When the break occurred seven men and two boys were at work in the lower story [of the powerhouse] and the first intimation they had that danger was near was by the rush of water into the

building. One of the men rose with the deluge and by a lucky chance struck an opening, through which he made his escape, being pulled from the water more dead than alive. Another was caught by a water spout produced by the rush of waters into the building and shot up through another opening, and he, too, was saved, as if by a miracle. The others were caught in a death trap and perished in the room where they were at work. . . . The water swirled around the building and then subsided almost as suddenly as it came. . . .

Once released from its confinement the water subsided rapidly, seeking a level with that below the dam, and it was then seen how the break had occurred. The dam was not toppled over, as many supposed it would be, but instead a large section, beginning near the center and extending toward the east bank, was moved bodily down the stream a distance of at least 40 ft. Another section, extending to within 30 ft. of the head-gate masonry [at the powerhouse] on the east end, was also moved down stream a distance of 40 or 50 ft. . . . It was not long before the section nearest the center also crumbled and disappeared. Had the remaining displaced section also tumbled down, the power house, which went down a few hours later, would probably have been saved. As it was, this section threw a heavy current against the power house, which eventually undermined the west wall of the building and caused it to collapse.

The Austin Dam remained in shambles for over a decade. The City of Austin did not have the means to undertake any major reconstruction, so the ruins stood as if in mockery of the puny efforts of humans to harness the Colorado. Finally, on July 29, 1911, the city signed a contract with William D. Johnson to

The 1937–39 Tom Miller Dam, built by the Lower Colorado River Authority at the site of the ill-fated 1893 and 1915 dams. Photograph by Steven R. Rae, 1971, courtesy Center for the History of Engineering, Texas Tech University, Lubbock, Texas.

rebuild the dam with a modified design that would incorporate some of the remaining portions of the structure. Under the agreement Johnson would be able to operate the rebuilt facility for the generation of electricity for a period of twenty-five years and then sell it to the city. According to Johnson's plans, the dam was reconstructed five feet higher than its original crest and was fitted with new headgate masonry, gates, flumes, turbines, generators, and tailrace.

With the work nearly complete in 1915, the dam was damaged by flooding, but the damage was repaired. This should have indicated design problems, but seemingly such dangers were ignored. The new structure was severely damaged again only a short time later, in September, 1915. Twenty-four of the new crest gates were carried away, the powerhouse tailrace was filled with debris, and the draft tubes to the powerhouse were blocked. The rebuilt but damaged dam and powerhouse stood abandoned for the next three years. Then in April, 1918, high water

further damaged the gate areas, and finally in June, 1935, yet another flood washed away most of the remaining gates and gate piers and destroyed a portion of the concrete spillway.

In 1937 the LCRA acquired the ill-fated site and for the first time constructed an adequate dam across the Colorado River at Austin. The present Tom Miller Dam has a 1,590-foot length composed of a gravity overflow section, a rebuilt hollow concrete dam with gated spillway, earth and rockfill sections, and a hydroelectric-generation station. Its maximum height is 100 feet from the riverbed to the top of the bridge across the spillway. The present reservoir, known as Lake Austin, has a capacity of 21,000 acre feet and a surface area of 1,830 acres. The reservoir is operated by the LCRA at an almost constant level to provide water to its hydroelectric plant. This station operates in coordination with the discharge from the turbines of the Marshall Ford power plant at Mansfield Dam, twenty-one miles upstream.

Location: The Tom Miller Dam, site of the two unsuccessful dams, is located across the Colorado River upstream from downtown Austin. It is most easily reached by taking Enfield Road to its intersection with Lake Austin Boulevard, from which point the dam can easily be seen just to the southwest. A paved road crosses the river just below the dam, giving additional good vantage points.

Suggested Reading:

"The Failure of the Austin Dam." *Engineering News* 43, no. 16 (April 19, 1900): 250–54.

"Hollow Reinforced-Concrete Structure Replaces Dam at Austin, Texas, Which Failed Fifteen Years Ago." *Engineering Record* 71, no. 22 (May 29, 1915): 672–73; no. 23 (June 5, 1915): 707–709; no. 24 (June 12, 1915): 750–51.

Taylor, Thomas U. *The Austin Dam.* U.S., Department of the Interior, Geological Survey, Water-Supply and Irrigation Paper No. 60. Washington, D.C.: Government Printing Office, 1900.

6. Austin "Moonlight" Tower Street Lighting System

Erected between 1894 and 1895, the Austin "Moonlight" Towers for ninety years have illuminated the streets of Texas' capital city. The towers represent the last-known surviving remnants in the United States of a street lighting scheme that was popular in the mid-1890s.

With the completion of the Austin Dam on the Colorado River in 1893, the treasury of the City of Austin was short on funds. The City Council, however, had promised the citizens that the new municipal dam would provide water power for a hydroelectric plant that would generate electricity to light the city and to operate a system of street railways. During the building of the dam, the city had put into use a narrow-gauge railroad line to carry supplies and equipment to the construction site. This railway line was no longer needed, so the municipal administration was able to make an agreement with the firm installing the hydroelectric equipment at the dam to trade them the railway line, which they would remove, in exchange for part of the cost for erecting a system of street lighting and for the dynamos at the dam.

Although the street lighting system built for Austin was a type in vogue at that time, it is considered unusual by modern standards. The Fort Wayne Electric Company of Fort Wayne, Indiana, erected a series of thirty-one wrought- and cast-iron towers throughout the city. The trussed towers were 150 feet tall and were mounted on 15-foot wrought-iron bases, for a

One of the "Moonlight" Towers as it appeared in 1897. Photograph courtesy Austin–Travis County Collection, Austin Public Library, Austin, Texas.

The "Moonlight" Tower at West Forty-first and Speedway. Photograph, 1975, courtesy Center for the History of Engineering, Texas Tech University, Lubbock, Texas.

total height of 165 feet. Unable to stand on their own, the towers were supported by heavy steel-cable guy wires. The trussed wrought-iron members gave the towers an appearance somewhat like that of oil derricks mounted on monopod bases. At the tops of the towers the construction crews installed groups of carbon arc lamps. According to the original contract of March 20, 1894, the towers were to emit a circle of light 3,000 feet in diameter, sufficiently bright so that the time could be read on an average watch on the darkest night. Work progressed on the towers from spring, 1894 and spring, 1985. The lamps were first lighted on the evening of May 6.

The Austin Moonlight Towers illuminated the city for their first forty years using the old-style carbon arc lamps. These lamps required nightly attention by city employees, who rode in buggies from tower to tower. These men reached the tops of the towers by way of special hand-operated elevators, which ran up the centers of the towers to give access to the lamps. In 1936 the carbon arc lamps were replaced by groups of six mercury vapor lamps atop each tower. These bulbs did not produce as much light, but they could be controlled by a switch at the base of each tower. A centralized control system for the towers was installed in 1942, when it was believed that a war emergency might require that the entire city be blacked out.

Through the years several of the Moonlight Towers have been lost. Two, for instance, were destroyed when they were struck by motor vehicles in the 1940s. There were no injuries in either instance, but both towers were damaged beyond repair. Corrosion and general deterioration have combined to force the removal of a few others. Increasing maintenance problems during the 1950s caused city officials to consider replacing the entire system with more ordinary street lights.

In the 1960s and 1970s, the aging Moonlight Towers were saved by the people they had served for so many years. When in 1964 the city attempted to take away one of the "unsafe" towers, the residents of Austin reacted by petitioning the City Council to return it. Realizing the popularity of the towers, the municipal administration in 1967 erected a new Moonlight Tower, patterned after the 1894 originals, in Zilker Park. In 1970 the tower at West Ninth and Guadalupe streets was honored with a historical marker from the Texas Historical Commission. This action was followed in 1975 by a recommendation from the Austin Historic Landmark Commission that fifteen of the surviving towers be given historic landmark status and thus protection by the city. Soon thereafter the tower lighting system was recognized by its acceptance into the National Register of Historic Places.

Today most of the Austin Moonlight Towers remain in service, illuminating the city. They are the last survivors of a once-popular system of street lighting. The pride of many Austin residents, they are truly one of the landmarks of the capital city.

Location: The Moonlight Towers are scattered throughout the older neighborhoods of Austin. The following locations are for the fourteen towers surviving of the fifteen given historic landmark status by the City of Austin in 1975: Canterbury and Lynn streets; City Park; East Eleventh and Lydia streets; East Eleventh and Trinity streets; Leland Street and East Side Drive; Pennsylvania and Leona streets; West Fourth and Nueces streets; West Ninth and Guada-

lupe streets (with historical marker); West Twelfth and Blanco streets; West Twelfth and Rio Grande streets; West Fifteenth and San Antonio streets; West Twenty-second and Nueces streets; West Forty-first Street and Speedway; Zilker Park (tower installed in 1967).

Suggested Reading:

Austin, City of. Historic Landmark Commission. Minutes, May 27, 1975. Typescript. City Hall, Austin, Tex.
"The Tower System of Electric Lighting." *Engineering News* 33, no. 5 (January 31, 1895): 72.

7. *Balmorhea Irrigation Project*

The Balmorhea Irrigation Project, dating from the late 1860s, in Reeves County is one of the few large, spring-fed irrigation systems in Texas; additionally, it is one of the handful of irrigation projects in the state to have received aid from the U.S. Bureau of Reclamation.

Indians in prehistoric times practiced irrigation with springwater flowing into Toyah Creek, and recorded irrigation in the area started about 1869. At that time waters were diverted from the stream into the Saragosa Ditch to irrigate fields of vegetables and feed crops raised to be sold to the U.S. Army post at Fort Davis, about thirty miles to the south. During

the next decade other canals were opened along Toyah Creek, the most prominent of them being the Murphy Ditch, about 1871. Through the 1870s, 1880s, and 1890s irrigation with springwaters from Toyah Creek expanded as farmers produced increasing amounts of alfalfa and other feed crops for a growing regional cattle industry.

The source of water for the irrigation along Toyah Creek consists almost exclusively of springwaters originating from the San Solomon and other springs, which come to the surface in a flat valley hemmed in by a horseshoe curve in the Davis Mountains. The springwater supply is occasionally supplemented by

Balmorhea Lake viewed from the Renz Dike. Water is stored in the reservoir until it is needed for irrigation purposes. Photograph by the author, 1981.

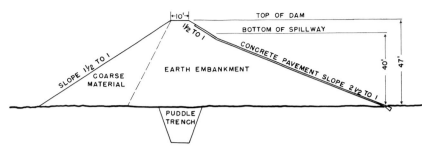

Cross-section of the highest point of the 1917 main dam, which impounds spring water and storm water to form Balmorhea Lake. Based on Vernon L. Sullivan, "Construction Methods Used in Building the Lower Reservoir of the Balmorhea Project," *Transactions of the American Society of Civil Engineers* 83, no. 1430 (1919–20): 313. Drawing by the author.

storm waters, principally from Madera Creek. Before any of the water resources were developed for irrigation, Toyah Creek flowed thirty-five miles to the northeast into Toyah Lake, a large natural alkali flat about five miles south of present-day Pecos.

By the turn of the century the irrigation system created along Toyah Creek consisted of five separate canals: (1) the Murphy or Clements Ditch, nine miles long, beginning at the south side of the San Solomon Springs and irrigating about fifteen hundred acres; (2) the Giffin Ditch, a mile long, originating at the Giffin Spring just north of the San Solomon Springs and irrigating about four hundred acres; (3) the Saragosa Ditch, two miles long, taken out on the north side of Toyah Creek about six miles below the San Solomon Springs and irrigating about fifteen hundred acres; (4) the St. Isabella Ditch, two miles long, starting on the north side of the creek about nineteen miles below the springs and irrigating about seven hundred acres; and finally (5) the Pruett Ditch, two miles long, taking its water from the south side of the creek twenty-six miles below the springs and irrigating about three hundred acres.

Development of the Toyah Creek valley increased substantially about 1906, when three land promoters named Balcolm, Morrow, and Rhea acquired fourteen thousand acres of supposedly irrigable land along the creek and began selling it to farmers. In the meantime, they laid out a new town, which they called Balmorhea, a name created from the first letters of their names. The town today is the commercial center of the agricultural district. Expansion reached its peak in 1909, when the irrigated area exceeded that for which water was available. The local irrigators organized themselves in 1914 as the Reeves County Irrigation District, which in 1917 became the Reeves County Water Improvement District No. 1.

To store excess water until it was needed for irrigation, the Reeves County Water Improvement District in 1917 constructed a still-operating dam and levee that created Lake Balmorhea, also known as the Lower Park Reservoir. The project also included the construction of a reinforced concrete diversion dam on Madera Creek, known as the Madera Diversion Dam. This five-hundred-foot structure diverted water into an inlet canal 2.8 miles long and leading to the actual storage reservoir. The reservoir itself was created by a thirty-nine-hundred-foot-long, forty-six-foot-high earthen dam combined with an earthen levee known as the Renz Dike. The water district at this time also constructed an outlet canal 2.5 miles long to connect the storage reservoir with the main canal on the south side of Toyah Creek.

The most interesting engineering aspect of the Balmorhea Project is the design and construction of the main dam at Balmorhea Lake. The structure was noted in engineering circles in its day for its economy of construction. Before work began on the project, the builders excavated a small ditch from Toyah Creek to the damsite to supply water for construction purposes. This water was used mainly for puddling a clay cut-off wall beneath the main dam structure, for soaking the various layers of earth to settle them as they were placed in position to form the dam, and to use in mixing concrete for the protective face of the structure.

The cut-off trench beneath the entire length of the dam was excavated by a steam dragline. It was dug as deep as twenty feet and varied in width from ten to forty feet. As soon as a section of the cut-off trench was excavated, a temporary clay dam was placed across its end and it was filled with water from the supply ditch. Selected clay then was gradually pushed into the water-filled trench from one end, making a complete puddle of the clay without having to mix it further. This was a very economical procedure.

As soon as the clay cut-off wall was completed, twenty-six dump wagons went to work moving earth into position to form the aboveground portion of the dam. They built the earthen embankment in layers three to four feet thick, each layer being flooded with water. Enough water was placed on each layer to

Stone- and concrete-lined canal carrying spring irrigation water through the heart of Balmorhea. Photograph by the author, 1981.

cause it to unite thoroughly with the moisture in the layer beneath so that the builders obtained a complete and uniform settlement of the earth.

After the earthen portion of the Balmorhea Dam was completed, the builders began laying a concrete facing on its upstream side to protect it from erosive wave action and from the effects of burrowing animals. After a concrete toe was laid at the base of the dam to serve as a footing for the facing, six-foot-wide strips were placed on the face of the dam to within two feet of its top. The slabs were laid alternately, and the entire concrete surface was reinforced by heavy wire netting. Two-inch step joints ran the entire length of the slabs. Through the combination of heavy wire netting reinforcement with step-type expansion joints, the surface of the paving was satisfactorily re-

inforced while it remained sufficiently flexible to withstand normal expansion and contraction of the concrete facing.

Employing the structures basically as described here, the Balmorhea Irrigation Project operated from the teens into the 1940s. During World War II, when food supplies became critical, the water district asked the U.S. Bureau of Reclamation to assist it in improving the water supply of the Balmorhea Project. Subsequent investigations showed that this could be done within a relatively short time and without requiring the use of large quantities of strategic materials. President Roosevelt authorized the improvement project on April 15, 1944, but work did not begin until June 19, 1946. At this time the Bureau of Reclamation began reconstructing selected portions of the Balmorhea system. It purchased the Phantom Lake Springs; constructed the Phantom Lake Canal, which carries water from the springs to the main canal near the San Solomon Springs; built the inlet feeder canal, which conveys spring flow from the main canal to Balmorhea Lake; and rehabilitated the Madera Diversion Dam on Madera Creek to divert storm waters into the reservoir. Much of the work consisted of placing concrete linings in portions of the two canals.

After the completion of the bureau improvements at the Balmorhea Project, the acreages irrigated did increase. With the passage of time, however, the flow from the springs has decreased, at least partly as the result of wells having been drilled in their vicinity. Despite the decreasing springwater supply, however, irrigated acreage in the Balmorhea system has remained in the thousands of acres, principally because of improved and enlightened use of the available water resources.

Location: The most convenient access to the dam and levee structures at Balmorhea Lake is by way of the paved extension of Houston Street, approximately 1.5 miles southeast of Balmorhea. The San Solomon Springs, the largest of all the springs feeding irriga-

tion water into the Balmorhea Project, are located within the Balmorhea State Recreation Area at Toyahvale, 4.4 miles southwest of Balmorhea on U.S. 290. The park is noted for its huge swimming pool, which incorporates the total flow of the San Solomon Springs. The park is open year round, with the swimming area open during the warm months of the year. The beautiful, tree-shaded area is an oasis in the desert.

Suggested Reading:

Sullivan, Vernon L. "Construction Methods Used in Building the Lower Reservoir Dam of the Balmorhea Project." *Transactions of the American Society of Civil Engineers* 83, no. 1430 (1919–20): 305–15.

Taylor, Thomas U. *Irrigation Systems of Texas.* U.S., Department of the Interior, Geological Survey, Water-Supply and Irrigation Paper No. 71. Washington, D.C.: Government Printing Office, 1902.

U.S. Department of the Interior. Water and Power Resources Service. *Water and Power Resources Service Project Data 1981.* Washington, D.C.: Government Printing Office, 1981.

8. *Bluff Dale Suspension Bridge*

The Bluff Dale Suspension Bridge, erected in 1890, is a classic example of the type of small suspension bridges erected on rural roads in Texas at the end of the nineteenth century. Moved from its original location to its present site in 1934, the structure remains in service as part of the Erath County road system.

The vicinity around Bluff Dale, a small community on the Paluxy River, was settled in the early 1870s. The town's history begins in 1889 when the Fort Worth and Rio Grande Railroad built through the area and placed a siding on land that had been donated by Jack Glenn for a town site. Because of its location near bluffs on the Paluxy, the town came to be called Bluff Dale. Soon it became a livestock shipping point on the railway for local ranchers.

The greatest impediment to the development of Bluff Dale was the lack of a bridge across the Paluxy. For a number of months local residents discussed the need for a bridge to provide them with communication eastward into Hood County. They genuinely felt that the lack of a bridge was retarding the economy in their part of the county.

In March, 1890, the Commissioners' Court of Erath County signed a contract with the Runyon Bridge Company, a partnership of E. E. Runyon with William Flinn, for the construction of three bridges across the Bosque River. Later in the year a fourth bridge was contracted for at Bluff Dale, spanning the Paluxy. According to the minutes of the Commissioners' Court meetings, this fourth structure was completed and accepted by the county on January 5, 1891. On this date the commissioners instructed the county treasurer to pay the Runyon Bridge Company "$3357.50 balance due said company on the contract of said company with Erath County for building of four bridges in the year 1890." Later in 1891, the county contracted with the Cunningham Bridge Company of Palo Pinto County, Texas, to build another bridge across the Paluxy west of Bluff Dale, but this structure should not be confused with the suspension bridge built on the east side of the community.

The Bluff Dale Suspension Bridge remained the principal crossing of the Paluxy River in eastern Erath County for more than forty years. When the graded

Looking south along the roadway of the Bluff Dale Bridge toward the village of Bluff Dale. Photograph by the author, 1983.

road between Stephenville and Granbury through Bluff Dale was designated State Route 10 in 1922, all of its traffic passed over the 1890 bridge. This continued for over a decade, until a new concrete bridge was constructed just downstream from the old suspension span in 1933. This is the site of the present-day U.S. 377 crossing.

About a mile and a half upstream, on the north side of Bluff Dale, a bridge was sorely needed by residents along the Berry's Creek Road, a graded road that leads northward from the community on the top of a divide west of Berry's Creek. The citizens in this area asked the county commissioners if the old bridge might be moved to give them convenient all-weather access across the Paluxy into Bluff Dale. Accordingly, in 1934 the county commissioners contracted Lee

Lewis to disassemble the suspension bridge and re-erect it at the new site. Work progressed through the spring of 1934, and by the time hot weather came, the bridge was back in use. It has remained in service there for more than fifty years.

As rebuilt in 1934, the Bluff Dale Bridge has a 140-foot suspension span combined with a 50-foot north approach and a 77-foot south approach. This gives it a total length of 267 feet. According to oral tradition, 25 feet was added to each approach at the time the bridge was rebuilt. Seven 7/8-inch steel cables on either side support the 10-foot, 4-inch-wide roadway. In March, 1983, county crews replaced the old wooden decking of the bridge with a heavy sheet steel surface to reduce maintenance costs. The towers supporting the cables consist of a 9-inch iron pipe on either side

County crew replacing the decking on the roadway of the Bluff Dale Suspension Bridge in March, 1983. Photograph by the author, 1983.

at each end of the suspension span and fitted with special cast-iron saddles to receive the cables. These towers extend approximately 12 feet above the roadway and support the bridge approximately 28 feet above low water in the Paluxy beneath.

Fortunately, the Bluff Dale Suspension Bridge has been recognized for its significance as a rare surviving example of a once-common bridge form. In the 1970s it received a historical marker from the Texas Historical Commission as well as listing in the National Register of Historic Places.

Location: The Bluff Dale Suspension Bridge spans the Paluxy River about seven hundred feet north of U.S. 377 in the Bluff Dale community. To reach the bridge, turn north from U.S. 377 on the first paved road west of the intersection of U.S. 377 with FM 3106. The turn-off is marked by signs that read "Berry Creek Rd." and "Historical Marker 700 Feet."

Suggested Reading:

Erath County, Tex. Commissioners' Court. Minutes, vol. E, pp. 88, 90, 101–102, 103, 152, 203. Regional Historical Records Depository, University Library, Tarleton State University, Stephenville, Tex.

Harris, Verna. "Bluff Dale Suspension Bridge." Typescript. 1977. 6 lvs. "Bluff Dale Suspension Bridge" file, Texas Historical Commission, Austin, Tex.

9. *Brazos Santiago Lighthouse*

The southernmost lighthouse on the Texas Gulf Coast, the Brazos Santiago Lighthouse, for almost ninety years served as a navigational aid at Brazos Santiago Pass between the south end of Padre Island and Brazos Island, about seven miles up the coast from the mouth of the Rio Grande. Today the century-old piers of the old lighthouse support the harbor pilot's office and a radio station at the Port Isabel Coast Guard Station.

The first lighthouse at Brazos Santiago Pass was erected in either 1852 or 1853. Called the Padre Island Beacon, it was a square, black wooden tower rising thirty-five feet above sea level and equipped with a weak fifth-order lens. Its light was visible for only about ten miles out to sea, but it was supplemented by the light emanating from the much taller Point Isabel Lighthouse (1852). The Padre Island Beacon served maritime interests for about a decade before it was destroyed by Confederate forces during the Civil War to prevent its falling into Union hands and becoming a lookout post.

The U.S. Department of the Treasury erected a new temporary light at Brazos Santiago in 1866, but it proved to be insufficient. Even so, it lasted until it was removed by a September, 1874, tropical storm that leveled the entire station, killing the keeper's wife

The truncated iron screw piles from the 1877–78 Brazos Santiago Lighthouse currently supporting the harbor pilot's office and a radio beacon station at the Port Isabel U.S. Coast Guard Station on South Padre Island. Photograph by the author, 1975.

and leaving hardly any signs that structures had ever been there.

After the 1874 destruction of the temporary beacon, Congress appropriated funds for the construction of a permanent lighthouse at the same site on the north side of Brazos Santiago Pass. The new structure was a sixty-foot lighthouse in which a wooden light station was placed atop an iron base of screw piles firmly anchored in the sands at the end of the island. The metalwork was fabricated under contract in Philadelphia, and its wooden parts were framed in Mobile, Alabama, with all the prefabricated parts shipped to South Texas. Work on the placement of the iron pilings and on the assembly of the ready-made parts for both the tower and its light station began in 1877. On March 1, 1878, the first light was exhibited.

The Brazos Santiago Lighthouse remained in service until Labor Day, 1951, when a fire destroyed the wooden portion of its superstructure. The lantern then was transferred to the top of the nearby U.S. Coast Guard Lifeboat Station building, where it operated for a while longer. After the fire, the upper level of the screw-pile lighthouse was removed, and a harbor pilot office and radio beacon station was erected on its truncated piles. This facility remains in service, perpetuating the use of the old Brazos Santiago Lighthouse site as a navigational aid.

Location: The remains of the 1877–78 Brazos Santiago Lighthouse, now the base for the Port Isabel harbor pilot office and a radio beacon station, are located at the Port Isabel U.S. Coast Guard Station at the extreme southern tip of Padre Island. It is accessible by crossing Laguna Madre on the Park Road 100 bridge from the town of Port Isabel and then turning south on the local paved road to the Coast Guard Station.

Suggested Reading:

Cipra, David L. *Lighthouses & Lightships of the*

Northern Gulf of Mexico. Washington, D.C.: U.S. Coast Guard, 1978.

Putnam, George R. *Sentinel of the Coasts: Log of a Lighthouse Engineer.* New York: W. W. Norton and Company, 1937.

10. Buchanan Dam

The Buchanan Dam is the uppermost of six dams owned and operated by the Lower Colorado River Authority (LCRA) on the Colorado River in Central Texas. Begun in 1931 and completed in 1938, the dam for almost half a century has impounded water for irrigation, municipal water supply, recreation, flood control, and hydroelectric-generation purposes.

The Central Texas Hydro-Electric Company, one of the Samuel Insull financial interests, began construc-tion of Buchanan Dam in April, 1931. Work pro-gressed for just over a year, until April 20, 1932, when it ceased because of difficulties stemming from the deepening economic depression. The construc-tion site lay quiet for the next three years, until the LCRA acquired the project. This agency proceeded with the construction, following plans similar though not identical to those prepared by the private power company. Even before the dam was finished, the river

Aerial view of Buchanan Dam, 1982. Photograph courtesy Lower Colorado River Authority, Austin, Texas.

View past the powerhouse toward two of the twenty-nine seventy-foot-span multiple concrete arches forming one of the sections of Buchanan Dam. Photograph by the author, 1981.

authority began deliberate impoundment of water. A flood in July, 1938, soon after the completion of the dam, brought the reservoir to full capacity for the first time. Seven months before, in January 1938, the first electricity generating unit went into operation.

Buchanan Dam is an exceedingly impressive structure that stretches 10,987 feet—over two miles—in length. Its maximum height is 145 feet, 6 inches, with its top standing at an elevation of 1,025 feet, 6 inches above sea level. Its overflow spillways are 5 feet lower. Starting at the south end of the dam, it consists of the following parts: an earthen gravity section forming the south abutment; twenty-three 35-foot-span multiple concrete arches; a 650-foot length of concrete and rock gravity section; twenty-nine 70-foot-span multiple concrete arches (above the area of the power plant); a gated spillway equipped with seven tainter gates 40 feet long by 25 feet, 6 inches high; a portion composed of natural rock with concrete gravity nonoverflow section; a gated spillway equipped with fourteen tainter gates 33 feet long by 15 feet, 6 inches high; a portion composed of natural rock with concrete gravity nonoverflow section; a gated spillway equipped with sixteen tainter gates 33 feet long by 15 feet, 6 inches high; and a concrete gravity overflow spillway 1,100 feet long.

The Buchanan Reservoir, formed by the dam, has a capacity of 992,000 acre feet of water at the spillway crest. Draining an area of approximately 31,250

square miles, the reservoir plays an important role in the overall operations of the LCRA, for water released from Buchanan Dam is used for power, irrigation, and municipal supply downstream at the other five dams owned by the authority. During ordinary operations, water released from Buchanan Dam is governed by the operation of the turbines in its powerhouse, although floodwater releases may be controlled by one or more of the gated spillway sections.

Even before Buchanan Dam was dedicated, the first of its three hydroelectric generators had begun producing electricity. Its three vertical generators are each 1,250-kw, 3-phase, 60-cycle, 7,200-volt, 171.4-rpm units manufactured by the Westinghouse Electric Corporation. Its two original Francis-type turbines were manufactured by the Newport News Shipbuilding and Drydock Company. They are 171.4-rpm turbines with 17,300 horsepower ratings at 131-foot head. The third turbine, which was placed in service in 1950 to expand generating capacity, is of similar design to the others and was made by the I. P. Morris Division of the Baldwin Manufacturing Company. All three of the generating units are controlled by Woodward cabinet-type governors located inside the concrete powerhouse.

Twelve-foot-diameter penstocks carry reservoir water to the turbines, each of the penstocks being equipped with fixed-wheel-type headgates. The third penstock is fitted with a wye and a butterfly-type valve used in controlling water flow from a pumpback system installed in 1950. The initial 1932 plans for the powerhouse had called for this type of valve from the S. Morgan Smith Company in each of the penstocks, but due to the suspension of construction in 1932, none of them were ever delivered. When such a valve was required for the addition of the third turbine in 1950, the low bidder, the S. Morgan Smith Company, found one of these unfinished 1932 butterfly valve cases still in storage. The valve assembly thus reached its original destination eighteen years late.

To conserve water for generating electricity, Buchanan Dam employs an interesting pumpback unit. Placed in service in May, 1950, it pumps water discharged from the turbines into the tail pond back into the reservoir during times of off-peak power demand. The water then is available for reuse during periods of peak electricity usage. Depending on the head of water available, approximately 1.5 kwhr of off-peak electricity produced by the generators will pump back into the reservoir enough water to generate 1.0 kwhr of electricity during peak demand. The equipment used for this work is an 84-inch, vertical 163.7-rpm Worthington centrifugal pump driven by a direct-connected Westinghouse 13,450-horsepower vertical electric motor.

Serving the Central Texas area for over forty-five years, Buchanan Dam is one of the most impressive engineering works on the entire Colorado River. It is readily accessible to visitors, and a public viewing area is provided at its south end.

Location: Buchanan Dam impounds water of the Colorado River on the Llano-Burnet county line, approximately ten miles west of Burnet on State Highway 29. Public parking is available at the south end of the dam near the LCRA offices and a commercial marina/restaurant area. There visitors may walk several hundred feet along the top of the dam. Many tourists, especially children, enjoy feeding bread to the huge carp that may be seen swimming just below the surface in a protected no-fishing area in front of the dam near its south end. The powerhouse is accessible from this area on a local paved road, but it is not open to the public. The extreme north end of the dam may be viewed from FM 690.

Suggested Reading:

Dowell, Cleo Lafoy, and Seth Darnby Breeding. *Dams and Reservoirs in Texas: Historical and Descriptive Information.* Texas Water Development Board Report 48. Austin: Texas Water Development Board, 1967.

Godfrey, F. A., and C. L. Dowell. *Major Hydroelectric Powerplants in Texas: Historical and Descriptive Information.* Texas Water Development Board Report 81. Austin: Texas Water Development Board, 1968.

11. *Buffalo Gap Railway Water System*

The Buffalo Gap Railway Water System, built between 1910 and 1911, is one of the best preserved early twentieth-century railway water systems in Texas. Today it is leased from its original builder, the Santa Fe Railway Company, by the town of Buffalo Gap. It remains in service to provide the domestic water supply for the municipality.

Buffalo Gap lies in a break across the Callahan Divide in east-central Taylor County, about sixteen miles south of Abilene. It takes its name from the herds of buffalo that beat a clearly defined trail through the gap before the arrival of the white settlers. The first community began to grow in the area when early ranchers drove longhorn cattle through the pass toward Kansas markets on the Western Trail. Buffalo Gap grew to such importance that by 1878 it was chosen as the county seat (but for only two years). In 1880 the Texas and Pacific Railway built across the northern part of Taylor County, and its residents voted to remove the county seat to Abilene. Since that time, Buffalo Gap has remained a ranching and market center.

Track-laying crews of the Panhandle and Santa Fe Railway reached Buffalo Gap on July 27, 1910. They were building a railroad line connecting Coleman, Texas, with Texico, New Mexico. About the time that the first steam locomotives reached the town, company crews began building a system to supply these engines with pure boiler water. Although railway company records indicate that the Buffalo Gap system was built during the second half of 1910, G. W. Harris, chief engineer of construction at Amarillo, wrote to C. A. Morse, chief engineer for the entire company system at Chicago, on December 5, 1911,

The 1910 concrete boiler house on the right with the modern metal pump house, erected in 1961 over the thirty-six-foot well at the left. Photograph by the author, 1975.

that at Buffalo Gap the "steel water tank is yet to receive [its] third coat of paint" and the "wood work in [the] pump house [is yet] to be painted." By this date, however, the system must already have been at least partially operational, even though the finishing touches remained to be made.

The effort undertaken by the railway company at Buffalo Gap for supplying its steam locomotives with boiler water created an interesting system. The sources of water developed in 1910 consisted of two large hand-dug wells. One of these was octagonal, measuring thirty-six feet deep and twenty-one feet in diameter; the other was thirteen feet deep by twelve feet square. Both were lined with concrete and their surface openings were protected by wooden covers. Company laborers erected a reinforced-concrete boiler house about seventy-five feet southeast of the thirty-six-foot well. This structure, on the west side of the tracks, originally housed a steam boiler and pumping equipment, which elevated water from the two wells. At one time a twelve-by-twenty-five-foot wooden coal bin stood at one side of the fifteen-by-twenty-six-foot boiler house for fuel storage.

Water from the wells was carried by a cast-iron pipeline to a large, cylindrical steel water standpipe about 650 feet south of the boiler house on the east side of the tracks. This standpipe was the standard 200,000-gallon pattern used by the Santa Fe throughout its system. It was built 24 feet in diameter and 60 feet tall and originally was painted black. Beside the

standpipe, convenient to the tracks, workers erected a 10-inch "Otto" water column on a concrete foundation. It was through this large metal fixture that crews actually "watered" the locomotives.

The Santa Fe Railway operated its water system at Buffalo Gap from late 1910 until it discontinued the

The concrete and metal cover over the thirty-six-foot hand-dug well, inside the current pump house building. Photograph by the author, 1975.

The 200,000-gallon standard-plan cylindrical steel standpipe erected by
Santa Fe Railway crews in 1910. Photograph by the author, 1975.

use of steam locomotives in the mid-1950s. The system fell into disuse until 1961. In that year the company leased its entire water system to the City of Buffalo Gap, which converted it to supply its municipal water distribution system. A new metal pump house was erected over the thirty-six-foot well, which was fitted with new pumping equipment, and the old disused concrete boiler house became a fireproof waterworks shop and warehouse. Electric pumps now elevate water from the thirty-six-foot well and pump it to the old cylindrical steel standpipe, now protected with aluminum paint. The tank provides both sanitary storage and gravity pressure for the entire distribution system, which carries water to residences and businesses in the town. Several years ago the standpipe was emptied and its access cover removed

so that the tank could be inspected. At that time it had gone seventeen years without cleaning, but city employees found that the only residue at the bottom of the tank was a mere half-inch deposit of clean, white sand.

Since 1961 the City of Buffalo Gap has leased the old Santa Fe Railway water system and maintained it in beautiful operating condition. It is one of the best preserved of all the early twentieth-century railroad water systems in Texas and one of only a handful of city waterworks in the state securing its entire supply from a hand-dug well.

Location: The 36-foot hand-dug well and old concrete boiler house for the water system stand on the west side of the Santa Fe tracks, just south of Elm

28

Creek on the west side of Buffalo Gap. The cylindrical steel standpipe, which can be seen from long distances, stands on the east side of the tracks, about 650 feet south of the well. The standpipe is accessible via Live Oak Street on the east side of the tracks; the old boiler house and 36-foot well are located at the end of a graded road leading from FM 89 north along the west side of the railway right-of-way.

Suggested Reading:

Baker, T. Lindsay. "The Buffalo Gap Waterworks."

Water: Southwest Water Works Journal 57, no. 10 (January, 1976): 6–8.
Johnson, Glenn, mayor of Buffalo Gap, to T. Lindsay Baker. Interview at Buffalo Gap, Texas, May 21, 1975. Typescript. 2 lvs. "Buffalo Gap Railway Water System" file, Texas Historic Engineering Site Inventory, Center for the History of Engineering, Texas Tech University, Lubbock, Tex.

12. Canadian River Wagon Bridge

Still spanning the Canadian River after almost seven decades, the Canadian River Wagon Bridge (1915–16) is one of the most impressive of all the multiple overhead truss bridges in Texas. Though today carrying only a natural gas pipeline, the old bridge stretches 3,255 feet and continues to withstand the floods that periodically rage down the Canadian valley.

The first attempt to place a wagon bridge across the Canadian River in Hemphill County came in 1888, only a year after the founding of the town of Canadian. On January 24 of that year, the county commissioners received a verbal petition to build a wagon bridge across the Canadian River just north of the new county seat of Canadian. The commissioners, deciding that such a structure would benefit the county, approved bonds in the amount of $9,000 for the project and began soliciting bids from various construction companies. They received bids from a number of firms for structures ranging in length from 880 to 1,800 feet at prices from $9,000 to

$17,500. Finally, in fall, 1888, the commissioners granted a contract for the bridge work. The contractors proceeded to erect a principally wooden bridge, which they completed in spring, 1889. Only a few months passed, however, before a major flood on the Canadian washed away much of the structure.

The Hemphill County Commissioners' Court then ordered a second bond election, this time for seventeen thousand dollars, to rebuild the damaged bridge more substantially. After the passage of the second bridge bonds, workers returned to the site and erected a new iron bridge, which incorporated elements of the damaged structure. Only a short time passed before a severe windstorm swept one of the iron spans into the river. The bridge company refused to repair the damage, which it felt was not its responsibility, and the county refused to expend funds for repairs it felt the company should undertake. Finally, a suit in federal court was settled in favor of the county, but in the meantime, the twice-damaged

The Canadian River Wagon Bridge (*left*) and Santa Fe Railway Bridge (*right*) washed out by floods in September, 1923. Local thrill-seekers are standing at the end of the bridge surveying the damage. Photograph courtesy Panhandle-Plains Historical Museum, Canyon, Texas.

The roadway of the Canadian River bridge from its south approach, about 1935. Photograph courtesy Texas Department of Highways and Public Transportation, Amarillo, Texas.

wagon bridge was abandoned. A quarter century passed before any further action was taken to provide the citizens of Hemphill County with a bridge.

In the years preceding World War I, a time when the "good-roads" movement was active in all parts of the United States, the residents of Hemphill County again began dreaming of a safe vehicular crossing for the Canadian. The lack of a secure route over the quicksands had for decades retarded the economic development of the northern part of the county, and local business leaders speculated about the commerce that a permanent bridge would bring to the town of Canadian. In response to local requests, the Texas

legislature passed an act in March, 1913, that authorized Hemphill County to sell bonds for the construction of roads and a wagon bridge across the Canadian River in the county. Several months passed, however, before further moves were made toward bridging the Canadian.

On February 11, 1915, the county commissioners received a petition from eighty-two Hemphill County voters requesting that they call an election to approve the issuance of $74,000 worth of bonds for the construction of "a wagon bridge across the Canadian River." After considering the petition, the commissioners called an election for April 20 of the same year. Feelings over the bond issue must have run high in Hemphill County, with the residents of Canadian strongly in favor and those in the outlying communities less eager to pay taxes to build a bridge principally for the benefit of the county seat. The local press reported that the election "was very interestingly contested throughout the county," as is evident from the results at the polls. Canadian represented the only precinct in the entire county voting in favor of the bond issue; all the other precincts voted overwhelmingly against it. The number of voters in Canadian, however, was so much greater than the number in the remaining eight precincts that the measure passed by seventy-five votes.

On July 25, 1915, the commissioners' court ordered the county judge to begin advertising for bids from contractors for the construction of a new steel wagon bridge across the Canadian, with the bids to be opened a month later. Several bridge companies made bids on the project, among them the Boardman Bridge Company, the Kansas City Bridge Company, the Missouri Valley Bridge Company, and the Kansas City branch house of the Canton Bridge Company of

The bridge erector's nameplate, dated 1916, atop the southernmost span of the Canadian River Wagon Bridge. Photograph by the author, 1983.

A representative Pratt through-truss span from the Canadian River Wagon Bridge. Based on Canton Bridge Company, Kansas City, Mo., "Bridge across Canadian River at Canadian, Hemphill County, Texas. Designed by Canton Bridge Company, Kansas City, Missouri," blueprint drawing (ca. 1915), in Engineering Department, Texas Department of Highways and Public Transportation, Amarillo, Texas. Drawing by the author.

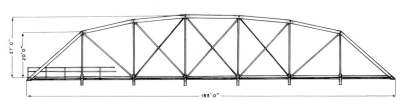

Canton, Ohio. The Canton firm received the contract as low bidder at sixty-six thousand dollars. Later the county revised the plans somewhat and agreed to pay the contractors an additional four thousand dollars.

The *Canadian Record* reported to its readers that the first members of the crew arrived at Canadian on December 28, 1915, "for the purpose of starting work on the wagon bridge." Three railway cars of materials had already arrived, and more were on the way. Work began first on the eighteen concrete piers that were to support the seventeen-span structure. These piers rested on steel footings, which were driven 65 feet into the sand of the riverbed. By February, 1916, half of the footings were in position, and by the next month five of the concrete piers were ready for the superstructure. The most imposing feature of the Canadian River bridge was its multiple overhead trusses. As initially built, the bridge consisted of seventeen identical 155-foot Pratt through trusses, which supported a roadway 16 feet wide and 2,635 feet long. Work progressed on the project through the spring and summer of 1916, and the bridge was opened to traffic in early August, 1916.

The Canadian River bridge remained in service for only about eight years. During high water in September, 1923, the Canadian cut a new channel around the north end of the bridge, leaving the structure intact but unusable. For a few days local civic leaders pondered the loss of their link over the Canadian, but soon they went to work. Through their efforts, the Texas Highway Department committed itself to pay three-quarters of the cost for extending the bridge four spans, 620 feet, to the north to cross the new channel of the river. The new spans were to be identical to those already in place. Within a matter of weeks the county commissioners called an election to approve the issuance of twenty-three thousand dollars in new bridge bonds to pay for the county's share of the project. In December, 1923, the county and state jointly accepted the bid of the Austin Brothers Bridge Company of Dallas, Texas, for the extension of the bridge.

Work began on the last day of 1923, continuing into the summer of 1924. During this time the structure not only was lengthened 620 feet to the north, but its entire wooden decking was renewed and all its steelwork repainted. Finally, a great celebration for the reopening of the bridge was held at Canadian on July 4, 1924. An estimated four thousand citizens and visitors participated in a ceremonial opening of the bridge, a free barbecue dinner, athletic events, auto races, and a grand ball. The addition of the four new spans gave the Canadian River bridge a total length of 3,255 feet, just over six-tenths of a mile.

The Canadian River Wagon Bridge remained in service until it was replaced by a new concrete highway bridge just downstream in 1953. Since its abandonment as a vehicular bridge, it has carried a natural gas pipeline across the river. Though its wooden roadway has been removed, the bridge stands today virtually as solid as when it was completed in 1916.

Location: The 1915–16 Canadian River Wagon Bridge spans the Canadian River parallel to the present-day U.S. 60–83 bridge on the north side of Canadian. Both ends of the structure are accessible on foot for observation by visitors.

Suggested Reading:

The Canadian Record (Canadian, Tex.), April 22, 1915, p. 1; December 30, 1915, p. 1; January 6, 1916, p. 1; February 10, 1916, p. 1; March 23, 1916, p. 1; March 30, 1916, [p. 6]; April 6, 1916, [p. 6]; April 13, 1916, [pp. 4, 8]; August 3, 1916, p. 1; August 10, 1916, p. 1; April 5, 1917, p. 1; October 4, 1923, p. 1; October 25, 1923, p. 1; November 29, 1923, p. 1; December 6, 1923, p. 1; January 3, 1924, p. 1; April 3, 1924, p. 1; April 17, 1924, p. 1; April 24, 1924, p. 1; May 1, 1924, p. 1;

May 15, 1924, p. 1; June 12, 1924, p. 1; July 3, 1924; p. 1; July 10, 1924, p. 1.

Hemphill County, Tex. Commissioners' Court. Minutes, vol. 4, pp. 276–81, 401–402, 408–10, 472, 492–94, 498–99, 508, 510, 597–600, 606–607. Office of County Clerk, Hemphill County Courthouse, Canadian, Tex.

Texas. State Highway Department. Construction and Maintenance Files for Project Control No. 30-5-2, Hemphill County. Manuscript and microfilm. Engineering Department, Texas Department of Highways and Public Transportation, Amarillo, Tex.

13. Canon Ranch Eclipse Windmill

The Canon Ranch Eclipse Windmill, erected about 1906, is the largest remaining operational wooden-wheel, turbine-type windmill in the United States. With a windwheel twenty-two and a half feet in diameter and mounted atop a wooden tower forty-two feet tall, it is a noted landmark in the ranch country of Trans-Pecos Texas.

The origin of the Eclipse windmills goes back to 1867 and a most unlikely place—a missionary station among the Ojibway Indians of Wisconsin. There the Reverend Leonard H. Wheeler and his son devised a windmill that automatically governed its speed of operation. Though not the first self-regulating American windmill, their machine proved to be one of the most successful. Wheeler secured a patent on his invention, which was manufactured under the brand name Eclipse by a succession of companies in a factory located at Beloit, Wisconsin.

During the nineteenth century, virtually all factory-made windmills were built of wood with some iron and steel parts, and they represented one of two basic styles: sectional wheel or solid wheel. The sectional-wheel mills had windwheels composed of several sections of blades that were pivoted on the ends of arms so that in increasing winds the individual sections could fold back to reduce the surface area exposed to the wind and thus reduce their speed. The solid-wheel mills, on the other hand, had wheels that were

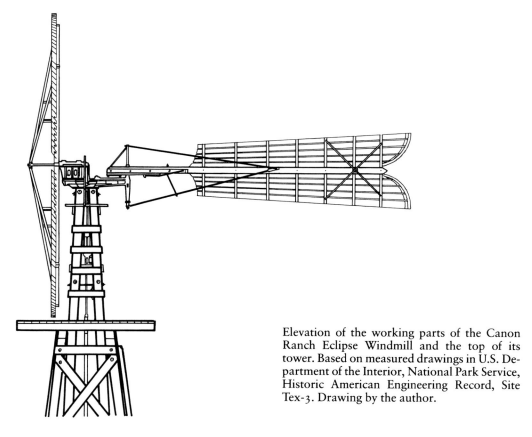

Elevation of the working parts of the Canon Ranch Eclipse Windmill and the top of its tower. Based on measured drawings in U.S. Department of the Interior, National Park Service, Historic American Engineering Record, Site Tex-3. Drawing by the author.

Windmiller and helpers preparing to lift the newly rebuilt 22½-foot-diameter windwheel of the Canon Ranch Windmill into position atop the tower during its most recent restoration. Photograph by the author, 1982.

rigid or solid. These wheels did not fold in, but rather retained a permanent circular configuration. Solid-wheel mills generally regulated their speed of operation through the use of a side vane, a small vane parallel to the windwheel that pushed the wheel away from the wind when its velocity grew too great. Eclipse mills are a classic example of the solid-wheel style.

During the nineteenth and early twentieth centuries, the larger size windmills, those sixteen or more feet in diameter, generally were termed "railroad" mills because they were frequently used to pump water for steam locomotives. The large-diameter mills also supplied water to municipalities, industries, and livestock on western ranches. As early as 1870, railroad-pattern Eclipse mills were being sold, and thousands of them were in use by the turn of the century. They

were made in sixteen-, eighteen-, twenty-, twenty-two and one-half-, twenty-five-, and thirty-foot sizes. For a few years between about 1905 and 1914, the maker, which by this time had become Fairbanks, Morse and Company, produced what it called a "Texas Pattern" Eclipse mill, which was the same as its railroad-pattern mills except that its castings were modified to give it capacity for longer pump strokes. The Canon Ranch Windmill is an example of the Texas Pattern.

All of the Eclipse windmills, whatever their size, were built predominantly from wood with iron and steel parts used to hold together those made from wood and employed where greatest strength was required. In operation, the turning motion of the large wooden windwheel was translated into a reciprocal

33

pump stroke by the action of a steel pitman connecting a crank plate at the back end of the main shaft with a steel pump rod beneath it. Each revolution of the wheel produced one stroke of the pump. A large hinged wooden vane directed the wheel into the wind. To govern the speed of operation, a side vane pushed the large wheel away from the wind as it increased in velocity. This reduced the surface area of the wheel exposed to the wind and slowed its speed. As the side vane pushed the wheel out of the wind, a linkage system raised a series of iron weights suspended within the tower. These weights served as a counterbalance of varying resistance against the pressure on the side vane, and they pulled the wheel back to face the wind squarely when its velocity decreased, giving the mill a more or less constant speed of operation.

The Canon Ranch Eclipse Windmill for many years pumped water from a drilled well and elevated it to a large reservoir on a hill adjacent to ranch headquarters. From that point the water flowed by gravity through a series of pipes to the various areas where it was needed. By the eve of World War II, the headquarters Eclipse had become recognized as a local landmark. It remained in service not because it was a relic but because it was the only mill available to the ranch owners at the time that was capable of pumping the amount of water needed.

In 1956 the power lines of an electric cooperative reached the Canon Ranch. The Eclipse was disconnected from the well and replaced by an electric pump, although the mill remained in place on its original tower. By this time the ranch owners realized

that their windmill was indeed a valuable piece of historic machinery. Since that time they have undertaken two restorations of the mill, most recently from 1979 to 1982. In the latter effort all of the wooden parts of the wheel and vane were replicated from original factory parts preserved either at the ranch or in the collections of the Panhandle-Plains Historical Museum in Canyon, Texas.

Because of its significance as a rare preserved example of a once-common piece of water supply equipment, in 1977 the Canon Ranch Eclipse Windmill was accepted into the National Register of Historic Places. In 1981, while the mill was being restored, architects prepared detailed, measured drawings of the mill and all its parts for inclusion in the Historic American Engineering Record, housed at the Library of Congress.

Location: The Canon Ranch Eclipse Windmill is located a number of miles over rugged roads into remote private property in eastern Pecos County and is not accessible to the public.

Suggested Reading:

Baker, T. Lindsay. *A Field Guide to American Windmills.* Norman: University of Oklahoma Press, 1985.
———. "The Story of the 'Railroad Eclipse.'" *Windmillers' Gazette* (Canyon, Tex.), 2, no. 2 (Spring, 1982): 3–4.
U.S. Department of the Interior. Historic American Engineering Record. Site HAER TX-3. Measured drawings and typescript. 1981. Library of Congress, Washington, D.C.

14. *Clear Fork of the Brazos Suspension Bridge*

After almost ninety years, the suspension bridge over the Clear Fork of the Brazos in Shackelford County remains in service. The handsome span located in scenic ranch country is one of the oldest operational suspension bridges in Texas and is a structure very worthy of inspection by visitors to the area.

During the mid-1890s the county commissioners of Shackelford County, who even then were meeting in the still-standing stone courthouse in Albany, began receiving repeated petitions and requests from the residents of Shackelford, Young, and Throckmorton counties to construct a bridge across the Clear Fork of the Brazos near its falls in the area of the J. A.

Matthews Ranch. In 1885 the county had built an iron truss bridge across the river upstream at Fort Griffin (described in entry no. 34), but this bridge was not on the route of travel for many local people. Rather than go out of their way via the Fort Griffin Bridge, they preferred to ford the river at a lower point to save a several-mile detour, except when high water forced them to use the Fort Griffin crossing.

On February 11, 1896, the Shackelford County Commissioners' Court met to address the need for another bridge across the Clear Fork. They agreed with local residents that a bridge was needed in the area of the falls, and they decided to advertise for

The Clear Fork of the Brazos Suspension Bridge along its roadway, showing wooden decking, metal tire treadways, concrete-filled and covered steel towers, and steel cables. Photograph by the author, 1977.

bids from contractors. Eighteen days later the commissioners met again on bridge matters, this time to open the bids that had been submitted by contracting firms. The Fluice-Moyers Company of Weatherford, Texas, as lowest bidder, received the contract to erect the bridge according to county specifications.

The contract with the builders called for a suspension bridge with a total length of 300 feet, including a 140-foot-long suspension span 40 feet over the river between two stone piers. The original document noted that the east approach was to be 116 feet long and the west approach 44 feet long. As work progressed the contractors suggested that the approaches be lengthened 5 feet on each end, a recommendation the county commissioners accepted. The roadway was to be 14 feet wide, with its joists made from 2-by-12-inch timbers and its decking from 2.5-by-8-inch lumber. The towers to support the steel cables were to be made from trussed steel members mounted on the cut-stone piers. Along either side of the roadway, the spans were to be reinforced with trussed steel stiffening members, which doubled as guardrails. The contractors were to receive $4,370 in payment.

The crew soon started excavating the footings for the piers and began preparing the cut-stone blocks from which the piers subsequently were built. Then the four steel towers were fabricated and put in place, after which time a temporary wooden catwalk was placed across the river so that workers could carry the individual steel wires back and forth to make the cables to support the roadway. An interesting detail of construction at the Clear Fork Bridge was the manner in which the cables from the towers to their anchors in the banks split as they descended from the tops of the towers.

According to the agreement between the county and the builders, the bridge was to be completed by June 15, 1896. The due date must have been met, for on June 20 the commissioners rode to the Clear Fork to inspect their new bridge. They probably met both before and after the inspection at the ranch home of County Judge J. A. Matthews, which was not far from the new structure. The commissioners then officially accepted the bridge, agreeing to pay an additional seventy-two dollars charged by the builders for the extra ten feet of approaches.

35

For almost ninety years the suspension bridge over the Clear Fork of the Brazos has given local residents a dependable crossing. The most significant alterations to the bridge structure were undertaken in the 1930s, when the steel towers were filled and covered with concrete and when the truss stiffening on the sides of the roadway between the towers was replaced. Otherwise the bridge stands today as it was built, a tribute both to the builders and to the taxpayers of Shackelford County, who wisely invested their money in 1896.

Location: The Clear Fork Suspension Bridge spans the Clear Fork of the Brazos in extreme northeastern Shackelford County. Access to the structure is convenient by way of a graded county road that leaves U.S. 283 at a point 9 miles north of Albany. The county road leads 7.9 miles northeast to the crossing. The suspension bridge may also be approached from the north by taking FM 2850 south 3.3 miles from State Highway 209 west of Woodson to a crossroads at the end of the pavement. From the crossroads, proceed south and southwest on a graded road 3.2 miles to the bridge.

Detail of the steel wire cables put into service in 1896, which support the suspension span of the Clear Fork bridge. Photograph by the author, 1978.

Suggested Reading:

Shackelford County, Tex. Commissioners' Court. Minutes, vol. 3, pp. 476, 487–88, 516–17. Office of County Clerk, Shackelford County Courthouse, Albany, Tex.

15. Cleburne Waterworks

Cleburne, the seat of Johnson County, was established in 1867 on the banks of two spring-fed branches of Buffalo Creek. Its waterworks system, in operation for more than a century, is typical of that for many small cities throughout Texas. It may, in fact, be taken as a case study in the development of such water systems in the state in the years since the late nineteenth century.

Before the establishment of a waterworks in Cleburne, its residents secured their water either from a series of free-flowing springs along the banks of Buffalo Creek or from shallow, hand-dug wells or cisterns on their own property. Residents who could afford the luxury paid to have water hauled to their homes or places of business.

Thomas U. Taylor, who later became the dean of engineering at the University of Texas, grew up in Cleburne during its early days, and on numerous occasions he reminisced about its early water system. In 1937 he remembered that "two or three men made their living by hauling water on two-wheel carts with a vertical barrel attached on a low platform strung to the axle. It was drawn by two horses. . . . The water was sold by the bucket full or barrel and each driver developed a trade and knew his route well. I lived across the street from one of these contractors, a Mr. Cunningham, and this was his only means of earning a living." Professor Taylor recollected in 1929 how he and other boys made spending money by carrying pails of water from the springs to local saloonkeepers: "In the early days the saloons would open at 4 o'clock in the morning, and the boys in the town . . . developed quite an industry and rivalry in carrying buckets of water to the opening saloons, selling them at five cents a bucket. The buckets were of uniform size, uniform shape, and were all made of cedar. I soon learned the homes of these saloon keepers and would waylay them to pledge me their morning bucket of water. Three buckets of water before breakfast was a good trade, amounting to fifteen cents."

The first real waterworks in Cleburne was built by the city in 1883–84. It collected water from several of the springs along West Buffalo Creek near the business district and carried it in vitrified clay pipes to a central collection well. It then was pumped directly into the mains to supply consumers in the center of the town by a walking beam–type pump actuated by a thirty-horsepower steam engine.

By 1887 the demand for water had outstripped the capacity of the springs. In that year the city began work on boring an artesian well to supplement the springwater supply, but difficulties prevented the completion of the project until 1891. In that year a total of four wells were drilled in the area of the springs on West Buffalo Creek near the West Henderson Street crossing.

Just before the wells were completed, the city administration entered into a contract with W. E. Moss to manage its water system. The municipality had encountered financial problems in running the waterworks, and its elected officials sought to solve the difficulties by contracting out its operation. According to the 1890 agreement, still known in Cleburne as the "Moss Contract," the businessman agreed to supply water to residences in the town at a flat rate of six dollars annually. Within two years the growth of the

population required that the water system be expanded, but Moss disagreed. He already had expended considerable amounts of money and refused to invest any more in the system. Perhaps under pressure from city officials, he sold his contract for operating the waterworks to Silas Lovelady, the man who had supervised the boring of the city's four artesian wells. The contract changed hands two more times before 1908, when the company running the system was placed in receivership. For the next four years it was managed first by William Battle and then by Arthur Chase, a civil engineer.

Finally, in 1912 the responsibility for operating the Cleburne Waterworks returned to the municipal administration. At this time the physical plant consisted of a brick and frame complex on the north side of West Henderson Street on the east bank of West Buffalo Creek, the site of the present-day Cleburne City Hall. Springfield Marine and Heine boilers supplied steam to operate the pumps in the system. The natural flow of the artesian wells had diminished to such an extent that compressed air had to be intro-

Looking east over the top of the brick and concrete pumpwell for the original 1883 Cleburne Waterworks, across West Buffalo Creek toward downtown Cleburne. Photograph by the author, 1975.

The 1891 Cleburne Waterworks pump house complex as it appeared about 1911. Photograph courtesy Office of City Manager, Cleburne, Texas.

duced into the wells continually to lift the water to the surface. Already by 1900 a partially submerged circular concrete reservoir and a steel standpipe had been constructed just over half a mile away to serve a new residential neighborhood.

The same year that the city resumed operation of the water system, it began construction of a new central pump house at the site of the old 1891 plant. The old buildings were razed, and a new brick central pumping station was erected in their place. It was so substantially built that it remained in service until it, too, was demolished half a century later.

In 1915 the Cleburne Waterworks was described as receiving its water from ten tubular wells, six and eight inches in diameter, between nine hundred and twelve hundred feet deep, all located near the main pump house. In this building three two-million-gallon Worthington pumps were powered by four nine-hundred-horsepower, hand-stoked Heine boilers pumping water both directly into the mains and into

storage reservoirs. The system in 1915 had twenty-five miles of cast-iron mains that varied from four to twelve inches in diameter. The average daily consumption for the city was 750,000 gallons. If consumers used water meters, they were charged 20 cents per thousand gallons, but most customers paid flat rates for their service. Charges for residences were $1.50 per quarter, $2.25 with bath, and $2.65 with bath and flush toilet.

One of the most interesting features of the early twentieth-century Cleburne Waterworks was the unusual system of underground tunnels, which collected water from the various wells and carried it to a sump beneath the main pumping station. Although this system may have existed earlier, it definitely is known to have been in use by the 1920s. Inside the pump house a 10-foot-square shaft went down 350 feet into the ground. At its base was a room 10 feet, 1 inch wide by 29 feet, 2 inches long, which was hewn into the solid rock. Beneath it was a sump the same width and

The partially underground pre-1900 concrete storage reservoir built on North Granbury Street. Photograph by the author, 1975.

ing areas. In 1926 new diesel engines were installed at the central pump house, and in 1932 a new Water Department office building was added. The underground aquifer supplying the system, however, was being depleted, and city leaders knew that an alternative source of supply had to be found. Consequently, in the 1960s a completely new water system was built employing water from a reservoir on the Nolan River west of the city. The old 1912 pump house was removed and a new city hall, library, and fire station erected on its site, but many of the older structures of the Cleburne Waterworks remain.

Location: The most interesting historic structures from the Cleburne Waterworks are the original brick and concrete collection well for the initial 1883 water system and the pre-1900 concrete and steel reservoirs built to serve new residential districts northwest of downtown. The brick and concrete collection well into which the flow of the springs on West Buffalo Creek was channeled still may be seen on the west bank of the creek just a few feet north of the current West Henderson Street (U.S. 67 west) bridge spanning the creek. This site is about three blocks west of the Johnson County Courthouse. Just below and to the east of the old collection well is the actual Buffalo Spring on which Cleburne was founded. For many years the spring has been covered, its flow directed through a pipe that protrudes from the concrete that covers the bed of the creek. The two old reservoirs are located on the city block on North Granbury Street bounded also by Mitchell Avenue and Baird and Warren streets. The most convenient route to these structures is north one-half mile on North Granbury Street from its intersection with West Henderson Street (U.S. 67), about five blocks west of the courthouse.

Suggested Reading:

"Fabled Spring Led to City Water System." *Cleburne Times-Review* (June 28, 1936), sec. 4, pp. 1, 5.
Guinn, Ernest E. "A History of Cleburne, Texas." M.A. thesis, University of Texas, 1950.

Installing the crankshaft in the new diesel engine at the main pumping station in 1926. Photograph courtesy Office of City Manager, Cleburne, Texas.

length and 6 feet deep. Access to this chamber was by way of an open electric elevator. Tunnels led from the underground room to seven of the artesian wells. Their flow, aided by the compressed air, passed into the sump, from which point the water was pumped to a surface reservoir by a 6-inch Worthington centrifugal pump.

With the passage of years, the Cleburne Waterworks was enlarged and improved. Gradually more wells were added to the system, most of them in newer parts of the town. Additional reservoirs were erected and mains laid to supply water to these grow-

16. *Congress Avenue Bridge*

The Congress Avenue Bridge, completed in 1910 and serving the citizens of Austin for three-quarters of a century, is known as one of the most graceful reinforced-concrete arch bridges in Texas. Although it has been renovated twice, the structure retains the basic appearance that it had seventy-five years ago.

39

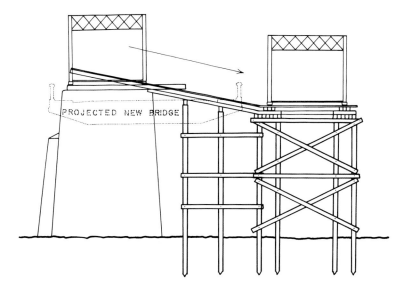

PROJECTED NEW BRIDGE

Method used to shift the spans of the old 1883 Congress Avenue iron truss bridge onto temporary wooden pilings to provide a crossing over the Colorado River during the construction of the current bridge from 1908 to 1910. Based on Waddell and Harrington, Consulting Engineers, Kansas City, Mo., "Bridge over the Colorado River at Congress Avenue, Austin, Texas, for Travis County. Details of Temporary Piers and Plan for Shifting Bridge," blueprint drawing, 1908, Engineering Department, District Office, Texas Department of Highways and Public Transportation. Drawing by the author.

Few of the thousands of commuters who daily pass over it ever consider that they are crossing the Colorado on a bridge built when the capital of Texas had fewer than thirty thousand inhabitants.

The story of the original Congress Avenue bridge is told under the heading of the Moore's Crossing Bridge (entry no. 63), for three spans from the original century-old Congress Avenue bridge are still in service at Moore's Crossing. The current bridge replaced the much older one in 1908.

For several years early in this century the residents of Austin and Travis County had agitated for the construction of a larger and stronger bridge across the Colorado. They felt that the old iron bridge was outmoded and not befitting the capital of a state with the area and wealth of Texas. Their efforts led to the passage of a substantial bond issue in June, 1908, for the construction of a new bridge as well as for other county road improvements.

The Travis County Commissioners' Court subsequently advertised for bids on the construction of a new reinforced-concrete arch bridge. On November 11, 1908, they granted a contract to the William P. Carmichael Company of Williamsport, Indiana, and Saint Louis, Missouri. The engineers who designed the attractive structure represented the firm of Waddell and Harrington of Kansas City.

The first step in the construction project was the shifting of the old bridge trusses to new temporary piers just to one side. This permitted continued public crossing of the river during the construction of the new bridge. Work began on the footings and later

on the wooden forms for the concrete abutments and six huge concrete piers. Forms were assembled for pouring the eight 32-foot-wide reinforced-concrete arches, each with a clear span of 110 feet, 9 inches. Each of these arches was reinforced with seventy pieces of 1¼-inch-diameter steel.

Through the use of vertical concrete members, the arches supported a concrete deck. This floor system was 50 feet wide, with 32 feet over the arches occupied by roadway pavement and interurban railway tracks. The overhanging portion of the deck was devoted to sidewalks and ornamental concrete railings, this outer 9 feet of the deck on either side being secured through the use of cantilever arms. The total length of the Congress Avenue Bridge as built in 1908–10 from end of handrail to end of handrail was 956 feet, 6 inches. Built at an expense of just over $200,000, the bridge cost the taxpayers approximately $4.00 per surface foot.

With only two interruptions, the Congress Avenue Bridge has remained in service for three-quarters of a century. As early as the 1930s, the county commissioners began receiving letters requesting the widening of the bridge, but no action was taken until after World War II. In 1952 the residents of Travis County had an opportunity to vote bonds for the widening of the structure. Although the proposition failed, its supporters continued their efforts.

In 1955 the City of Austin, Travis County, and the Texas Highway Department came to an agreement under which they jointly shared the cost of widening and repairing the bridge. By narrowing the walkways

The concrete arch Congress Avenue Bridge being built alongside the 1883 iron truss bridge that preceded it at the site for a quarter of a century. Photograph courtesy Austin–Travis County Collection, Austin Public Library, Austin, Texas.

and replacing the old ornamental concrete railings with metal, highway engineers were able to give it an effective roadway forty-four feet wide. Work began in spring, 1956, and was completed in September of the same year.

Few people thought about the Congress Avenue Bridge again for another twenty years while its four lanes of traffic remained open. In 1975, however, the outer two lanes were closed because state highway engineers found the cantilevered outer lanes in deteriorating condition. This situation required major repairs for the first time in the history of the bridge.

Over the next five years the Congress Avenue Bridge underwent significant reconstruction. Texas Highway Department engineers directed the removal of all portions of the bridge above the arches and piers. Crews then placed prestressed-concrete box girders from pier to pier, removing much of the weight from the old concrete arches but at the same time retaining their historic profile. In the process the engineers widened the structure slightly, giving it five lanes of traffic as well as space for both pedestrians and cyclists. The project was completed in early 1980, with a ceremonial reopening of the refurbished old bridge on May 19.

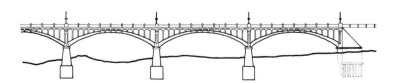

General plan of the 1908–10 Congress Avenue Bridge, showing one abutment, three piers, and three reinforced-concrete arches. Based on Waddell and Harrington, Consulting Engineers, Kansas City, Missouri, "Bridge over the Colorado River at Congress Avenue, Austin, Texas, for Travis County. General Layout," blueprint drawing, 1908, Engineering Department, District Office, Texas Department of Highways and Public Transportation, Austin, Texas. Drawing by the author.

41

Looking north along the Congress Avenue Bridge in the early 1950s, showing its original walkways, ornamental concrete railings, and lamp standards. Photograph courtesy Photographic Archives, Texas Department of Highways and Public Transportation, Austin, Texas.

Location: The Congress Avenue Bridge spans the Colorado River at the foot of Congress Avenue in downtown Austin.

Suggested Reading:

"Colorado River Bridges" vertical file. Austin–Travis County Collection, Austin Public Library, Austin, Tex.

"A New Reinforced Concrete Bridge across the Colorado River, Austin, Texas." *Engineering News* 63, no. 25 (June 23, 1910): 713.

17. *Copano Bay Causeway*

The Copano Bay Causeway (1930–31), preserved today by the State Department of Parks and Wildlife as a public fishing pier, is a classic example of the type of timber highway bridges constructed on the Texas coast half a century ago.

As early as 1928 preliminary plans were being prepared in Austin for a bridge across Copano Bay, a large but shallow inland extension of Aransas Bay, about forty miles up the coast from Corpus Christi. The project was planned jointly by the Texas Highway Department and Aransas County, the state and county agreeing to share the cost of construction in a two-thirds to one-third ratio. The bridge was needed not only to connect the communities of Rockport and

Fulton on the Live Oak Peninsula with the Lamar community on the Lamar Peninsula, but also to lessen the distance that motorists were required to drive in travel northeastward along the coast from Corpus Christi. Prior to the causeway's construction, they had to travel a number of miles inland to skirt Copano Bay.

In early January, 1930, the Texas Highway Department advertised for bids from contractors for the proposed bridge project. By January 22 the department had received several bids, and it awarded the contract to the Southwest L. E. Myers Company. The firm had two hundred working days in which to complete the causeway. Work began on February 15,

1930, but it went more slowly than had been expected, and the structure did not reach completion until early 1931.

As constructed, the Copano Bay Causeway consisted of 468 nineteen-foot wooden spans resting on bents with four creosoted piles each. Of the spans, 149 were southwest of a bascule draw-span, and 319 were to the northeast. The steel draw-span section was 62 feet, 3 inches long and provided a 39-foot, 3-inch clearance for boats and barges passing from landlocked Copano Bay into open Aransas Bay. The total length of the causeway was 8,955 feet. In addition to the structure itself, it had 1,305-foot and 1,605-foot earthen approaches at its southwest and northeast ends, respectively. The timber spans supported a 6-inch-thick concrete roadway 20 feet wide. Originally, the earthen approaches were covered with shell surfacing 18 inches thick and 20 feet wide. The average depth of the water over which the bridge passes is only 6 feet, although in some places it is considerably deeper. The top of the roadway was placed only 12 feet above mean low tide.

The steel bascule draw-span on the Copano Bay bridge was built according to the standard plan for such structures used by the State Highway Department in the 1930s. The actual ironwork was fabricated for the contractors by the International Steel and Iron Company of Evansville, Indiana. Shipped to the construction site in pieces, it was assembled at Copano Bay and its concrete counterbalances were poured in place. These two large weights facilitated the raising and lowering of the span with the hand-operated equipment that was installed between 1930 and 1931. Watchmen were provided with spartan quarters adjacent to the draw span, and they were required to tend it twenty-four hours a day to allow the passage of vessels through the bridge.

As built in 1930–31, the Copano Bay Causeway served the traffic needs on the Gulf Coast for twenty years with virtually no alterations. Since it never received the full force of any tropical storms, it survived without the reconstructions needed by other coastal bridges. In the 1950s the causeway at Copano Bay was improved by the addition of electrical equipment

Looking northeast along the 1930–31 Copano Bay Causeway, showing at the right the new concrete causeway, which replaced the old causeway in the 1960s. Photograph by the author, 1981.

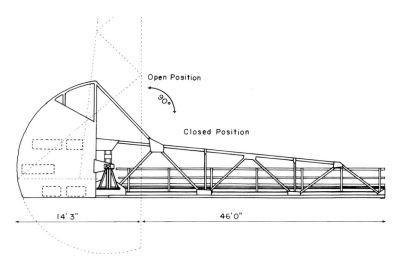

The Texas Highway Department standard-plan bascule draw-span of the type installed at the Copano Bay Causeway in 1930. Based on Texas, State Highway Department, "Texas State Highway Department Hand Operated Steel Bascule Span Sept. 1929," blueprint drawing, File Control No. 179–10, Calhoun County, Design Department, Texas Department of Highways and Public Transportation, Yoakum, Texas. Drawing by the author.

to raise and lower its bascule span and to replace the kerosene lamps that for two decades had been used for nighttime lighting. Other improvements to the bridge during the decade included the renovation of the decking on the draw span, replacement of the fenders at water level on both sides of the draw span, and the construction of an additional bridge tender's residence, garage, and supply room. With these slight changes, the old timber trestle remained in service into the mid-1960s.

Increasing traffic over the Copano Bay bridge during the late 1950s and early 1960s prompted plans for replacing the old wooden structure with a new concrete causeway. Whenever a boat or barge needed to pass through the timber bridge, long lines of automobiles backed up waiting for the draw span to close. The delays caused a considerable inconvenience to the traveling public and led to demands for the replacement of the trestle. Consequently, in 1964 the Texas Highway Department let a contract for the construction of a completely new concrete causeway parallel to the old one. Stretching 9,230 feet across the bay and including a high-rise section 50 feet above the water that provides 75 feet of horizontal clearance for vessels, the new bridge was dedicated on October 20, 1966, in honor of President Lyndon B. Johnson.

As soon as the new concrete bridge opened to the public, the old causeway was transferred to the Texas Parks and Wildlife Department. The bascule span and several hundred feet of timber trestle were removed from its center section and the two ends were converted to become the Copano Bay Causeway State Fishing Pier. The two bridge ends remain in the custody of the state Parks Department and today are outfitted with mercury vapor lamps; fish-cleaning facilities; rest rooms; and concessions selling bait, tackle, snacks, cold drinks, and other supplies. A small fee is charged to fish from the old bridge.

Location: The old Copano Bay Causeway stands above the shallow waters of Copano Bay parallel to the current concrete causeway carrying State Highway 35 across the bay, 3.5 miles northeast of Fulton.

Suggested Reading:

"New Bridge across Copano Bay." *Texas Highways* 13, no. 12 (December, 1966): 28–30.
Texas. State Highway Department. Construction and Repair Files on Project Control No. 180–4. Manuscript and microfilm. Engineering Department, Texas Department of Highways and Public Transportation, Corpus Christi, Tex.

18. Corpus Christi Seawall

The Corpus Christi Seawall (1939–40) has successfully protected Corpus Christi from the reoccurrence of the devastation it suffered from a great

hurricane in 1919. The attractive structure is seen by thousands of visitors annually.

The severe tropical storm that struck Corpus Christi

Looking south along the Corpus Christi Seawall between the harbor entrance and the marina. Photograph by the author, 1975.

with tremendous force on September 14, 1919, killed 284 persons and destroyed an estimated twenty million dollars' worth of property. Much of the city lay only about 5 to 9 feet above sea level, and the storm tides reached 11.5 feet above that. The entire low-lying section of the city was flooded and then struck by drifting timber and debris, which battered down virtually everything in its path. After the hurricane had passed, the residents of the city found themselves isolated from the world in terms of rail, wire, and highway communication.

The Corpus Christi disaster led the Texas legislature in 1921 to grant to the city for twenty-five years a portion of the state property taxes contributed by seven Gulf Coast counties (Nueces, Jim Wells, Jim Hogg, Duval, Brooks, Kleberg, and Willacy) for the construction of a breakwater and seawall. Funds deriving from this remission of tax reve-

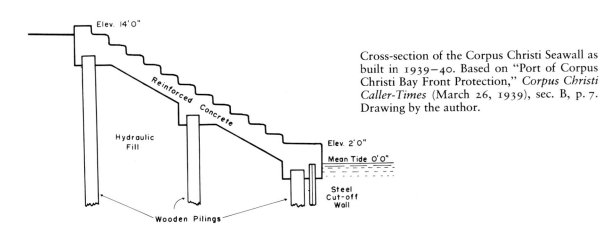

Cross-section of the Corpus Christi Seawall as built in 1939–40. Based on "Port of Corpus Christi Bay Front Protection," *Corpus Christi Caller-Times* (March 26, 1939), sec. B, p. 7. Drawing by the author.

45

nues were not great during the first years, but they enabled the city to start building a stone breakwater several thousand feet long and a short distance off-shore. Work began on the project in 1921 and continued through 1926. Although the breakwater was not as high as had been desired by municipal leaders, it was all that could be built with the funds available.

By 1938 an additional $900,000 in remitted taxes had accumulated. This larger amount was due in part to increased values of taxable property caused by the discovery of oil fields and the expansion of agriculture and ranching in the seven counties. With this money in hand and more expected, the City Council of Corpus Christi decided that the time had come to expand the protective structures on the bay front. Applications were made for Public Works Administration assistance, but no support was forthcoming from the New Deal agency. In June, 1939, the Texas legislature extended the tax remission period for an additional ten years, giving the city an expected $1.5 million to complete the planned bay-front improvement.

After city engineering staff and officials inspected other seawalls elsewhere along the Gulf and Atlantic coasts, they returned to Corpus Christi to plan a step-type concrete wall resting on creosoted pine pilings. Other features of the planned structure included a sheet-steel cut-off wall beneath the concrete toe of the seawall and hydraulic fill backing to support it from behind. The structure was planned to extend from the entrance of Corpus Christi harbor a distance of approximately twelve thousand feet to bluffs on the south side of the city.

To undertake the construction project, Corpus Christi had to purchase from private owners the entire area between Water Street and the actual bay front. This strip two hundred to five hundred feet wide and the length of the proposed seawall was mostly poorly drained land that at the time had comparatively little commercial value. Its acquisition gave the city complete control of its bay front, and in time it permitted the construction of recreational areas and the beautifully landscaped Shoreline Boulevard just behind the seawall.

Before construction began on the seawall, the contractors made test borings into the ground at three-hundred-foot intervals along the line of the proposed structure. From the data they obtained, they were able to determine the proper lengths for the sheet-steel cut-off wall at the front base of the seawall as well as those for the creosoted pine pilings that would

support it. The lengths for the sheet steel in the cut-off wall varied from fifteen to thirty-four feet, and the wooden piles varied in length from twenty-nine to fifty-four feet.

After the borings were made, the contractor used hydraulic fill methods to create an earthen mound along the proposed line for the seawall. His men then excavated a trench for the toe of the seawall and in this area drove into position the sheet-steel pilings for the cut-off wall. In the meantime, other crews built up the long earthen mound so that the fill was carried up to grade along the line of the wall. The earth then was covered with a temporary layer of construction paper on which the concrete would be placed.

The seawall was designed to be laid in forty-foot sections with interlocking expansion joints at the ends of each section. The weight of the concrete is supported on the creosoted wooden pilings set at ten-foot centers. The thickness of the reinforced concrete slab is twelve inches, and it is faced with "steps" with one-foot, six-inch tread and one-foot risers. Starting one foot, six inches below mean tide level, the seawall rises fifteen feet, six inches, making it stand two feet, six inches above all known flood tides.

One of the interesting problems encountered by the engineers in building the Corpus Christi Seawall was the matter of draining flood- and rainwaters from the downtown business district of the city. This situation was complicated by the existence of a considerable arroyo draining a part of the main commercial area. To handle the flow of water from the commercial area above the bluff, the designers planned a nine-foot, horseshoe-shaped, closed pressure sewer, which extended upstream from the base of the bluff at Broadway to discharge at the seawall. At each street intersection, the seawall was designed with gravity sewers provided with twin sets of automatic one-way gates for draining floodwaters through the structure into the bay. Additional protection for the downtown business district was provided in 1947 with the construction of a large horseshoe-shaped structure under Water Street connected to two large pump stations, which force storm water into the bay during periods of high tide and above-normal rainfall.

Along with the actual seawall construction came an accompanying project to provide a safe harbor for small boats. Built within the protected area behind the refurbished 1920s breakwater, this marina was designed with a minimum of eight feet of water. Access and parking are provided by three land masses, two T-shaped and one L-shaped, which were con-

A shrimp boat docked at the 1939–40 marina on the bay front in Corpus Christi. Photograph by the author, 1975.

structed using a steel shear pile perimeter, dead-men tie-backs, and hydraulic fill. To this day the marina serves as a recreational focus for the entire bay-front area.

For more than forty years the Corpus Christi Sea-wall has protected the city from tropical storms. Equally important, it has given the residents of the city the feeling of security that has permitted them to make Corpus Christi the beautiful city it is today.

Location: The Corpus Christi Seawall stretches over two miles along the bay front at the east side of Cor-pus Christi. Its vantage points are numerous along Shoreline Boulevard.

Suggested Reading:

Noyes, E. N. "The Corpus Christi Sea Wall Project." *Civil Engineering* 9, no. 9 (September, 1939): 536–38.
"Port of Corpus Christi Bay Front Protection." *Corpus Christi Caller-Times* (March 26, 1939), sec. B, pp. 6–7.

19. *Corsicana Oil Field Discovery Well*

Drilled in 1894 for water, not oil, the discovery well for the Corsicana Oil Field opened production in the first commercially successful oil field west of the Mississippi. This field brought the modern petroleum in-dustry to Texas and set the stage for the unprece-dented oil discoveries on the Texas Gulf Coast less than a decade later.

By 1893 the residents of Corsicana had outgrown

47

The forest of derricks that grew up in Corsicana by 1898. Photograph courtesy Navarro County Historical Society, Corsicana, Texas.

their outmoded 1883 waterworks, and they began requesting a new system to serve the town. Accordingly, the Corsicana Water Development Company incorporated the next year with $100,000 in stock to drill an artesian well and provide its water to consumers through a system of mains. This firm contracted with Horace G. Johnston, Elmer H. Aiken, and Charles Rittensbacher, men who had drilled other successful artesian wells in the vicinity, to sink a water well in the town of Corsicana.

In the spring of 1894, Johnston, Aiken, and Rittensbacher began boring a well at a site about a block south of the Cotton Belt Railroad tracks on South Twelfth Street. Work progressed fairly smoothly until the drillers reached a depth of 1,027 feet (on June 9). To their great dismay, crude oil began to spurt over the floor of their rig. This meant that they would have to case off the oil-bearing level to prevent the petroleum from contaminating the artesian flow that they were seeking. Despite the "problems" caused by the petroleum, the men continued their effort, finally

reaching water at 2,470 feet. To the three drillers, the oil was nothing more than an annoyance.

News of the discovery, however, soon spread. Oil-production leases were sold covering the entire vicinity. The largest of several firms organized to exploit the discovery was the Corsicana Oil Development Company. It secured leases covering about ten thousand acres around the artesian well site. The firm then made an agreement with two oilmen from the East, John H. Galey and J. M. Guffey, to drill five wells in exchange for a half interest in all the company's oil and gas leases. Their first well was sunk on a town lot about 200 feet south of the city well. In October, 1895, the drillers found oil at 1,040 feet, but the natural flow from the well was only about 2.5 barrels a day. They continued drilling the other four wells, however, and found better producers in 1896 and 1897. Even as these initial exploratory wells were being drilled, numerous other small production companies began drilling their own wells in the neighborhood. As early as 1896, the Corsicana Field in

The first railway tank car loaded with oil shipped from Corsicana. Photograph courtesy Navarro County Historical Society, Corsicana, Texas.

An early-day rotary drilling rig from Corsicana on exhibit in the National Museum of American History of the Smithsonian Institution in Washington, D.C. Photograph courtesy Smithsonian Institution.

Navarro County had become recognized as the main contributing element in Texas oil production, which in that year jumped from 50 to 1,450 barrels annually. By 1897 production had risen to 65,975 barrels from forty-seven wells.

Petroleum was found at depths of 1,000 to 1,040 feet, where the oil-bearing sand layer was from 10 to 40 feet thick. After a drill bit struck the sand, it usually took a day for the free-flowing oil to reach the surface, although a few wells spouted it upward with more force. Derricks sprang up in yards, gardens, and horse lots throughout the town, sometimes only feet apart. Corsicana quickly changed from a quiet little backwater into a bustling, crowded, boisterous young city filled with overcrowded boardinghouses and hotels. Residences that had not rented for years were

leased at premium prices. The *Dallas Morning News* reported to its readers that "Corsicana is one city in Texas that is full up . . . every business house in the city has a tenant, a condition of things, so far as business houses are concerned, that has not existed for years."

Oil production at Corsicana continued to grow and finally outstripped local demand. An outlet was needed, but no one knew where or how to sell the oil. Solving the problem in 1898, Joseph Stephen Cullinan established a refinery (this, the first refinery in the Southwest, is discussed in entry no. 21). At the plant, workers processed the crude oil into more marketable products, which Cullinan then arranged for sale by the Standard Oil Company.

One of the greatest contributions of the Corsicana

Field was its role in the development and testing of rotary oil-well drilling rigs. Until the 1890s virtually all well drilling was done with cable-tool rigs. These machines literally pounded holes in the ground through the repeated striking of heavy drill bits. Once the material was pulverized, bailers were sent down on the cable to remove the loose rock and earth. These rigs operated satisfactorily in hard formations, but in softer formations like those at Corsicana they often caused the holes to cave in.

The methods and ideas of several early drillers contributed to the evolution of the modern rotary drilling system at Corsicana. At least three men had used elements of the system in the late nineteenth century. Two of them, M. C. and C. E. Baker, came to Corsicana as drillers from Yankton, Dakota Territory, soon after the initial discovery at the artesian well, and they brought with them elements of their prototype rotary drilling rig. In their first machine, water was poured down the well through a hollow drill pipe, and the pulverized debris was washed up on the outside to the surface. The drill bit turned or rotated as the water was forced downward. Initially, operation was by means of a horse turning a "horse power"—geared device, but later steam engines were added to the machinery. Such rigs made it possible to penetrate with comparative ease the vast areas of soft, unconsolidated material in the Texas Gulf Coast region.

Among the men who observed the Bakers' new equipment were Johnston, Aiken, and Rittensbacher—the drillers of the discovery well. They saw their greatest opportunities in manufacturing drilling rigs rather than in actually boring the wells, so they set up a small plant in Corsicana for making the equipment. Working together they perfected a rotary drill system by 1901 that combined hydraulic, screw, and abrasive principles. Marketed as the Gumbo Buster, it was an immediate success. They and their successors continued producing and selling these and other types of drilling equipment until 1944, when their plant was purchased by the Bethlehem Supply Company.

One of the most lasting effects of the development of the Corsicana Oil Field was the conservation legislation passed by the Texas legislature as a result of the Navarro County experiences. Disapproving of the great waste of valuable oil that occurred at Corsicana, the legislators passed a law that prohibited drilling into a second oil-bearing level without encasing the wells passing through the first. They also enacted statutes requiring that all abandoned wells be plugged and that natural gas not be burned for illumination purposes between 8:00 A.M. and 5:00 P.M.

The Corsicana Oil Field, the first commercially successful oil field west of the Mississippi, is still an area of petroleum activity. Second and third booms hit Navarro County in the 1920s and 1950s, and the county remains a substantial producer. Its claim to fame, however, is as the birthplace of the modern Texas petroleum industry.

Location: The discovery well for the Corsicana Oil Field is preserved as a historical monument in Petroleum Industry Park, across from the Wolf canning plant in the 400 block of South Twelfth Street in Corsicana. There visitors may examine the wellhead of the discovery well and read historical markers erected by the state and by the Texas Mid-Continent Oil and Gas Association. Adjoining the park to the south is the preserved early twentieth-century H. C. Nicoll welding shop, which also has an interpretive historical marker.

Suggested Reading:

Dunn, Jane G. "A History of the Oil Industry in Navarro County." M.A. thesis, Baylor University, 1967.
Rister, Carl Coke. *Oil! Titan of the Southwest.* Norman: University of Oklahoma Press, 1949.
Warner, C. A. *Texas Oil and Gas since 1543.* Houston: Gulf Publishing Company, 1939.

20. *Cuero Hydroelectric Plant*

Established in 1896, the Cuero Hydroelectric Plant is one of the oldest hydroelectric plants in Texas and represents a classic example of the type of hydroelectric facility that began appearing in the state during the 1890s.

The Cuero Hydroelectric Plant consists of a masonry dam across the Guadalupe River and an adjacent powerhouse at the east end of the dam. In 1896 the Buchel Power and Irrigation Company began constructing the dam and first generating station. As early as 1891 there already had been an electric company in Cuero producing current with a steam engine

The Cuero Hydroelectric Plant as it appeared about the turn of the century with its wooden powerhouse. Photograph courtesy Texas State Library, Austin, Texas.

and a Heisler dynamo, but brothers Otto and C. August Buchel with other financial backers created a separate firm to compete with the already-existing company.

The Buchel Power and Irrigation Company constructed a 220-foot masonry dam across the Guadalupe and at its east end erected a wooden powerhouse. Construction progressed through 1897, with the company's lines first carrying power to Cuero in March, 1898. For a while the Buchel Company competed with its predecessor in the electricity business, the Cuero Light and Power Company, but

within a year the earlier firm sold its holdings to the Buchel brothers. The hydroelectric plant operated with dynamos powered by two American turbines with a 10-foot working head, which gave them approximately four hundred horsepower. An auxiliary steam engine was added to the system to produce electricity at times of insufficient stream flow.

In 1903 the wheel pit at the plant was enlarged, three new fifty-inch Samson turbines were added, and the height of the dam was increased two feet. Much of this new work, however, was damaged in 1908, when the entire plant burned to the water's edge. That same

The dam and powerhouse at the Cuero Hydroelectric Plant. Photograph by the author, 1975.

Two of the 1920s vertical turbines in place in the wheelpit at the Cuero Hydroelectric Plant. Photograph by the author, 1975.

year a group of local businessmen bought the Buchel brothers' hydroelectric plant and organized themselves as the Cuero Light and Power Company. They rebuilt the entire generating facility, using the old dam, and started the plant again on December 28, 1908. In 1911 the owners raised the crest of the dam another three feet, three inches, giving it a total height of fifteen feet, three inches. At this time, they also replaced the old American turbines with three new fifty-six-inch Samson turbines.

In 1914 the hydroelectric facility was purchased by the Texas Southern Electric Company, which built the present concrete wheel pit at a cost of thirty thousand dollars. This firm soon reorganized as the Texas Gas and Electric Company. In 1920 it went into receivership, operating under the receiver's control for almost two years. In 1922 the Cuero plant was purchased at auction by the firm of Morrison and McCall, which operated it for about three years.

Soon after this purchase, the Guadalupe River flooded severely, and a huge barrage of driftwood several miles long struck the dam, pushing off a section 7

Interior of the powerhouse at the Cuero Hydroelectric Plant, with its three 1922 Allis-Chalmers 375-kw, 2,300-volt vertical generators. Photograph by the author, 1975.

feet, 8 inches high and leaving the plant without power. While the dam was being repaired with a reinforced-concrete section, an auxiliary steam power generator provided electricity to the town. On April 3, 1922, during another flood, high water cut around the west end of the dam, opening a new channel 125 feet wide. To correct this damage, the dam was extended to the west across the gap to its present length.

In 1922 Morrison and McCall installed the existing generating equipment at the Cuero Hydroelectric Plant. This consists of three vertical three-phase, sixty-cycle, 2,300-volt, 200-rpm generators with 375-kw capacity, made by the Allis-Chalmers Manufacturing Company. Below these generators in the wheel pit were placed three vertical turbines also made by Allis-Chalmers. These are of the fixed-blade propeller type with a capacity of 550 horsepower with a fifteen-foot head.

With its 1920s generating equipment and a modified 1890s dam, the Cuero Hydroelectric Plant continued to operate for the next forty years with comparatively few changes. Morrison and McCall owned and ran the plant until they sold it to the Texas Central Power Company in 1925. In the next year the owners changed their name to the Central Power and Light Company. This firm built an increasingly large power network throughout Central Texas during the subsequent decades, a network in which the Cuero facility contributed a constantly decreasing proportion of electricity. The old Cuero plant was finally shut down on October 20, 1965, because its capacity had grown so small contrasted with that of the total system that it was no longer commercially feasible to operate it. Since that time the powerhouse has stood silent, with most of its equipment intact.

Location: The Cuero Hydroelectric Plant is located on private property on the Guadalupe River about two miles north of the town of Cuero and is not generally accessible to the public.

Suggested Reading:

Buchel Power and Irrigation Company, Cuero, Tex. *Prospectus . . . the Water Power and Transmission Plant of the Buchel Power & Irrigation Company, at Cuero, De Witt County, Texas.* Cuero, Tex.: Star Print, [ca. 1896]. Photocopy available at the Center for the History of Engineering, Texas Tech University, Lubbock, Tex.

Godfrey, F. A., and C. L. Dowell. *Major Hydroelectric Powerplants in Texas: Historical and Descriptive Information.* Texas Water Development Board Report No. 81. Austin: Texas Water Development Board, 1968.

21. Cullinan Oil Refinery

The J. S. Cullinan Oil Refinery, established in 1898, was the first major oil refinery in the southwestern United States. Many of its original structures, including one of its brick and sheet iron stills, still survive. The site has the additional distinction of having been the birthplace of the Mobil Corporation.

In October, 1897, Joseph Stephen Cullinan, an experienced petroleum refiner from Pennsylvania, visited Corsicana at the invitation of the town's mayor. Local business and civic leaders had wanted him to come there to evaluate the possibility of establishing a refinery to process at least some of the oil that was coming from the growing Corsicana Oil Field. The oilman already was planning a trip to California, so he routed his travel through Texas. He was sufficiently impressed with the opportunities at Corsicana to stay for several days and make plans to refine the oil he found there.

Cullinan entered into an agreement with a number of local oil producers for them to supply him with 150,000 barrels of oil at fifty cents a barrel. In return he proposed to start an integrated operation consisting of producing, storing, refining, and marketing petroleum. His idea included connecting the wells to proposed storage tanks at the refinery by pipelines. The processed petroleum from the refinery would then be shipped to markets by rail.

Having made these plans, Cullinan set off for the East to seek backing for the Corsicana refinery project. He found the support he needed and proceeded to order material for the construction of the pipelines, tanks, and refinery. His backers, however, reneged on their promises of financial assistance. Cullinan was forced to locate new investors to fund his project. Meeting in Saint Louis with one of his old friends, Calvin N. Payne of Titusville, Pennsylvania, he explained to him that he had found a dependable supply of crude oil in the Corsicana Field, that the material

A brick and sheet iron petroleum refining still at the J. C. Cullinan Oil Refinery. Photograph by the author, 1975.

for his planned system was already on its way to Texas, and that he desperately needed $150,000 to complete the project. Payne conferred with Henry C. Folger in New York. There he convinced the capitalist to supply the money Cullinan needed. Consequently, in early 1898 the three men, Cullinan, Payne, and Folger, met to form the J. S. Cullinan Company to collect, refine, and market the oil from the Corsicana Field. They then made arrangements to sell their entire production to the Waters-Pierce Oil Company, a Standard Oil subsidiary.

With money in hand, Cullinan returned to Corsicana in spring, 1898, to await the arrival of his materials and equipment. In the meantime, E. R. Brown, a young assistant refinery superintendent from the Standard Oil refinery at Olean, New York, arrived on the scene. Cullinan had seen that Brown, who was not yet thirty, was a man of unusual ability, and he

hired him to supervise the construction and later the operation of the Corsicana refinery.

Brown and Cullinan chose a twenty-acre site on the south side of Corsicana for their plant. It was located only about a mile from the producing area of the Corsicana Field and was conveniently near the line of the Houston and Texas Central Railroad. On June 6, 1898, they broke ground for the new facility, which began operation when the first still was fired on Christmas Day. Petroleum refining at this time consisted mainly of boiling crude oil until it vaporized, catching the vapors as the oil passed through heat stages, and then condensing those vapors back into liquid form. The main products of the Cullinan Refinery were kerosene, fuel and lubricating oil, and a small amount of gasoline. The initial capacity of the plant was five hundred barrels of crude daily.

Cullinan remained at the Corsicana refinery until

Buildings at the Cullinan Refinery about the turn of the century. Photograph courtesy Navarro County Historical Society, Corsicana, Texas.

1901, when he left for the Spindletop Oil Field near Beaumont. Among his activities during his turn-of-the-century residence in Corsicana were two notable efforts to develop new uses for petroleum. In 1898 he and his brother fitted a Cotton Belt steam locomotive with a special device that allowed it to burn oil rather than coal. Similar experiments were being conducted about the same time in other parts of the country. The success of the Cullinan brothers, however, resulted in 1901 in the Houston and Texas Central Railroad conversion of its locomotives to oil as a fuel. Cullinan also devised a program of sprinkling oil on unpaved streets as a means of preventing dust from blowing. This gave Corsicana the claim of having the only "dustless streets" in Texas. In 1902, a year after he went to Beaumont, Cullinan left the J. S. Cullinan Company to devote himself to interests in the Spindletop field. There he was instrumental in the same year in forming the Texas Company, which he later served as president.

After Cullinan's departure from Corsicana, the refinery he had built passed through several reorganizations. The firm first became the Corsicana Refining Company, then the Navarro Refining Company, then John Sealy and Company, and finally, in 1911, the Magnolia Petroleum Company. This last firm was the direct predecessor of the Mobil Corporation.

The J. S. Cullinan Refinery, birthplace of Magnolia

An artist's conception of the Cullinan Refinery in its heyday, around the turn of the century. Courtesy Navarro County Historical Society, Corsicana, Texas.

Houston and Texas Central Railroad steam locomotive No. 334, the first of that firm's engines to be converted from coal to oil as fuel after its feasibility had been demonstrated at Corsicana. Photograph courtesy Navarro County Historical Society, Corsicana, Texas.

and Mobil and the first refinery in the Southwest, remains intact today. Although it has not been used for refining in many years, the facility is still an important pipeline terminal on the system of the Mobil Pipe Line Company, a subsidiary of the Mobil Corporation.

Location: The J. S. Cullinan Oil Refinery is located on the southern outskirts of Corsicana at the west side of FM 709, one mile south of its intersection with State Highway 31. Although the compound containing the old refinery is not open to the general public, most of the surviving turn-of-the-century structures can be seen from the highway.

Suggested Reading:

Dunn, Jane C. "A History of the Oil Industry in Navarro County." M.A. thesis, Baylor University, 1967.
Magnolia Pipe Line Company, Dallas, Tex. *Welcome to Magnolia.* Dallas: Magnolia Pipe Line Company [ca. 1957].

22. *Daisy Bradford No. 3 Oil Well*

The East Texas Oil Field, the largest oil field in the contiguous United States, was opened up by the discovery of oil at the Daisy Bradford No. 3 Oil Well a few miles west of Henderson in Rusk County. This field for over half a century has been a major source of petroleum for the United States.

The success at the Daisy Bradford No. 3 is credited to the dogged determination of Columbus Marvin Joiner, a native of Center Star, Alabama. As a young man he read law, became an attorney in Tennessee, where he served as a state legislator, and in 1897 moved to Oklahoma. There he began dealing in oil properties, making and losing two fortunes in petroleum before turning his attention to Texas in 1926. Despite the prevailing beliefs of knowledgeable geologists to the contrary, Joiner felt that vast pools of oil lay beneath portions of East Texas. His opinions were shared by a small number of other people, among them a group of Oklahoma City speculators who in 1919 purchased oil leases on about twelve thousand acres in Rusk County. The businessmen missed a few areas in the county, and Joiner proceeded to secure leases there.

Joiner asked his geologist, Dr. A. D. Lloyd, to study maps of the areas encompassing his leases to advise him where he might have the best prospects for strik-

C. M. "Dad" Joiner signing oil lease papers in East Texas. Photograph courtesy Special Collections, Ralph W. Steen Library, Stephen F. Austin State University, Nacogdoches, Texas.

Automobiles carrying sightseers who converged on the Daisy Bradford No. 3 Well in October, 1930. Photograph courtesy East Texas Oil Museum, Kilgore, Texas.

ing oil. Lloyd recommended an area roughly seven miles west of Henderson. There Joiner had a lease on parts of the old Andrew H. Miller property, owned in the 1920s by one of his descendants, Mrs. Daisy Bradford. In one of the poorer parts of the state, the farm was in an area of mixed cultivated fields and pastures scattered on rolling hills that in places were covered with oak, pine, and sweet gum trees. The local residents raised cotton, sweet potatoes, and corn in an almost subsistence life-style.

Joiner began work on the Bradford farm in summer, 1927. He and his men moved their used equipment on heavy, mule-drawn wagons and started erecting a wooden derrick where they proposed to drill. Some of the timbers for the derrick came from trees that stood on the farm. Drilling of the Daisy Bradford No. 1 proceeded for six months, but then Joiner was forced to abandon the well. The derrick and rig were skidded several hundred feet to a new site, but months passed before he was able to raise enough capital to

begin drilling anew. Finally, work began on a second well, but it too was abandoned as a dry hole.

In March, 1929, work began on a third attempt at the Bradford farm. The eyes of East Texas watched the activities at the flimsy timber derrick fitted with worn-out equipment and a pair of mismatched boilers. Onlookers even gave the boilers names, Big Joe and Little Joe. Joiner, who was just a year short of seventy, came to be known locally as Dad. Work continued on the Daisy Bradford No. 3 until by January, 1930, it had reached 1,530 feet. Activity again was suspended while Joiner traveled about the countryside trying to raise more money by selling additional parts of his oil leases. The operating funds for the drillers got so low that even when they returned to work the only fuel they could afford for their boilers was wood chopped from the scrubby pines on the farm. Fortunately, Joiner was able to raise enough money to continue on down to a depth of 3,592 feet, where the men found a trace of oil in early September, 1930. Favorable in-

C. M. "Dad" Joiner (third from left, wearing a tie) shaking hands with his geologist, Dr. A. D. Lloyd, at the Daisy Bradford No. 3 soon after Joiner had struck oil. Photograph courtesy East Texas Oil Museum, Kilgore, Texas.

dications from a drill-stem test induced an oil field supply company to provide Joiner with enough casing to attempt to put the hole into production, so work progressed until October 3, 1930, when a crowd of expectant spectators applauded as the drillers blew in a well that gushed oil over the top of the derrick.

Only days after the discovery the *Oil and Gas Journal* described the scene at the well:

> For the past week oil scouts, geologists and lease brokers have been hovering near the well, many of them sleeping in their cars or on improvised beds during the last three nights, and people from the farms and surrounding towns have practically been camping on the well waiting for it to come in and

blow off the top of the crown block. Hastily erected hamburger stands have been having large and quick turnovers of their stock, and cheese sandwiches have been selling at 15 cents per, slabs of cheese melting before the onslaught of the hungry mob as if it were fried chicken, and Mrs. Bradford's farm house is surrounded at meal time by many hungry people who are attracted by the sign outside the house, "Meals 75 cents, inside." . . .

One man about the well was highly elated to tell how his wife had given Mr. Joiner $125 for a sublease on 8 acres only a stone's throw from the test, and on October 2 selling 4 acres of the 8 for $10,000 and a well which will be drilled. . . . Several other such sales were made by Mr. Joiner to

The Daisy Bradford No. 3 as it appears in production today. Photograph by the author, 1983.

raise a little cash now and then to keep things moving, making real profits for those who were really benefactors in time of need, but who acquired holdings for a song in comparison to the prices they would now command.

An almost instant boom hit economically depressed Rusk County. A tent city called Joinerville sprang up like a mushroom at the point where a dirt road turned off the Henderson highway to the new well. A contemporary report noted that "cloth penants [*sic*] wave in the breeze in the new town" advertising that lots could still be purchased cheaply but that they would "probably rise in price . . . as the town is enlarged."

The center of the activity, however, was Henderson itself. Not only were the hotels and rooming houses filled with new arrivals, but owners of private homes also began renting all their unoccupied rooms, no matter what size or condition. "All spare rooms are now bringing in dividends to the owners," a reporter noted. The eating places were doing a "rushing business," and the county courthouse was a beehive of activity, with hundreds of leases being bought and sold. Abstract companies filled up all extra space in the building with stenographers who worked overtime every day except Sunday "knocking out records for prospective clients, who are writing and calling for completed abstracts by the dozens."

The Daisy Bradford No. 3 was only the start of a much larger boom in East Texas. Two months later, on December 19, the Bateman No. 1 Lou Ella Crim came in near Kilgore, and much of the feverish lease and promotion activity shifted there. Then on January 26, 1931, a third major well, the Arkansas Gas and Fuel Company No. 1 Lathrop well, blew in near Longview. This indicated to all observers that the geologists had been wrong and that indeed a vast pool of oil existed beneath several counties of East Texas. Because their geologists had advised them that such resources could not exist in the region, most of the

major oil companies had not entered the early lease play, leaving much of the development in the field to independent operators. By July, 1931, 1,100 wells had been drilled in the new field, with 3,396 drilled by the end of the year. The number of wells drilled was phenomenal, the week of October 28, 1931, witnessing the completion of 172 wells, an average of just over one an hour. From its discovery in October, 1930, through 1944, the East Texas Oil Field produced an amazing 2,104,173,790 barrels of crude oil, over twice as much as any other field in the history of the United States to that time.

Location: The Daisy Bradford No. 3 Oil Well is sufficiently hidden in the back country of the East Texas Oil Field that many local residents have never visited the site. It can be reached, however, on paved roads. The simplest route to the well site begins by taking State Highway 64 about 2.4 miles east from Turnertown to the Pioneer Park roadside rest area. From the east end of the rest area, drive in a generally northerly direction on a meandering, roughly paved county road 1.2 miles to a T intersection. Avoid turns onto any of the unpaved roads that branch from the road. At the T intersection, turn right onto another paved county road and proceed a half mile eastward, passing a large sheet-metal-roofed barn to the first paved road branching to the left. Take this paved road north 0.3 mile to a small fenced parking area adjacent to a granite historical marker commemorating the Daisy Bradford No. 3 Well. The well itself is located about seventy-five yards down the grassy hill directly behind the marker.

Suggested Reading:

Bredbert, L. E. "Bringing in Rusk County Discovery." *Oil and Gas Journal* 29, no. 21 (October 9, 1930): 50.
Rister, Carl Coke. *Oil! Titan of the Southwest.* Norman: University of Oklahoma Press, 1949.

23. *Dallas—Oak Cliff Viaduct*

Connecting the cities of Dallas and Oak Cliff and spanning the Trinity River and its flood plain, the Dallas—Oak Cliff Viaduct in its day was one of the longest reinforced-concrete arch bridges in America. Since its dedication in 1912, it has served as a continuous link between the two cities and even today is used by thousands of motorists.

The first bridges between Dallas and Oak Cliff were erected in the mid-nineteenth century, one as early as 1855, but from time to time they all were put out of commission at least temporarily by seasonal flooding on the Trinity River. Local residents accustomed themselves either to commuting to work across the river in boats or to waiting for the waters to recede

Looking northeast along the Dallas–Oak Cliff Viaduct near downtown Dallas. Photograph by the author, 1983.

and for the bridges to be repaired before they went from one side to the other. This situation persisted until the great Trinity River flood of late May, 1908. This inundation completely washed away all the existing bridges, stopped all rail communication with downtown Dallas, and flooded residences in much of the area. This disaster convinced the citizens of Dallas County that the time had come to build a permanent bridge to ensure a tie between Dallas and Oak Cliff.

Less than a year later, in April, 1909, the county engineer advertised for competitive plans for the design of a concrete viaduct to connect Dallas with Oak Cliff. A committee of three experts was appointed to evaluate the proposed designs. From fifteen submissions they chose the plans drawn up by Ira G. Hedrick, a member of the engineering firm of Hedrick

and Cochrane of Kansas City, Missouri. They accepted Hedrick's designs as originally prepared, with only two minor exceptions, the alterations being a change in pier footings and a slight widening of the roadway. This proposed structure was to include reinforced-concrete arch spans, concrete girder spans, one ninety-eight-foot steel span, and earthen embankments at the extreme ends of its approaches.

While the plans were being drawn and then evaluated, the county commissioners of Dallas County proposed the sale of bonds in the amount of $609,796.75 to fund the construction of a permanent viaduct across the river. The voters approved the proposal in April, 1910, and county commissioners opened bidding for the actual construction project. The recipient of the major portion of the contract was the firm of Corrigan, Lee and Halpin of Kansas City, with

Elevation of a typical portion of the Dallas–Oak Cliff Viaduct and of its Trinity River crossing. Based on Victor H. Cochrane, "The Dallas–Oak Cliff Viaduct," *Engineering Record* 63, no. 13 (April 1, 1911): 357. Drawing by the author.

the contract for the concrete pilings for the piers going to the Gulf Concrete Construction Company of Houston. The entire project was supervised by the firm of Hedrick and Cochrane as consulting engineers. By October, 1910, work had begun.

The first stage of construction consisted of preparing the footings for the concrete piers, which would support the arch portion of the structure. At the locations for the piers for the arch spans, men used special machines to drive steel cores into the ground. After reaching an average depth of about fourteen feet, they withdrew the cores and poured concrete into the holes to form the pilings. Concrete footings were used throughout, with the exception of cypress timber pilings employed beneath the piers of both sides of the ninety-eight-foot steel span.

After the placement of the piles was completed, the principal contractors began their phase of construc-

seventy-nine feet, six inches from center to center of piers. At the point where the viaduct crosses the actual channel of the Trinity River, the U.S. Corps of Engineers required that there be a total vertical clearance of sixty feet from the normal low-water level to the bridge. Already at this date plans were being considered for the construction of a Trinity River barge canal, and the authorities felt that this clearance would be necessary for the passage of barges and other vessels beneath the bridge. To provide this vertical clearance, a ninety-eight-foot steel girder span was put into place. Its four steel girders were encased in concrete so that they would have an appearance uniform with that of the remainder of the structure. The approaches to the viaduct consist of earth fill and concrete girder trestles.

After the pier construction was completed, complex wooden forms were erected and steel put in place for

Sectional elevation of a typical reinforced-concrete arch span in the Dallas–Oak Cliff Viaduct. Based on "Reinforced-Concrete Viaduct between Dallas and Oak Cliff, Texas," *Engineering News* 65, no. 13 (March 30, 1911): 394. Drawing by the author.

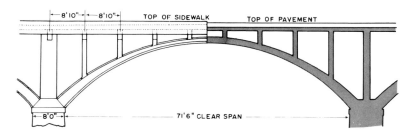

tion work with the actual piers. As the viaduct was designed, it includes several different types of piers. The ordinary piers for the arch section of the bridge are massive concrete structures carrying the arches high above most recorded flood levels. Every fifth pair is made stronger than the others in case the arch on the other side of the pier should fail. The two piers on each side of the span across the riverbed are of special design, as they support not a concrete arch span but rather the ninety-eight-foot steel girder span. Both the ordinary and the so-called abutment piers are pierced longitudinally by two openings nine feet wide and spanned at their tops by arches.

Reinforced-concrete arches make up most of the length of the Dallas–Oak Cliff Viaduct. Fifty-one in number and poured in position, they have a clear span of seventy-one feet, six inches and measure

pouring the reinforced-concrete arches. These were made in continuous pours that averaged about fourteen hours after all form work was completed. Then the roadway sections were poured and the ornamental concrete guardrails, which were poured separately, were put in place. The lamp standards at each pier were poured in position.

Coming from Houston Street in downtown Dallas, the bridge angles to the right at the end of its approach at an angle of 47° 44′. This northeast approach, 439 feet long, is at an ascending grade of 2.8 percent. The roadway proceeds over concrete arches to the steel Trinity River span on a level grade. After passing over the river, the viaduct continues over concrete arches in the same direction at a slight descending grade of 0.74 percent to the point where it meets its approach spans at the southwest end, after which the grade is maintained to its juncture with Lancaster Avenue. The total length of the viaduct, including its approaches, is 6,562 feet. The clear horizontal span of the 98-foot steel girders across the river channel is 90 feet. The bulk of the structure consists of its fifty-one reinforced concrete arch spans, which constitute 4,055 feet of the total length.

The contractors completed the Dallas–Oak Cliff Viaduct in early 1912, with the official opening on February 22. Impressive festivities accompanied the dedication ceremonies, which included public speakers, a parade of vehicles across the newly completed bridge, the singing of "America" by thousands of children from the schools of Oak Cliff and Dallas, and the release of carrier pigeons to spread the message of the opening of the bridge to different parts of the two cities, all concluded by an evening of "music in the air and . . . fireworks illuminating the heavens."

Herbert Gambrell, at the time a boy, was the first one to cross the officially opened viaduct, much to the chagrin of parade officials. He recalled years later that he was "right up front" near the lead automobile, which was to carry the officials across the viaduct in the opening parade. Gambrell was on his new bicycle, and after the chain was let down for the vehicles to pass over the bridge, he noticed that the driver of the lead car had stalled it. This blocked all the other automobiles. "When I saw him get out to crank start it, that was all I needed." Young Gambrell was off across the bridge, the first person to cross it after it was officially opened.

Since 1912, the Dallas–Oak Cliff Viaduct has served as a reliable tie between the two cities. The viaduct itself has changed very little. In the 1930s the Trinity River channel was straightened and two huge earthen levees placed on either side of it. Their construction meant that only a portion of the viaduct actually was needed to provide a roadway from levee to levee, but no changes were made in the bridge. On February 26, 1973, the traffic flow across the viaduct was changed from two-way to one-way, carrying motorists from Houston Street in downtown Dallas southwest to Oak Cliff. Today it still carries thousands of commuters between the two cities, few of them aware that they are crossing the Trinity on a bridge built at a time when there were more horses than automobiles in Dallas County.

Location: The Dallas–Oak Cliff Viaduct carries one-way traffic from Houston Street in downtown Dallas across the Trinity River and its present-day industrial area to the suburb of Oak Cliff. It may be viewed either from its roadway, although stopping is prohibited, or from any of the several cross streets that pass beneath it in the old Trinity River floodplain.

Suggested Reading:

Noyes, E. N. "Construction of the Concrete Viaduct between Dallas and Oak Cliff, Texas." *Engineering Record* 66, no. 19 (November 9, 1912): 520–22.
"Reinforced-Concrete Viaduct between Dallas and Oak Cliff, Texas." *Engineering News* 65, no. 13 (March 30, 1911): 392–94.

24. Dallas Union Terminal

The Dallas Union Terminal, built between 1914 and 1916, is one of the handful of truly magnificent railway stations in Texas. It continues to serve both rail traffic and motorcoach service in downtown Dallas.

Around the turn of the century, each of the railway companies serving Dallas either had a separate depot or leased space in a terminal owned by some other line. Thus, if a traveler needed to change from one railroad to another, he or she was forced into the inconvenience of transferring from one depot to another, sometimes across town. The first attempt to solve this problem came in 1906, but it failed because of a lack of agreement among the railroad companies. In 1911 proposals were made for a more comprehensive solution to the Dallas station problem.

In March, 1912, the Union Terminal Company was organized to build a union station to serve all the railways carrying passengers to and from Dallas. The stock in the new firm was jointly owned by eight railroads: the Gulf, Colorado and Santa Fe; the Chicago, Rock Island and Gulf; the Missouri, Kansas and Texas of Texas; the St. Louis, San Francisco and Texas; the Houston and Texas Central; the St. Louis Southwestern; the Trinity and Brazos Valley; and the Texas and Pacific. The construction of the union station was conducted under the direction of the terminal company, which also operated the complex when it was completed.

The site chosen by the Union Terminal Company for its passenger facility was on the western edge

Dallas Union Terminal, now dominated by the tower of the Hyatt Regency Hotel, seen from the Ferris Plaza in downtown Dallas. Photograph by the author, 1983.

Interior of the second-floor main waiting room of the Dallas Union Terminal as it appears today. Photograph by the author, 1983.

63

of the Dallas central business district. The station proper was built on the west side of Houston Street between Jackson and Young streets. The complex covered a considerable area, much of it occupied by railway yards, repair and service areas, and express handling facilities. Most of this area was leased by the terminal company from various railways already occupying the ground, but a smaller area for the passenger facility was purchased from private owners at a cost to the terminal company of about $1.75 million. The site had been occupied by a flour mill, a grain elevator, and several warehouses. One of the major reasons for the selection of this specific site was its proximity to the Dallas–Oak Cliff Viaduct (1912), which gave the location convenient access to the Oak Cliff district across the Trinity River. Much of the acreage acquired by the terminal company for its railway yards and support facilities required extensive filling due to its occasional flooding by high water from the Trinity River before the construction of its levee system in the 1930s.

The Dallas Union Terminal Company employed Jarvis Hunt, a nationally known designer of monumental railway stations, to prepare plans for its terminal. Hunt today is probably best remembered for his huge Kansas City Union Terminal, one of America's great passenger stations. For Dallas, which at the time had only about 140,000 people, he designed a smaller but very impressive structure. Construction began in March, 1914, and continued until October 8, 1916, when the terminal opened to passengers. The official dedication ceremonies came six days later, on the opening day for the State Fair of Texas in Dallas.

The Dallas Union Terminal occupied three main levels. In designing the structure, Jarvis Hunt attempted to separate the functions of the building into its three distinct floor levels to increase the efficiency of circulation through the depot. It was possible, for instance, for a passenger to walk directly into the station and to a train without having to pass through either the ticket lobby or any waiting room. The architect estimated that only about 30 percent of the station patrons would require the use of waiting rooms, so he placed them away from traffic circulation on the second floor. To protect the travelers from the dangers associated with the railroad tracks and yet provide them with access to the trains, an elevated passageway over the tracks was provided from the second floor of the station. This passageway proved to be very unpopular with the traveling public, however,

because of the number of steps required. The other alternative, tunnels beneath the tracks, was impractical in 1916 because of occasional flooding from the Trinity River. Baggage was handled on two enclosed freight-elevator-equipped "bridges" spanning the tracks.

The station building for the Dallas Union Terminal measures 281 feet, 6 inches long and 134 feet wide. Standing three stories tall, it is approximately 70 feet high. The building rests on concrete foundations that extend 28 feet down to limestone bedrock. The walls are a combination of structural steel components and load-bearing masonry. Heavy concrete sections encase most of the steel members to protect them from fire damage and corrosion. The front and side exteriors consist of a 6-foot base of Vermont granite with all the remaining exterior faced with "Tiffany white combed enamel brick" and terra cotta.

The main entry to the terminal from Houston Street is through four groups of doors on the east side of the station. These originally led either into a ticket lobby or directly to stairs to the elevated passageway to the tracks. A semicircular ticket office with fourteen sales windows was located between the two central entrances, and the baggage area occupied the entire west side of the ground floor. A carriage entrance, still covered by a cast-iron marquee canopy supported on large chain braces, is found at the north end of this floor. The second floor of the station contained the waiting rooms and dining facilities. High windows line the side and end walls of this area, and a high, vaulted ceiling spans the main waiting room. Lighting was provided to the large central waiting room by four beautiful cast-iron chandeliers containing rings of incandescent fixtures. Furnishings consisted of sixteen heavy double wooden benches flanked by radiators fitted with cast-iron grills. Around the main waiting room were several smaller waiting rooms designated for women, "matrons," smokers, and blacks. The third floor housed railway and terminal company offices and related facilities. This level extends only over the north and south ends of the building and occupies the area between the open area above the main waiting room.

As was true of most large public railway terminals in its day, the Dallas Union Terminal exhibited a curious combination of advanced railway technology with classical detailing and formal visual features. This presents a dramatic contrast of two different schools of thought in design. In the Dallas terminal the two forms provide an interesting transition from the steel, smoke, and steam of trackside to the refinement and grandeur found in the urban face of the waiting rooms and gleaming white building exterior.

The passenger station itself represented only a small fraction of the Dallas Union Terminal Company buildings and leased properties. The nature of railway equipment demanded large amounts of space for its service, storage, and repair. The terminal complex consequently contained a large number of auxiliary structures. Among these were a 320-foot-by-56-foot express freight building, a reinforced-concrete powerhouse, locomotive and coach service and repair facilities, including an engine roundhouse, coaling platform, water standpipe, an interlocking switch system employing two switch towers, and a "layover station" for trainmen in Dallas between runs.

As early as the 1930s, alterations were being made to the Dallas Union Terminal. The greatest objection to the building design was the required climbing of stairs to the second floor to reach the overhead passageway leading to the tracks and then the descending of a second flight of steps to the actual platform for boarding. Most of the substantive changes to the terminal were undertaken between 1947 and 1950, according to plans prepared in the mid-1940s by architect Wyatt C. Hedrick. Twenty years after the construction of the terminal, the Trinity River had been leveed and the danger of high water in the station area removed. This permitted the construction of a tunnel to replace the elevated passageway to the tracks. At this time the two overhead baggage bridges also were removed and replaced by simple grade-level baggage crossings. The addition of the tunnel leading to the platforms eliminated the need for the second-floor waiting rooms, so the ground floor lobby was "modernized" by removing the semicircular ticket office and adding new seating. Architect Hedrick at the time felt that travelers would continue to use the second-floor waiting rooms, so he provided escalators to this area, but the old upper-level waiting rooms went virtually unused.

After the completion of the modifications to the station in 1950, the Dallas Union Terminal for the next two decades gradually declined. At the time of its construction, the general consensus was that railway travel would continue to expand for the foreseeable future, but beginning in the 1920s railroad passenger traffic began diminishing steadily. Finally in 1969, the last railroad tenant of the station, the Texas and Pacific Railway, discontinued its passenger service to Dallas. The grand old station seemed doomed.

In 1972 the City of Dallas purchased the Union Terminal station building. Within two years it reopened as the Dallas Transportation Center, with the inauguration of Amtrak rail passenger service on March 14, 1974. The ground floor of the building now serves not only as a rail station, but also as a lobby for the Surtran motorcoach service to and from the Dallas–Fort Worth Regional Airport. Current plans are to preserve the station building with only minor alterations.

Location: The Dallas Union Terminal stands on the west side of Houston Street between Jackson and Young streets at the west side of the Ferris Plaza (1924) in downtown Dallas. It is open to the public as the Dallas Transportation Center.

Suggested Reading:

Fildes, Steve. *Dallas Union Station.* Dallas, Tex.: City of Dallas Building Services Department [1975].
"New Union Passenger Facilities at Dallas." *Railway Age Gazette* 61, no. 20 (November 17, 1916): 889–94.

25. Don Patricio Causeway

The Don Patricio Causeway, built with private capital in 1927, was the first bridge to link Padre Island with the Texas mainland. In addition, it holds the distinction of having been one of the more unusual bridges ever constructed in the state.

The builder was Col. Sam Robertson, one of the first promoters of tourism on Padre Island. In the 1920s Robertson purchased extensive tracts of land on the island, erected picturesque wooden hotels on each end to cater to tourists, and even attempted to build a rudimentary road the entire length of the island. Among the many projects for which he is remembered is his long wooden bridge, built to make his hotels and other developments more accessible to visitors. He named it Don Patricio in honor of Pat Dunn, from whom he had purchased his island property. For several months Robertson's men worked at a pile driver, pounding a total of 3,903 wooden pilings

The Don Patricio Causeway in its heyday, sometime between 1927 and 1933. Photograph courtesy Texas Department of Highways and Public Transportation, Corpus Christi, Texas.

all the way across Laguna Madre from the Flour Bluff area near Corpus Christi to Padre Island. The distance was more than 3 miles. As the piles were driven, timber crosspieces were mounted on them to support four wooden troughs. Toward the end of construction, Robertson's men erected a tollhouse at the Flour Bluff end of the bridge, and there, beginning with the opening of the bridge on July 4, 1927, they began charging holiday seekers three dollars a car for crossing over to the island. After paying their fees, the drivers steered their vehicles into the troughs and made their way 3.25 miles over the causeway to the island, all the way attempting to keep tires from rubbing too roughly on the sides of the troughs. On

their return, they came back over the bridge in the troughs on the other side. There was no way to turn back, and once on the bridge there was no place to stop in the event of mechanical problems.

Colonel Robertson seems to have done remarkably good business operating his toll bridge. In July, 1927, when he opened the causeway, he received tolls from eighteen hundred motorists going over to the island; 2,500 cars followed in the next month. Although the Great Depression slowed the traffic flow across the toll bridge, it seems to have remained a money-making venture. The peak month in 1931, for instance, saw 1,156 vehicles cross. Even the drivers who did not use the bridge to get to Padre Island contributed to Colo-

View along the lines of surviving wooden pilings from the 1927 Don Patricio Causeway as they now appear. Photograph by the author, 1975.

nel Robertson's coffers, for he also operated the only two ferries serving the upper end of the island at the time.

The causeway went out of service in 1933, and Texas lost one of its most striking bridges. A number of years passed before another bridge was built to take its place. Although the troughs have been gone for many years, most of the wooden piers from the Don Patricio Causeway still may be seen stretching across Laguna Madre, and the name of the old bridge is perpetuated by Don Patricio Road on the southwestern side of the city of Corpus Christi on the old route to the bridge.

Location: The three rows of wooden pilings from the Don Patricio Causeway may still be seen extending across much of Laguna Madre. They are probably best viewed from the John F. Kennedy Causeway, which carries Park Road 22 from Corpus Christi across to Padre Island.

Suggested Reading:

Smylie, Vernon. *The Secrets of Padre Island.* Rev. ed. Corpus Christi, Tex.: Texas News Syndicate Press, 1972.
Texas. Highway Department. "Route Report Padre Island." Manuscript and typescript notebook. [Ca. 1931]. Engineering Department, Texas Department of Highways and Public Transportation, Corpus Christi, Tex.

26. Droemer Brick Yard

The most successful of several early brickmaking enterprises in the Lee County area, the Droemer Brick Yard is significant today because it preserves most of the structures and equipment used by its owners in late nineteenth-century and early twentieth-century Texas brick manufacture.

The builder of the Droemer brick-manufacturing plant was Christian Droemer. A native of Germany, he lived for a time in Madrid, Spain, where he learned the craft of brickmaking, before immigrating to Texas. About 1870 he established a brickyard on the out-skirts of Giddings, which for almost three-quarters of a century served Lee County residents. Droemer and his sons produced thousands of unmarked bricks used throughout the entire area, some of them even being used in the construction of the current Lee County courthouse. Most of the equipment and buildings remain intact from the brickmaking days.

Christian Droemer's family worked together in their business, the children being responsible for moving clay from a pit to a storage building where it was allowed to dry. Older family members mixed the

The domed brick kiln built by John Ewald Droemer in 1924. Photograph, 1976, courtesy Center for the History of Engineering, Texas Tech University, Lubbock, Texas.

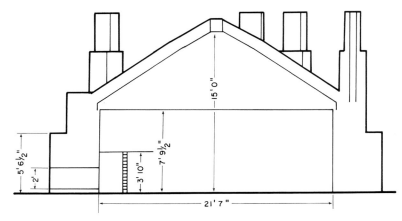

Cross-section of the 1924 Droemer kiln. Based on 1972 manuscript field-measured drawing in "Droemer's Brick Kiln" file, Texas Historical Commission, Austin, Texas.

clay with water to the correct consistency and molded it into the proper shape with wooden forms. The "green" bricks then were shifted to the sun to dry for several days before they were carefully stacked in a rectangular updraft kiln, the foundations of which are still visible. This open-top kiln remained in use for firing bricks until 1924, when John Ewald Droemer, a member of the third generation of the family in Texas, took steps to increase the efficiency of the yard.

He purchased a hand-operated brick press to make more uniform bricks. It produced bricks averaging 8¼-by-4-by-2¼ inches. The same year he razed the old rectangular kiln and replaced it with a more modern downdraft structure. This domed kiln is the most striking feature of the entire brickyard today. It is circular with ten flue stacks rising from its 4-foot, 6-inch-thick brick walls. A central dome rises 15 feet above the center of a 21-foot, 7-inch open space within the kiln.

Droemer family members carefully stacked unfired bricks inside the circular kiln, carrying them inside through two large doors on either side. It took three to four weeks to prepare the thirty-two thousand bricks that filled the kiln to capacity. Family members then fired the bricks by placing burning post-oak logs into six arched openings, called "eyes," which encircle the base of the kiln. The heat from the burning logs passed up the interior walls before being deflected downward through the bricks into openings in the hollow floor. It passed to the outside through the ten flues. After the firing was complete, the kiln was allowed to cool, and the finished bricks were removed through the two doorways. The entire interior of the 1924 kiln is coated with a thick, green, vitreous glaze. Since the Droemer bricks were unglazed, this coating probably originated from a chemical reaction between the post-oak fuel and the sand in the bricks.

Just a few feet southeast of the circular kiln stands a corrugated sheet-steel clay storage and molding shed. Even today it remains complete with its brick press, a hammermill used to pulverize clay, and a system of wooden hoppers, chutes, and conveyors. John Ewald Droemer adapted his hand press so that he could power it with a farm tractor, and his home-made system of levers and pulleys improvised to accomplish this end exhibits amazing ingenuity.

As early as 1890 the family had purchased a hand-operated repress machine designed to give the bricks sharper and more uniform edges, but it proved to be slow and unwieldy in actual use. It soon ended up in a nearby pasture, where it lies to this day. The entire area of the brickyard is littered with cull bricks, which were rejected and never sold. At one time or another they were used for almost everything from constructing chicken coops to paving a livestock area.

Because of increased competition from larger and more modern brickyards employing natural gas as a fuel and railways for shipping, the Droemer family was forced to discontinue brick production in 1940. Since that time, some of their equipment and structures have been converted to alternative uses, such as the storage of farm equipment and tools. The old circular kiln itself was used for a while as a storage building, but today it stands empty, its dome seemingly on the verge of collapse.

Location: The Droemer Brick Yard is located at Droemer Industries on Old Serbin Road at the southwestern outskirts of Giddings. The site is on private property and not generally accessible to the public, although its structures are visible from the county road.

Suggested Reading:

Killen, Mrs. James C., ed. *History of Lee County.* Quanah, Tex.: Nortex Press, 1974.

27. Eagle Lake Irrigation System

Eagle Lake, a natural lake about 2.5 miles east of the Colorado River in eastern Colorado County, has the distinction of having been in 1899 the source of the first water used for large-scale rice irrigation in the Colorado River Valley. Since that time the storage capacity of the natural lake has been increased, and it has continued for over eighty years to provide irrigation water to fields in the surrounding area.

According to oral tradition, Eagle Lake takes its name from a Karankawa Indian legend. In the story an Indian maiden chose between two suitors by asking the warriors to swim across the lake, climb a tree, and return to her with a young eagle. The town of Eagle Lake, located just north of the lake, was an Anglo-American settlement before Texas became a republic. The family of Frank J. Cooke, one of Stephen F. Austin's colonists, settled near the lake in 1835, and was later joined there by other immigrants. By 1859 the community, built on the site of a former Indian village, became a station on the Buffalo Bayou,

Brazos and Colorado Railway. It grew slowly through the remainder of the nineteenth century, and in the 1900 census showed only 1,107 inhabitants. The year before, however, an event occurred that changed the history of the town and its region.

In 1899 William Donovant irrigated 250 acres of rice with water that he pumped from Eagle Lake. His experiment proved to be so successful that many other people emulated him. In 1900 thirty thousand acres of rice were planted in the Colorado River Valley, and the next year fifty-six thousand acres were planted. Water to irrigate most of this agricultural development came from the Colorado River and its tributaries, as well as from drilled wells. Donovant, however, continued to use the water from the natural reservoir, which at the time was described as "a beautiful, clear, fresh-water lake . . . covering an area of about 2,500 acres and having an average depth of 8 feet."

William Donovant's 1899 system for irrigating his

The inlet canal that carries Colorado River water into Eagle Lake for storage until it is needed for irrigation. Photograph by the author, 1981.

The present-day pumping facility that elevates water from Eagle Lake into the main canal to be carried by gravity flow to the fields for irrigation. Photograph by the author, 1981.

rice fields consisted of elevating waters from Eagle Lake with a 12-inch Van Wie double-suction pump, which had a capacity for four thousand gallons per minute. The pump had for its power source three steam boilers, which he had removed from the Lakeside Sugar Refinery, another of his ventures, and had installed together with a two-hundred-horsepower steam engine. The pump raised the water 27 feet into a 350-foot flume, which carried it to his main canal leading to the fields.

Within a year the waters of Eagle Lake came to be used by a second irrigator, the Eagle Lake Rice Irrigation Company. Also known as the Vineyard and Walker Canal System, it likewise secured its supply of irrigation water directly from the natural reservoir. Since the lake lacked sufficient water to supply both systems, each irrigator was forced to build his own canals and pumping plants to pump water from the Colorado River and transport it to the natural lake, from which it was pumped a second time to the fields.

Over the past eighty years a number of efforts have been undertaken to increase the storage capacity of Eagle Lake through the construction of levees. At the present time there are approximately fifty-three hundred feet of earthen embankments averaging about six feet high, which create a reservoir with a capacity of ninety-six hundred acre feet and a surface area of about twelve hundred acres, a considerably smaller surface area than reported at the turn of the century.

The lake provides a means for storing water that is diverted from the Colorado River at times when excess floodwater is available, this water being conducted to the lake by means of an earthen canal. This role, however, has lessened in importance since the 1930s because dams constructed upstream by the Lower Colorado River Authority (LCRA) regulate the river flow. Permit No. 1493 issued in 1949 by the State Board of Water Engineers allows the diversion of sixty thousand acre feet of Colorado River water annually to irrigate approximately twenty-five thousand acres supplied by the lake. The lake today is operated by the LCRA, which purchased the formerly privately owned irrigation system on January 31, 1983.

Location: Eagle Lake is situated due south of the town of Eagle Lake, about 2.5 miles east of the Colorado River. Access to the mouth of the inlet canal that feeds river water into the reservoir and to the pumping facility that elevates water into the main irrigation canal is via a short paved private road leading east from FM 102, about 1.4 miles south of its intersection with U.S. 90A inside the town. On the way one passes the site of William Donovant's Lakeside Sugar Refinery, which is interpreted by a historical marker. The area at which the inlet canal empties into the lake is popular with local anglers, who claim to have caught some very impressive fish, but most visitors find the even larger alligators that inhabit the waters to be far more impressive. The fields irrigated from the lake are mostly east and south of the town.

Suggested Reading:

Dowell, Cleo Lafoy, and Seth Darnby Breeding. *Dams and Reservoirs in Texas: Historical and Descrip-* *tive Information.* Texas Water Development Board Report 48. Austin: Texas Water Development Board, 1967.

Taylor, Thomas U. *Irrigation Systems of Texas.* U.S., Department of the Interior, Geological Survey, Water-Supply and Irrigation Paper No. 7. Washington, D.C.: Government Printing Office, 1902.

28. *East Navidad River Bridge*

One of the many fine nineteenth-century iron bridges in Fayette County, three of which are listed on the National Register of Historic Places, the East Navidad River Bridge for a century has carried vehicular traffic across that stream near the Dubina community.

On May 12, 1885, a delegation of residents from southern Fayette County attended the regular meeting of the County Commissioners' Court in La Grange. They carried with them a written petition requesting that the commissioners consider the need for a permanent bridge to span the East Navidad River on the road between Dubina and High Hill. The petitioners

The 1885 East Navidad River Bridge viewed from its own wooden roadway. Photograph by the author, 1981.

must already have presented their request orally to the individual commissioners, for at the same meeting the commissioners appointed six local residents as a bridge committee to investigate the need for a new bridge and the conditions at whatever site they might recommend. They also were authorized to recommend the dimensions for the proposed bridge and to estimate its approximate cost. The Fayette County residents appointed to the committee were W. J. Hildebrand, C. Proetzel, Joseph Peter, C. Baumgarten, J. Muzny, and R. Wolters. At least two of them had been signers of the initial petition.

In May and June, 1885, the members of the East Navidad River Bridge Committee did investigate. They decided that the best location for the structure would be where the existing road crossed the stream at a ford. They recommended to the county commissioners that the proposed structure be eighty feet long with a twelve-foot roadway. They presented the officials with two sets of figures representing the estimated cost for such a bridge: $3,100 for a heavy-duty structure and $2,850 for a lighter-weight alternative. The committee endorsed the heavier choice. Committee members also reported that they themselves would collect "a sufficient sum of money" from private individuals to pay for the construction of approaches to the proposed overhead truss span.

After accepting the report of the East Navidad River Bridge Committee, the Fayette County commissioners authorized the committee members "to enter into contract in the name of Fayette County with some reliable Bridge Company for the material & building of said bridge at the place designated," provided that the cost of the project did not exceed $3,100 for a heavy-duty structure.

The committee under its instructions from the county commissioners made an agreement with the King Iron Bridge Company of Cleveland, Ohio, for the construction of a bridge over the East Navidad River. Later in the year, bridge company crews appeared in Fayette County; their prefabricated bridge was shipped by rail to Texas in pieces. They first excavated footings for the tubular steel piers, which, after being put in place and braced, were filled with concrete. Then they erected a temporary falsework and assembled the members of the overhead Pratt truss span, which stretched eighty feet between the piers. As this work was being conducted, the crews also installed thirty-five-foot steel girder approach spans at each end of the bridge. All the spans in place, the workers installed wooden decking in position to form a roadway, and the East Navidad River Bridge was ready for its first traffic.

Since its opening in 1885, the bridge has provided a dependable crossing on the county road linking Dubina with High Hill. Operating today with a five-ton weight limit, it continues to carry local traffic. Spanning the slowly flowing East Navidad River amid large oak trees draped with Spanish moss that hangs above the heads of grazing cattle, it has one of the most beautiful settings of any bridge in Texas.

Location: The East Navidad River Bridge carries local traffic across the East Navidad River in southern Fayette County a few miles northeast of Schulenburg. The most convenient route to take to see the bridge is north from U.S. 90 a distance of 2.1 miles on FM 1383 to the Dubina community and then seven-tenths of a mile west via graded Fayette County Road 480 to the actual crossing.

Suggested Reading:

Fayette County, Tex. Commissioners' Court. Minutes, vol. 2, pp. 510, 526–27. Office of County Clerk, Fayette County Courthouse, La Grange, Tex.

29. Elissa

Launched in 1877 in Scotland and today preserved in Galveston, the *Elissa* is the oldest seaworthy square-rigged iron sailing ship in the world. Unlike most preserved historic ships, which are found in dry dock or are permanently moored in harbors, the *Elissa* is a genuinely operational sailing vessel and makes periodic trips into open sea. She has the distinction of being the oldest vessel listed on Lloyd's Shipping Register in London.

In October, 1877, the *Elissa* was launched by Alexander Hall and Company at its shipyard in Aberdeen, Scotland. Hall custom built the four-hundred-ton, 150-foot bark to order for Henry F. Watt of Liverpool. Unlike older wooden vessels, the *Elissa* had both superstructure and hull made from wrought iron, the most popular ship-building material of its day. She remained commercially active for almost a century.

Work being conducted in rebuilding the hull and superstructure of the *Elissa* while it was still in Greece in 1977–78. Photograph courtesy Galveston Historical Foundation, Galveston, Texas.

The *Elissa* at sea in the Gulf of Mexico in 1982. Photograph courtesy Galveston Historical Foundation, Galveston, Texas.

On her maiden voyage the *Elissa* carried Welsh coal from Britain to Brazil, and for decades she carried a variety of cargoes as she competed with steamships for her share of the maritime trade. Her owner made his living from the portion of the commerce that the steam vessels had not yet taken over. Thus the *Elissa* often was drawn into smaller ports. Among her destinations were harbors in Europe, South Amer-

Galveston Historical Foundation volunteers aloft in the rigging of the *Elissa*. Photograph courtesy Galveston Historical Foundation, Galveston, Texas.

ica, Canada, and the United States, as well as more distant ports in Burma, India, and Australia. She is known to have delivered bananas to and loaded cotton in Galveston in both 1883 and 1886.

In 1898 Henry Watt sold the ship to the first of a number of subsequent owners. For fourteen years she sailed under the Norwegian flag before being sold just before World War I to Swedish owners and then in 1930 to Finnish owners. In 1918 her first auxiliary

motors were added, and through the years her masts were shortened and finally removed. Sailing in the Scandinavian coastal trade until 1960, the *Elissa* then was sold to Greek owners for use on the Mediterranean. There her last vestiges of a sailing vessel were removed, and she was used solely as a motorship.

As early as 1961, maritime historians had begun watching the *Elissa*, hoping that she might be saved for posterity. The ship's future, however, seemed uncertain at best. By the mid-1960s she had fallen into the hands of petty smugglers in Greece, who are thought to have used her to transport illicit bonded American cigarettes between Yugoslavia and Italy. In 1970, however, an opportunity presented itself for preservationists to purchase the *Elissa*.

During the 1960s, historic preservation groups in Galveston had started searching for a square-rigged sailing vessel with ties to the city that they might restore and preserve as part of Galveston's maritime heritage. They learned of the availability of the *Elissa,* and in 1975 the Galveston Historical Foundation purchased the decrepit old ship. A crew was sent to examine the vessel, and plans were initiated to restore it in Greece. Later study showed that it was practical in terms of time and money to rebuild only the hull and superstructure of the iron ship there and then tow it across the Atlantic for its full restoration in Galveston. The basic work on the hull was conducted in Greek shipyards between 1977 and 1978, the ship was towed to Galveston in 1979, and work began on

the remainder of the restoration, a project that took three additional years.

The *Elissa* was restored as an actual operating sailing ship of the 1870s. This was a very time-consuming and expensive effort, one aided by numerous foundations, corporations, and historic preservation agencies, as well as by the donation of thousands of volunteer work hours. Finally, in December, 1981, the vessel was moved to her permanent berth at Pier 21. There, work continued on the restoration, with the restored *Elissa* making her first actual voyage under sail into the Gulf of Mexico on Labor Day, 1982.

Location: The *Elissa* is berthed at Pier 21 near the Strand Historic District in downtown Galveston. It is open to the public for a nominal admission charge, which is applied to its maintenance.

Suggested Reading:

Sea History no. 15 (Fall, 1979), special issue featuring the history and restoration of the *Elissa*.

30. El Paso and Southwestern Railroad Rio Grande Bridge

The El Paso and Southwestern Railroad Bridge (1902) across the Rio Grande above El Paso is one of two very similar structures spanning the river in the same general area. It is particularly noteworthy because of its unusual size for the region.

For many years the bridge was the primary Rio

An El Paso and Southwestern passenger train crossing the newly completed Rio Grande bridge about 1902. Photograph courtesy Southwest Collection, El Paso Public Library, El Paso, Texas.

Detail showing the beautifully preserved condition of the ironwork composing the spans of the 1902 El Paso and Southwestern Railroad Bridge. Photograph by the author, 1975.

Grande crossing for the El Paso and Southwestern Railroad. This company was founded in 1902, the year that it built the bridge, principally to transport ores from the great open pit mines of Arizona and New Mexico to the already well-established smelting works in El Paso. (The El Paso Smelter is discussed in entry no. 31.)

Because the route of the El Paso and Southwestern Railroad westward into New Mexico required that it pass through some unusually rugged country, a route that required the construction of a 1,000-foot tunnel, the bridge carrying the line across the Rio Grande had to meet special demands. Not only did it have to be a comparatively high bridge, standing 86 feet above the riverbed, but it also had to be built at a grade of 0.8 percent toward the west to give an increase in elevation to aid locomotives in pulling their loads through the rough terrain in that direction. Spanning the entire floodplain of the Rio Grande, the bridge as built was an impressive 1,692 feet, 6 inches long.

Construction on the Rio Grande Bridge began in April, 1902. The initial work consisted of excavating the footings for the concrete and steel piers that in time would support the bridge. These foundations were dug, and then wooden pilings were driven into the excavated areas to an average depth of 26 feet to provide sufficient footing for the piers that would be placed above them. The pier system for the bridge consisted of six massive concrete piers to support the central spans and six smaller steel towers to support

the steel-girder approach spans. The bodies of the large concrete piers were poured with an average height of 49 feet, and they measure 28 feet, 5 ½ inches by 14 feet, 5 ½ inches at their bases. They have a batter of ¾ inch per foot, and the upstream faces bear a projecting V. The steel tower rests on much smaller concrete piers.

After the foundation and pier work was completed by the Missouri Valley Bridge and Iron Works of Leavenworth, Kansas, in August, 1902, a second contracting firm began work on the steel superstructure. The contractor for this phase of the work was the Phoenix Bridge Company of Phoenixville, Pennsylvania, a firm known for its major bridge projects throughout the country. Although the steel girder spans of the approaches were put in place by cranes, the erection of the larger and heavier five parallel chord spans, each 181 feet long, required much greater effort. These spans were assembled one at a time, with the first part of the work being the placement of wooden falsework to support the truss members as they were positioned. It took four or five days to erect the falsework to support one span and then about the same length of time to assemble the prefabricated parts of the span. Then the falsework was disassembled, moved into position for the next span, and the process repeated. Once the steel superstructure was in place (on October 4, 1902), it was fitted with eight-inch-by-eight-inch wooden crossties six inches apart as a base for laying rails across the nearly completed structure. With all the details of construction completed, the finished bridge was turned over to the railroad company, which laid the rails across and put it into service.

The El Paso and Southwestern Bridge is as impressive statistically as it is physically when viewed by visitors. It consists of five 181-foot parallel chord steel deck spans resting on the six large concrete piers. These are coupled with eight 70-foot steel-deck girder spans supported on the steel towers. Each end of the bridge leaves the side of the valley from large concrete abutments. The structure was designed to carry a live load of two steam locomotives with 40,000 pounds on each driver pulling a train load averaging 4,000 pounds per linear foot. Its dead load capacity was estimated at the time of construction at 2,300 pounds per linear foot. The entire weight of the ironwork in the bridge is 1,311 tons.

The El Paso and Southwestern Bridge remained in daily service for many years, but after the complete acquisition of the line by the Southern Pacific Railroad in the middle of the twentieth century, its use decreased since that company already owned a comparable bridge only a short distance away. The old El Paso and Southwestern Bridge remains in service, however, and it stands in beautiful condition, perhaps as much due to the aridity of the environment as to maintenance. It is a most impressive legacy of the railroading heritage of far West Texas.

Location: The El Paso and Southwestern Railroad Bridge spans the Rio Grande at the north side of the ASARCO Smelter in El Paso. It is most easily seen

from U.S. 85 (Doniphan Drive) in the area between the smelting works and the slightly older and somewhat similar Southern Pacific Railroad bridge a short distance upstream.

Suggested Reading:

Thompson, R. A. "The Rio Grande Bridge of the El Paso & Southwestern R. R. near El Paso, Tex." *Engineering News* 69, no. 15 (April 9, 1903): 322–23.

31. El Paso Smelter

The El Paso Smelter is one of the best-known smelting works in Texas. Located on a prominent hill between the Rio Grande and Interstate 10 just northwest of El Paso, it is seen by thousands of motorists daily, though few of them have ever entered its gates or considered its historical significance.

The El Paso Smelter officially opened on August 29, 1887, at a site that Robert Safford Towne had purchased in the spring of that year. He built the initial facility in collaboration with the Kansas City Consolidated Smelting and Refining Company and transferred ownership of the land to that firm the next year. Six years earlier Towne had begun developing lead and silver mines in northern Mexico. Feeling that it would be advantageous to begin a smelting works in El Paso, he joined with the Kansas City firm in building a smelter to process ores not only from his

own mines but also from others in Mexico and in the southwestern United States.

It took only five months to build the initial El Paso Smelter. In 1890 the plant was described as having the following equipment and facilities: four ore roasters, six blast furnaces, four eighty-horsepower and one fifty-horsepower steam boilers, two twenty-five-horsepower engines for operating the blast furnaces and pumping water for stacks, one forty-horsepower engine at the sampling works, one four-horsepower engine for generating electricity by an Edison dynamo, one twelve-thousand-gallon Dean duplex pump for elevating water from the Rio Grande to the plant, and one laboratory equipped with a telephone for communications. The smelter at this time employed about 250 men; the skilled workers were sent by the Kansas City Consolidated to El Paso, and

The El Paso Smelter about 1890, showing its early buildings and its steel-reinforced wooden chimney. Photograph courtesy Southwest Collection, El Paso Public Library, El Paso, Texas.

77

Operations at the El Paso Smelter during the early 1900s. Photograph courtesy Southwest Collection, El Paso Public Library, El Paso, Texas.

the common laborers were Mexicans who had entered the country prior to the enactment of strict immigration laws.

The most striking visual feature of the first El Paso Smelter was its hundred-foot-tall chimney. Made from wood, lined with thin sheet metal, and reinforced by a metal framework on the outside, it led gases from the blast furnaces to the open air above the smelter. Despite its combustible nature, it served its purpose well with only a small initial cost.

A major national event affected the development of smelting in El Paso: the passage of the McKinley Tariff in 1890. This protective measure, in part urged by smelter operators using domestic ores in other parts of the country, placed a tax of one and a half cents per pound on lead smelted from ores imported from any foreign nation. Since the El Paso Smelter in its early years depended primarily on Mexican ores, the passage of the tariff covering imported lead ores greatly reduced its profits. The smelter owners assessed a per-

centage of the metals smelted as their fee for processing ores, so their revenues depended directly on the profits derived from selling smelted metals. The initial effect of the McKinley Tariff was reduced production at the smelter, but this was followed by the development of new ore sources within the United States, mainly in New Mexico and Arizona.

In March, 1899, the American Smelting and Refining Company was formed when seventeen corporations and one partnership, among them the Kansas City Consolidated Smelting and Refining Company, merged to form one large smelting trust. It contained virtually every large firm in the business, with the exception of M. Guggenheim's Sons. The new company, known as ASARCO, the American Smelting and Refining Company, controlled sixteen smelters, eighteen metal refineries, and numerous mines, but it encountered financial and management difficulties during its first years of existence. In 1901 the Guggenheim family entered the financially ailing ASARCO by purchasing a majority of its stock. Thereafter the wealthy northeastern family controlled ASARCO and its El Paso facility.

Less than three months after the Guggenheim family entered the company, a disastrous fire almost completely destroyed the El Paso Smelter. Beginning in the engine room on the morning of June 10, 1901, the flames spread quickly through much of the smelting works. By the time it was brought under control four hours later, the fire had destroyed most of the facility. Reconstruction began as soon as insurance investigators had completed their reports, and the new plant that began operation the next year was acclaimed in the mining press as "one of the largest and best equipped labor- and time-saving smelters in the world." The rebuilt smelter boasted seven lead fur-

naces and a 3,250-ton copper furnace, each with independent flue systems and stacks. The El Paso Smelter had entered the copper-smelting business. Crude oil supplied from the Spindletop Oil Field by the Waters Pierce Oil Company fueled the furnaces.

In 1910 work began on a completely new copper-smelting facility at the El Paso Smelter. Completed on December 16, 1911, it covered three acres and was equipped to burn oil. It consisted of reverberatory furnaces and Wedge roasters with a capacity of six million to eight million pounds of copper ore monthly. This construction marked the beginning of truly large-scale copper smelting at the plant. Much of the copper ore processed in El Paso came from the Santa Rita Mines in New Mexico.

For the next decades most growth of the smelter

General view of the El Paso Smelter, including its 610-foot reinforced-concrete chimney. Photograph by the author, 1975.

79

was gradual, with the exception of the addition of a new zinc-smelting plant in 1946. This facility reprocessed slag from ores already smelted, using newer technology to remove zinc, which before could not be recovered economically.

The most prominent feature at the El Paso Smelter since the middle of this century has been its great 610-foot concrete chimney, on its completion in 1950 the tallest in the world. Built for ASARCO by the Custodis Construction Company of Chicago, a firm that specializes in industrial chimneys, the stack serves the lead smelter at the plant. The base of the great concrete chimney measures 66 feet, 6 inches in diameter, and its top is a foot thick and 16 feet in diameter. Construction of the chimney required thirty-three hundred cubic yards of concrete and forty-one tons of reinforcing steel.

One of the landmarks of El Paso, the El Paso Smelter remains in operation every day of the year, smelting ores from throughout the southwestern states. Although constantly growing and adding new structures and equipment, it retains a surprising number of historic buildings and pieces of machinery. The offices are still housed in a two-story, yellow-painted brick building with wooden galleries that ap-

pears in 1880s photographs. Inside one still finds the original decoratively painted cast-iron payroll safe, today preserved as a relic of former days. Scattered through the smelting works are such historic structures and equipment as the early twentieth-century El Paso Laboratory, an impressive 1912 Nordberg high-efficiency air-blowing engine, the circa 1916 primary gyratory ore crusher, 1916 copper converters, and a fine 1917 electrical switchboard on the east side of the powerhouse.

Location: The El Paso Smelter is located between Interstate 10 and U.S. 85 (Doniphan Drive) on the northwest side of El Paso. As an operating industrial facility, it is not open to the public, although many of its operations may be observed from a distance from the highways on either side.

Suggested Reading:

Lee, Mary Antoine. "A Historical Survey of the American Smelting and Refining Company in El Paso, 1887–1950." M.A. thesis, Texas Western College, 1950.
"El Paso Smelter" vertical file. Southwest Collection, El Paso Public Library, El Paso, Tex.

32. *El Paso Waterworks*

The history of the El Paso Waterworks presents an interesting account of how water resources were developed for domestic and industrial use in the largest city in Trans-Pecos Texas. The story of water supply at El Paso, however, goes back much further than one might expect.

The initial supply of water in the El Paso valley came from the Rio Grande and the many Spanish colonial acequias, or open irrigation ditches, that took their flow from the river. The acequias date from Spanish settlement in the El Paso area in the seventeenth century. These ditches continued to provide not only agricultural water but also that for domestic purposes for many El Paso residents until the late nineteenth century. As early as 1873, the Anglo city administration of El Paso had begun regulating the use of the open ditches because of their importance as sources of domestic water. The first ordinances prohibited bathing in the canals, throwing refuse into them, or otherwise polluting their waters, and another soon established the office of water commis-

sioner to supervise the maintenance of the canals. By 1875 the city aldermen passed the first of several ordinances requiring all persons who used acequia water within the city limits to perform maintenance work on the ditches in proportion to the amount of water they used.

With the passage of years, El Paso residents developed supplemental sources of domestic water. The best known of these means was the delivery of fresh water to homes and business places by the *aguadores,* teamsters driving two-wheel and later four-wheel carts and wagons fitted with wooden or steel water tanks. These businessmen, following established routes through their territories, carried soft, filtered water to all parts of the city. Some of the carts were highly ornamented. A reporter for the *Lone Star,* a local newspaper, on March 18, 1882, noted that he had seen one of these vehicles "tastefully decorated with business advertisements painted in every color known to the Art." In addition to water delivered by the *aguadores,* a small proportion of the local supply

Two El Paso *aguadores* with their burro-drawn water carts about the turn of the century. Photograph courtesy Southwest Collection, El Paso Public Library, El Paso, Texas.

came from a limited number of hand-dug wells within the city.

The charter for the first company desiring to supply water to El Paso consumers was filed with the Texas Department of State on March 31, 1881, but the firm was never able to deliver any water. The businessmen who formed the entity, known as the El Paso Water Company, sold their rights to Sylvester Watts of Saint Louis, Missouri, on April 29, 1882. Watts guaranteed the City Council that he would carry out the obligations of the former water company and that he would build the system that the El Paso Water Company had been unable to construct. He soon erected and equipped a pump house near the Rio Grande that elevated river water to an earthen reservoir at the site of the present-day Sunset Heights Reservoir, near the intersection of West Cliff and North El Paso streets. From this reservoir water flowed by gravity through riveted steel pipes to consumers in the central part of the city. The river water proved to be generally unsatisfactory for drinking purposes, so the business of the *aguadores* remained strong. By 1883 a silting reservoir had been added to the system, but still many consumers felt that the

water from the Watts system was not potable. By this time a rising cry was beginning to be heard from consumers who protested the charges that Watts made for his water service, prices more than double those charged by operators of comparable systems in other parts of the country.

To improve the quality of the water entering the system, in 1891 Watts began providing well water from a large hand-dug well excavated near the banks of the Rio Grande. Located at a site about in line with Third Street extended, he erected a new pump house and had workmen excavate a large well sixty-five feet deep, eighteen feet in diameter at the top, and fourteen feet in diameter at the bottom. From its base perforated pipes were pushed out in four directions to increase percolation into the well. Known as the Watts Well, it continued to provide domestic water to consumers until 1918. This source of supply produced extremely hard water, with more than a thousand parts per million of dissolved solids. Many consumers found this water as unsatisfactory as that from the river, and they continued to buy water that was shipped in by rail from Deming, New Mexico, or from various mountain towns in New Mexico, and

81

The 1937 art deco–style pump house at Well No. 17 of the El Paso Waterworks system. Photograph by the author, 1975.

sold by the *aguadores*. Fifteen to twenty of the water wagons were still in service as recently as 1910.

In 1902 the contract between Sylvester Watts and the City of El Paso expired. The City Council granted to the Watts Engineering Company, a firm that claimed to succeed to all the rights and privileges of Sylvester Watts and the old El Paso Water Company, permission to operate the El Paso Waterworks under a license that the council might revoke at any time. On November 3, 1902, the City Council awarded a franchise to W. J. Davis to construct and maintain an adequate new water system for El Paso. The next year the Davis franchise was conveyed to the International Water Company. Its plan was to drill a series of wells on the mesa east of the city and supply pure underground water from these projected wells by gravity flow to consumers. In time it did succeed in drilling several wells in the new area, but at the same time it purchased the old well, plant, and distribution system belonging to the Watts Engineering Company. Soon it began pumping hard water from the old Watts Well into the system, polluting the fresh water from the wells on the mesa. Although the firm provided better service than that given by Watts, the citizens tired of the poor water quality and the inability of the International Water Company to expand its mains into the newer parts of the city. Finally, in 1910 the City of El Paso purchased the entire plant and system of the International Water Company.

From 1910 to the present, the El Paso Waterworks has been owned and operated by the City of El Paso. The wells on the mesa proved to be a fine source of water for the first few years of municipal ownership, but in time their supply began to dwindle. Further exploration revealed strong wells in the area of the Montana Well Field, but they too diminished by the mid-1930s. During the first decades of city ownership, a number of new reservoirs, including the Sunset Heights Reservoir (1916), the Davis Reservoir (1923), and the Woods Reservoir (1932–33), were constructed to increase storage capacity and to serve new parts of the city. New pumping techniques introduced in the 1930s boosted the supply from the wells in the mesa and Montana fields, but it was obvious to city leaders that additional water would have to come from the Rio Grande. An initial treatment plant for river water was placed in service in 1943, and the capacity for treating surface water has been increased several times.

Perhaps the most significant event in the history of the El Paso Waterworks since the middle of this century was the establishment of the El Paso Public Service Board. On May 22, 1952, the City Council passed Ordinance 752, which reorganized the city Water Department and placed it under the supervision of the Public Service Board. The board consists of five members, four of them appointed by the City Council for staggered five-year terms and the fifth being the mayor. According to the ordinance creating it, the board is to "operate and manage the system with the same freedom and in the same manner as ordinarily enjoyed by the Board of Directors of a private corporation." This makes the board a semi-independent government corporation, a status giving it considerable independence in its operations. Since its establishment, the El Paso Public Service Board has successfully operated and expanded the El Paso Waterworks so that it continues to provide a dependable supply of water to the residents of Texas' westernmost city.

Location: A number of historic structures remain part of the El Paso Waterworks system. Perhaps the oldest is the modified but still operating 1916 Sunset Heights Reservoir, located near the intersection of West Cliff and North El Paso streets. The 1923 Davis Reservoir remains in service in a city block bordered on three sides by San Diego and Gold avenues and Indiana Street. The 1932–33 Woods Reservoir, also still in service, may be seen from Rim Road near its intersection with Brown Street. Finally, Well No. 17, with its beautiful 1937 art deco concrete pump house, may be seen at the intersection of San Antonio and Tornillo streets.

Suggested Reading:

Nicoll, Marion C. "Brief History of the El Paso Water System from 1881 to 1921." M.A. thesis, Texas Western College, 1951.

Wallace, Christopher M. *Water Out of the Desert.* Southwestern Studies No. 22. El Paso: Texas Western Press, 1969.

33. Fort Davis Military Water System

Actually three different water systems operating at different times, the Fort Davis Military Water System contains perhaps more preserved elements than any other nineteenth-century military water system in Texas. For this reason it deserves more than passing notice.

The 1846–48 war with Mexico added vast new territories to the United States, including the present

The pumpwell and pump house that provided Fort Davis with water from 1883 until its abandonment as a military post in 1891. Photograph by the author, 1975.

states of New Mexico, Arizona, and California. Texas had joined the Union only months before the outbreak of the war. Interest in the new western lands quickened with the discovery of gold in California in 1849. Intent on reaching the new goldfields, but at the same time wishing to avoid winter snows, thousands of gold seekers made their way across the continent on the southern overland route. A vital segment of this route was the San Antonio–El Paso road.

To protect travelers on this road from Indian attacks, the U.S. Army established Fort Davis in October, 1854. The post was named for Jefferson Davis, then secretary of war and later president of the Confederacy. For the next thirty-seven years, with a five-year interruption during and immediately after the Civil War, the post provided protection and a stopping place for travelers on the San Antonio–El Paso overland route as well as a stop for a few years on the Butterfield Overland Mail. The garrison at Fort Davis also participated in important campaigns against hostile Apache and Comanche Indians, as well as against border bandits, during its existence as a military post.

During its first years, the source of water for Fort Davis was Limpia Creek, outside and three-quarters of a mile north of the post grounds. Soldiers used wooden water wagons to carry the limited supply from the stream to the post compound. A correspondent in 1870 noted that the stream was "clear, pure and cold."

Despite the high quality of the Limpia Creek water, officers at Fort Davis started looking for a more convenient source of supply. As early as 1870, the post commander was considering the use of water from a spring that was adjacent to the post corrals on the southeast side of the complex, this despite warnings that it was "always regarded as unhealthy." Apparently the desire for convenience outweighed fear of waterborne illness, for by the mid-1870s the spring had become the sole source of drinking water for the post. Soldiers built a stone retaining wall around the spring to protect it from pollution, but their work appears to have been to no avail.

In June, 1878, the post surgeon at Fort Davis wrote to his superiors to "call attention to the spring from which all water used at the Post is derived." He reported, "There is a defect in that the water passes through the wall below the surface and rises directly into the drainage ditch. This ditch becomes higher than the spring by rapid pumping, and, as a consequence, the ditch drains back into the spring nearly

every time the water tank is filled. This ditch is the resort of pigs, and I have observed them wallowing in it within six feet of the spring." This condition, judging from the remains of the retaining wall preserved today, was not remedied, although the surgeon proposed specific work to do so.

The problems with the Fort Davis water supply continued until the 1880s, when the army built a completely new waterworks system patterned after those used in the eastern states. In April, 1883, two military officers and one civil engineer surveyed the site of the fort and drew up plans for the construction of a new system. Built over the next three years, it secured its supply from a collection well that was excavated near Limpia Creek, north of the post compound. From the collection well steam pumps in an adjacent stone pump house elevated the water two hundred feet to two large cypress tanks located at the summit of a steep rock ledge between the well and the fort. The first tank, purchased in 1883, held 33,000 gallons, and the second one, added in 1886, held 31,200 gallons. From these wooden tanks a main waterline led downward toward the fort complex. About halfway down the side of the mountain it passed through a smaller stone reservoir. Its purpose may have been to reduce the pressure on the system so that ordinary hydrants and fixtures could be used. Once the main line reached the fort, branch lines carried water by gravity to most of the post buildings. This new waterworks-type system was built between 1883 and 1886, although some additions were made as late as 1888. By the time it was completed it included almost eighteen thousand feet of cast-iron pipe, three pumps, two boilers, and two large cypress tanks. The total investment between June 23, 1883, and January 12, 1888, was $10,397.81. This system served the fort until the post was abandoned in June, 1891.

After the troops left Fort Davis, some of the buildings were occupied by civilians as residences, and some of the former government property was removed and used for completely different purposes. The staves from the two large water tanks, for instance, were taken from the top of the ridge where the tanks had been erected and were reused in the construction of corral fences in the neighborhood. Over the years most of the old fort buildings deteriorated, some of them to near collapse. Believing that Fort Davis should be preserved as a monument to the struggles of the pioneers with the Indians, a number of citizens began a movement to preserve it. Judge

David A. Simons of Houston, one of the leaders of the preservation group, bought the property in 1946 and started rebuilding some of the buildings. Then in 1961 Congress authorized the purchase of the fort complex, a purchase effected on January 1, 1963. Since that time the old post has been administered as the Fort Davis National Historic Site by the National Park Service, which has undertaken the stabilization, restoration, or reconstruction of most of the post buildings, including parts of its historic water system.

Location: The Fort Davis National Historic Site is located on the northern edge of the town of Fort Davis. The 1870s stone retaining wall still stands around the former spring in the corral area of the fort. Visitors pass this site, now adjacent to the tourist picnic area, as they drive on the paved roadway that leads into the fort complex. The 1883 stone collection well and pump house are located at the extreme north boundary of the national historic site and are most conveniently accessible from State Highway 118 at a point

three-tenths of a mile west of its intersection with State Highway 17 on the extreme northern outskirts of Fort Davis. Both structures are clearly marked with signs. The sites of the two cypress reservoirs atop the ridge between the pump house and the fort present little for visitors to see, but the remains of the stone reservoir halfway down the side of the ridge are accessible to visitors who do not mind walking through brush and across rough, rocky ground. From the stone reservoir site one can clearly see the disturbed ground that covers the century-old main waterline as it leads toward the fort complex.

Suggested Reading:

Scobee, Barry. *Old Fort Davis.* San Antonio, Tex.: Naylor Company, 1947.
Utley, Robert M. *Fort Davis National Historic Site, Texas.* U.S. Department of the Interior, National Park Service, Historical Handbook Series No. 38. Washington, D.C.: Government Printing Office, 1965.

34. *Fort Griffin Iron Truss Bridge*

The Fort Griffin Iron Truss Bridge, erected in 1885, has carried vehicular traffic across the Clear Fork of the Brazos for over a century. The bridge was erected under contract for Shackelford County by the King Iron Bridge Company, one of the largest of the late nineteenth-century firms specializing in building prefabricated bridges for states, counties, and cities.

Answering the demands from its constituents for an all-weather crossing over the Clear Fork of the Brazos between the towns of Albany and Throckmorton, the Commissioners' Court of Shackelford County on February 11, 1885, made the decision to build a bridge near the town of Fort Griffin. On that day the commissioners instructed the county clerk to write to several bridge companies to request proposed plans and specifications for a structure adequate for the crossing point. Three months later the commissioners met to consider the materials submitted to them by the bridge firms. After examining the plans and specifications, they ordered that bonds be issued in the amount of ten thousand dollars for the construction of a bridge, and they stated for the record that they would spend no more than that amount on the project. At the same meeting they ordered the publication of advertisements soliciting bids from contractors for the bridge.

On June 10, 1885, the county clerk read to the assembled commissioners the bids he had received from four companies for the construction of an overhead truss bridge across the Clear Fork. The firms bidding on the project were the King Iron Bridge Company of Cleveland, Ohio; the Wrought Iron Bridge Company of Canton, Ohio; the Penn Bridge Works of Beaver Falls, Pennsylvania; and the Kansas City Iron Bridge Company of Kansas City, Missouri. The King Iron Bridge Company, with a low bid of $8,050, won the contract. The next day the Commissioners' Court again met on bridge matters, officially awarding the contract for the project to King, provided it posted bond in the amount of $12,000 within a month's time, which it did.

Work soon began on the banks of the Clear Fork near Fort Griffin. Bridge company men began digging the footings for two large piers and started cutting the limestone blocks from which they later built the piers. They erected a temporary wooden falsework to support the prefabricated iron and steel members as they assembled the truss span of the bridge. About this time they also put into place the steel girders that support the two approach spans.

As erected by the King Iron Bridge Company in 1885, the Fort Griffin Bridge has a total length of 226

Southwest along the approach to the main span of the 1885 Fort Griffin Iron Truss Bridge over the Clear Fork of the Brazos. Photograph by the author, 1981.

feet. The Pratt overhead truss span itself is 110 feet long, with the northeast approach measuring 72 feet and the southwest approach 44 feet. The total width of the truss structure is 20 feet, giving a roadway 13 feet, 6 inches wide. The abutments for the approaches are made from limestone, as are the two large piers that still support the truss span 40 feet above low water in the river. The roadway itself consists of large wooden timbers, which today are protected by two 9-inch steel plate runners. The original railings, still in place, were made from 2- and 3-inch wrought-iron pipe.

The completed bridge was inspected by members of the Commissioners' Court on September 30, 1885. Some of the members were dissatisfied with the lime-stone in the northeast pier, and the bridge was not accepted for the time being. On the same day the commissioners ordered the clerk to advertise for bids for the construction of more substantial approaches to the bridge, a minor project undertaken in the fall of 1885. Then, apparently in light of the doubts concerning the durability of the northeast pier, the commissioners asked the King Iron Bridge Company to put up a bond of four thousand dollars to guarantee that the bridge would stand for the next two years.

The doubts of the county commissioners seem to have had little basis, for the Fort Griffin Bridge not only still stands but it also remains in service carrying rural traffic across the Clear Fork of the Brazos. So far as can be ascertained, an interesting 1886 county ordinance continues in force regulating this traffic. On February 11, 1886, the County Commissioners' Court authorized the painting and placement of signs at each end of the Fort Griffin Bridge warning travelers that they were liable for a five-thousand-dollar fine if they drove or rode across the bridge "faster than a walk" or drove more than twenty head of cattle or horses across the span at one time.

Due to the high quality of construction and the high standard of maintenance that it has received for a century, the Fort Griffin Bridge remains in virtually the same condition today as when it was erected in 1885.

Location: The Fort Griffin Iron Truss Bridge spans the Clear Fork of the Brazos River near Fort Griffin in northeastern Shackelford County. Access to the bridge is via a graded county road that leads northwest from

U.S. 283 approximately one mile south of the present-day highway bridge across the Clear Fork. A prospective visitor should drive through a cattleguard northwest on the gravel county road about five-tenths of a mile to the first crossroads, turn right to drive another four-tenths of a mile northeast to the structure. The bridge is located within a mile of the very interesting Fort Griffin State Historical Park, which is strongly recommended for any visitors who are interested in frontier or regional history.

Suggested Reading:

Shackelford County, Texas. Commissioners' Court. Minutes, vol. 2, pp. 235, 248–49, 260–63, 276–79, 283, 305, 399; vol. 3, pp. 450, 582. Office of County Clerk, Shackelford County Courthouse, Albany, Tex.

35. *Fort Worth Stockyards*

The Fort Worth Stockyards for decades were known as the largest and most important livestock market in the American Southwest. Although today reduced in size and scope, the Fort Worth yards remain a significant market center for Texas livestock.

As early as 1875, efforts were undertaken to establish a commercial market with packinghouses in Fort Worth, but all the pioneer ventures ended in failure.

It was not until 1889 that the semisuccessful Fort Worth Union Stockyards were established. Opening for business on January 19, 1890, and covering 206 acres of land, its operators claimed that they had the "finest yards south of Chicago." Only weeks after they opened, on February 7, a group of Fort Worth capitalists, joined by J. R. Hoxie of Chicago, founded the Fort Worth Dressed Meat and Packing Company

Now-quiet packinghouses at the Fort Worth Stockyards. Photograph, 1975, courtesy Center for the History of Engineering, Texas Tech University, Lubbock, Texas.

The well-weathered sign welcoming visitors to the Fort Worth Stockyards District. Photograph, 1975, courtesy Center for the History of Engineering, Texas Tech University, Lubbock, Texas.

to process meat from animals purchased at the yards. Although Fort Worth had both stockyards and a packing plant, most of the livestock entering the yards was sold to packeries elsewhere and shipped to the northern states. The Fort Worth facility operated at a loss until it was purchased in 1893 by G. W. Simpson of Boston, who hoped to put it on a money-making basis. As part of his plan, Simpson and Fort Worth business leaders incorporated the Fort Worth Stockyards Company, but they too met financial difficulties, some of them stemming from the panic of 1893.

Simpson, as well as many Fort Worth business leaders, felt that their best hopes for profits and perhaps even for the future of the city lay in attracting major meatpacking companies to North Texas. Consequently, they formed a committee to subscribe funds with which to bring one of the "Big Five" meatpackers to Fort Worth. The committee negotiated with both the Swift and Armour companies, finally coming to an agreement whereby it would provide each firm with fifty thousand dollars as inducement to establish packinghouses in Fort Worth. The money was raised by the fall of 1901. Soon both firms began preliminary work to establish their packinghouses in the city. The stockyards company was reorganized with J. Ogden Armour as president and E. F. Swift as vice-president; about the same time, railway spurs

were built to serve the sites for the two new facilities. Work on the packing plants began in January, 1902, with the cornerstones for both being laid in March of that year. Within a matter of months they began operation.

During their early years, the Fort Worth Stockyards experienced a tremendous boom. In five years' time the area surrounding the new facilities changed from one with just a few scattered houses to the incorporated City of North Fort Worth, with a population of ten thousand, all supported by the stockyards, the packeries, and their auxiliary operations. Within this five-year period the Fort Worth Stockyards achieved the sale of a million cattle and calves within one calendar year. The peak sales years, however, came in wartime markets with sales of 3.5 million head in 1917 and 5.25 million head in 1944.

To the uninitiated the Fort Worth Stockyards appeared to be an endless maze of railway sidings, stock pens, and chutes, all of which were dominated by the huge Armour and Swift packinghouses. To those who worked there, however, the complex was an orderly place where cattle, hogs, and sheep were efficiently bought, sold, shipped, or slaughtered. Several different business entities cooperated to make the stockyards function as an integrated economic unit. These included the Fort Worth Stockyards Company, the Fort Worth Belt Railway Company, numerous commission houses, the two large and several smaller packinghouses, livestock buyers, and the Stockyards National Bank.

The Fort Worth Stockyards Company owned the yards and all the facilities for unloading, sheltering, feeding, and watering the animals. It secured its operating funds by providing feed and by charging a daily yardage fee. The Fort Worth Belt Railway Company owned and served the tracks that led from the main railroad company trunk lines, and it was paid switching charges for each railway car that it handled.

The commission companies, acting as the representatives of the livestock owners, were responsible for selling individual owners' cattle or other stock. Each of these firms was allotted certain pens into which the stock raisers' animals were driven from the railway cars. The commission men ordered feed and water for the animals consigned to them and offered them for sale. The commission companies employed several salesmen, who were responsible for negotiating the sale of the animals to buyers. Interestingly, it was customary for only one buyer at a time to negotiate with a salesman, with all the transactions completed by a word or a gesture, no written contracts being prepared. A number of buyers were always present at the Fort Worth Stockyards. These men represented not only the Swift and Armour packeries, but also smaller packing plants and even northern packeries. The sales were based on the price of the stock per hundred pounds live weight.

After a salesman and a buyer had negotiated a purchase, the animals were driven to a scale house operated by the Stockyards Company to be weighed. As soon as the total price was stamped on the scale ticket, the responsibility of the commission merchant ended. The buyer then drove the animals to his own pens, where he kept them until he was ready to ship them to other locations or to slaughter them. Trading ended at three o'clock in the afternoon. All sales were for cash only. Thus on the afternoon of the same day that sales took place, the commission merchants were able to settle up their accounts with their clients, the stock raisers. From the money due the rancher or farmer, a deduction was made for the railroad transportation. The commission merchant refunded this amount to the Stockyards Company, which had paid for the transportation on receipt of the stock. Also deducted were the yardage fees, insurance fee, feed bill, and the commission merchants' own fees. The Stockyards National Bank for many years provided facilities for the financial transactions at the stockyards. Their offices made it possible for a rancher or farmer to get immediate cash after the sale of stock and to have it transferred to a local bank without delays or difficulties.

During the 1950s the stockyards receipts at Fort Worth began a decline, which has continued to the present. Among the numerous factors that created the problems were an increasing growth of country livestock auctions nearer the actual livestock-producing regions, the growth of large commercial feedlots, and a change in livestock transportation from railroads to trucks. As a result of these changed conditions, the two large packinghouses in Fort Worth, Armour and Swift, closed down their outmoded plants in 1962 and 1971, respectively, leaving behind only smaller meatpacking facilities. The stockyards today continue to handle moderate numbers of cattle, but by no means the millions sold annually during the boom years.

Although the actual livestock-related activities at the stockyards have declined over the last thirty years, their vicinity has become one of the more important commercial and entertainment areas in Fort Worth, which still boasts of being "Cowtown" and "Where the West Begins." The stockyards district today is a center of restaurants and clubs, clothing stores and art galleries, all of which capitalize on the "cowboy" and "western" reputation of Fort Worth. The continuing revitalization plans for the area call for more galleries, small shops, restaurants, and even a theater in the old Exchange Building and in the former horse and mule barns, now known as Mule Alley. The Fort Worth Stockyards are still alive and well, though not what they used to be, and they remain an interesting place to visit.

Location: The Fort Worth Stockyards area is most easily accessible on Exchange Avenue just east of North Main Street (State Spur Route 496), about five-tenths of a mile south of its intersection with State Highway 183 on the northwest side of Fort Worth. This turning is 2.6 miles north on North Main Street from the Tarrant County Courthouse in downtown Fort Worth.

Suggested Reading:

Barksdale, E. C. *The Meat Packers Come to Texas.* University of Texas, Bureau of Business Research,

Texas Industry Series No. 7. Austin: University of Texas, Bureau of Business Research, 1959.

Newman, Ruth G. "The Industrialization of Ft. Worth." M.S. thesis, North Texas State College, 1950.

Pate, J'Nell. "The Fort Worth Stockyards Company as a Big Business Enterprise." *Panhandle-Plains Historical Review* 52 (1979): 63–74.

36. Franklin Canal

The first large-scale irrigation effort in the El Paso valley, the Franklin Canal, was built by a group of local capitalists between 1889 and 1891. In 1912 the system was acquired by the U.S. Reclamation Service, which renovated and enlarged it. Today the Bureau of Reclamation still owns it, although the El Paso County Water Improvement District No. 1 conducts its day-to-day operation and maintenance.

The initial Franklin Canal system consisted of a dam on the Rio Grande that diverted water into an earthen canal stretching down the El Paso valley for about thirty miles. The dam itself was built diagonally into the river and only extended about halfway across, but this diverted sufficient water into the head of the canal. The diversion site was not far above what then was considered to be downtown El Paso.

Headgates at the diversion point for Rio Grande waters flowing into the Franklin Canal on the northwest side of El Paso. In the background is the 1902 El Paso and Southwestern Railway Bridge. Photograph by the author, 1975.

A segment of the Franklin Canal flowing through an El Paso neighborhood shortly after the canal's renovation by the U.S. Reclamation Service about 1915. Photograph courtesy Southwest Collection, El Paso Public Library, El Paso, Texas.

During its early years, the canal had only earthen sides and bottom and a capacity of 175 cubic feet per second. It was 30 feet wide at its head, but it decreased in size as it passed down the valley to only 15 feet wide at Fabens, where unused flow returned to the river. The system was designed to irrigate about thirty thousand acres of agricultural land, but the supply of water in the Rio Grande was so erratic and unpredictable that in the mid-1890s only about three thousand acres actually received the benefit of its irrigation.

Construction of the Franklin Canal cost its private owners a total of $150,000. Within only about eight years another $70,000 had to be spent for repairs and protection against overflows. After a while, the affairs of the original company were placed in the hands of a receiver, and then the property was purchased by one Thomas Worthington of Manchester, England, as trustee for the bondholders.

The greatest problems of the Franklin Canal for its first two decades, however, were not financial. The difficulty was an unpredictable water supply. At times the Rio Grande was a raging torrent and at others it barely flowed. The only solution was the construction of a large storage reservoir upstream from the El Paso valley. There a dam could impound floodwaters when the river was at flood stage and store them for when they were needed. For years the idea of an international dam above El Paso was discussed, but when the time came to build a storage reservoir, it was not near El Paso. Instead the U.S. Reclamation Service chose to build its large Rio Grande water storage project at Elephant Butte, eighty miles upstream, near present-day Truth or Consequences, New Mexico.

Although the new dam on the Rio Grande was built many miles upstream, the needs of the El Paso valley farmers were not forgotten. As work progressed at Elephant Butte, the Reclamation Service in 1912 purchased the entire diversion and delivery works of the old Franklin Canal. During the major construction at the damsite, smaller crews began a systematic reconstruction and renovation of the Franklin Canal. By 1916 some portions of the canal had been lined with concrete, its diversion works had been repaired and its heading enlarged, and its capacity for irrigation had been increased to forty thousand acres. With a dependable supply of irrigation water released from the Elephant Butte Dam when it was needed in the El Paso valley, all the farmers received a reliable flow for the first time.

The Franklin Canal had a steeper grade than was necessary for proper flow of irrigation water. Consequently, Reclamation Service engineers designed special drop structures, which later were built at several locations along the canal to control the velocity of water for highland irrigation. A novel plan used for these structures consisted of constructing cylindrical gates, which were counterbalanced and could be adjusted to allow a discharge that would produce the proper speed of flow to prevent either erosion or silting in the canal.

With urban growth in the El Paso valley, much of the land formerly irrigated by the Franklin Canal has been consumed by residential, commercial, and industrial construction. This has resulted in water rights being shifted from formerly irrigated areas to different areas. The volume of flow in the Franklin Canal has remained more or less constant, and it remains in service as an integral part of El Paso valley irrigated agriculture.

Location: The diversion works for the Franklin Canal are located on the Rio Grande just above the international boundary between the United States and the Republic of Mexico. The water is diverted into a canal known as the American Canal for the short distance that it flows from the dam to a point where it passes beneath Doniphan Drive. Becoming the Franklin Canal here, it flows parallel with the Rio Grande through the railway yards adjacent to downtown El Paso before it gradually deviates farther from the river as it flows in a generally easterly and then southeasterly direction down the valley. Among the many good vantage points from which the canal may be viewed are the small bridges that carry streets across the canal as it flows through El Paso. The canal also may be seen with ease for the several miles that it parallels Alameda Avenue (State Highway 20), beginning at Presa Street in Ysleta and continuing to the point where the canal leaves Alameda Avenue several miles southeast near Passmore Road.

Suggested Reading:

"Cylinder Drops for Irrigation Ditches." *Engineering News* 75, no. 24 (June 15, 1916): 1144.

Lawson, L. M. "Concrete Lining, Franklin Canal, Rio Grande Project." *Engineering News* 72, no. 11 (September 10, 1914): 540–43.

Lee, Willis T. *Water Resources of the Rio Grande Valley and Their Development.* U.S. Department of the Interior, Geological Survey, Water-Supply and Irrigation Paper No. 188. Washington, D.C.: Government Printing Office, 1907.

37. *Galveston Causeway*

Erected between 1909 and 1912, the Galveston Causeway for more than seventy years has linked Galveston Island with the Texas mainland. Noted for its graceful beauty, the bridge has survived numerous tropical storms that have wreaked havoc on lesser engineering works in the same area.

As early as the 1850s railway trestles had been built across Galveston Bay to connect the port city of Galveston with the rest of the state. These wooden structures, often damaged or destroyed by storms as well as by the action of *Teredo navalis* sea worms, were never truly permanent. At the time of the great September, 1900, hurricane, for instance, three wooden railway trestles spanned the bay, not to mention the crossing afforded by the steel Galveston Highway Bridge (1893), discussed in entry no. 39. The three

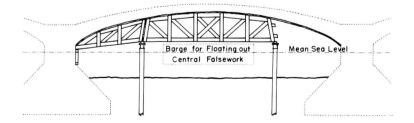

Simplified drawing showing the method used to float into position and then secure temporary wooden falsework to support forms and reinforcement for pouring the concrete arch spans in the Galveston Causeway. Based on "The Construction of the Galveston Causeway," *Engineering Record* 63, no. 21 (May 27, 1911): 578. Drawing by the author.

Forms and reinforcing steel positioned for pouring several of the concrete arch spans near the center of the Galveston Causeway, ca. 1911. Photograph courtesy Rosenberg Library, Galveston, Texas.

railway trestles had been built by the Gulf, Colorado and Santa Fe Railway; the Galveston, Houston and Henderson Railroad; and the Galveston, Harrisburg and San Antonio Railway.

All four of the bridges across the bay were destroyed in the 1900 storm. At the height of the hurricane, an ocean liner broke free from its moorings at one of the Galveston piers and was driven by the fury of the winds completely through all four bridges. Of the four structures, the trestle belonging to the Santa Fe Railway was the least damaged. With a great effort it was rebuilt in nine days' time to restore rail transportation to the stricken city and to carry a temporary eight-inch water line to residents. For the next few years the single-track Santa Fe trestle remained the sole link between Galveston Island and the mainland. Although passenger trains were able to cross the span in ten minutes and freight trains in fifteen minutes, there were almost always delays at one end or the other. The delays were seldom longer than five minutes for passenger trains, but freights often were delayed longer, especially during times of peak passenger service. During the months of heaviest freight traffic, the cotton-loading season from August to March, between sixty and seventy-five trains crossed the temporary one-track trestle daily. The management of the railway companies could not endure the bottleneck at the bridge indefinitely, so railroad officials and municipal leaders began agitating for the construction of a permanent causeway to carry both rail and highway traffic across the bay.

The first definite action toward the construction of

The parade of vehicles across the Galveston Causeway on the day of its dedication, May 25, 1912. Photograph courtesy Rosenberg Library, Galveston, Texas.

a new combined highway and railway bridge took place in early 1906. At this time a committee consisting of city and county commissioners was appointed to make initial plans for a causeway. The next year they submitted their plans for a permanent reinforced-concrete bridge, which was expected to cost approximately two million dollars. At the request of local residents, the Texas legislature passed a bill that allowed Galveston County to issue bonds for the construction of a causeway, to tax property owners fifteen cents per hundred dollars valuation for the payment of these bonds, and to lease the right-of-way over the structure to steam and electric railway companies.

When the bond election was held, the residents of Galveston County voted emphatically, 1,446 to 70, in favor of the issue. This action placed the entire causeway project in the hands of the County Commissioners' Court, and the causeway committee dissolved itself. For the next year a number of long and discouraging meetings took place among the county commissioners and representatives of the various railway companies interested in the potential use of a new causeway. Finally, on December 15, 1908, the entities came to an agreement. The county offered the railroads certain space on the structure for a period of ninety-nine years, for which the companies agreed to pay $575,000 of the construction costs, one-tenth when the contract was let, and the remainder in installments. The agreement also included a provision whereby other railways might gain access to the city via the new structure by paying agreed sums to the

Work being conducted on January 29, 1921, at the mainland end of the Galveston Causeway during its 1917–22 reconstruction. Photograph courtesy Rosenberg Library, Galveston, Texas.

four companies first involved. The parties to the agreement were the county, the three railroads crossing the bay in 1900, and the newly organized Galveston-Houston Electric Railway Company, which at the time was building an electric interurban railway to connect the two Gulf Coast cities.

On April 26, 1909, the county auditor advertised for bids from construction firms for the contract to build the Galveston Causeway. The specifications basically were those prepared three years earlier by the Concrete Steel Engineering Company of New York for the former causeway committee. After the bids were received, the county awarded the contract to the A. M. Blodgett Construction Company of Kansas City.

The Galveston Causeway as originally built consisted of earthen embankments on both Galveston Island and Virginia Point (or mainland) ends, twenty-eight reinforced-concrete arch spans, and a steel draw-span. The structure stretched across the bay a distance of 10,675 feet, just over two miles. Of this distance, 8,219 feet, 9 inches of the causeway in reality consisted of earthen embankments: 3,696 feet, 5 inches on the Virginia Point end and 4,523 feet, 4 inches on the Galveston Island end. It carried a two-lane, brick-paved highway, one electric interurban track, and two steam railway tracks. The arch section as completed in 1912 comprised twenty-eight 70-foot reinforced-concrete arches, fourteen on each side of a large central draw-span. All the piers rested on creosoted wooden-pile footings.

The Scherzer rolling-lift drawbridge on the Gal-

veston Causeway was one of the largest of its kind in the world. It weighed 3,293,000 pounds, 700 tons of which was in actual steel and the remainder of which consisted of five hundred cubic yards of concrete used as a counterbalance. This span provided a one-hundred-foot clear opening for the passage of ships into Galveston Bay. Its lift mechanism was operated by two fifty-horsepower electric motors furnished with current from the interurban line. To support the immense weight of the drawbridge, a very large concrete pivot pier was constructed. The draw span was fabricated by the Penn Bridge Company of Beaver Falls, Pennsylvania.

The greatest part of the structure, as completed in 1912, consisted of the earthen embankments on either end of the concrete arch section. These in effect were earthen berms protected by concrete slabs and retained by walls of concrete sheet pilings. The fill for the embankments was moved to the site by hydraulic fill techniques using dredges and large centrifugal pumps. Through both the earthen embankment and the concrete arch sections of the causeway passed a thirty-inch-diameter cast-iron water main. It served as an auxiliary pipeline to carry Galveston its water supply from artesian wells near Alta Loma on the mainland. At the drawbridge the water main left the causeway and crossed under the draw span thirteen feet below the natural bottom of Galveston Bay.

One of the most interesting aspects of the construction of the causeway was the operation of the construction camp built by the contractors at the island end of the structure. It included housing for workers,

The Galveston Causeway with its Scherzer rolling-lift drawbridge in raised position, as seen from Virginia Point today. Photograph by the author, 1981.

offices, railway yards, a pier into the bay, and such construction works as a concrete casting yard, a blacksmith shop, and a sawmill. The first three months' effort by the contractors was devoted to the preparation of this camp as a base of operations for the remainder of the project. The camp was dominated by three buildings, all of two-story frame design with their first floors raised six feet above the ground. The first of these held general offices, a store, and foremen's quarters; the second provided white workers' housing; and the third gave quarters for black laborers. When the camp was working at full capacity, it accommodated 450 men who were housed 6 to a room, each room with three double beds. In an effort to prevent the spread of illness or disease, all the windows and doors to dining rooms and kitchens were provided with two sets of screens and all the toilets for workers were placed on the dock over the water of Galveston Bay. With these and other precautions, the health of the camp was described as remarkably good, considering its size and the semitropical climate.

The completed Galveston Causeway was dedicated by the governor in a large celebration on May 25, 1912. This ceremony culminated the efforts of the

city and county of Galveston to secure a permanent tie with the Texas mainland. This "permanent" link, however, operated for only about three years before it was placed out of commission by a hurricane in August, 1915 (the first severe tropical storm to strike Galveston after the disastrous 1900 hurricane).

The central portions of the causeway, the concrete arch and steel draw-spans, survived with only slight damage. The earthen embankment sections at both ends, however, in the words of an engineer at the time, "collapsed like an empty barrel with the hoops removed." Although the concrete sheet pilings remained in place, the water and wind during the storm simply washed away the earth fill and the concrete retaining walls collapsed toward the center. For two years the causeway remained unusable, with its earthen approaches washed out. The intact concrete arch and draw sections mockingly stood by themselves in the center of the bay. A temporary wooden trestle, hastily erected, served as the only dry link with the mainland.

In late 1917 reconstruction work began. During the course of this work most of the original earthen embankments were replaced with concrete arches similar to the ones that had withstood the storm, thus making the causeway the continuous arched structure that visitors see today. The island end now contains forty-two arches, and the Virginia Point end contains sixty-five. The new arched sections were built with the same width and traffic capacity as the earlier arched portions. On each end of the reconstructed causeway the contractors built reinforced-concrete abutments with earth fill behind them. To avoid the problems encountered in the original earthen embankments, these new abutments were designed after the pattern of the Galveston Seawall and were V shaped, coming to a point where the actual concrete arches of the bridge began.

Reconstruction work continued from late 1917 to early 1922, at which time the structure returned to normal service. Since its reopening, it has served with only brief intermissions as a link between Galveston and the Texas mainland. Because of its historical significance, the structure was placed on the National Register of Historic Places in 1975.

Location: The Galveston Causeway stretches across

Galveston Bay between Galveston Island and the Texas mainland, roughly parallel to the modern Interstate 45 bridges. The Virginia Point end of the causeway is accessible by a local paved road leaving the southernmost exit from the interstate highway before it crosses Galveston Bay. The island end of the bridge is accessible via a city street off Port Industrial Boulevard, which runs parallel to the railway tracks leading to the causeway. The brick-paved roadway of the structure has been closed to public vehicular traffic for many years, but it is possible to walk on this roadway from either end.

Suggested Reading:

"Construction Methods Employed in Building the Galveston Causeway." *Engineering Record* 66, no. 2 (July 13, 1912): 41–43.
"The Construction of the Galveston Causeway." *Engineering Record* 63, no. 21 (May 27, 1911): 576–78.
"The Galveston Causeway." *Engineering Record* 62, no. 16 (October 15, 1910): 424–26.

38. Galveston Grade Raising

After Galveston was devastated by the great September, 1900, hurricane, the surviving inhabitants took several direct actions to protect their city from any future disaster. Their most famous effort was the construction of the noted Galveston Seawall along the entire oceanfront (discussed in entry no. 42). Along with the seawall came a less well known but even

more impressive effort to raise the grade of the entire city to protect it from flooding.

Construction of the initial section of the Galveston Seawall took place between 1902 and 1904. The seawall alone, however, could only break the force of waves striking the seaward side of the city. To protect the inhabitants from the flooding that always accom-

Spectators watching the work of the dredge, *Holm,* moored in the canal dug through the city of Galveston to provide the dredges with access to the areas requiring fill. Photograph courtesy Rosenberg Library, Galveston, Texas.

A large pipe from one of the dredges discharging mixed sand and water into a canal that carried it to an area requiring fill during the grade-raising operation. Photograph courtesy Rosenberg Library, Galveston, Texas.

panies major hurricanes, the municipal government undertook the almost unbelievable task of increasing the elevation of the entire city—raising its grade. In an amazing effort between 1903 and 1911, the elevation of the populated portion of Galveston was raised as much as sixteen feet, seven inches. This project provided a solid backing behind the new seawall and at the same time directed the drainage of the city toward Galveston Bay.

The sand composing Galveston Island is particularly well suited for making fill, but the available sources were so located that it was difficult to devise an economical means of moving it to where it was needed. It was not feasible to excavate it from the part

of the island west of the city, for this was the only direction into which the city could grow. Obtaining sand from this area offered the additional drawbacks of expense and difficulty in transporting it several miles to the areas requiring fill. Another potential source of sand for the project was from the Galveston beaches. Since most of the fill was to be placed on the seaward side of the island, dredging of ocean sand from this area seemed promising. The removal of sand from this area, however, might expose the footings for the new seawall to erosion and subsequent damage.

The most feasible source for sand proved to be the area between the two jetties at the entrance to Gal-

Utility mains at Twenty-fifth Street and Broadway already moved to the level at which they will be buried when the area is flooded with hydraulic fill. The grade in this neighborhood was later raised ten feet, burying these pipes eight feet underground. Photograph courtesy Rosenberg Library, Galveston, Texas.

An area with its grade already raised on the right while the area on the left has its buildings raised and placed on new foundations in preparation for the placement of hydraulic fill. Photograph courtesy Rosenberg Library, Galveston, Texas.

veston Harbor because the removal of fill material from this area would deepen the harbor entrance. Unfortunately, the jetties were located four miles from the area of the city to be raised, and this location placed them beyond the limits of ordinary hydraulic dredging operations.

The City of Galveston opened bidding on the contract for the grade-raising project in 1903. The method for moving the fill material was left to the discretion of the contractors bidding for the job. Needless to say, engineers puzzled over how to move the vast amounts of fill economically. The answer came from P. C. Goedhart of Düsseldorf, Germany, who also was a senior member in the firm of Goedhart and Bates in New York. This company received the contract for moving the earth in the grade-raising operations at a rate of 18.5 cents per cubic yard of fill delivered where required.

Goedhart's plan called for excavating sand from the channel between the jetties with hydraulic hopper dredges and then conveying it in these vessels by way of a canal dug through the area to be filled. The Goedhart and Bates firm sublet the contract for excavating the channel to Charles Clarke and Company for seven cents per cubic yard of material moved. This in itself was a substantial task, for approximately 1.5 million cubic yards of earth were moved to create the three-mile canal two hundred feet wide and twenty feet deep.

The hopper dredges used in the Galveston project were of unusual size and capacity and had certain features that were different from those in any dredges that had been used in the United States up to that time. Produced in German shipyards, they sailed across the Atlantic to Galveston under their own power. The smallest of the four dredges was about

160 feet long and 28 feet wide. Its hopper had a capacity for over five hundred cubic yards. The vessel was filled by a specially designed 22-inch centrifugal pump and emptied by a similar pump of the same capacity. Each of the three larger dredges had a capacity nearly three times that of the smaller vessel. Their pumps filled and emptied a load using the same machinery.

In the actual filling operations, the dredges discharged a load of mixed water and sand through long pipes at selected points along the temporary canal. The contractors were allowed to fill sixteen city blocks at one time, and they could take earth from any street in the section to be filled for constructing dams and ditches to confine the sand or return excess water to the canal. As the work progressed, the canal was filled in with sand up to the same grade as the surrounding land. About twelve million cubic yards of earth fill were required to raise the grade to the specified level, and nearly fifteen million cubic yards had to be moved, including filling the canal, before the project was completed. Work on the graderaising began in December, 1903, and continued until February, 1911. During subsequent years, smaller grade-raising projects were undertaken in western sections of the city.

The grade-raising effort was financed by the City of Galveston with some assistance from the state. The contracted cost of moving fill was $2,080,745, but this sum did not include the cost of the vast efforts by individuals and the city and county governments in related operations. More than two thousand dwellings had to be raised to the new levels. Larger buildings for which raising was more economical than tearing down and rebuilding were lifted by the ordinary methods of house-raising. New foundations then were built under them before the sand fill reached their sites. Smaller buildings were raised and supported on wooden posts, carefully braced to prevent the inward rush of sand and water from undermining them.

One of the most interesting aspects of the Galveston Grade Raising was the necessary relocation of all public services in the city. This included moving water, gas, and sewer mains, as well as street railway tracks and electricity, telegraph, and telephone lines. The populated districts of Galveston were raised an average of eight feet, although the area immediately behind the seawall was raised sixteen feet, seven inches. This change in grade required a corresponding change in the levels of all utilities, not to mention sidewalks, fences, and outbuildings. Because of the

depths to which all sewers and other underground pipes would have become buried, it was deemed necessary to raise them also to correspond with the new grades. This had the beneficial effect of improving the flow within the sewer system, which never previously had had sufficient grade for proper operation.

Gas, water, and sewer mains, after an initial period of experimentation, were moved in the following manner. Workers first excavated down to the mains to expose them completely. Then they used chain blocks on tripod derricks to lift them until they reached the proper levels. Men filled in the trenches under the lines to avoid breaking joints and interrupting service. Once raised to a level where they could not be supported on the soil, the mains were carried on temporary supports. When they reached their new grades, they were braced by firm struts nailed to timbers driven into the ground on either side of the pipes. In this way the mains could withstand the inward rush of sand and water that in time buried both mains and supports.

The appearance of the raised portion of the city, which included practically all its residential districts, was somewhat similar to that of a desert town with no vegetation. All landscaping had to be done again. As quickly as it could be managed, homeowners started the long, expensive task. Topsoil from the mainland was brought in and spread over the new fill. Grass, shrubs, and trees were planted, and new flower gardens were laid out. Oleanders and palms, which grew quickly in the climate, were widely used by both the citizens and the municipal government to beautify yards and streets; Galveston in time became known as the "Oleander City." Within a remarkably short time, most visible traces of the massive grade-raising operations had disappeared.

Location: During the Galveston Grade Raising, the elevation of most of the populated districts of the city was increased at least several feet. The depth of fill was greatest immediately behind the Seawall, was twelve feet at Avenue P, ten feet at Broadway, and eight feet at Avenue A, decreasing at a rate of one foot per fifteen hundred feet from the Gulf toward the bay. A few signs of the massive engineering work still may be seen, but they are not common. The cast-iron fence at Ashton Villa, located at 2324 Broadway, for instance, was not raised fully at the time of the grade raising, and it can be seen emerging rather awkwardly from the sand that surrounds it. The brick kitchen of the Samuel May Williams house at 3601 Avenue P also was not raised, even though the remainder of the residence was, so today it stands at a lower level than do the wooden portions of the structure.

Suggested Reading:

"Raising the Grade of Galveston." *Railroad Gazette* 36, no. 1 (January 1, 1904): 6–8.
"The Relocation of Public Service Systems during the Grade Raising of Galveston, Tex." *Engineering Record* 54, no. 11 (September 15, 1906): 299–302.

39. Galveston Highway Bridge

The 2.5-mile Galveston Highway Bridge, opened to the public on November 15, 1893, was acclaimed in its day as the longest highway bridge in the world. It held the additional distinction of being second longest among all bridges only to the great Lake Pontchartrain railway bridge. The impressive structure stretched 11,309 feet across Galveston Bay. Connecting the port city with the Texas mainland for only seven years, the structure was swept away by the 1900 Galveston hurricane.

For forty-five years Galveston residents discussed the construction of a vehicular bridge across Galveston Bay. Although railway trestles had spanned the bay since the 1850s, no wagon bridge had ever been built. Finally in 1893, Galveston County undertook such a project, even though only a very limited amount of money was made available to fund the effort. The projected bridge had to be not only long but also economical to build.

The plans settled on by the county commissioners called for a bridge made partly from steel bowstring arches resting on concrete piers and partly from wooden timbers. The bridge was designed with eighty-nine fixed steel spans for a metal structure 7,432 feet long, combined with wooden trestle approaches 3,877 feet long. In April, 1892, the commissioners awarded a contract for the project to the Missouri Valley Bridge and Iron Works of Leavenworth, Kansas. This firm began its work in November, 1892, and completed the project in October, 1893.

The first work by the contractors centered on constructing the concrete piers. They were mounted on wooden pile foundations placed in the following manner: Watertight temporary iron caissons slightly

The bowstring-arch section of the 1893 Galveston Highway Bridge. Photograph courtesy Rosenberg Library, Galveston, Texas.

larger than the piers were sunk at the proper locations. Then earthen material at their base was removed to a depth of two or more feet. If workers found a hard bottom, they immediately set to work with a pile driver and sank between seventeen and twenty-four wooden piles. If they were unable to find a solid bottom, they instead placed a grillage made from twelve-inch wooden timbers drift-bolted together on top of the piles as a sound base for pouring concrete.

After the piles were driven and while the caisson was still in position, workers placed a mold for the concrete over the piles and prepared it for pouring concrete. These molds came in two sections, the first extending just above the water level and the second forming the upper portion of the pier. Concrete was poured into these molds and allowed to set before they were removed. The standard piers were twenty-two feet, six inches long and two feet, six inches wide just below their coping, which projected three inches on all sides over the main body of each pier. The ends were rounded and both ends and the sides were designed with a batter of one-half inch to the foot.

After the concrete piers were finished, crews on barges floated the prefabricated and assembled bowstring arches into position. The trusses then were raised to the proper level and bolted into place on anchor bolts, which had been embedded in the concrete. The eighty-one-foot-long spans in the bridge were divided into four twenty-foot panels each. The top and bottom chords consisted of heavy steel angle members riveted together to form T sections, and the web members were attached to them through the use of gusset plates. The trusses were mounted eighteen feet apart, providing the space for a wooden roadway. While the truss spans were being put into position, pile drivers were at work driving the piles for the timber trestle approaches and the remainder of the work on the wooden portion of the bridge was being completed.

To permit the passage of barges and boats through the bridge, a swing span was built on one large octagonal concrete pier. Footing for this pier came from sixty-three wooden piles. After the large concrete pier was completed, the work crews put in place a 226-foot, 3-inch steel swing span. This span rotated atop the pier by the action of a pinion gear attached to the swinging span, which was turned by the watchman with a large crank in his shelter house on the span.

When the Galveston Highway Bridge was completed, it was of considerable interest to the engineering community at large not only because of its impressive length but also for its remarkably low construction cost. Initially, the contract called for a project costing $183,000, but a small extension of the trestle approaches and a few unexpected expenses brought the total up to $191,986, amazingly low for a structure this size. The engineering press noted that "the steel work is unquestionably light, but the traffic will be light also," adding that "the alternative presented appears to have been to have a fairly efficient, light bridge . . . or to have no bridge at all."

The highway bridge remained in service until it was swept away by the great 1900 Galveston storm. After the hurricane passed, only the crumpled remains of a few truss spans, portions of concrete piers, and broken-off tops of wooden pilings still stood. After the storm its role was taken first by ferries, then by reconstructed wooden railway trestles, and finally, in 1912, by the reinforced concrete Galveston Causeway, which included a vehicular road at one side.

Location: No remains of the 1893 Galveston Highway Bridge are visible. The bridge crossed the bay in the approximate area of the two modern reinforced-concrete highway bridges. Thus, when one drives between the mainland and Galveston Island, one necessarily goes over the general area of the 1893 bridge.

Suggested Reading:

Baker, T. Lindsay. "1893 Galveston Bridge Praised." *Galveston Daily News* (May 19, 1974), sec. B, p. 1.
"The Galveston County (Tex.) Highway Bridge." *Engineering News* 31, no. 10 (March 8, 1894): 204–205.
"A Great Bridge." *Galveston Weekly News* (November 16, 1893), p. 16.

40. Galveston Jetties

The growth of Galveston, the most important nineteenth-century port on the Texas coast, was retarded for much of its history by a major navigational impediment: the continued accumulation of sandbars at the entrance to its harbor. This natural phenomenon prevented many larger oceangoing ships

Workers constructing the pine stake and sea cane gabions for use in the 1874–77 gabionade jetty project at Galveston. Men on the right are assembling gabions; those on the left are coating one with protective concrete. Photograph courtesy U.S. Army Engineer District, Galveston, Texas.

from even entering the harbor and forced shippers to "lighter" their cargoes to and from these vessels. In other words, more shallow-draft boats and barges had to load and unload goods at the larger ships anchored outside the harbor and then carry these cargoes to and from the docks. This was an expensive and time-consuming process and greatly restricted the tonnage moving through the port.

The sand accumulations were completely natural. Sand and silt are automatically carried to the coast by fresh-water streams that empty into it. The generally southwesterly currents of the Gulf pick up this suspended sediment and carry it farther along the shore, depositing it to create the coastal islands such as Galveston Island. Among the points where sediment from the fresh-water streams enters the Gulf is the mouth of Galveston Harbor, a three-mile-wide gap between the east end of Galveston Island and the tip of the Bolivar Peninsula. When the currents carrying this fresh water and its sediments meet the natural ocean currents, the velocity of the former decreases and the sediments automatically drop to the bottom. This tendency toward the deposit of sediments is further enhanced by the action of tides washing across the wide three-mile gap, often further slowing the speed of the silt-laden waters and causing them to release sediment. Whenever and wherever this occurs, sandbars are created.

Two distinct sandbars formed at the entrance to Galveston Harbor. The outer bar, 4.5 miles from shore, had a depth of twelve feet and an inner bar had a depth of nine feet, six inches. The two bars remained impediments to trade from the founding of Galveston in the 1830s until the final solution of the problem in the late 1890s. The inner bar grew sub-

stantially after obstructions were sunk in its area during the Civil War.

As early as 1857 the state of Texas allocated $23,000 for improving Galveston Harbor, but it was forty years and millions of dollars later before effective measures were taken to clear its entrance. Much of the early funding went to pay for expensive and ineffective dredging. Among the well-meaning but unsuccessful efforts was that by the citizens of Galveston in 1869. In that year they appropriated $170,000 to construct a wooden pile jetty more than a mile into the Gulf. Although the scheme failed, it did point the way toward the eventual solution of the problem. The answer took the form of building structures that would restrict the available space for the passage of waters flowing in and out of the harbor. If the channel were sufficiently restricted, the waters would flow fast enough to carry sediment farther into the Gulf before depositing it, thus keeping the entrance of the harbor clear of sandbars.

In 1874 the U.S. government began major efforts to improve the entrance to Galveston Harbor. In that year the U.S. Army Corps of Engineers initiated its "gabionade" project. This ill-fated effort attempted to channel the flow of currents in and out of the harbor entrance between two rows of large "gabions." These structures were pine stake boxes with sea cane wattling measuring six by six by twelve feet, coated with cement inside and out, and filled with sand. They were stacked in rows on the bottom of the harbor entrance to create a channel through which tidal currents were expected to flow. Work on the project proceeded until 1877, when it was abandoned as a failure. The sand-filled gabions fell to pieces and were never seen again.

Placement of granite blocks to form part of the solid rock Galveston Jetties in July, 1896. Photograph courtesy National Archives, Washington, D.C.

After the abandonment of the gabionade project, the Corps of Engineers decided on another design for the jetties to channel the flow of water through the entrance of the harbor to scour it clean. Beginning in 1880, the corps began constructing "mattress-type" jetties composed of alternate layers of brush and heavy stones. These structures were planned to extend 10,220 feet into the Gulf from the east end of Galveston Island and from the west end of the Bolivar Peninsula. They were to be 5 feet below the mean tide level and 12 feet wide at the tops on their shore ends. They were to slope gradually upward toward the surface and to increase in width to 24 feet at the tops of their extreme ends. Work progressed on the "mattress" project from 1880 to 1886, when it too was suspended. At this time it was discovered that the brush mattresses were being eaten away by *Teredo navalis* sea worms. Slowly, the new jetties, which had cost over a million dollars to build, sank to the ocean floor. A nineteenth-century writer reported that by 1893 "there was little to indicate that such a thing as a completed mattress jetty had ever existed." The sandbars still blocked the entrance of Galveston Harbor to all but shallow-draft vessels.

As time passed and more and more unsuccessful projects were undertaken to make Galveston a true deep-water port, demands for a successful solution to the problem grew in parts of the country where at first they might not be expected. Galveston rep-

resented the nearest potential deep-water port for much of the Rocky Mountain West and Central Great Plains. Promoters of economic development in cities like Denver and Wichita realized that if major international shipping were able to use Galveston, their areas would be the ones to benefit through cheaper transportation for their products. The development of Galveston harbor would save as much as seventeen hundred miles of rail transportation to reach a deep-water port. Thus congressmen from states like Colorado, Kansas, and Arkansas joined those from Texas in supporting funding to improve the harbor at Galveston.

After two unsuccessful attempts to construct jetties at Galveston, the Corps of Engineers finally developed a plan that proved to be a singular success. The revised design, chosen in 1890, called for the construction of two solid rock jetties stretching from either side of the harbor entrance into the Gulf of Mexico to the point where they reached a depth of thirty feet of water. This meant that the south jetty, the one starting at the east end of Galveston Island, would reach six miles into the ocean, and the north jetty from the Bolivar Peninsula would extend five miles to sea. At their seaward ends the jetties would be seven thousand feet apart.

The cores of the two jetties were built from native Texas sandstone and their tops and sides covered exclusively with huge chunks of Texas granite. The granite riprap gradually was increased from three-quarters of a ton at the shore ends to not less than ten tons nor more than fifteen tons at the outer ends. The only exception to these specifications was at the shore end of the south jetty, where sandstone was used both inside and outside. As the jetties were extended into the sea, railway tracks were laid atop them to facilitate the movement of rock for further construction. A railroad line carried the huge pieces of stone from Galveston to the south jetty site, but there were no railway connections at the Bolivar Peninsula for the north jetty work. The contractors there used first a railway ferry and later barges to transport the rock from which the north jetty was built. As completed, the jetties stood five feet above mean low tide, twelve feet wide at the top, and had slopes on their sides at the natural grade taken by the rock as it tumbled down from above.

Construction of the solid rock jetties began in 1890 and continued through 1898. By 1895, however, the beneficial results of the project already were becoming apparent to everyone. The depth of water over the outer bar increased from twelve feet, its natural depth, to seventeen feet, six inches, and the inner bar had virtually disappeared with an increase in water depth from nine feet, six inches to twenty-four feet, six inches. By the turn of the century the channel had deepened to between twenty-five feet, six inches and twenty-eight feet.

The improvement to the entrance of Galveston Harbor, including the expenditures for the unsuccessful projects, cost the taxpayers approximately eight mil-lion dollars, but the benefits far outweighed the expense. As a result of the project, the Central Great Plains and Rocky Mountain West received a deep-water port only a thousand miles away, about half the distance to East Coast ports. The economic benefits to Texas cannot be measured. Even today the 1890s solid rock jetties, repaired through the years, remain in service keeping the entrance to Galveston Harbor open to shipping.

Location: The Galveston Jetties extend seaward in a generally easterly direction from the extreme east end of Galveston Island and from near the western tip of the Bolivar Peninsula. The South Jetty may be reached by taking the paved road past the bait houses eastward from the northeast end of Seawall Boulevard in Galveston. The North Jetty is accessible via a local road just southeast of State Highway 86, about 1.7 miles east of the ferry landing at the west end of the Bolivar Peninsula.

Suggested Reading:

Axelrod, Bernard. "Galveston: Denver's Deep-Water Port." *Southwestern Historical Quarterly* 70, no. 2 (October, 1966): 217–28.

Howell, Charles W. "Improvement of Entrance to Galveson Harbor." *Transactions of the American Society of Civil Engineers* 6, no. 163 (1878): 223–30.

Sherman, W. J. "The Galveston Harbor Works." *Engineering News* 37, no. 11 (March 18, 1897): 162–63.

41. *Galveston Military Fortifications*

Fortifications to protect the harbor at Galveston, Texas, predate even the establishment of Galveston as a town. Located in three separate areas, two on Galveston Island and one on the Bolivar Peninsula, all the major defensive works may at least be observed from some distance, with some of them having complete public access. Many visitors find them among the most fascinating of all the engineering works in the Galveston area.

The first fortifications at Galveston were erected near the present site of Fort Travis on the Bolivar Peninsula between 1816 and 1817 by Francisco Xavier Mina during Mexico's revolution against Spain. Here the rebellious troops drilled while awaiting reinforce-ments and while planning a campaign into Mexico. Four years later the same general area was occupied by a mud fort built by men under the leadership of Dr. James Long, an American filibusterer who came to Texas in an unsuccessful attempt to wrest it from Mexican rule. His young wife, Jane, remained behind at the fort with only her daughter and a slave girl through the winter of 1821–22 awaiting the return of her husband, only to learn that he had been killed. Today Jane Long is known as the "Mother of Texas" because she was the first woman of Anglo-American descent to enter Texas and because she bore the first known child of such parentage in the state.

Three major military installations that once guarded

Construction of Battery Thomas Davis at Fort Travis about 1898. Photograph courtesy Galveston County Beach and Parks Department, Galveston, Texas.

Galveston harbor survive. Although none today serve military purposes, they are still known as Fort Travis, Fort San Jacinto, and Fort Crockett. Fort Travis is located in the area of the earlier forts from the first two decades of the nineteenth century on the Bolivar Peninsula. The site also was occupied during the Civil War by a battery and at the time was known as Fort Green. The early history of Fort Travis, however, finds it located at the east end of Galveston Island. It was built as an octagonal defense work for the Republic of Texas in 1836 and was named in honor of William Barret Travis, the commander at the Alamo. It mounted six- and twelve-pound guns taken from the steamer *Cayuga,* which for a matter of days in late April, 1836, had housed a temporary capitol for the Republic of Texas. The new post was commanded by James Morgan and remained occupied until 1844.

The name Fort Travis was applied in 1898 to a new federally constructed defensive work erected on the strategic Bolivar Peninsula in the area of the earlier forts built by Mina, Long, and the Confederate army. The U.S. government purchased ninety-eight acres and on this site constructed a substantial reinforced-concrete system of gun emplacements and bunkers to protect the east side of the entrance to Galveston Harbor. These facilities were enlarged several times in the early twentieth century, and during World War I and World War II.

Fort San Jacinto is located across the harbor entrance from present-day Fort Travis, at the east end of Galveston Island in approximately the same area as the original 1836 Fort Travis. It was built to guard the west side of the harbor entrance. It was named for the Texan victory at the Battle of San Jacinto, and its site was reserved for public purposes by an act of the Republic of Texas on December 9, 1835, and by a joint resolution of the U.S. Congress on March 1, 1845. The site, however, lay vacant until 1898. In that year,

The abandoned remains of gun emplacements and bunkers at Fort San Jacinto. Photograph, 1975, courtesy Center for the History of Engineering, Texas Tech University, Lubbock, Texas.

at the time of hostilities with Spain, the Department of War initiated construction of a reinforced-concrete fortress known as Fort San Jacinto. Work progressed on the major construction project until its completion in 1901, although the first garrison arrived at the facility as early as April 20, 1898. Fort San Jacinto was occupied from the 1890s through the end of World War II, with the exception of a brief period after the great 1900 Galveston storm, and it was the original headquarters for the Galveston harbor defenses.

The third major element in the Galveston military fortifications is the portion best known to the public. Fort Crockett is located just behind Seawall Boulevard on the oceanfront of Galveston. It was established in 1897 and named for David Crockett. Its role

was to defend the western end of the port city from attack by sea. Occupied from 1897 to 1900, the facility, like forts Travis and San Jacinto, was not garrisoned for the years immediately following the Galveston hurricane. By 1911, however, it had become a mobilization center during border troubles with Mexico. It was about this time that the large two- and three-story concrete barracks, quartermasters' stores, and other buildings were erected at the post. They were notable in their day because they were constructed by the "Aiken System of Flat Wall Construction." In this method the reinforced-concrete walls were poured and set in an almost horizontal position and then raised into their vertical position with special screw jacks. The most impressive feature at Fort

The World War II–era earth-sheltered, concrete-lined gun emplacement at Fort Crockett. Photograph, 1975, courtesy Center for the History of Engineering, Texas Tech University, Lubbock, Texas.

Crockett, however, is the huge World War II–vintage earth-protected and concrete-lined gun emplacement from which long guns once pointed toward the Gulf.

Since the end of World War II, the roles of the three major Galveston military fortifications have changed drastically. Fort Travis today has been converted to the Fort Travis Seashore Park, administered by the Galveston County Beach and Parks Department. Fort San Jacinto stands deserted, a haven for rattlesnakes. The only operating military area at the site, the Fort Point Coast Guard Station, is not part of the original facility. Fort Crockett is used jointly by the Coast Guard and the U.S. Army Corps of Engineers for personnel housing. Other buildings at Fort Crockett are used by Galveston College and the Texas A&M University Moody College of Marine Sciences and Maritime Resources as office, laboratory, and teaching space, as well as housing offices for the National Marine Fisheries Service.

Location: Fort Travis, now better known as the Fort Travis Seashore Park, is accessible to the public near the tip of the Bolivar Peninsula. It may be reached by visitors who take the free Bolivar Ferry on State Highway 86 from Galveston across the harbor entrance to the peninsula. Fort San Jacinto, located on the extreme east end of Galveston Island, may be observed from some distance from the top of the seawall at the east end of Seawall Boulevard. The gun emplacements and attractive concrete buildings of Fort Crockett stand just behind the seawall on Seawall Boulevard in the area just west of Forty-fifth Street and may be seen quite easily.

Suggested Reading:

Darst, W. Maury. "Galveston's Harbor Defenses." *Texana* 10, no. 1 (1972): 51–54.
"Fort Crockett Makes City Strategic Center of Nation's Defenses." *Galveston Daily News* (August 15, 1939), sec. G, p. 4.
Hardman, R. C. "Unit Wall Concrete Building Construction, Fort Crockett, Texas." *Engineering News* 66, no. 26 (June 27, 1912): 1205–1206.

42. *Galveston Seawall*

Through most of the nineteenth century, Galveston was noted as the foremost port on the Texas Gulf Coast. Its history, however, was dramatically affected when the port and resort city was struck by a devastating hurricane on September 8, 1900. This storm came to be known as the greatest natural disaster in Texas history, having killed an estimated six thousand residents and destroyed approximately thirty-six hundred homes. The death and destruction was caused principally by the force of the extreme winds coupled with a fifteen-foot high tide, which swept over the entire city.

In the wake of the storm, Galveston leaders organized several distinct but related efforts to rebuild and protect their city. For one of these endeavors, the City Commission and County Commissioners' Court appointed a board of engineers to report on a means for protecting the city from a recurring disaster. The board, consisting of Brig. Gen. H. M. Robert, the former chief of U.S. Army Engineers, and Alfred Noble and H. C. Ripley, presented its formal report on January 25, 1902. It recommended the construction of a solid concrete wall over three miles long along the oceanfront of the city as a barrier to the sea, raising

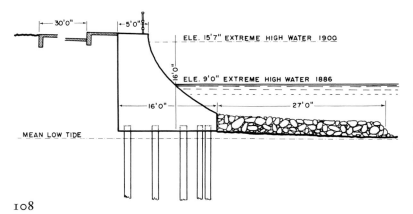

Original plan for the Galveston Seawall as submitted by Messrs. Robert, Noble, and Ripley in 1902. The basic design was followed in subsequent seawall construction. Based on "Plans for the Protection of Galveston from Floods," *Engineering News* 47, no. 17 (April 24, 1902): 344. Drawing by the author.

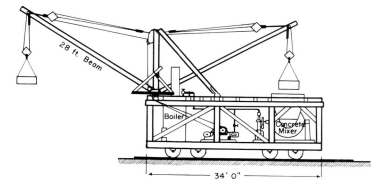

Side view of one of the concrete mixing and handling machines used in the construction of the early sections of the Galveston Seawall. Drawing shows the relative positions of the boiler, steam engine, and concrete mixer on the lower level as well as the use of two derricks for handling raw materials and mixed concrete. Based on "Concrete Mixing and Handling Machines for the Galveston Sea-Wall," *Engineering News* 49, no. 3 (January 15, 1903): 55. Drawing by the author.

the grade of the city to reduce the danger from flooding, and the construction of a protected embankment behind the proposed concrete seawall.

The design proposed by the board was for a concrete gravity section sixteen feet wide at its base one foot above mean low water. The seaward face of the concrete structure was to be curved, with its upper portion vertical so that it would deflect large ocean waves upward to prevent them from passing over the wall into the city.

Galveston County undertook the construction of the massive concrete structure. The consent of the taxpayers was necessary for the project, and on March 20, 1902, in an overwhelming vote, the citizens approved a tax levy of 50 cents on each $100 valuation on property to pay interest and principal on bonds in the amount of $1.5 million to pay for the effort. On September 19, 1902, the county closed a contract with the firm of J. M. O'Rourke and Company of Denver to build the seawall. The first pile was driven at the foot of Sixteenth Street on October 27,

1902, and the immense project was completed almost two years later, on July 29, 1904.

The wall was built on a foundation of vertical wooden pilings, which were protected from undermining on the seaward side by wooden sheet pilings, which further were protected by stone riprap 3 feet thick and 27 feet wide. The concrete sections of seawall were built in two steps. First a base 16 feet wide and 3 feet thick was poured to provide a foundation for the section placed above it. This concrete base completely covered the tops of the wooden pilings. The upper portion of the seawall was built in 50-foot interlocking sections, which were reinforced with 1¼-inch square steel rods set within the concrete.

The magnitude of the project may be seen in the volume of material that went into the initial 3.5-mile section. Used in its construction were fifty-two hundred railway carloads of crushed granite, eighteen hundred carloads of sand, one thousand carloads of cement, twelve hundred carloads of round wooden pilings, four thousand carloads of wooden sheet pil-

Concrete being mixed and poured during the construction of one of the early sections of the Galveston Seawall. In use is one of the special concrete mixing and handling machines built especially for use on the Galveston project. Photograph courtesy Rosenberg Library, Galveston, Texas.

The initial section of the Galveston Seawall soon after its completion in 1904. Photograph courtesy Rosenberg Library, Galveston, Texas.

ings, thirty-seven hundred carloads of stone riprap, and five carloads of reinforcing steel.

Interesting machines were employed to mix and deliver the concrete for the seawall. These specially built mixing and handling machines moved behind and parallel to the long construction site on steel rails. The two machines consisted of double-deck cars measuring sixteen-by-thirty-four feet, which rolled on eight wheels. They carried on their lower decks steam boilers and engines as well as concrete mixers, and their upper decks provided working platforms. At the front end of the cars were twin derricks fitted with twenty-eight-foot booms, one handling raw materials and the other moving mixed concrete in one-yard batches. Raw materials consisting of portland cement, sand, and gravel were loaded onto the upper working level from adjacent railway cars; from there they were placed in measured amounts in the concrete mixers. The mixed concrete was dumped from the mixing machines into skips at track level. The skips filled with concrete were elevated by the second derrick to the actual places where mixed concrete was needed.

While the county seawall was being built along the oceanfront between the south jetty and Thirty-ninth street, Congress authorized the construction of another section of seawall along the front of the Fort Crockett Military Reservation, between Thirty-ninth and Fifty-third streets. This work followed the basic design of the county section and was conducted from December, 1904, to October, 1905.

The first test of the new protective structure came in 1915, when Galveston again was subjected to a severe tropical storm. This hurricane crossed the Texas coast about thirty miles southwest of Gal-

veston, and the seawall proved the adequacy of its design by preventing a recurrence of the damage of fifteen years earlier. Only twelve residents lost their lives in the storm, and the total property loss was far, far less than in 1900. One of the remarkable incidents of the storm was the destruction of the schooner *Allison Doura* on the seawall. Caught about a hundred miles at sea from Galveston, the sailing vessel loaded with sisal was driven before the storm with her captain and crew helpless. The ship was thrown onto the seawall near Thirty-ninth Street, her two anchors catching in the toe of the wall and the schooner being pounded to pieces at its top. Fragments of the ship's hull, masts, and cargo were strewn all over the western portion of the city.

New sections of the seawall continued to be added. The first of these came in 1918, when an east extension to the structure was built by the federal government to run from Sixth Street to Fort San Jacinto for the protection of the military installation. Its progress was interrupted by a less intense storm in September, 1919, which prevented completion until March, 1921. Another extension 2,860 feet eastward across the Fort San Jacinto Reservation was made between May, 1923, and January, 1926. Galveston County built a 2,800-foot addition to the west end of the seawall in 1926 and 1927. This gave the wall a total length of 7.29 miles. Finally, in 1950 Congress authorized the construction of an additional 3-mile southwest extension of the seawall similar in design to the existing walls to protect the newer western portion of the city.

Beach sand at Galveston is essential for the protection of the toe of the seawall. Because of reduction in the amount of beach sand through the wave action of tropical storms after the construction of the first sections of seawall, an effort was initiated in the mid-1930s to augment the natural replenishment of beach sand through the construction of sheet steel pile groins (later rehabilitated with stone extending from the seawall into the surf). A series of thirteen of these groins, each five hundred feet long and fifteen hundred feet apart, was built between Twelfth and Fifty-ninth streets from 1936 to 1939. They have successfully caused the accumulation of sufficient quantities of beach material, most of it below mean low tide level, to keep the toe of the seawall well protected.

Today the Galveston Seawall remains the city's principal protection against the destructive forces of hurricanes. In addition to serving this function, it is one of the most often seen and most popular historic engineering works in the state. Because of its location on the sea front of a resort city, it is a very appealing place for social gatherings. It has been popular for bicycle riding, walking, sunbathing, and evening serenading for decades, and it will most likely remain so for decades to come.

Location: The Galveston Seawall stretches over ten miles for virtually the entire length of Seawall Boulevard along the oceanfront of Galveston and is accessible to the public at all points.

Suggested Reading:

Davis, Albert B., Jr. *Galveston's Bulwark against the Sea: History of the Galveston Seawall.* Rev. ed. Galveston, Tex.: U.S. Army Engineer District, Galveston, 1961.

"The Galveston Sea Wall." *Engineering Record* 48, no. 1 (July 4, 1903): 14–16.

"Plans for the Protection of Galveston from Floods." *Engineering News* 47, no. 17 (April 24, 1902): 343–44.

The Galveston Seawall near its southwestern end. Photograph by the author, 1981.

43. Galveston Waterworks

Still employing most of its 1895 components as well as elements even older, the Galveston Waterworks is one of the most interesting of all the municipal water systems in Texas. It provides a dependable supply of fresh water to the port city, which is surrounded on all sides by the saltwater of the Gulf of Mexico and Galveston Bay. Securing its supply of fresh water from almost twenty miles away in an area on the mainland near the town of Alta Loma, the system transports this water through an original 1895 cast-iron pipeline to the city, passing beneath Galveston Bay for two miles.

For the city's first fifty years, the only water supply for Galveston came from individual cisterns and shallow hand-dug wells. The cisterns were the favored source of supply because their collected rainwater was fresh to the taste, whereas the wells almost always delivered only brackish water. The first recorded proposal to construct a waterworks for Galveston came from Col. J. S. Thrasher in 1870. He suggested securing a supply from a body of water known as Sweet-water Lake, located about five miles from the city, but in 1871 the city aldermen decisively rejected his plan.

During the next decade the City Council changed its opinion regarding the construction of a waterworks. The members of the council realized that Galveston desperately needed some type of water system for fire protection. Consequently, on February 2, 1880, they appropriated ten thousand dollars to sink an experimental artesian well near the southeast corner of the Ball High School campus. Drilled by the firm of Maxey and Nixon of Saint Louis, the well reached a depth of seven hundred feet before it reached water. Because it provided no natural artesian flow at the surface, however, the aldermen considered the experiment only a qualified success. As happened to virtually all the wells in the city, the fresh groundwater soon turned salty.

Five more years passed before any further steps were taken to establish a water system for Galveston. By this time the city had a population of about twenty-five thousand, virtually all of whom relied for

View up the side of the 1895 Alta Loma standpipe, still a part of the Galveston water system. Photograph by the author, 1973.

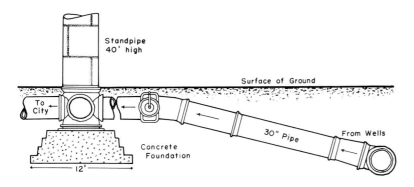

Cross-section of the 1895 Alta Loma stand-pipe, showing its foundation and the mains leading to and from the structure. Based on "The Galveston Water-Works," *Engineering Record* 34, no. 7 (July 18, 1896): 122. Drawing by the author.

their drinking water on supplies of rainwater stored in cisterns. The water problem was not so severe during the wet months of the year, but even then water was conserved for use in times of dry weather. When Galvestonians wanted to bathe, they generally went to the bay, the Gulf, or a nearby bayou, or else used brackish water from a well. Finally, in 1885 W. C. Connors of Dallas constructed a fire-protection water system that covered part of the downtown business district. Using water pumped directly from Galveston Bay, the system, leased by the municipal government, helped to protect a small part of the city from a disastrous fire that burned forty blocks of buildings on November 13, 1885.

After the 1885 fire, the city aldermen decided that the time had come for Galveston to have its own complete waterworks system. The councilmen decided to build a system using artesian wells, which would provide water for both fire protection and domestic and industrial use. Work began on the system in 1887 with the construction of a pump house and reservoir at Thirtieth Street and Avenue H. Completed in 1888, both of these structures, though altered, exist today. The city sank a series of thirteen wells at eight-hundred-foot intervals along Avenue G (Winnie Street) between Seventeenth and Forty-first streets. Although all the water from the string of wells was highly impregnated with salt, it was used together with the fresh water from individual cisterns until the new system was built a few years later.

Soon after the city sank its wells along Avenue G, Jacques Tacquard, a rancher near Hitchcock, about fifteen miles inland from Galveston, drilled one of the first truly fine artesian wells in the area. His 1887 well suggested to local leaders that they, too, might find a comparable flow of fresh water if they drilled deep enough. Accordingly, in 1889 the Galveston city fathers appropriated funds for drilling a 3,000-foot

well within the city. They hoped that it would penetrate rock and provide fresh water to solve the city's water woes. Begun in early April, 1891, it was drilled until it reached a depth of 3,070 feet without either passing through rock or striking a fresh-water aquifer. After this disappointment city officials realized that they would have to go to the mainland if they were to secure an adequate and reliable supply of fresh water.

By this time more and more individuals had secured strong artesian wells on the mainland in the area around Hitchcock. It was here that the Galveston City Council determined it would go for water. Accordingly, it hired a civil engineer, Wynkoop Kiersted, to design a system securing its supply from a series of artesian wells on the mainland and transporting this flow to the island through a pipeline. About the same time, council members accepted special inducements from the promoters of the Alta Loma community to locate the wells in that area a few miles beyond Hitchcock.

Contractors began construction on the new Galveston water system on September 12, 1894. They sank a series of thirty artesian wells near Alta Loma in the general area of the Santa Fe Railway tracks. An influent pipe connected these wells and carried their flow to a cast-iron pipeline leading from Alta Loma 18.7 miles by gravity flow to a receiving tank at the old 1888 waterworks pump house in the city. From that point it was pumped into standpipes and directly into the mains for distribution. The complete system was finished and placed in operation on August 19, 1895.

Among the most interesting features of the Galveston system were the collection mains and large forty-eight-inch-diameter, forty-foot-tall steel standpipe erected near the head of the pipeline. The purpose of the standpipe, which is still in use, was to

The 1895 pipeline that still carries fresh water from the mainland to Galveston. Photograph by the author, 1982.

provide an emergency escape valve for the water entering the pipeline should any extreme pressures occur at the wells or at the head of the line. The designer of the system also realized that at some date in the future the system would require pumping as the artesian flow decreased, and he designed the standpipe so that it could become part of the pressure system when pumping would be added. At a later date the original standpipe was raised an additional twenty feet.

The laying of the pipeline was a remarkable engineering feat. It consists of 12-foot lengths of 30-inch-diameter cast-iron pipe. Carrying water 11 miles from near Alta Loma to the edge of Galveston Bay, it crosses beneath the bay a distance of 10,352 feet and then runs an additional 4.75 miles to the central pumping station in the city. The sections of the pipeline on shore consist of lengths of class B pipe 1 inch thick and weighing 3,661 pounds; the underwater section is composed of class D pipe 1⅛ inch thick and weighing 4,485 pounds per 12-foot length. The

line from Alta Loma to Galveston crosses a most forbidding swamp and marsh area. As soon as crews dug through the muck, they placed the pipe in the ground with its bell ends pointed toward the supply station. The minimum depth for covering the pipes was 18 inches, with the earth heaped over the pipes where they could not be covered otherwise. Filling proceeded as soon as the laid pipe was inspected.

Beneath the waters of Galveston Bay, the pipe was laid in a three-foot trench excavated by a specially built dredge. For the underwater work, eight pieces of pipe were assembled and the joints were poured with molten lead and caulked in the usual manner on a wharf to form ninety-six-foot sections. Each of these sections, weighing about twenty tons, was moved from the wharf by a barge using trusses to support the pipe. Eight large chains, one around each length of pipe, held the assembly in place as it was lifted from the wharf. After it was elevated, the assembly was moved a short distance and then lowered until the pipe, with wooden plugs inserted in each end, was about half submerged and semifloated in the bay water. Moving the pipe in this fashion reduced the load on the barge enough to dispense with the use of heavy counterweights. Next a tug towed the barge into position and the pipe, with the plugs removed, was lowered into place underwater. A diver then went down to guide the spigot end into the bell of the pipe already in position. The joint was forced into its full length by strong rigging of ropes and blocks on the barge. The diver caulked the joint and the barge returned to Galveston for another eight-member section of pipe. During most of the underwater pipe laying, only one ninety-six-foot section of pipe could be installed in one day, especially on the northwest end of the line, where a hard bottom clay stuck to the dredge bucket. The first section of the two-mile underwater line was laid on November 30, 1894, and the last was put in place on May 6, 1895.

The contractors, finishing their work on the Galveston waterworks on schedule, turned the system over to city officials on August 19, 1895. The system functioned without major difficulties until the great Galveston hurricane of September 8, 1900. The storm virtually destroyed all the aboveground parts of the water system in the city. It not only demolished the upper stories of the 1888 red brick pump house, but it also damaged portions of the pipeline under the bay. Within a few weeks the city restored the system to at least partial operation, but four years passed before the central pump house was rebuilt into an even more attractive building than it had been before the storm. Because of occasional damage to the pipeline section under the bay, an auxiliary main was laid within the structure of the 1912 Galveston Causeway as a security measure. In 1916 the old 1895 line under the bay was renewed. It was removed from its initial three-foot trench, inspected, and then relaid in a parallel trench ten feet deep to give it further protection from storms and damage from ships. As the water supply from the original wells on the mainland diminished, several different forms of pumping were added through the years to the facilities at Alta Loma. Today the system there is served by a pump house that went into service in 1939. Most of the supply now comes from wells located farther inland.

Location: The head of the thirty-inch diameter 1895 cast-iron pipeline is located within the city limits of the new municipality of Santa Fe, Texas, in an area that in the past was considered part of Alta Loma. The original forty-eight-inch-diameter steel standpipe still stands at the intersection of State Highway 6 and Avenue H in Santa Fe. The 1939 Galveston Waterworks pump house, successor to much older structures that once stood in the area near the standpipe, is located southeast of Alta Loma beside State Highway 6. The 1895 pipeline runs roughly parallel to and between State Highway 6 and the Santa Fe Railway tracks much of the distance between Alta Loma and Galveston Bay, but the line is buried and difficult to see. One of the few points where it may be seen easily is its crossing over a small stream just a short distance southeast of the old standpipe. The 1888 Galveston Waterworks pump house, as rebuilt in 1904, still stands at Avenue H and Thirtieth Street in Galveston and continues to be part of the functioning waterworks system.

Suggested Reading:

Baker, T. Lindsay. "The Remarkable Cast Iron of the Galveston Waterworks." *Cast Iron Pipe News* 42, no. 1 (Winter, 1974–75): 4–8.

"The Deep Artesian Well at Galveston, Tex." *Engineering News* 28, no. 33 (August 11, 1892): 222–25.

Peek, R. H. "Artesian Water Supply of Galveston, Tex." *Engineering News* 39, no. 9 (March 3, 1898): 138–39.

44. *Gonzales Hydroelectric Plant*

The site of hydroelectric generation since the early 1890s, the Gonzales Hydroelectric Plant recently has returned to service after two decades of neglect. It is one of the pioneer hydroelectric plants in Texas.

The initial hydroelectric-generating facility on the Guadalupe River at Gonzales was constructed between 1891 and 1892. It consisted of a simple dam across the river providing a head of nine feet of water to power three turbines. These turbines, sixty inches, sixty-six inches, and seventy-two inches in diameter, produced the motive force that operated a cotton gin, a gristmill, pumps for the town water system, and an electric light plant. Floodwaters destroyed the first dam, and in 1917 it was replaced by a larger dam, which provided an improved head of approximately fifteen feet of water to power the turbines.

In 1925 the Texas Central Power Company purchased the Gonzales Hydroelectric Plant from its private owners, Messrs. Spooner and Lewis. Upon acquiring title to the property and the rights to use the Guadalupe River water, the power company undertook a major renovation of the plant. It kept the 1917 dam, but its crews built new concrete turbine pits, turbine pit forebay, and a brick powerhouse above them. In the pits they installed three Leffel two-hundred-rpm turbines with a capacity of five hundred horsepower at a fifteen-foot head. Above these Francis-type turbines they replaced the old generating equipment in the powerhouse with three Westinghouse vertical generators. These were four-hundred-kw, three-phase, sixty-cycle, twenty-three hundred-volt, two-hundred-rpm units.

The Gonzales Hydroelectric Plant operated on the natural flow of the Guadalupe River for most of its history. This meant that from time to time during low water the power plant necessarily ran below its capacity. The situation changed with the impoundment of water upstream at the Canyon Reservoir on June 16, 1964. Since that time the flow has been partially regulated by releases from that reservoir.

The Gonzales Hydroelectric Plant as it appears today. Photograph by the author, 1983.

Because of the comparatively small generating capacity of the Gonzales facility, the Central Power and Light Company, successor to the Texas Central Power Company, ceased operating it in November, 1965. The electric company removed all the generators and control equipment and abandoned the turbines to rust in the pits below. The powerhouse fell victim to vandals, but fortunately it suffered no major structural damage. In late 1970 the City of Gonzales purchased the old plant primarily to protect the intake for the city water supply located a short distance upstream from the dam. The site remained quiet for a few years, but in 1976 city leaders began considering the idea of returning the old hydroelectric plant to service.

In 1978–79 the City of Gonzales employed an outside consulting firm to study and report on the potential for refurbishing the hydroelectric plant to provide a portion of the Gonzales electric power supply. The report stated that the old facility could supply 10 percent of the electricity consumed by the town, and in so doing it could earn a profit for the municipal

government. The consulting engineers recommended installing new generators over the old 1920s turbines, which surprisingly were still in usable condition. James Leffel and Company, makers of the original turbines, completely rebuilt them, and they are now back in place in the old pits. The historic plant, abandoned for almost two decades, returned to service in April, 1983, again supplying electric power to the residents of Gonzales.

Location: The Gonzales Hydroelectric Plant is located just southwest of the intersection of St. Michael and Water streets on the Guadalupe River at the southwest side of Gonzales. Most of its major parts are readily visible from the public right-of-way.

Suggested Reading:

Godfrey, F. A., and C. L. Dowell. *Major Hydroelectric Powerplants in Texas: Historical and Descriptive Information.* Texas Water Development Board Report No. 81. Austin: Texas Water Development Board, 1968.

45. *Granite Mountain Quarry*

The Granite Mountain Quarry, which has produced high-quality stone for almost a century, traces its origins to the construction of the present Texas capitol during the mid-1880s. The site of the quarry is as impressive as the famous capitol constructed from its stone, for it is a remarkable 166-foot-tall dome of solid pink granite, which covers approximately eighty acres.

In November, 1881, the Texas statehouse in Austin burned. Even before this occurred some state officials had been considering the erection of a larger building to replace it, but the destruction of the old structure forced the legislators to take immediate action. Accordingly, in 1882 the Sixteenth Texas Legislature appropriated approximately three million acres of the state public domain in the western Panhandle region to finance the construction of a new statehouse. It authorized the formation of a Capitol Board consisting of the state governor, treasurer, attorney general, comptroller, and land commissioner to dispose of the land at not less than fifty cents an acre and with the proceeds therefrom to erect the structure.

One Mattheas Schnell from Illinois accepted the contract offered by the state, taking the land in payment. He then brought in a group of financiers who purchased three-quarters' interest in the project, forming what was known as the Capitol Syndicate. Elijah Meyers, the architect who drew up the plans for the building, originally called for the use of limestone in its construction and the contract bid was based on the use of this material. Later investigations proved, however, that the limestone available in the Austin area was unsatisfactory. As Land Commissioner W. C. Walsh later remembered, "Throughout the various layers of stone, iron pyrites were found imbedded, and these upon exposure to air disintegrated and stained the stone in rusty streaks." Such material obviously could not be used.

For a number of weeks, the Capitol Board haggled with the members of the Capitol Syndicate over how to resolve the question of what type of stone to use in the building. The northern capitalists suggested using Bedford limestone from Indiana, but the Texas officials did not want to use "imported" stone in their capitol. In the meantime, the three owners of Granite Mountain forty-five miles to the west in Burnet County made a surprising offer. Lacking the capital to develop a quarry at the mountain, but at the same time realizing that their property would be of much greater value if a quarry could be started there, they offered to the state at no cost all the granite that might be needed for the construction of the new capitol. With the offer of all the granite that was needed free for the taking, the state officials recommended the use of this material instead of limestone. The syndicate members refused because of the greater cost of handling and cutting the much harder granite. A compromise was struck when the contractors agreed to use granite from Burnet County if the state would furnish convict labor for cutting the stone, would construct a narrow-gauge railway line from Burnet to the quarry, and would rebuild the wagon road be-

The architect's original rendering in which he presented his general design for the state capitol. Photograph courtesy Texas State Library, Austin, Texas.

The Granite Mountain Quarry a century ago. Photograph courtesy Texas State Library, Austin, Texas.

tween Burnet and Austin. The Austin and Northwestern Railroad Company already connected the two towns.

Work soon began at Granite Mountain, but unexpected problems arose. Protesting the use of convict labor to quarry and cut the stone, the International Association of Granite Cutters boycotted the entire construction project, warning all its members to stay away from Austin. Unable to secure skilled stonecutters in America because of this labor action, the Capitol Syndicate recruited eighty-six Scottish stonecutters, bringing them to the United States under contract with their transportation expenses paid. Eventually, sixty-two of the Scottish workers reached America to begin work on the project. The Knights of Labor filed suit against the Capitol Syndicate in the Federal District Court in Austin for violation of the Alien Contract Labor Law and eventually won their case. By the time the litigation finally wound its way through the courts, however, the new building in Austin was completed and most of the Scotsmen had returned home. The capitol itself officially opened on May 16, 1888.

The construction of the state capitol was only the beginning for the Granite Mountain Quarry. Since the 1880s it has been the major source for the Texas pink granite used in building construction projects throughout the United States, not to mention its use in monuments, memorials, and even in such projects as the Galveston Jetties. The most beautiful collection of buildings made from the well-known Texas stone are the State Capitol and the public edifices that surround it. Among these imposing buildings in Austin are the Sam Houston Office Building, the Texas Supreme Court Building, the Texas Employment Commission Building, and the Lorenzo de Zavala State Library and Archives Building.

Today the Granite Mountain Quarry is operated by

Penitentiary convicts shaping columns of Granite Mountain pink granite for use in the construction of the state capitol. Photograph courtesy Photographic Archives, Texas Department of Highways and Public Transportation, Austin, Texas.

The Granite Mountain Quarry as it now appears. Photograph, 1976, courtesy Center for the History of Engineering, Texas Tech University, Lubbock, Texas.

the Texas Granite Corporation, and it continues to supply its beautiful stone to customers in all parts of the United States as well as overseas.

Location: The Granite Mountain Quarry is located 1.2 miles west of Marble Falls on FM 1431. It is an operating industrial facility and is not accessible to the public, but much of the quarry work done can be seen from the highway, which passes very near the site.

Suggested Reading:

Allen, Ruth Alice. "The Capitol Boycott: A Study in Peaceful Labor Tactics." *Southwestern Historical Quarterly* 42, no. 4 (April, 1939): 316–26.

Andrus, M. Walter. *Behind This Cornerstone.* Austin: Chapman Printing Company, 1956.

Ramsdell, Charles W. "Memories of a Texas Land Commissioner, W. C. Walsh." *Southwestern Historical Quarterly* 44, no. 4 (April, 1941): 481–97.

46. Hangar Nine

Erected as a temporary structure in 1918, Hangar Nine is the oldest surviving military aircraft storage and repair structure in the United States. Located on Brooks Air Force Base in San Antonio, it currently houses the Edward H. White II Museum of Flight Medicine and is open to the public.

When the United States entered World War I in 1917, the responsibility for its aerial operations lay with the Aviation Section of the U.S. Army Signal Corps. At this time it had a mere thirty-five trained pilots and only about two hundred training planes, most of them of questionable military value. Once the country entered the war, it made great strides in increasing and improving both the manpower and the aircraft of the Aviation Section. By October of the next year, American industry had produced almost

An aerial review for the secretary of war at Brooks Field on May 19, 1927. Photograph courtesy National Archives, Washington, D.C.

fourteen thousand military aircraft and about forty-two thousand aviation engines.

In the meantime, the army recruited thousands of men for service in its air corps and it began instructing them in aircraft operation and maintenance at eighteen leased or hastily constructed flying schools in various parts of the country. One of these installations was Brooks Field, at the time outside San Antonio. The War Department chose the Alamo City for military training facilities because of its mild climate, convenient transportation facilities, and good water supply. Delighted by the prospect of securing yet another military camp for their area, members of the San Antonio Chamber of Commerce put together an 873-acre tract south of the city and offered it as a site for the proposed training field. The army accepted, with military and civilian officials breaking ground for the facility on December 8, 1917. The first aircraft landed at the new base on March 28, 1918, by which time the contractors had completed much of their major construction at the site.

Among the initial buildings erected at Brooks Field were a series of wood-frame hangars forming a segmental arch along the north side of a northeast-southwest turf runway. The ninth hangar in the row was the present-day Hangar Nine. Most of the World War I–vintage buildings at the base have been re-

moved, but Hangar Nine has survived. In the 1960s the Department of Defense announced that it too would be demolished, but by that time aviation and military history enthusiasts had realized the historical significance of the building, the last World War I hangar in the country. Together with local historical groups, they requested and received Air Force permission to restore the old hangar in line with modern safety standards so that it could be preserved for future generations.

The hangar itself is a rectangular-shaped, two-story wood-frame building with a low pitched gambrel roof supported on wooden trusses held together with their original bolts. Its sides are covered with white-painted weatherboarding and rows of six-over-six windows, and its ends consist of large sliding doors. At the north side of the building stands a rectangular flat-roofed frame wing, which was built at the time the hangar was constructed. The inside walls remain unsealed, and the wood trusses stand exposed, thus allowing visitors to observe clearly the inner structure of the hangar. Its floor is the original concrete slab poured in 1918.

The list of historical personages associated with Hangar Nine seems almost endless. Among the men who took their flight training at Brooks Field, later Brooks Air Force Base, from 1918 to the 1950s were

Charles Lindbergh, the first man to fly solo across the Atlantic; Elwood Quesada, a pioneer in mid-flight refueling, who later became the chief administrator of the Federal Aviation Agency; and Hoyt Vandenberg, Nathan Twining, Thomas D. White, and Curtis LeMay, all of whom later became chiefs of staff of the Air Force. Some of the better-known flight instructors who taught at Brooks Field, all of whom at times undoubtedly had dealings in Hangar Nine, included Russell Maughn, the first pilot to make a "dawn-to-dusk" flight across the United States; John Macready, who wrote two of the earliest texts for flying instruction and who set an open cockpit altitude record of 40,800 feet; and Claire Chennault, who became the leader of the World War II "Flying Tigers."

Edward H. White, the father of astronaut Edward H. White II, took his flight training at Brooks Field, graduating in June, 1930, only a matter of months before his son was born. For this reason Hangar Nine in 1968 was renamed the Edward H. White II Museum for its long association with the White family.

Location: Hangar Nine, also known today as the Edward H. White II Museum of Flight Medicine, is located on the Inner Circle Road at Brooks Air Force Base on the southeast side of San Antonio. Access to the building and museum is by way of the Main Gate to the base on Military Drive (Loop 13).

Suggested Reading:

Bullard, John W. "A Brief History of Brooks Air Force Base." Offset printed. 1 lf. Available at Edward H. White II Museum of Flight Medicine, Brooks Air Force Base, San Antonio, Tex.

Hangar Nine as restored in the 1960s. Photograph by the author, 1978.

47. *Harris County Dome Stadium*

The Harris County Dome Stadium, erected between 1962 and 1965 and known to most Texans as the Astrodome, was the first large domed sports stadium ever built. Because its design and construction presented numerous engineering problems that had never before been met, it is the only post–World War II project included in this book.

The idea of creating an enclosed sports stadium for Houston is credited to Harris County judge Roy Hofheinz. A millionaire entrepreneur who had served as mayor, state legislator, and even as manager for Lyndon Johnson's first political campaign, Hofheinz on two occasions while mayor in the mid-1950s inspected Rome's ancient Colosseum. While in Rome he learned that the Colosseum had been fitted with a *velarium,* or movable awning, which slaves, with the aid of crude machines, could pull over the stadium to protect spectators from the elements. Impressed with the idea of building a covered stadium, Hofheinz reputedly declared, "If those Romans could put a lid on

The Harris County Dome Stadium on September 3, 1963. Photograph courtesy Engineering Department, Harris County, Houston, Texas.

their stadium, so can we. . . . We'll build a stadium that will make Emperor Titus's playhouse look like an abandoned brickyard." This he proceeded to do.

At the request of the Harris County Commissioners' Court, the Fifty-fifth Texas Legislature created the Harris County Park Commission. A bill introduced later enabled the county to submit a revenue bond to local voters, which they approved in 1958, to establish the Houston Sports Center. In 1961 the county electorate approved a general obligation bond to erect the covered stadium that Judge Hofheinz had envisioned.

The Harris County Dome Stadium was and is one of the engineering marvels of the twentieth century. It is a domed circular steel and concrete structure sufficiently large to provide playing fields for either football or baseball. With an outer diameter of 710 feet and a clear span of 641 feet, 8 inches, it covers approximately nine acres. The roof rises 208 feet above the surface of the playing field. Seating is arranged on six levels so that there are six front rows. The building contains forty-five thousand seats for baseball. Seats at field level are in two movable stands, which rotate 35 degrees from baseball to football position and increase the seating to fifty-two thousand for the latter. For boxing matches, speaking engagements,

conventions, and musical performances sixty-six thousand seats can be made available.

The steel dome that covers the Astrodome consists of a framework of five-foot-deep lamella trusses. This design was chosen principally because it could provide even stress distribution. The dome has a rise of ninety-three feet (a radius of six hundred feet) and rests on seventy-two columns. The key to the success of the dome is a welded-steel tension ring at its circumference. Weighing 750 tons, this ring holds the entire 2,150-ton dome structure together. Tests of a model in the McDonnell Aircraft Company wind tunnel in Saint Louis demonstrated to the designing engineers that the structure could withstand hurricane wind gusts of 165 miles per hour and sustained winds of 135 miles per hour.

The erection of the dome structure presented special problems. To support the lamella trusses and auxiliary roof members during their erection, thirty-seven temporary steel towers were built to provide landing points for the various trusses. The erection towers, similar in appearance to oil derricks, were 20 feet square at their bases and tapered to 10 feet square at the 100-foot level, from which point they continued up to their final heights from 170 to 207 feet. First the meridian ribs at the center of the dome

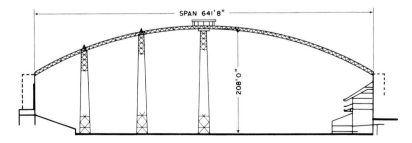

Cross-section of the Harris County Dome Stadium under construction, showing typical placement of its temporary erection towers. Based on Louis O. Bass, "Unusual Dome Awaits Baseball Season in Houston," *Civil Engineering* 35, no. 1 (January, 1965): 64. Drawing by the author.

View from the top of the dome under construction. Photograph courtesy Houston Metropolitan Research Center, Houston Public Library, Houston, Texas.

were put into place. Then the roof structure, one sector at a time, was put into position until the steel erection was completed. The roof assembly project took approximately four months and was finished on schedule. Upon completion, the towers were removed; the deflection of the dome was 4³/₁₆ inches; the design deflection had been 4¼ inches.

Another important element in the design and con-

Interior of the Harris County Dome Stadium almost two decades after its completion. Photograph by the author, 1981.

struction of the stadium was the selection of a covering for its roof. Since the roof was never intended to open or close, its covering was permanent. The building contains approximately forty-six hundred individual skylights, their pattern being selected to provide for the acoustical needs of the structure. These light-admitting coverings were made from two layers of acrylic plastic to control condensation. The outer layer is transparent to admit light; the inner layer is diffusive to scatter light through the building.

Heating and cooling presented major problems for the designers. The interior of the structure is entirely climate controlled by equipment with sixty-six hundred tons of cooling capacity. The system circulates approximately 2.5 million cubic feet of air per minute while admitting 250,000 cubic feet of fresh air. Smoke and hot air are drawn out through openings in the top of the domed roof.

The stadium was carefully planned for handling thousands of sports enthusiasts conveniently. The seating was designed so that spectators enter the stadium about the middle of the six levels and proceed either up or down on ramps or escalators to their seats. Parking surrounds the building, with space for over thirty thousand vehicles. Eight traffic arteries radiate from the parking areas. Inside the building there is sufficient space in restaurants and dining facilities to feed an estimated 3,250 people at one time. The spectators need never miss any of the sports action, for eight technicians work a 474-foot electronic scoreboard with fifty thousand colored lights.

A structure as remarkable today as when it was completed, the Harris County Dome Stadium is one of Texas' most impressive engineering efforts.

Location: The Harris County Dome Stadium is located southwest of downtown Houston convenient to Interstate Loop 610, U.S. 90A, and State Highway 288. Tours of the stadium are available at regularly posted hours most days of the year.

Suggested Reading:

Bass, Louis O. "Unusual Dome Awaits Baseball Season in Houston." *Civil Engineering* 35, no. 1 (January, 1965): 63–65.
Jefferson, T. B. "Welded Steel Frames World's Largest Clear-Span Domed Stadium." *Welding Engineer* 49, no. 6 (June, 1964): 55–57.

48. High Bridge over the Pecos

Renowned in both fact and fiction, the High Bridge over the Pecos River Canyon (1891–92) was the most spectacular of all the historic bridges in Texas. It held the distinctions of being not only the highest bridge in the United States, but also the third highest bridge in the entire world. The structure remained in service until it was replaced with another high bridge nearby during World War II.

Known to railway historians as the Pecos Viaduct, the High Bridge over the Pecos was built to solve a number of problems that for a decade had plagued the Galveston, Harrisburg and San Antonio Railway in crossing the Pecos River in western Texas. When this subsidiary of the Southern Pacific Lines was first built westward from San Antonio toward El Paso between 1881 and 1883, the Pecos River Canyon presented its most serious physical obstacle. Originally the tracks led steeply and with many curves from the high surrounding plains dropping three hundred feet through the Rio Grande canyons to the mouth of the Pecos on the Rio Grande, where they crossed the Pecos on an ordinary iron truss bridge. The line then led in an equally steep and circuitous route back to the level plains above. This route required the construction of two tunnels, 3,600 feet of wooden trestles, 2,730 feet of iron bridges, and most significantly, it involved 2,926.2 degrees of curvature and a total of 902.27 feet of rise and fall in elevation.

Most of the original line through the Rio Grande gorges was through soft sandstone crisscrossed with seams and fissures. The canyon walls were so prone to rock falls that the railway company had to employ watchmen day and night to patrol the line to prevent any derailments caused by obstacles on the track.

Section of the High Bridge over the Pecos as completed in 1892. Based on Julius Kruttschnitt, "The Pecos Viaduct," *Proceedings of the Engineering Association of the South* 6 (August, 1894): plate 1. Drawing by the author.

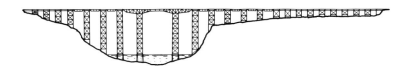

The High Bridge over the Pecos in its heyday. Photograph courtesy estate of Roger Fleming and the Institute of Texan Cultures, San Antonio, Texas.

More important than this, however, was the fact that the 1880s line required steep grades and sharp curves both in and out of the canyon. These conditions demanded short trains, slow speeds, and high fuel consumption. In short, the original route to and from the Pecos crossing was not only dangerous but also very expensive to operate.

For the next decade various plans for eliminating the difficulties were proposed, but the solution did not come until 1890. In that year a railway engineer again investigated the country on either side of the Pecos Gorge. He determined that approaches to the canyon could be made at comparatively slight expense about 3.5 miles upstream from the first crossing. This route completely eliminated the sharp curves and steep grades, but it required that the company erect a viaduct across the Pecos Canyon that would be taller than any others that had ever been attempted in the United States.

The bridge to span the Pecos Canyon was designed

between 1890 and 1891 by the Phoenix Bridge Company of Phoenixville, Pennsylvania. After planning the structure, this firm proceeded to erect it under contract to the Southern Pacific Company. A secondary contract for the stone and concrete piers and footings was let to Ricker, Lee and Company of Galveston, which also held the contract for grading the new roadbeds leading up to the canyon sides at the bridge site.

Ricker, Lee and Company began work on the viaduct with the foundations and piers. Their effort began in early March, 1891, and was completed on November 21 of the same year. All the piers and footings were founded on solid rock, which presented no problems on the canyon walls. The contractors met difficulties, however, in the bottom of the canyon, which was filled with dozens of feet of boulders and debris. Some of the boulders in the bottom of the gorge were so large that it was difficult for the crews to determine when they had struck solid rock. In the

125

case of pier number nine, only about five feet of the pier was visible at the surface, though it measured fifty-five feet from its base deep in the rocky debris. The piers were made from concrete and local limestone, although seven of the most important footings had copings cut from Texas pink granite originating from the Granite Mountain Quarry in Burnet County (see entry no. 45).

After the construction of the piers and footings, as well as the completion of the tracks leading to the east and west sides of the construction site, Phoenix Bridge Company crews began work on the wrought-iron and steel towers and spans. Starting on November 3, 1891, the workers completed the east half of the viaduct on December 30, 1891, a remarkably short time for the effort involved. Then they shifted to the west end of the span on January 8, 1892, finishing the second half of the bridge on February 20.

The Pecos Viaduct as completed stood 320 feet, 10¾ inches above the average water flowing in the Pecos River far below. It measured 2,180 feet long, including a combined cantilever and "suspended" lattice span 185 feet in length over the actual watercourse. The ironwork alone weighed 1,820 tons.

During the construction of the High Bridge, an incident occurred that involved one of the most colorful residents of Trans-Pecos Texas, Judge Roy Bean. As justice of the peace he held court in the nearby town of Langtry. Only one fatal accident took place during the erection of the viaduct, and it brought Bean to the construction site. A portion of the structure being erected had collapsed, and ten workers had fallen, seven of whom were killed. Judge Bean rode muleback from Langtry to hold inquest into the deaths. Beside each of the seven corpses he purportedly pronounced the same verdict: "This man seems to have come to his death by timbers falling on him." He then turned his attention to the three wounded men, pronouncing the same verdict over them though they were still alive. An onlooker interrupted Bean. "Those men are not dead, Judge," he said, to which Bean reputedly replied, "That's all right. They ain't dead yet, but they will be. You don't think I'm going to ride that mule back up here later just to do what I'm doing now." Despite being pronounced dead, the three men survived to tell the tale.

After the Phoenix Bridge Company completed the ironwork on the viaduct, railway company crews installed electrical signal equipment to place the structure in service. A special train carrying dignitaries officially opened the bridge to rail traffic on March 31, 1892. For the next half century the Pecos Viaduct stood as one of the most famous landmarks in all West Texas. Because of its strategic importance, it was guarded by U.S. Army troops during both World War I and World War II and was protected by Texas Rangers during the Mexican Revolution early in this century. It served as settings for motion pictures, for remarkable equestrian feats by horsemen, and even for trick flying by Gen. Jimmy Doolittle, who successfully piloted an open-cockpit plane beneath the bridge by tipping its wings to clear the towers.

Spectacular though it was, the High Bridge grew obsolete as locomotive and train weights increased over the years. The Southern Pacific Company strengthened the viaduct on two occasions, in 1909–10 and in 1929, each time increasing its carrying capacity considerably. After the attack on Pearl Harbor and subsequent growth of rail traffic, company officials realized that the old bridge might not be able to carry all the weight that it could be called on to bear and might become a "bottleneck" on the highly important southern transcontinental railway link.

Topographic studies revealed that a suitable site existed about a quarter mile downstream for a second railway bridge. Just over a year after the outbreak of hostilities, the company successfully applied to the Office of Defense Transportation for construction materials for a new bridge. Work began on a new single-track viaduct on concrete piers in August, 1943, and the first main line train passed on December 21, 1944. This newer structure, which remains in service today, consists of a number of continuous cantilever and plate girder spans stretching 1,390 feet across the canyon.

After the opening of the new bridge, the 1890s Pecos Viaduct was kept as a standby for five years. In 1949 the Southern Pacific sold the individual spans from the bridge to various states and local governments for use as shorter bridges across streams in their individual jurisdictions. Most of the other parts of the metal structure went to scrap dealers. Initially, plans had been made for the purchase of the entire structure by the government of Guatemala for use in that country, but the deal fell through, resulting in the piecemeal sale of elements from the historic old bridge.

Today the site of the 1891–92 High Bridge is marked by surprising surface remains. The aban-

Detail of metal members, originally part of the 1892 High Bridge over the Pecos, that were left behind when the structure was dismantled in 1949. Photograph by the author, 1975.

doned earthen railway embankments lead up to its old abutments, and a huge concrete locomotive water tank still stands empty at one side of the gorge. The entire area of the former bridge is marked by footings, piers, and various pieces of scrap iron that were not removed when the structure was dismantled over thirty-five years ago.

Location: The High Bridge over the Pecos carried the main line of the Southern Pacific Railway across the Pecos River about 3.5 miles above its mouth. The bridge site, just upstream from the current 1943–44 railway bridge and on private property, cannot be seen from the present-day U.S. 90 crossing west of

Comstock. Located over 2 miles away in rough ranch country, it may be viewed from a distance from the roadside rest area on U.S. 90, about 5.7 miles northwest of the highway bridge crossing over the Pecos.

Suggested Reading:

"Bridging Pecos Made Rail History." *Texas Professional Engineer* 6, no. 2 (March–April, 1947): 2–3, 22–23.
Kruttschnitt, Julius. "The Pecos Viaduct." *Proceedings of the Engineering Association of the South* 6 (August, 1894): 9–19.
"The Pecos Viaduct." *Engineering News* 29, no. 1 (January 5, 1893): 2–4.

49. *Houston 1879 Waterworks*

Almost hidden behind the Bayou Pumping Station (1926) near downtown Houston, portions of the original 1879 Houston Waterworks pumping facility still may be seen. Although not part of the first waterworks in Texas, the structures here represent some of the oldest intact waterworks remains in the state.

Throughout Houston's pioneer years from the 1830s to the late 1870s, its residents took their drinking water directly from nearby Buffalo Bayou, from shallow hand-dug wells, or from cisterns collecting rainwater. This scheme proved satisfactory during the early decades, but in time the need for a citywide domestic water system and for an adequate fire protection system prompted civic leaders to consider building a waterworks to serve the growing community.

The question was discussed through the mid- and late-1870s, resulting in the City Council's authorizing a New Yorker, James M. Loweree, to construct a waterworks under a franchise from the city. His twenty-five-year contract called for his making available 3 million gallons of water daily, constructing a 150,000-gallon reservoir, supplying free water to three public fountains, and providing pressure that would throw six streams of water through fifty feet of hose to a height of one hundred feet. In return, Loweree received the right to lay water mains through the city and to charge consumers for the water they used.

The private waterworks company erected a dam on Buffalo Bayou above the Preston Street Bridge, laid its

Houston Waterworks about the turn of the century. At the center of the complex stands the still-surviving circular pumpwell with its conical roof. Photograph courtesy Harris County Heritage Society, Houston, Texas.

mains, built a pumping plant, and started pumping water from Buffalo Bayou into the system. At the time, the bayou was a clear, flowing stream, and no one complained about water quality. The local press described it as "free from all impurities and . . . pure and wholesome to drink." The original pumping plant, built just north of Buffalo Bayou, consisted of a circular brick pumpwell about twenty-eight feet in diameter located next to a rectangular brick pump house equipped with steam pumping equipment. Loweree operated the system for about three years and sold it in 1881 to a group of local businessmen headed by former mayor T. H. Scanlan. Organized as the Houston Water Works Company, they soon began to encounter difficulties that grew year after year for the next quarter century.

Perhaps the most serious deficiency in the Houston system was its inability to provide sufficient water pressure to fight fires effectively. The city suffered a number of serious conflagrations during the 1880s and 1890s, and often the water system did not give enough pressure for water from the hoses to reach above the first stories of the burning buildings. The disaster that finally caused city officials to take action, however, was the destruction by fire of the city hall and market complex in 1901. During this fire there was not enough pressure to force water even to the roofs of the burning buildings.

In addition to the water system's being wholly inadequate to provide fire protection, it failed in yet another important way. Its owners were either unable or unwilling to provide consumers with pure drinking water. Although the Buffalo Bayou water was potable in the late 1870s, by the 1880s and certainly by the 1890s, it had become increasingly polluted with both domestic and industrial wastes. Until 1887 the

The 1879 pumpwell from the original Houston Waterworks, abandoned and nearly buried at the southwest corner of the waterworks compound at the Bayou Pumping Station. Photograph by the author, 1981.

bayou was the only known source of water, but in this year the first successful artesian well was bored in the city, and a vast resource of artesian flow was discovered. By the next year the Houston Water Works Company had started drilling its own wells, using this water in its system when possible, but its operators persisted in occasionally using bayou water when the wells did not provide sufficient supply. This led to an almost continuous outcry of citizens and elected officials against the use of the impure surface water.

Since water from the polluted bayou continued to flow through the mains even after the turn of the century, the water system itself increasingly came to be considered a health menace. As early as 1902 the City Council considered purchasing the system to regulate the purity of the water entering the mains. At this time the system consisted of fifty-five artesian wells and a total of sixty-five miles of mains. The next year the city offered Scanlan and his business partners $750,000 for the system, but they turned down the offer. Discussions continued over the next three years, and finally in 1906 the Houston voters authorized and approved a $434,700 bond issue for the purchase. Coupled with funds already in the city treasury, the municipality bought the entire system for a total of $901,700. Since that time the Houston Waterworks has been operated as a division of the municipal administration. Underground water served as its sole source of supply until 1954, when water from Lake Houston was also introduced.

The original 1879 Houston Waterworks pump house and pumpwell continued to be used into the

early years of this century, and they remained intact at least as recently as the eve of World War I. Since that time, however, the pump house has been razed, leaving only its foundations. The old circular brick pumpwell with its conical concrete roof was converted for many years into a sand trap for a well in the artesian supply system. It remained in use in this altered role at least into the late 1970s, at which time it was abandoned altogether. About this time it was placed on the National Register of Historic Places. It stands today as an important legacy to the early history of the Houston Waterworks and as one of the oldest surviving waterworks structures in the state.

Location: The original pumpwell for the 1879 Houston Waterworks, together with the buried foundations for its pump house, may be seen in the extreme southwest corner of the waterworks compound at the Bayou Pumping Station, located at 27 Artesian Street, almost in the shadow of Interstate 45 near downtown Houston.

Suggested Reading:

Baker, T. Lindsay. "Houston Waterworks: Its Early Development." *Water; Southwest Water Works Journal* 56, no. 4 (July, 1974): 37.

Carroll, B. H., Jr. *Standard History of Houston Texas.* Knoxville, Tenn.: H. W. Crew, 1912.

McComb, David G. *Houston, the Bayou City.* Austin: University of Texas Press, 1969.

50. Houston Ship Channel

The Houston Ship Channel, which makes present-day Houston third among the nation's ports in tonnage handled, was conceived as early as the 1820s, predating even the founding of the city. The story of the channel construction is one of gradual and intermittent excavation and dredging, which finally in this century resulted in the completion of a deep-water channel from the Gulf of Mexico to the industrial districts of metropolitan Houston.

The modern Houston Ship Channel roughly follows the course of Buffalo Bayou. Running west to east, this body of water offered early settlers a means of communication and transportation in the days before railroads. The stream was widest and deepest from its mouth on the San Jacinto River upstream to Brays Bayou, where Harrisburg was established in 1826, but it was passable by shallow-draft boats as far upstream as White Oak Bayou. Vessels reached the mouth of the San Jacinto River and access to Buffalo Bayou by sailing across Galveston Bay, although in the process they had to cross first the sandbars at the entrance to Galveston Harbor and then the shoals at both Red Fish Bar and Clopper's Bar.

As early as the 1820s, Buffalo Bayou served the local transportation needs of settlers along its banks. With the establishment of Houston in 1836, vessels soon began attempting to reach that point on the bayou, sometimes with success and sometimes not.

The first steamboat to arrive there was the *Laura*, on January 22, 1837, leading the way for other vessels to venture up the bayou.

From the 1830s through the 1870s, efforts were undertaken by both the Houston municipal government and the state government, as well as by private companies, to clear, widen, and deepen the channel of Buffalo Bayou to enhance its capacity for navigation. In the summer of 1839, for instance, the city aldermen formally established "the Port of Houston," and even earlier that year had cleared snags and sandbars from five miles of Buffalo Bayou. This type of work continued spasmodically for the next forty years. Much of the effort by local businessmen in promoting their city as a port was devoted to securing the legal establishment of Houston as a port of delivery by the federal government. This major goal was accomplished on June 14, 1870, when Congress gave it that designation.

The next major step in the development of the ship channel came in 1873. In that year Charles Morgan, owner of extensive shipping interests along the Gulf Coast, purchased rights for the use of portions of Buffalo Bayou for navigation purposes. Over the next three years his dredges for the first time cleared a channel south of the San Jacinto River that opened the route to the bayou for genuine oceangoing ships. In the meantime, the U.S. Army Corps of Engineers

The S.S. *Merrymount* loading 20,300 bales of cotton destined for Liverpool, England, at the Houston Ship Channel in November, 1919, only five years after the waterway opened to deep-water vessels. Photograph courtesy Houston Metropolitan Research Center, Houston Public Library, Houston, Texas.

Upper end of the Houston Ship Channel seen from the air. Photograph courtesy Port of Houston Authority, Houston, Texas.

excavated a channel across Red Fish Bar, removing that impediment to navigation.

The U.S. government in time assumed the major role in the development of the waterway. In 1880 a bill was introduced in Congress for the purchase of the "Buffalo Bayou Ship Channel" from the Morgan interests. A decade passed before direct action was taken, but on May 2, 1892, the federal government paid $92,316.85 for Morgan's improvements to the channel, and it reopened for free public use.

From the 1870s through the 1880s, a great many efforts had been undertaken to widen and deepen the Buffalo Bayou waterway, but the improvements failed to endure. The banks constantly washed into the channel, and Houston residents dumped increasing amounts of sewage into the bayou, turning portions of it into an open cesspool. Adding to these difficulties was the deposit of new snags and logs in the

bayou after each heavy rain. Even so, by 1896 the channel had been dredged to a depth of ten feet for its entire length.

As soon as the jetties at the entrance to Galveston Harbor began successfully removing the sandbars there, making Galveston a true deep-water port, Houston leaders began clamoring for further improvement to the channel serving their city. Consequently, in December, 1897, Congress appropriated funds for deepening the channel. Combined with later appropriations, this funding permitted the Corps of Engineers to dredge the channel across Galveston Bay to a depth of seventeen feet, six inches. On June 13, 1902, President Theodore Roosevelt signed a bill providing one million dollars for improving the ship channel to Houston. Three years later Congress altered the project to make the terminus of the waterway a point of Buffalo Bayou known as Long Reach, the site of the present-day turning basin at the head of deep-water navigation.

In 1909 the Texas legislature passed a bill allowing the creation of navigation districts, which could issue bonds for the improvement of harbors and related facilities. In December of the same year a delegation of Houston businessmen met with members of the Congressional Rivers and Harbors Committee and in so doing set a precedent that later was followed in many other parts of the country. They offered to share with the federal government the cost of dredging the Houston Ship Channel to a depth of twenty-five feet. With a favorable response to their offer, the Houstonians returned home to convince the local voters to support their plan. In January, 1911, the residents of Harris County voted to form the Harris County Houston Ship Channel Navigation District and passed a bond issue for $1.25 million to match federal funds to deepen the waterway. Prior to this time no local interests had ever made such substantial offers to share the cost of navigation improvements, but since then the federal government has adopted a policy of undertaking no such projects without the promise of local contributions and assurances that the port facilities would be publicly owned and accessible to all potential users.

Through the combined local and federal effort, the Houston Ship Channel was dredged to a depth of 25 feet between 1912 and 1914. The project reached its completion more than a year ahead of schedule, on September 7, 1914. The first seagoing vessel to use the new channel was a 184-foot schooner drawing 16 feet, 6 inches of water, the *William C. May,* which docked at the Southern Pacific wharves downstream from Houston on September 26. The ceremonial opening of the waterway followed on November 10, with President Woodrow Wilson pushing a pearl-topped button in Washington to set off cannons beside the turning basin as part of the dedication festivities.

Since the opening of the Houston Ship Channel to deep-water vessels and the realization of the dreams of Houston's becoming a major port, the waterway has been widened and deepened several times. Port authority officials and Corps of Engineers officers realized that the area along the channel would become the site of major industrial facilities not only because of its deep water but also because of its abundant fresh-water supply and sufficient elevation to protect building sites from the danger of flooding during

tropical storms. In 1919, 1922, 1929, 1935, 1948, and 1958, Congress passed bills to widen and deepen the channel, these works resulting in the eventual deepening of the waterway to forty feet.

By 1964, the fiftieth anniversary of the deep-water channel to Houston, the U.S. government had spent a total of $64 million for the ship channel improvements and maintenance, and the local government had contributed $28 million in port facilities. In the anniversary year the port facilities were yielding $148 million annually in taxes, and the channelside industries were valued at an estimated $3 billion. The facilities employed approximately 55,000 persons and paid them an estimated $314 million in wages and salaries annually. By the 1980s it was estimated that the ship channel generated approximately $3 billion annually for the local, state, and national economies and that the jobs of 159,000 Texans were in some way related to the activity of the Port of Houston. Through the successful cooperation of the federal government with local entities, the meandering, snag-filled Buffalo Bayou of the nineteenth century had converted Houston into one of the most important ports serving the United States.

Location: The Houston Ship Channel follows the course of Buffalo Bayou from the turning basin in Houston to its confluence with the San Jacinto River and thence to the waters of Galveston Bay. Perhaps the most interesting viewing point onto the waterway is at the Houston Turning Basin, where an elevated visitors' observation platform and free public parking are available. To reach this area, drive northwest on Clinton Drive from Loop 610 just over two miles to the well-marked entrance to the parking area. This entrance is just southeast of North Wayside Drive. Another way to view the channel is from the Port of Houston Authority inspection vessel, the *Sam Houston,* which carries visitors who have made prior appointments on its daily trips on the waterway.

Suggested Reading:

Alperin, Lynn M. *Custodians of the Coast: History of the United States Army Engineers at Galveston.* Washington, D.C.: Government Printing Office, 1977.
Sibley, Marilyn McAdams. *The Port of Houston.* Austin: University of Texas Press, 1968.

51. Humphrey Direct Action Pumping Plant

Constructed between 1914 and 1915 on the banks of the Rio Grande below Del Rio, the Humphrey Direct Action Pumping Plant used the first large Humphrey explosion pump installed in the United States. The facility and adjacent gas-generating plant were built to irrigate several thousand acres of land on the G. Bedell Moore estate, now Rancho Rio Grande, in Kinney County.

The property owners contracted with Alexander Potter, a New York consulting engineer, to prepare plans for the most economical pumping plant to suit the requirements of their site. Because of the expense of construction and maintenance, the owners already had decided against using a more traditional gravity canal system, choosing instead to pump water from the Rio Grande into canals serving their fields. Potter investigated both centrifugal and explosions pumps, even traveling to England to examine the successful use of Humphrey direct action pumps at London's Chingford Waterworks. He recommended the use of a sixty-six-inch Humphrey pump for the site on the Rio Grande. The actual pump was made by the Humphrey Gas Pump Company of Syracuse, New York.

Construction began on the Texas facility in 1914. The plant as built consisted of a cylindrical pump house, the actual Humphrey pump and connected steel play pipe, a surge tank to receive the elevated water from the play pipe, and an adjacent facility for the generation of producer gas to power the pump.

One of the most unusual features of the installation on the Rio Grande was its fuel. As several thousand of the acres proposed to be irrigated were covered with mesquite scrub, this wood was chosen to fuel the producer-gas plant. Made by the Standard Gas Power

Company of New York, the gas-producing equipment employed an Akerlund vertical down-draft generator with a water pan on top and a vapor ring around its combustion belt. When using moderately dry mesquite, the facility had a capacity of five million BTU per time unit necessary, generated in the form of gas.

The pump house was located beside the Rio Grande on a stone ledge that crossed the river and created a slight fall. Below water level in the river an intake equipped with an automatically controlled valve admitted water into the lower level of the pumping facility. The pump house itself was a twenty-eight-foot-diameter cylindrical reinforced-concrete structure with its top at ground level and its base extending to below normal low water level in the river. Because of dangers involved in using its gas fuel, special attention was given to ventilating the pump house with forced-air blowers.

The operation of a Humphrey pump is most unusual by today's standards because of its ability to elevate water without the use of pistons or other large moving parts. A charge of gas and air was exploded within the chamber of the pump above the water surface. This explosion drove the water within the pump downward, closed the water and inlet valves of the pump, and produced an upward motion in a column of water in the steel play pipe. The inertia of this moving water column permitted the burned gases to expand to a point below atmospheric pressure, at which point both the exhaust and water valves opened. There then followed a return surge downward in the play pipe back into the pump until the water reached the exhaust valves and closed them by impact. This was followed by a second forward surge set up by the trapped and compressed gases within the pump. Pres-

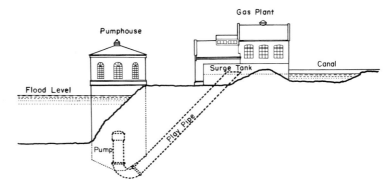

General elevation of the Humphrey Direct Action Pumping Plant as designed by Alexander Potter. Based on "America's First Large Direct-Explosion Pump Will Irrigate Texas Lands," *Engineering Record* 71, no. 19 (May 8, 1915): 597. Drawing by the author.

Overall view of the slowly deteriorating Humphrey Explosion Pump complex, with the Rio Grande in the background. Photograph by the author, 1975.

sure then fell below atmospheric level again, at which time a fresh charge of gas and air was drawn into the pump. This fresh charge was compressed by a second return surge and ignited by an electrical spark to begin the cycle again. The period of oscillation in Humphrey pumps depends on the length of the column of water in the play pipe; in the case of the Rio Grande plant, the cycle was twelve explosions per minute.

Water passing from the upper end of the play pipe

View past the surge tank toward the producer gas-generation building at the Humphrey Pump complex. Photograph by the author, 1975.

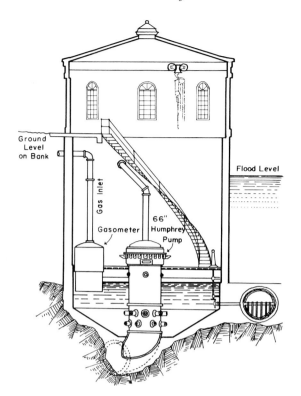

Cross-section of the circular concrete pump house and its Humphrey Pump as it operated in 1915. Based on "America's First Large Direct-Explosion Pump," p. 597. Drawing by the author.

with great velocity entered a reinforced-concrete surge tank measuring twelve-by-thirty-six feet. From this tank it passed into the head of a main canal. The surging waves were visible for considerable distances down the canal.

The Humphrey Direct Action Pumping Plant on the Rio Grande functioned for only a short time. After about three months of intermittently successful operation, it was closed. The foundation for the huge sixty-six-inch pump was unable to withstand the impact of the repeated explosions, and the pump tore itself loose several times. Finally, after several repairs, the plant was left to the ravages of time. A few years ago the heavy equipment at the bottom of the pump house was removed, and since that time the structure has been allowed to fill with water to the natural river level. Although the site has been abandoned for over sixty years, the buildings are remarkably well preserved, despite their almost ghostly appearance.

Location: The Humphrey Direct Action Pumping Plant is located on the privately owned Rancho Rio Grande in Kinney County and is not accessible to the public.

Suggested Reading:

"America's First Large Direct-Explosion Pump Will Irrigate Texas Lands." *Engineering Record* 71, no. 19 (May 8, 1915): 596–98.
"A Humphrey Direct-Acting Explosion Pump for Irrigation Service at Del Rio, Texas." *Engineering News* 72, no. 16 (October 15, 1914): 794–96.
Trump, C. C. "The First Large American Humphrey Pump." *Engineering News* 73, no. 4 (January 28, 1915): 154–58.

52. International and Great Northern Railroad Station

The International and Great Northern Railroad passenger station represents one of only two surviving early twentieth-century railway depots in San Antonio. The fine structure reflects not only the tastes of its day but also the prosperity of both the railway and the city early in this century. It is one of the landmarks of the Alamo City.

The International and Great Northern Railroad had its beginnings in two railway companies established just after the Civil War. The first of these was the Houston and Great Northern Railroad (H&GN), which received its charter from the state legislature on October 22, 1866, during its first session after the Civil War. Actual railway construction, backed by both eastern and local capital, did not begin until after Texas had been readmitted to the Union in 1870, but soon thereafter H&GN lines stretched from Houston to Palestine. The second progenitor of the International and Great Northern was the International Railroad Company, chartered by the legislature on August 5, 1870, to build from Fulton, Arkansas, to Laredo, Texas, on the Mexican border. This company merged with the H&GN in 1873 to become the International and Great Northern Railroad (I&GN). In 1879 this new company extended its tracks into San Antonio, reaching the city only two years after the arrival of the first railroad there. The I&GN erected a station in the city that served its

Looking northwest to the International and Great Northern Station. Photograph by the author, 1975.

needs until early in this century, when company officials deemed it necessary to erect a new passenger station that better reflected its affluence and the importance of the city as a point on its lines.

The I&GN in 1906 employed architect Harvey L. Page to design for it a new depot to serve San Antonio. Drawing on the then-popular Mission Revival style, he planned a beautiful tan brick structure with steel superstructure, which incorporated many of the architectural features found in the San Antonio missions. The depot is one of the finest of all the Mission Revival buildings in the state.

The San Antonio station of the I&GN takes the basic form of a Greek cross. Barrel vaults radiate from its central dome, which dominates the structure. The exterior facades are symmetrical and similar in style. The four corners are ornamented by three-story bell towers, which frame mission-style parapets at the center of each side. Large stained-glass "rose windows" were placed on the east and south facades, their general style being taken from that of windows in the San Antonio missions. Around these openings are carved the words, "International & Great Northern—The Texas Railroad." The entrances on the east and south sides have hipped, green tile roofed canopies to protect travelers from the elements. Originally, a landscaped park was on the south side of the building.

Inside the depot the main waiting room is covered by a large copper-roofed dome. A bronze statue of an Indian, a motif frequently used by the I&GN during the era, surmounts the dome. A gallery with cast-iron balustrades on the second floor provides access to office areas located there. Ornamental details on the interior are drawn from Art Nouveau, Prairie, and Victorian styles.

The International and Great Northern Railroad Station served as one of the transportation centers for San Antonio from its opening in 1907 until after World War II. With the purchase of the line by the Missouri-Pacific Railroad Company in 1924, the building became known as the Missouri-Pacific Station. During the 1950s and 1960s the volume of rail passenger traffic dwindled to a single train north and south daily. Already the railway company had reduced station maintenance to a minimum. In 1958 the park area to the south was converted into an asphalt-topped parking lot, and the next decade saw the removal of train sheds, lunchroom, newsstand, and public-address system. Finally in 1970 the railroad closed the station and in 1973 sold the entire complex to an individual.

Location: The International and Great Northern Railroad Station stands at the corner of Medina and Houston streets, just west of downtown San Antonio.

Suggested Reading:

Missouri-Pacific Railroad Company, Saint Louis, Mo. Building Record File for Passenger Depot and Train Shed, San Antonio, Tex. Manuscript. 1924–73. Photocopy in "San Antonio Railroad Depot" file, Texas Historic Engineering Site Inventory, Center for the History of Engineering, Texas Tech University, Lubbock, Tex.

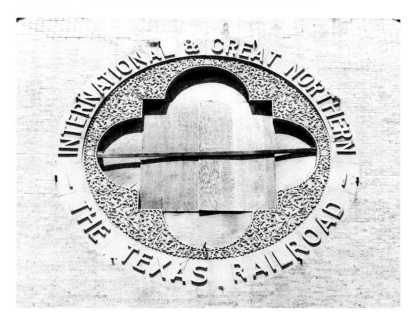

Detail of the stonework around the rose window on the south side of the International and Great Northern Station. Photograph by the author, 1975.

53. *Justiceburg Railway Water System*

The Justiceburg Railway Water System (1911–12) represents a classic example of the means employed by railroads early in this century to develop surface water supplies for their steam locomotives in semi-arid country. The high state of preservation found in the Justiceburg system makes it a particularly significant historic engineering site.

In building its cut-off line connecting Brownwood, Texas, with Clovis, New Mexico, a route planned to reduce the distance that Santa Fe trains traveled between the ports of Houston and Galveston and the West Coast, railroad construction crews reached the hamlet of Justiceburg in Garza County on April 17, 1911. The community had been established only about four years earlier, when a store opened for

business on the J. D. Justice Ranch. After the arrival of the railroad, its construction crews began an extensive effort to develop and store surface water on a nearby tributary of the Double Mountain Fork of the Brazos River.

The storage structure for the Justiceburg system is a 450-foot-long earthen dam. The surprisingly large structure stands approximately 25 feet above the former bed of the tributary and is faced with concrete on its upstream side to reduce seepage. When completely filled, the reservoir covers 76.5 acres, although silting over the years has reduced its storage capacity. The original 16-foot-by-22-foot, two-story reinforced-concrete pump house still stands at the north side of the reservoir. Access is by way of a 100-foot wooden

The pump house, catwalks, and inlet tower erected by the Santa Fe Railway at Justiceburg Lake in 1911–12. Photograph by Steven R. Rae, 1971, courtesy Center for the History of Engineering, Texas Tech University, Lubbock, Texas.

catwalk mounted on railway rails with concrete footings. Beside the ramp is a rectangular, concrete-lined pit, which in 1912 held the kerosene used to fuel the first pumping engine. Today both the cover to the fuel storage pit and the old pump are gone, replaced by more modern electric pumping equipment housed in the same concrete building. Extending beyond the pump house toward the center of the lake is a second catwalk 300 feet long. It also is supported on rails with concrete footings in the bottom of the lake. It leads to another prominent feature of the system, a large cylindrical inlet tower. Standing about 30 feet tall, the inlet tower consists of roughly laid red brick on a concrete foundation. It is 12 feet in diameter at its base, tapering to 10 feet in diameter at its top. Three intake pipes are visible at different positions, each allowing water to be drawn from a different level.

From the pump house a buried water pipeline leads to the Santa Fe Railway tracks and then northwest along the right-of-way to a steel deck girder bridge spanning the Double Mountain Fork of the Brazos. Here the pipeline emerges from the ground to pass across the river, supported beneath the bridge. At the other side the line again goes underground, following the right-of-way northwest to Justiceburg.

A cylindrical riveted steel water tank erected by the Santa Fe between 1911 and 1912 stands on the southwest side of the tracks in the little community. The water line leads here. The pipeline crosses under the tracks opposite the tank, leads through valves in a small wooden valve house beside the tank, and then passes into the storage structure. Interesting graffiti from the 1920s still may be read on the wooden sides of the valve house. The steel tank was built according to the Santa Fe Railway standard plans of the day. It is twenty feet in diameter and stands fifty-six feet tall, giving it a capacity of about 130,000 gallons. On its black painted side the now-dim Santa Fe name may still be read.

As the Justiceburg system originally operated, the kerosene-fueled pump forced water from the reservoir through the pipeline to the steel tank. A second set of pipes carried the water under gravity pressure from the tank to a swivel-type "water elevator," or free-standing water spout, located between the main-line track and a siding adjacent to the tank. There the train crews conveniently were able to fill the locomotive tenders with water. More water was needed by the locomotives headed northwest, for they were pulling the grades that would lead them to the Cap Rock Escarpment a few miles farther along the line.

It is uncertain precisely when the Justiceburg System actually went into operation, although it is known that the dam was completed on June 17, 1912. Time was necessary for the reservoir to fill with water to a usable level, but we may assume that the system did begin functioning sometime before the end of the year. It continued in operation until 1954, when the Santa Fe discontinued the use of steam locomotives along its line from Brownwood to Clovis. After it ceased using the system, the company gave it to the local community, which has maintained it.

Location: The most prominent structure in the Justiceburg Railway Water System is the large black standpipe beside the tracks in the village of Justiceburg. The water pipeline is most easily visible as it passes under the 1911 Santa Fe plate girder bridge crossing the Double Mountain Fork of the Brazos. This bridge is parallel with and only a few dozen feet from the current U.S. 84 bridge spanning that same stream a short distance southeast of Justiceburg. The reservoir, today known as Justiceburg Lake, lies just east of U.S. 84 down a dirt road that leaves the hardtop 1.5 miles southeast of the community.

Suggested Reading:

Harper, Carl. "Building the Santa Fe Railway through the South Plains." *West Texas Historical Association Year Book* 11 (1935): 73–92.
Santa Fe Splinters. Microfilm. 34 vols. Southwest Collection, Texas Tech University, Lubbock, Tex.

54. *Kelly Plow Works*

The Kelly Plow Works was the only full-line agricultural implement manufacturer in the southwest in the nineteenth century. Just over a century ago the foundry and plow works at Kellyville in Marion County produced over half of the agricultural tools and implements manufactured in the entire state.

The Kelly Plow Company had its beginning near Marshall, Texas, in 1843. There, John A. Stewart began making crude plows in a shop owned by a man named Sanders. Five years later he moved his plow patterns and personal tools to a new location known as Four-Mile Branch. The site was four miles west of booming Jefferson, the head of steam navigation in northeast Texas, and it was a popular camping spot for teamsters coming and going from Jefferson. With his brother-in-law, Stewart ran a general repair shop, where he also made plows and smelted small amounts of native hematite ore into iron with a small charcoal-fueled pocket furnace.

In 1852 George Addison Kelly, a native of Greene County, Tennessee, joined the business enterprise. With his father he moved to a farm in Natchitoches Parish, Louisiana, in 1849, and arrived in Jefferson three years later as a crew member of a steamboat. In Jefferson, he took his first employment with John A. Stewart as a foreman for the slaves working in his foundry and shop. Kelly realized that there was a ready market in Texas for cowbells and various types of iron hollowware, so he took an extended trip to the iron foundries of Kentucky to study their operations. Becoming familiar with what at the time were the latest methods of production, he returned to Marion County and introduced many of these concepts into the Stewart foundry. Profiting financially from

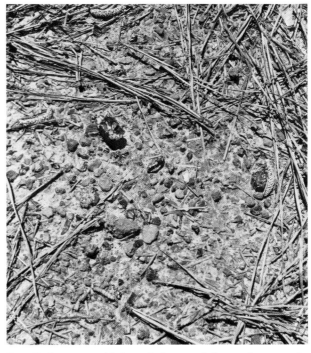

Detail of century-old slag, cinders, and charcoal among the pine needles on the ground at the site of the Kelly Plow Works. Photograph by the author, 1981.

139

The present-day roadside rest area that prior to 1882 was occupied by the foundry and manufacturing complex of the Kelly Plow Works. Photograph by the author, 1981.

his efforts, Kelly bought a share of the business in 1858, and on the death of Stewart two years later became the sole owner. With the outbreak of the Civil War in 1861, Kelly converted the factory from the manufacture of agricultural tools to military supplies, mainly cannonballs.

After the close of the war, George A. Kelly returned his plant to domestic production. Already in 1860 he had developed his "Blue Kelly" plow, which after the war became one of the standard products of his factory. In time "Blue Kelly" became almost synonymous with "plow" in Texas. After the pioneer Nash Iron Furnace (discussed in entry no. 64) ceased production during the war, George Kelly purchased all its equipment and a stockpile of pig iron and transferred the additional tools to his factory at Four-Mile Branch. With Nash's equipment added to his own,

Kelly began large-scale iron smelting. In 1874 he rebuilt the furnace, but it never operated as profitably as he had hoped. Despite this, however, Kelly's production was so high that the *Engineering and Mining Journal* could report that he made and sold ten thousand plows during 1877 alone.

In 1880 the Kelly Plow Works employed approximately forty skilled workers at $2.00 a day as well as a hundred common laborers at $1.00 a day. In this year Kelly smelted over three thousand tons of Marion County iron ore in his charcoal-fueled furnaces. The smelting works produced a total of $36,000 worth of pig iron, but the operating expenses were so high that Kelly made little profit from its sale. He did, however, have the distinction of being the most important manufacturer of agricultural implements in Texas, making more than half of the $140,000 worth produced. Among the range of Kelly products were plows, cotton planters, cultivators, harrows, corn planters, grain drills, and cane mills. Before the end of 1880, however, the Kelly Plow Works suffered a disastrous fire. As the foundry had never made the profits that Kelly had desired, he abandoned his charcoal-fueled furnaces and devoted his interests exclusively to manufacturing.

Two years after the fire and after Jefferson had begun to decline when the railroad bypassed it, Kelly decided to shift his factory operations to a more promising location. After moving all the equipment that he was able to salvage, he opened a new factory at Longview under the name of the G. A. Kelly Plow Company. There it operated well into this century as the only full-line agricultural implement factory in the Southwest.

The site of the Kelly Plow Works at Four-Mile Branch in Marion County is today known as Kellyville, from the town that grew up around the factory during the 1860s and 1870s. After the plow works moved to Longview, most of the residents departed as well, converting Kellyville into a ghost town. The state of Texas marked the site of the plow works with a granite monument in 1936, and then the Kelly heirs deeded the site of the former factory to the state for

use as a roadside rest area. The manufacturing plant occupied the general area where today one finds an open pavilion and tennis courts. The entire ground surface in most of the park is still littered with century-old slag, cinders, and pieces of charcoal, some of the earth being black with the debris. North of the factory site near the present-day Kansas City Southern Railway tracks one may view the Kelly family cemetery as well as the Kellyville Negro cemetery.

Location: The Kelly Plow Works stood at the site of the present roadside park on the north side of State Highway 49 approximately half a mile northwest of its intersection with FM 729. The park is approximately four miles west of Jefferson.

Suggested Reading:

Dugas, Vera Lee. "Texas Industry, 1860–1880." *Southwestern Historical Quarterly* 70, no. 2 (October, 1955): 151–83.
"Progressive Plant That Is Making Implement History." *Hardware & Implement Journal* (Dallas, Tex.) 24, no. 24 (December 22, 1919): 17.
"Progress of the Iron Industry in Texas." *Engineering and Mining Journal* 25, no. 8 (February 23, 1878): 135.

55. *Lake Wichita Dam*

The Lake Wichita Dam (1900–1901) created in its day the largest body of surface water in the state of Texas. Surviving floods and poor maintenance for decades, the dam still may be seen on the southwest side of Wichita Falls.

The idea of the Lake Wichita Dam came from the mind of Wichita Falls businessman and promoter Joseph Alexander Kemp. A native of Clifton, Texas, Kemp moved to Wichita Falls in 1883. There, he opened a mercantile business that furnished supplies to the Indian reservation at Fort Sill, Oklahoma. As he made his fortune, Kemp through the years participated in the organization, promotion, and building of banks, milling companies, and railroads. At one time or another he served as the president of four different short-line railways. Among his many ventures, most of which had as their goal the promotion of both Wichita Falls and his own financial interests, was the construction of a reservoir to provide domestic water

to the residents of Wichita Falls and to supply irrigation water to area farmers.

Returning to Wichita Falls in a driving rainstorm in the mid-1890s, Joseph Kemp routed his travel via high ground to avoid flooding. From one of the vantage points along the way, he looked across the valley of Holliday Creek, at the time filled with storm water, and conceived the idea of building a dam across the valley to create a reservoir. Although statistical data were lacking on the available runoff from the watershed of the creek, Kemp felt certain that there would be sufficient water for both domestic and irrigation needs. At the time the only source of domestic water in the city was a series of riverbed wells, and no irrigation was being practiced.

Seeking the aid of engineers, in 1896 Kemp planned the construction of an earthen dam across Holliday Creek southwest of the city. With blueprints in hand, he sought financial support for his idea, but for years

Pavilion erected at Lake Wichita in 1909 shortly after it opened to the public. Photograph courtesy Panhandle-Plains Historical Museum, Canyon, Texas.

he met only disappointment. The Texas Constitution of 1876 prohibited the issuance of public bonds for water or reclamation projects, and Wichita Falls did not have the means to construct a dam to impound its own water supply.

Since public funding appeared to be unavailable, in the late 1890s Kemp turned to private investors to collaborate with him in the effort. He joined with Martin Lasker, a wealthy Galveston miller, and other backers to create the Lake Wichita Company. They purchased the land that would be inundated in the valley for twenty dollars an acre as soon as a survey of the area was completed in 1900. In the meantime

Wichita Falls authorized Kemp, Lasker, and their associates to build a waterworks system to serve the community. To do so they formed the Wichita Falls Water Works Company. While their workers began construction at the damsite, other employees started work on the pumping facilities, reservoirs, and system of mains for the waterworks.

Teams of mules pulling scrapers started moving earth into position to form a quite long earthen dam. The structure, 23 feet tall, was built 6,250 feet long and 20 feet wide at its top. No efforts were taken to protect either its upstream or downstream faces. Two 36-inch pipes with gate valves were placed near the

Looking southeast along the top of the Lake Wichita Dam today. Photograph by the author, 1975.

142

The outlet canal at the point at which it passes from beneath the Lake Wichita Dam in the area of the natural channel for Holliday Creek. Photograph by the author, 1975.

center of the dam at the bed of Holliday Creek to provide an outlet for water, which passed through an open ditch to be used downstream. No separate spillway was constructed; instead, a gap in the hills about half a mile to the southeast happened to be at the right elevation to serve the purpose. After the dam was completed in 1901 and the reservoir was filled with water, Lake Wichita covered twenty-two hundred acres and had a total storage capacity of fourteen thousand acre feet of water. It was 21 feet deep at its deepest point, with an average depth of approximately 6 feet, 10 inches—very shallow by modern standards.

Lake Wichita became the beauty spot of the Red River Valley. Orchards sprang up in the irrigated district downstream, but the most impressive activity took place around the dam itself. In 1909 a two-story concrete pavilion was built to provide dining and entertainment facilities on a pier over the lake waters. A street railway line soon extended from the city to the lake, where tourist facilities sprang up almost overnight. Within only a short time baseball teams from the eastern states began wintering at Wichita Falls,

and beside the dam an amusement park was built and even a horse racetrack was constructed. Next came a large hotel complex, with Lake Wichita achieving at least a regional reputation as a resort.

Just as quickly as it had developed, however, the lakeside boom came to an end. Fire swept through the amusement and hotel area, leaving only the pavilion. Twenty years later even the pavilion ceased to stand, the weight of its concrete floors having caused it to collapse on itself. In late 1913 the dam was threatened by floods, and it barely held. Although the owners discussed strengthening the structure, for lack of funds the only repair undertaken was the installation of timber flashboards at the top of the upstream face. In 1915 a concrete ogee spillway was constructed at the site of the natural spillway.

Since World War I the story of Lake Wichita has been concerned mostly with its problems. Among the difficulties is its nature as an earthen structure. On numerous occasions the dam has nearly collapsed under the pressures of impounded floodwaters. Its only actual failure was a break in 1901, just after it was built, but the residents of Wichita Falls since that time have felt uneasy with the dam upstream from the city. Another problem is that the ownership of the dam has changed several times, with most of the owners not giving the structure the maintenance that it has deserved. Water loss presents yet another difficulty. The reservoir is located over a sandy loam soil, which is noted for its high permeability, causing much of the water stored in the reservoir to disappear into the ground. This situation is coupled with high evaporation losses from such a shallow reservoir. After petroleum was discovered in the watershed above the reservoir, the water quality deteriorated because of salt pollution originating from the oil wells. This salinity increased even further when naturally salty water from a newer reservoir above Lake Wichita was diverted into the lake.

In 1920 Wichita Falls purchased the Lake Wichita Dam and all the area covered by its impounded water. Already its ownership had changed three times. The city continued to use the lake as a source of water for the municipal waterworks until 1947, and it remained a source of water for irrigation until 1950. Its principal use today is for limited recreation by local citizens and as an emergency source of cooling water for an electricity-generating station.

Location: The Lake Wichita Dam lies across the valley of Holliday Creek just west of the Wichita Falls

State Hospital on the southwest side of Wichita Falls. The most convenient access to the dam is via FM 2380 (Kemp Street) from the city. The spillway, which is located about half a mile southeast of the dam on the other side of the state hospital, may be seen a few yards northwest of FM 2380, just above the Wichita-Archer county line.

Suggested Reading:

Dowell, Cleo Lafoy, and Seth Darnby Breeding. *Dams*

and Reservoirs in Texas: Historical and Descriptive Information. Texas Water Development Board Report 48. Austin: Texas Water Development Board, 1967.

Saikowski, Ron. "Lake Wichita." Typescript. 1971. "Lake Wichita" file, Texas Historic Engineering Site Inventory, Center for the History of Engineering, Texas Tech University, Lubbock, Tex.

56. Landa Rock Mill

Erected by Joseph Landa in 1875, the Landa Rock Mill stands beside the Comal River in New Braunfels. It is a handsome combination of New England mill architecture and Texas German craftsmanship. For over a century it has been used for milling purposes.

New Braunfels was established by German immigrants in 1845, but they soon were followed to the area by non-Germans, who began investing their money in the community. One of these persons was William W. Meriwether, who had operated mills and plantations in Shelby County, Tennessee, before coming to Texas. In June, 1847, he purchased 480 acres on the banks of the Comal River at New Braunfels, an acreage that encompassed the Comal Springs, which form the head of the river. Meriwether's slaves dug a millrace to a site that he had chosen for the erection of a gristmill, which the blacks also built. As the years passed Meriwether added a flour mill, a sawmill, and a cotton gin. He operated the enterprise for about a dozen years before selling it to Joseph Landa in 1859.

The 1875 Landa Rock Mill, today part of the milling complex of the H. Dittlinger Roller Mills Company on the Comal River in New Braunfels. Photograph by the author, 1978.

144

Landa was a Jewish immigrant to Texas who had been born in Prussia in 1811. He came first to New York in 1843, moving to San Antonio two years later. There, he made investments in real estate and other ventures, but in 1847 he moved his residence to the newly established town of New Braunfels. For a number of years, Landa observed Meriwether's mill complex, dreaming of building it into an even more substantial commercial enterprise. His opportunity came in 1859, when Meriwether offered to sell him his entire milling property and business.

Landa's milling business prospered. In 1875 it had grown to such an extent that he decided to erect a completely new mill on the site of Meriwether's old structure. Accordingly, he built a handsome three-story cut limestone mill, which became known locally as the Landa Rock Mill. It remains intact today, and water still flows beside the building in the old 1847 millrace.

Landa's Rock Mill measures thirty-by-seventy-four feet and is oriented north and south. Its basement originally held the turbines, which powered milling machinery in the upper floors. The ground, second, and third floors were built with large open spaces and a row of six wooden columns down the middle. The stone walls average twenty-eight inches thick at ground level and gradually decrease in thickness at each story to eighteen inches at the third floor. Above the upper story is a low attic beneath a ridge roof with a four-in-twelve pitch.

Landa's milling business was profitable for a num-

ber of years, but by the early 1890s it began suffering from competition from other mills using more modern equipment (he was still using old-style millstones for all his grinding). Thus, in 1891 Landa and his son, Harry, bought a larger turbine and installed an up-to-date Hungarian Roller Mill system. This returned the Landa Rock Mill to a money-making basis, and it remained an important industry in New Braunfels for the next two decades.

The Landa family owned and operated the mill until 1927, when they sold it to an investment company. Today it forms part of the H. Dittlinger Roller Mills Company complex and is used for storing grain and feed. Although it originally stood in the open, through the years a number of random buildings have been built on two sides of the old 1875 mill, obscuring its view from these directions.

Location: The Landa Rock Mill stands on the north side of Landa Street near the entrance to Landa Park in New Braunfels.

Suggested Reading:

Haas, Oscar. *History of New Braunfels and Comal County, Texas 1844–1946.* Austin, Tex.: Steck, 1968.
U.S. Department of the Interior. Historic American Buildings Survey. Site Tex 3251. Typescript. 1972. Library of Congress, Washington, D.C.

57. *Lavaca Bay Causeway*

Erected between 1930 and 1931 on the main highway link along the Texas Gulf Coast between Corpus Christi and Galveston/Houston, the timber Lavaca Bay Causeway stands preserved today as a fishing pier operated by the Texas Parks and Wildlife Department. The structure is typical of the long wooden trestles built in coastal areas by the State Highway Department half a century ago.

The Lavaca Bay Causeway served as an integral part of the coastal highway. Before its construction, traffic was forced to divert inland a number of miles to go around Lavaca Bay. Plans were drawn for the construction of a causeway across Lavaca Bay in the late 1920s, and in 1930 the Texas Highway Department advertised for bids on the project, with the con-

tract going to J. DePuy of San Antonio. Work on the job began later in 1930 and was finished in April, 1931, at a total cost of $546,903.

As completed in 1931, the causeway consisted of 539 19-foot treated-timber spans combined with a 62-foot, 9-inch movable bascule span over the navigation channel in and out of Lavaca Bay. The total length of the structure was 10,305 feet, not including earthen approaches. The individual wooden bents supporting the bridge consisted of 4 creosoted timber piles driven into the bottom of the shallow bay, which were capped by 12-inch-by-14-inch-by-22-foot treated timber caps. Sway braces and sashes were bolted to connect and stabilize the piles above mean high tide level.

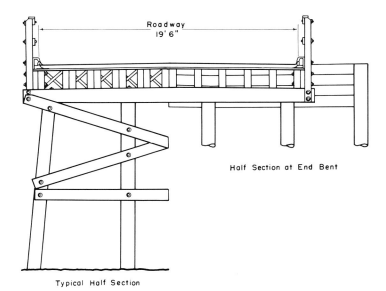

Roadway
19' 6"

Half Section at End Bent

Typical Half Section

The bents and roadway of the 1930–31 Lavaca Bay Causeway seen at a typical bent and at the end bent. Based on Texas, State Highway Department, "Timber Trestle with Concrete Floor[,] 19 Ft. Span[,] 19'-6" Roadway[,] Jan. 1930," measured drawing, 1930, Design Department, Texas Department of Highways and Public Transportation, Yoakum, Texas.

Stringers connecting the timber bents measured 6 inches by 18 inches by 20 feet long and were mounted at 1-foot, 10½-inch centers. These also were made from treated timber, mostly fir. Atop the wooden superstructure a 5¼-inch reinforced concrete deck was poured to provide a curbed roadway 19 feet, 6 inches wide.

The bascule draw-span for the causeway consisted of a steel superstructure fabricated elsewhere and shipped to the construction site for assembly. Providing about forty feet of actual horizontal clearance, the span was counterbalanced by two huge concrete weights on either side of the roadway. It was designed to carry the weight of a typical ten-ton truck. As installed in 1930–31, the bascule span was hand operated by bridge watchmen who worked in a small house adjacent to the draw span. When the bascule span was raised, the roadway at each end of the span

was protected with a log chain connected to the railings, a rectangular black-on-yellow stop sign, and, at night, a red kerosene warning lamp. By the 1940s a small wind-power electric generator was added to provide a limited amount of power for lighting purposes.

The Lavaca Bay Causeway suffered several times from encounters with tropical storms. One of the most serious of these storms came in August, 1942, when the structure was heavily damaged. Repairs were undertaken in March, 1943, and completed in August, 1944, at a cost of $452,230. The bridge had hardly reopened to traffic before it again was damaged by a tropical storm in 1945, this time not so severely. Serious damage again came to the causeway during Hurricane Carla in 1961, but by this time it had been replaced by a newer structure.

On March 3, 1959, a contract was granted by

The Lavaca Bay Causeway after severe hurricane damage in August, 1942. Photograph courtesy Photographic Archives, Texas Department of Highways and Public Transportation, Austin, Texas.

Looking northeast along the 1930–31 Lavaca Bay Causeway as converted into a state park fishing pier. The new concrete causeway is at the left. Photograph by the author, 1982.

the State Highway Department to Elmer C. Gardner, Inc., of Houston to build a completely new causeway across Lavaca Bay. Work began on March 19 on a five-million-dollar project that was completed in summer, 1961. The new causeway was the longest bridge ever built in Texas and the first built on dry land and moved in pieces to the site. The 2.2-mile-long structure was also the first large prefabricated concrete bridge erected in the state. More than 388 individual parts and sections of the structure were prestressed and precast at a nearby shore plant built especially for the purpose. Another first on the project for Texas was the use of sonar to locate approximately a million yards of hydraulic fill material used in the approaches. The new causeway, which was dedicated on July 1, 1961, now carries State Highway 35 traffic over the bay without the need for a draw span be-cause it crosses the navigation channel with one hundred feet of horizontal clearance and forty-five feet of vertical clearance.

A year and a half after the opening of the new concrete causeway, on January 14, 1963, the Texas Highway Department transferred the old wooden causeway to the State Parks and Wildlife Department for development as a public fishing pier. The two ends of the bridge at Port Lavaca and Point Comfort, totaling thirty-two hundred feet of causeway, were preserved, and the central section of the structure was removed. The remaining portions were provided with lights, fish-cleaning facilities, rest rooms, and concessions providing fishermen's needs. With the two ends of the bridge crossing Chicken Reef, the location is ideal for sea trout, and the old causeway is a popular resort for Gulf fishermen.

Location: The two preserved ends of the 1930–31 Lavaca Bay Causeway, known today as the Port Lavaca Causeway State Park, extend into the bay from Port Lavaca and Point Comfort about four hundred yards southeast of the current 1961 concrete causeway on State Highway 35.

Suggested Reading:

"Lavaca Bay Causeway." *Texas Highways* 7, no. 4 (April, 1960): 2–7.
Texas. State Highway Department. Construction and Maintenance Files for Project Control No. 179–10, Calhoun County. Manuscript and microfilm. Design Department, Texas Department of Highways and Public Transportation, Yoakum, Tex.

58. Los Ebanos Ferry

Transporting vehicles and pedestrians across the Rio Grande between Texas and the Republic of Mexico, the Los Ebanos Ferry is the last ferry operating on the Rio Grande and the only hand-pulled international ferry on the borders of the United States. It perpetuates a form of river crossing that a century ago was perhaps the most common of all in Texas.

The Los Ebanos Ferry is a so-called cable or hand-pulled ferry. The vessel itself is a simple steel scow, a modern version of the wooden boats used in the past. It accommodates two or at most three vehicles. A heavy steel cable anchored on two ebony trees, one on each side of the Rio Grande, keeps the boat from drifting downstream. These beautiful trees, common in the vicinity, give Los Ebanos its name. Two pulleys rolling on the long steel cable across the river are linked to the boat by two short lengths of cable.

Motive power for the ferry is human. Several men, who sometimes are recruited from among the drivers of the vehicles being carried, pull on a rope attached to anchors on each side of the river. Two men can pull the ferry from the Texas side toward Mexico, but four

Vehicles from the American side preparing to take the Los Ebanos Ferry across the Rio Grande to Mexico. Photograph by the author, 1981.

Men pulling the Los Ebanos Ferry across the Rio Grande to the American side in 1965. Photograph courtesy Photographic Archives, Texas Department of Highways and Public Transportation, Austin, Texas.

or five are needed to pull against the current to bring it back to the American side.

The river crossing at Los Ebanos is centuries old. Early residents from the Mexican side of the river crossed here on their way to the salt flats at El Sal del Rey about forty miles to the northeast. The first recorded visitors to the area, however, were explorers and colonists under José de Escandón in the 1740s. Los Ebanos was the site of a hostile entry into Texas by Mexican soldiers during the war with Mexico in 1846, as well as of the crossing into Mexico of Texas law officers hot on the trail of rustlers with five hundred head of stolen cattle in 1874.

For many years Los Ebanos was a center of smuggling, especially during Prohibition. Most of the illegal activity took place just upstream around a hairpin turn in the river at a place called La Grulla. Known as the "Smugglers' Paradise," it was renowned throughout South Texas for rough activity. To crack down on the smugglers, in 1950 the U.S. Border Patrol established a station at nearby Los Ebanos. Today it is the international border station that serves the ferry, which was also established in that year. Since that time it has had the distinction of being the only government-licensed, hand-pulled ferry on any American border.

The Los Ebanos Ferry, although made from steel, varies little from its predecessors used throughout Texas during the nineteenth century. Consisting only of the scow, a cable fitted with pulleys, and a rope for pulling, it operates seven days a week year round. It only closes when the water is high and the current too strong. The trip to Mexico and back takes about ten minutes, but during times of heavy traffic as many as a dozen cars may wait in line as much as an hour to cross. Pedestrians, however, may ride across anytime. A small fee is charged for automobiles and an even smaller fee is charged for pedestrians.

Location: The Los Ebanos Ferry crosses the Rio Grande just southwest of the village of Los Ebanos in Hidalgo County. Access to the ferry is via FM 886, which leads southward from U.S. 83 to the village. From the town square, proceed south and southwest a few hundred yards to the ferry and its adjacent U.S. Customs station.

Suggested Reading:

"Los Ebanos Is Home of the Last Ferry Working on the Rio Grande." *Monitor* (McAllen, Tex.) (November 11, 1981), sec. D, p. 12.

Pinkard, Tommie. "Hop a Ferry to Mexico." *Texas Highways* 30, no. 1 (January, 1983): 32–35.

59. *Lucas Gusher*

Known as the birthplace of the modern petroleum industry, the Lucas Gusher (1901) was the discovery well for the Spindletop Oil Field near Beaumont. The development of this field established the importance of Texas as an oil-producing state, a role it has maintained since that time.

Two individuals were instrumental in the discovery of oil at Spindletop. The first of these, Pattillo Hig-

149

The Lucas Gusher flowing uncontrolled in January, 1901. Photograph courtesy Spindletop Museum, Beaumont, Texas.

gins, a native of Beaumont, was a self-taught geologist and engineer although he had completed only the third grade. Handicapped in adolescence by the loss of an arm in a shooting accident, Higgins first developed the idea that petroleum might be located beneath a slight dome-shaped mound that rose twelve to fifteen feet above the surrounding coastal plain south of Beaumont. The elevated point had received its name, Spindletop, years before because heat waves rising from the prairie around it gave the trees growing on its crest the seeming appearance of a spinning top. Realizing the potential value of petroleum and having studied geological reports on the Texas Gulf Coast region, Higgins in 1892 organized the Gladys City Oil, Gas, and Manufacturing Company to explore for oil and develop the area commercially. Plagued by failures in drilling, Higgins went to backer after backer seeking the funds he needed to continue his search.

In the course of his efforts, Higgins met Anthony Francis Lucas, an immigrant engineer from the Hapsburg Empire, who for a number of years had engaged in mining salt from coastal salt domes in Louisiana. At the turn of the century Lucas knew probably more than any other man in America about these geologic structures and their potential for producing not only salt but also petroleum. Lucas and Higgins jointly drilled an experimental well on the Spindletop mound, which both of them knew was the top of a salt dome. They reached a depth of only 575 feet before abandoning their effort as a failure. Then through the firm of James Guffey and John Galey of Pittsburgh, Pennsylvania, the two men secured additional financial support from Andrew Mellon to conduct five more tests. All the leading petroleum experts believed that the Texas coastal area contained no deposits of petroleum in commercial quantities, so the Beaumont entrepreneurs were acting against virtually all expert opinion.

Higgins and Lucas contracted with Alfred and James Hamill, reputable well drillers from Corsicana, to sink their test wells at Spindletop. Beginning in October, 1900, they progressed on a well until January 10, 1901. On that morning things began happening that neither of the drillers had ever experienced before. As they were lowering a new rotary bit into the well, drilling mud began to bubble up over the working platform. It grew into a stream of mud shooting up into the wooden derrick. The pressure continued to increase, forcing several hundred feet of drilling

Roughnecks in the Spindletop Field during its second major boom, during the 1920s. Photograph courtesy Lufkin Industries, Inc., Lufkin, Texas.

pipe upward, knocking the crown block from the top of the derrick and scattering the pipe around the area like pieces of spaghetti. Quiet followed for a few minutes, the drillers returning to the well to inspect the damage. As they began clearing away the debris, they heard a sound that they could compare only to that of a gigantic cannon blast. Again mud and rocks began shooting from the well, followed by a terrific column of gas. Within seconds the gas turned to a column of heavy greenish black petroleum, shooting into the sky a hundred feet above the top of the derrick.

Soon Anthony Lucas reached the site of the gusher that would bear his name, only to be followed by hundreds and later thousands of spectators who came to witness the spectacular geyser of oil. It shot so high into the air that people on the upper floors of the Jefferson County Courthouse, about four and a half

miles away in downtown Beaumont, could see it clearly. Few of the viewers, however, realized what an unusual event they were observing, for up to this time nowhere else in the world had such a gusher been seen, except in the oil fields of Russia.

The well flowed uncontrolled for six days and then was not completely capped until January 19. In the meantime, a huge lake of oil was formed by earthen dikes around the well. On March 3 sparks ignited the stored oil, but the fire was controlled without damaging the well itself. Within a matter of days all of the land in the Spindletop area was covered with leases for the production of petroleum, and numerous landowners made fortunes overnight. Property in the proved area of production eventually sold for a minimum of $200,000 per acre, with one tract selling for $900,000 an acre. A mad rush of drilling ensued,

The site of the Lucas Gusher, marked today only by the less than attractive footing for the 1941 granite monument that once recorded the events of the Spindletop discovery. Photograph by the author, 1983.

with scores of wells being drilled as close together as possible and with each leaseholder attempting to secure as much oil as quickly as possible before it was drained away by wells belonging to others. In its first ten years the Spindletop Field produced 42,773,650 barrels of oil, the peak year coming in 1902 with the production of 17,420,949 barrels. No comparable production had ever been known in America. An even greater year came in 1927, when drilling reached a lower horizon to produce 21,255,935 barrels in a twelve-month period.

Today petroleum is still produced at the Spindletop Field, although the well at the actual Lucas Gusher has been capped for many years. The site was marked by a fifty-eight-foot granite monument in 1941. Among the honored guests at the dedication of the marker were Pattillo Higgins, "the father of Spindletop," and Alfred Hamill, one of the drillers of the original well. Land subsidence caused by sulfur mining in the vicinity of the marker, however, forced its removal to another site in 1955. Today it stands adjacent to the Gladys City Boom Town reconstruc-

tion, a living history museum operated by Lamar University in Beaumont, about three-quarters of a mile north of the actual well site.

Location: The site of the Lucas Gusher is marked by the concrete footings for the 1941 monument on the south side of the slight mound known as Spindletop on the southern side of Beaumont. The well site, which is on private property, is located approximately five hundred yards northeast of West Port Arthur Road, about 1.1 miles southeast of its intersection with U.S. 69-96-287. Anyone interested in the Lucas Gusher should consider visiting the Gladys City Boom Town reconstruction as well as the Spindletop Museum, both on the nearby campus of Lamar University.

Suggested Reading:

Clark, James A., and Michel T. Halbouty. *Spindletop.* New York: Random House, 1952.
Rister, Carl Coke. *Oil! Titan of the Southwest.* Norman: University of Oklahoma Press, 1949.

60. *McDonald Observatory*

Funded by the bequest of northeast Texas banker William Johnson McDonald, the McDonald Observatory upon its completion in 1939 had the second-largest telescope in the world, an eighty-two-inch reflector. This great instrument remains in full use every clear night and has become the center of a complex of

Surveying the site for the McDonald Observatory in the early 1930s. The transit is set up on its tripod at the center of the site where the eighty-two-inch telescope later was located. Photograph courtesy University of Texas McDonald Observatory, Mount Locke, Texas.

other astronomical telescopes, which cluster around it atop Mount Locke in the Davis Mountains of Trans-Pecos Texas.

William Johnson McDonald, born in Lamar County, Texas, on December 21, 1844, was a self-made man. He grew to maturity on a farm, served briefly in the Confederate army, and returned home to read law while working as a teacher and printer. After becoming an attorney at Clarksville, he entered banking, advancing to the presidency of three different financial institutions. Moving to Paris, Texas, where one of his banks was located, he resided there for the remainder of his life. A man of moderate temperament and hard work, he never married, but devoted himself to his business interests, the study of natural sciences, and occasional travel. He died on February 8, 1926, leaving most of his estate to the University of Texas to erect and equip an astronomical observatory.

The efforts of distant relatives to contest McDonald's will delayed university acquisition of the bequest, but the six-year interim gave university officials sufficient time to make proper preliminary plans for the establishment of an observatory. During this time H. Y. Benedict, president of the university and himself trained as an astronomer, was contacted by Dr. Otto Struve, director of the University of Chicago Yerkes Observatory, and by Robert M. Hutchins, president of the University of Chicago. The latter institution had a large staff of outstanding astronomers

and decades of experience in operating astronomical observatories. Benedict had realized that the McDonald gift, though generous, was not sufficiently large both to build an observatory and to endow its staff and operation. During the course of a ten-minute telephone call, Hutchins and Benedict agreed on a plan for broad long-term cooperation between the two universities in constructing and then staffing the planned observatory. According to this agreement the University of Texas would pay for the observatory and retain its ownership, and the University of Chicago would pay for all salaries and half of the operating expenses for a thirty-year period. Use of the equipment would be shared by the two institutions for the duration.

With the agreement reached for collaboration between the two universities, the next step in planning the observatory was to determine its optimum location. During the summer of 1932, two Chicago astronomers took an extended trip by truck through western Texas, New Mexico, and Arizona using a four-inch telescope to test the quality of various observing locations. As the results failed to indicate that any of the areas in Arizona or New Mexico were superior to sites in far West Texas, the decision was made to locate the observatory in the Davis Mountains region. The site finally chosen was on an unnamed mountain peak sixty-eight hundred feet in elevation, located largely on a ranch established years

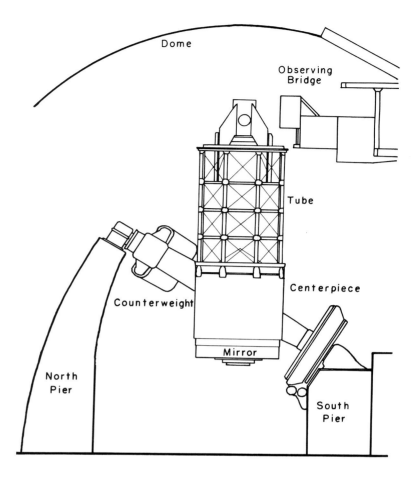

The major elements of the eighty-two-inch telescope at the McDonald Observatory. Based on Otto Struve, *The Birth of the McDonald Observatory,* Contributions from the McDonald Observatory, ser. 2, no. 1 (Austin: University of Texas, 1962), p. 4. Drawing by the author.

before by G. S. Locke. His granddaughter, Mrs. Violet Locke McIvor, donated two hundred acres to the project, a gift matched by the Fowlkes family, the owners of adjoining property. The site was named Mount Locke in honor of the pioneer settler.

The next steps in founding the observatory were the construction of a road to the site and the selection of a company to build the telescope and structure to house it. A road past Mount Locke already was being built at the time by the Texas Highway Department. The state legislature authorized the agency to construct a spur to the summit of the mountain, a project finished in October, 1933. Finding a company to build the telescope and see its production and installation through to completion, however, was not as simple a matter as building a gravel road up the side of the mountain.

Otto Struve, who served as director for both the McDonald Observatory and the University of Chicago Yerkes Observatory, wrote to all the major build-

ers of telescopes, asking them to submit proposals for the project. Soon the list of potential bidders was reduced to two firms, the Warner and Swasey Company of Cleveland, Ohio, and J. W. Fecker of Pittsburgh, Pennsylvania. Both companies had built large reflecting telescopes, but finally the former was chosen because it was thought that its heavy two-pier mounting for the telescope was superior.

The heart of the reflecting telescope at the McDonald Observatory is its 82-inch mirror. This great reflector, 11¾ inches thick at its edge and weighing fifty-six hundred pounds, was poured of Pyrex glass at the Corning glass works on December 31, 1933. The careful grinding, shaping, and polishing that followed began on October 19, 1934, and continued for four years. The reflecting surface of the glass disc consists of a thin coating of aluminum, which was deposited by evaporation of the metal in a high vacuum. When the great mirror was completed in Cleveland, it was shipped in a guarded express railway car

Erection of the steel dome for the McDonald Observatory at Mount Locke. Photograph courtesy University of Texas McDonald Observatory, Mount Locke, Texas.

to Alpine, Texas, from which point it was moved to the observatory by truck.

By the time the great mirror reached Texas, the McDonald Observatory building was ready to receive it. The structure itself is a steel, domelike shell that completely surrounds but does not at any point touch the telescope or its mounting. This design prevents any possible vibrations. The shell also was made by the Warner and Swasey Company in its Cleveland factory. All the steel parts were fabricated there and the dome itself preassembled and then taken apart for the company engineers and officials to be certain that all the parts went together properly. It is designed so that the dome-shaped top can rotate and open to allow

The metal dome housing the eighty-two-inch telescope as seen today. Photograph by the author, 1975.

observation in any part of the heavens. Steel construction work began in July, 1934, and was completed in November, 1936.

Under the huge metal dome is the reinforced-concrete two-pier mounting that actually supports the telescope. With footings in bedrock, this mount holds the assembly solidly and without vibration while the astronomers use the huge but delicate telescope.

The 82-inch telescope at the McDonald Observatory was dedicated on May 5, 1939. It has been the scene of numerous major astronomical discoveries, but perhaps the most significant was W. A. Hiltner's finding of interstellar polarization. Much of our knowledge of objects in our solar system, of the evolution of stars, and even of the size of the observable universe, has come from the study of light collected by this great telescope. Since its construction in the 1930s, other telescopes have been added on Mount Locke to supplement its work and to undertake research not possible with the aging equipment.

The most prominent addition was the construction of a new 107-inch telescope only a hundred yards away from the older 82-inch. Placed in operation in 1969, it was built jointly by the University of Texas and the National Aeronautics and Space Administration.

Location: The McDonald Observatory is located at the summit of Mount Locke at the end of Texas Spur 78. The spur leaves scenic State Highway 118 approximately 15.5 miles northwest of Fort Davis. A new interpretive center near the base of Mount Locke explains to visitors the operation of the observatory complex. Although the old 82-inch telescope is not open to the public, visitors are welcome at the summit, where they may watch operations at the 107-inch telescope from a special viewers' gallery.

Suggested Reading:

Struve, Otto. *The Birth of McDonald Observatory.* Contributions from the McDonald Observatory, ser. 2, no. 1. Austin: University of Texas, 1962.

61. Matagorda Lighthouse

First established in 1852 and rebuilt twenty years later, the Matagorda Lighthouse is the oldest lighthouse in active service on the Texas coast. Its slender tower for over a century and a quarter has provided a landmark by day and a beacon by night marking the entrance to Matagorda Bay at Pass Cavallo.

The story of the Matagorda Lighthouse begins in 1848. Late that year the U.S. Treasury Department purchased the site for a lighthouse at the extreme north end of Matagorda Island from Levi Jones. Difficulties arose in government acquisition of title to the property in part because the Texas attorney general was not available in Austin when he was needed during the negotiations to secure the title. Delays dragged on into 1851, with the collector of customs at Galveston complaining that for unknown reasons the state official seemed to be attempting to sabotage the entire lighthouse project. Finally, however, on November 7, 1851, the attorney general notified Gov. Peter H. Bell that the transfers of title were complete and that all was satisfactory.

In October, 1850, Congress had appropriated fifteen thousand dollars for the construction of a lighthouse at the pass, but the initiation of the project had been delayed by the slow transfer of title for the property. Construction finally began in June, 1852. The structure erected was a seventy-five-foot prefabricated iron tower on a concrete and pile foundation. Within the tower a spiral cast-iron staircase around a central pier provided access from the base to the lantern area at its apex. There the lamps were placed within a glass lens protected all around by thick glass windows. The keeper exhibited the first light at Pass Cavallo on December 31, 1852.

The Matagorda Lighthouse served local shipping until after the outbreak of the Civil War. As happened to virtually all the Texas lighthouses during the conflict, Confederate forces attempted to render the tower unserviceable for Union military operations. Sometime in late 1861 or early 1862, rebel troops dismantled the operating parts of the light and removed them from the site, leaving the tower vacant until December, 1862, when other Confederates attempted to destroy it with explosives. An anonymous writer in the weekly *San Antonio Herald* on January 24, 1863, reported that the soldiers had failed in their effort "to blow up the light house at Pass Cavallo," adding that since its actual light mechanism had been taken away it could "be used by our enemy only as a look out, and for this purpose their mastheads serve them

The Matagorda Lighthouse after it was rebuilt and its height increased fifteen feet in 1873. Photograph courtesy National Archives, Washington, D.C.

equally well without the risk of capture." The tower must have suffered significant damage, however, for the U.S. Lighthouse Board after the war in 1867 reported that "the cast-iron tower at this station was much injured by the rebels in an attempt to blow it up, several of the [iron] plates being broken. During the war the sea encroached upon the site to such an extent that, owing to the undermining of the foundation, the tower was in danger of falling. It was consequently taken down, and the iron sections composing it stored upon the highest point of the island."

The board erected a temporary beacon at the south side of Pass Cavallo, but it was damaged in an August, 1868, storm. About this time an inventory was made of the surviving iron plates from the 1852 tower and new plates were cast to replace the broken or missing ones. The design of the tower was altered to increase its height from seventy-five to ninety feet. When the time came to rebuild it, its location was shifted west about two miles because of beach erosion at the original site. Returning to service in 1873, the Matagorda Lighthouse operated without serious incident until it was struck by a severe hurricane in August, 1886. This storm, which destroyed the nearby port town of

Indianola, swept away everything at the station except the iron tower and the heavily damaged keeper's house. The storm rocked the tower so strongly that it bounced a piece of the lens out of its frame and smashed it on the deck of the lantern.

Since 1873 the Matagorda Lighthouse has remained an active aid to navigation. Although it is now automated and has no keepers in residence, it continues to flash its beam of light out to sea marking the entrance to Matagorda Bay.

Location: The Matagorda Lighthouse stands at the north end of Matagorda Island several miles out to sea from Port O'Connor. The island itself is now administered as a wildlife refuge by the U.S. Department of the Interior. The lighthouse is accessible to visitors who can provide their own boat transportation to the dock at the old Matagorda Island Air Force Base and are willing to walk approximately three miles each way to the lighthouse, which is kept locked; the foundations from the former lighthouse keepers' houses and auxiliary structures; and a small cemetery.

General view of the Matagorda Lighthouse as it appears today. Photograph by Range Control Officer Charles D. Turner, 1975, courtesy the photographer.

Suggested Reading:

Baughman, J. L. "Taps for Texas Lighthouses." *Houston Chronicle* (June 29, 1952), magazine section, pp. 6–7.

U.S. Department of the Treasury. Light-House Board. "Report of the Light-House Board, November 2, 1867." In U.S. Department of the Treasury, Secretary, *Report of the Secretary of the Treasury on the State of the Finances for the Year 1867,* pp. 194–239. Washington, D.C.: Government Printing Office, 1868.

Woodward, Earl F. "Internal Improvements in Texas in the Early 1850's." *Southwestern Historical Quarterly* 76, no. 2 (October, 1972): 161–82.

62. Medina Dam

The Medina Dam, the principal feature of the Medina Irrigation Project, was built between 1911 and 1912 to impound floodwaters on the upper Medina River west of San Antonio. On its completion it was acclaimed as the fourth-largest dam in the United States and the largest in Texas. The entire project, one of massive scale, was undertaken exclusively with private funds, all of which were raised by the promoter of the project, Dr. Fred Stark Pearson.

The idea of building a dam to store floodwaters on the Medina River for use in irrigation downstream was developed by Alexander Y. Walton as early as the mid-1890s. For a number of years he attempted to interest engineers and capitalists in the idea, but he failed until 1909. In that year, through the intermediary services of engineers living in San Antonio, Walton's concept attracted the attention of Dr. Fred Stark Pearson, an international builder of large dams and hydroelectric plants. At the time Pearson was engaged in a major project in Mexico, so on his travels

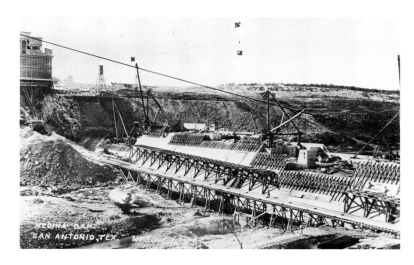

Construction of the Medina Dam during 1912. Photograph courtesy Texas State Library, Austin, Texas.

to that site he stopped off in Texas to investigate the potential on the Medina.

Pearson grew interested in the prospects of the Texas project, but before making any decisions he employed several engineering firms to conduct detailed examinations of the site, its geology, and the potential for irrigated agriculture proposed for an area about twenty-five miles to the south. Only after receiving favorable reports did he make the decision to undertake the effort and seek capital to finance it. Most of Pearson's backers were in England, so he went to them for support in the spring of 1910. Within a relatively short time he sold approximately six million dollars' worth of stock in the venture. As soon as the support was guaranteed, the Medina Irrigation Company formed under the laws of Texas to build and in time to operate the irrigation system. Its first effort, which took about a year, involved purchasing the lands of all the individuals whose properties would be inundated by the proposed reservoir, not to mention the acquisition of the lands to the south, which were to be irrigated.

In spring, 1911, actual work began at the site. The Medina Irrigation Company made an agreement with the Southern Pacific Railroad for the construction of a temporary nineteen-mile spur railway line from the nearest station, Dunlay, to the damsite. Meanwhile, work began on the building of a large construction camp to serve as a base of operations. The chief engineer for the irrigation company in 1912 described the camp as consisting of "ten or twelve small cottages for superintendent, engineer and general foreman, bunkhouses and ten houses for skilled labor and foremen, all of whom are white, together with the neces-

sary storerooms, machine shops, commissary, a well-equipped small hospital, etc." The camp also had its own artesian wells, a huge rock crusher, and even an electricity-generating plant. The engineer added that "the common laborers are all Mexicans, who are paid from $1.25 to $1.50 a day and furnished with shacks or tents. The average force . . . is about 2000 men." The laborers, many of whom were recruited in Mexico and brought their families with them, lived in an area west of the spillway and reached their temporary shelters by way of a bridge, the ruins of which are still visible in the spillway canyon.

The first actual work on the large concrete dam consisted of excavating its footings. The men dug down to solid rock in the area upon which the dam later was built. At the center they struck rock about twelve feet down, but they dug the sides as deep as twenty-five feet in places. At the bottom of the excavation, large holes were drilled into the solid rock, later to be plugged with concrete, to give the foundation a permanent anchor into the rock.

The first concrete was poured for the Medina Dam on November 10, 1911, beginning the major phase of work in the construction project. The effort continued, twenty hours a day, six days a week, for the next year. The last structural concrete was poured on or about November 24, 1912. The huge concrete job was done in a remarkably short one year's time.

The design was for a gravity dam 164 feet high with a vertical upstream face. It measures 128 feet wide at the riverbed and 25 feet wide at its top. The downstream face drops vertically 8 feet from the top and then curves to a plane surface with a 66 to 100 slope. The principal mass of the structure, between

Looking across the Medina Dam along its upstream face. Photograph by
the author, 1975.

600 and 700 feet long, lies within the walls of the
Medina River canyon, and the wings at each end extend back to form the total 1,580-foot length. The
spillway, located at the west end of the dam, is a natural limestone saddle. Excess water passes over this
spillway and then down a ravine to the natural riverbed
below the dam. The main reservoir, Medina Lake,
covers 5,575 acres when the water is at spillway level.
It is eighteen miles long and has a maximum width of
about three miles. The reservoir capacity is about
254,000 acre feet.

A number of smaller engineering works join with
the principal dam in forming the water system for the
Medina Irrigation Project. Four miles below the storage dam is a much smaller concrete arch gravity
diversion dam. Water released from the main dam is

diverted here into a main canal with a six-hundred-
second-foot capacity, which carries it twenty-four
miles to the areas to be irrigated toward the south.
The diversion dam, unlike the Medina Dam, is an
overflow structure with its entire crest serving as
spillway. It is 50 feet high, 44 feet wide at its base, and
440 feet long. To avoid costly excavations through
rock in rough country, the main canal below the diversion dam includes two reinforced-concrete inverted
siphons and several flumes in its route to the irrigated
farms.

As originally planned, the Medina Dam was to release waters to irrigate lands owned by the company
in Medina, Bexar, and Atascosa counties. The long-
range goals of the company included the establishment of towns, the sale of agricultural lands, and the

Detail of gate controls atop the Medina Dam. Photograph by the author, 1975.

continued sale of irrigation water to the buyers. The hopes of the promoters, however, were never fully met because of an unexpected series of unfortunate circumstances. The first major difficulty befalling the Medina Irrigation Company was a drought. Months passed after the completion of the project before there was sufficient rainfall in its watershed to impound even enough water to test the main canal, much less to irrigate. It was impossible to sell any of the agricultural lands until the reservoir had sufficient water to support irrigation on those lands. Consequently, the sale of farms was delayed until 1914. Then World War I broke out in Europe, complicating communications with the English backers of the project and impeding Pearson's access to British capital. In these circumstances the Medina Irrigation Company went into receivership. Believing that the finances of the project could be salvaged by a reorganization of the company, Pearson and his wife sailed for England aboard the *Lusitania*, in May, 1915. On the seventh of that month, a German submarine torpedoed the liner and sank it, with the loss of 1,195 lives, among them those of Dr. and Mrs. Pearson.

After Fred Pearson's death, federal bankruptcy courts greatly limited the activities of the Medina Irrigation Company. It was able to lease irrigated farms at five dollars per acre, but it could do little more. The English bondholders decided after the war that they would rather sell the project than reorganize it, but for years they received no reasonable offers. Finally in 1927 a firm known as San Antonio Suburban Irrigated Farms purchased the system, but in 1930 it too went into receivership. The holdings then were purchased by another company known as Medina Irrigated Farms, which operated the project until it passed into the possession of the Bexar-Medina-Atascosa Counties Water Improvement District No. 1, the present owner of the system. The entire Medina Irrigation Project continues to operate today, providing irrigation water to farms served by the dams and main canal built over seventy years ago.

Location: The Medina Dam, the key engineering work in the Medina Irrigation Project, forms Medina Lake on the upper Medina River, about 40 miles west of San Antonio. The most convenient access to the dam is via FM 471 north 14.9 miles from Castroville to its juncture with FM 1283. Turn northwest and proceed an additional 6.8 miles to an intersection with a graded county road. Turn southwest and drive about 2.5 miles via the graded road past the Mico community beside the lake to the dam itself. Visitors may walk across the 1,580-foot top of the dam, but vehicles are prohibited from its narrow roadway. The offices of the Bexar-Medina-Atascosa Counties Water Improvement District No. 1 are located at Natalia, named for Dr. Pearson's daughter Natalie.

Suggested Reading:

Kearney, C. H. "Construction Methods on the Medina Valley Irrigation Project, Texas." *Engineering Record* 66, no. 23 (December 7, 1912): 632–34.
Kuehne, Cyril Matthew. *Ripples from Medina Lake.* San Antonio, Tex.: Naylor Company, 1966.

63. Moore's Crossing Bridge

Serving the citizens of Travis County for over a century, the fine iron truss bridge that now spans Onion Creek at Moore's Crossing in the southern part of the county has origins that go back to Austin in the 1870s. The three overhead truss spans in this present-day structure constituted half of the superstructure forming a bridge erected across the Colorado River at the foot of Congress Avenue a century ago. In 1915, after the original bridge had been replaced with the current Congress Avenue Bridge, these three spans were simply moved to their current location and reerected.

As early as 1840, the year after its founding, Austin boasted ferries carrying traffic across the Colorado River, but it was not until the mid-1870s that any action was taken to erect a permanent bridge to take their place. On November 29, 1875, the Commissioners' Court of Travis County signed an agreement with C. Baker of Saint Joseph, Missouri, allowing him to erect a toll bridge across the river within three blocks of the foot of Congress Avenue. According to the agreement, still preserved in the county courthouse, Baker agreed to build "a good, & safe Bridge across the Colorado . . . and keep the same in constant repair for the space of ten years." In return the county commissioners granted him the right to operate the bridge as a money-making venture by charging tolls to travelers who crossed it.

Mr. Baker did not waste any time while he was securing permission to erect his bridge. Already he had started organizing the Travis County Road and Bridge Company, of which he was the principal stockholder, to undertake the construction and then operation of the bridge. On December 2, 1875, only three days after the commissioners granted Baker the right to build the bridge, the newly formed company filed with the county clerk a copy of its charter, another copy of which was filed the next day with the Texas secretary of state. Of 740 shares of capital stock in the company, C. Baker held 400.

Little immediate progress was made on the project. A dispute arose in 1876 between the bridge company and the heirs of James Gibson Swisher, who operated a ferry across the Colorado near the bridge site. The company wished the far end of its bridge to rest near the site of the ferry landing on property owned by the Swisher heirs. This family had resided in the Austin area since 1846, and James G. Swisher had been a signer of the Texas Declaration of Independence and had fought in the Texas Revolution. The family was very well known in the Austin area, and they certainly were not people who could be pushed around. Finally in early 1877 the Swisher heirs came to an agreement whereby they granted to the bridge company the right to place the south end of its projected structure on their property and agreed to cease operating the

Looking south across the 1880s Colorado River bridge from the toll house at the foot of Congress Avenue, about 1886. Photograph courtesy Texas State Historical Association, Austin, Texas.

The 1880s Colorado River bridge during the late nineteenth century, showing all six overhead truss spans and its five cut-stone piers. Photograph courtesy Austin–Travis County Collection, Austin Public Library, Austin, Texas.

ferry as soon as the bridge began carrying traffic. They also permitted the company to extend a road across their property southward to the road's crossing over Bouldin's Creek, where the firm was to erect a much smaller bridge.

With the question of the right-of-way settled, the Travis County Road and Bridge Company proceeded to erect its bridge across the Colorado. Its initial effort was the construction of a wooden bridge that lasted for only a few months. After the bridge opened, it was severely damaged by the destruction of most of its first span. Drovers had attempted to drive a herd of cattle across the wooden bridge, but the animals began milling around on the first span rather than proceeding across. Their weight was too great and caused the timbers beneath to give way. The beasts fell an estimated fifty feet to the water below, where most of them drowned. The wooden bridge closed, and the ferry returned to its normal activity of carrying people and vehicles across the Colorado.

After the disastrous failure of their wooden bridge, the board members of the Travis County Road and Bridge Company decided that they would have to replace it with a structure that the traveling public could trust. Consequently, they signed a contract with the King Bridge Company of Cleveland, Ohio, to build an iron truss bridge in place of the wooden failure. Crews from the bridge erection company appeared in 1882 and went to work on the foundations. They constructed substantial cut-stone abutments at each end of the proposed structure and erected a series of five stone piers an impressive 30 feet long by 12 feet wide. This stonework supported six pin-connected Pratt overhead truss spans, which had been fabricated by the contractors. Five of these spans measured 150 feet in length, and the one nearest to Congress Avenue was 160 feet long. Including gaps between the truss spans, the total length of the structure was 913 feet, 6 inches.

On January 22, 1884, the bridge opened to the toll-paying public. The toll schedule had been set by Travis County back in 1875, when it gave C. Baker the right to erect a bridge, and included the following rates:

loaded wagons drawn by six horses, mules, or oxen
$1.00

loaded wagons drawn by four horses, mules, or oxen .75

loaded wagons drawn by two horses, mules, or oxen .50

half of these fees for any of the above vehicles if empty

any vehicle drawn by one horse, mule, or ox .25

horsemen .10

footmen .05

loose horses, mules, or cattle per head .05

loose sheep, hogs, or goats per head .025

For almost three years the Travis County Road and Bridge Company operated its bridge across the Colorado River. In 1886, however, the county decided that it wanted to purchase the structure so it could function as a free public bridge. As part of the negotiations, the county and the bridge company employed Niles Meriwether, a civil engineer from Memphis, Tennessee, to inspect the bridge. His report, filed on June 13, 1886, discussed the bridge, its design, and its state of repair in a favorable light. He estimated that it would cost $73,120 to build an equivalent

Looking north across the three 1880s truss spans of the Moore's Crossing Bridge at roadway level. Photograph by the author, 1982.

bridge if the county decided to do so. Meriwether noted that the Congress Avenue bridge was of a type commonly used for highway and railway purposes and that the Austin structure was "one of the best examples I have seen built by the King Bridge Company."

The county commissioners offered the Travis County Road and Bridge Company seventy-three thousand dollars for the structure and agreed to assume payment on the balance of the bonds held by the King Bridge Company for money owed them on the construction project. By autumn, 1886, the county had consummated its purchase and had opened the bridge to the public, with William Turney appointed as bridge keeper. Among his responsibilities was the enforcement of a series of regulations concerning the bridge, which had been issued by the county commissioners. Among these rules promulgated on Decem-

ber 6, 1886, were the prohibition of riding across the bridge "at a gait faster than a walk," the restriction of herds of horses or cattle crossing the bridge to fifty or fewer, and the prohibition of any vehicle bearing any "flying banners, or anything else calculated to frighten animals or teams." The rules also prohibited sitting "upon the railing of the Bridge" or "loafing . . . upon the Bridge." For their efforts in supervising traffic across the structure, Turney and his successors were paid forty-five dollars per calendar month with no days off.

The county operated the Congress Avenue bridge until late 1891, when it turned the structure over to the City of Austin. The municipality had extended its boundary to include both ends of the bridge, and the county commissioners decided that the city should assume its maintenance. In reality, the county retained ownership of the structure, and the city shared its maintenance expenses. The old structure remained in service until 1910, when the present concrete bridge took its place.

In 1915 the county moved three of the 150-foot spans from the old bridge to Moore's Crossing over Onion Creek south of Austin. The Commissioners' Court received bids from five companies on the project to build a bridge across the lesser stream using spans from the former structure. As the low bidder, the Austin Brothers Bridge Company of Dallas, Texas, on July 28, 1915, received the contract at $4,600. Work began by late summer, but in mid-September the plans were changed. Instead of using just the three old overhead truss spans, the contractor and the Commissioners' Court jointly decided to increase the height of the concrete piers by three feet and to add an extra sixty-foot span at the north end of the bridge. The additional span, a Warren truss, cost the county only an extra $580, but the added concrete work brought the final expense up to $5,965.50.

Only a few months passed before the Moore's Crossing Bridge was destroyed by flood. All three of its main spans were washed downstream. The three remaining spans from the 1880s Colorado River bridge were moved from Austin to the site on Onion Creek and placed on higher concrete piers. The flood-damaged sixty-foot span at the north end of the bridge was replaced with the current eighty-two-foot Warren truss span. Since that time the bridge has carried rural traffic over Onion Creek.

In 1886 engineer Niles Meriwether wrote of the iron truss bridge: "If kept well painted . . . [and] the flooring and joists renewed . . . I know of no reason why this bridge may not be of service for years and years." He could have had no idea that the structure would serve the taxpayers of Travis County so well, for the three old iron trusses remain in use to this day—one of the most remarkable of all the survivors from the Austin of a century ago.

Location: The Moore's Crossing Bridge spans Onion Creek just to the south of Bergstrom Air Force Base in southern Travis County. It may be reached by taking a graded county road a short distance west from the Michalk Store on FM 973 at a point 3.1 miles south of its intersection with State Highway 71.

Suggested Reading:

"Colorado River Bridges" vertical file. Austin–Travis County Collection, Austin Public Library, Austin, Tex.

Travis County, Tex. Commissioners' Court. Minutes, vol. C, p. 292; vol. E, pp. 368–69, 379–406, 440–41; vol. F, pp. 393–94, 620; vol. M, pp. 473, 488–91, 526, 583. Office of County Clerk, Travis County Courthouse, Austin, Tex.

64. Nash Iron Furnace

The Nash Iron Furnace operated in present-day Marion County from 1847 into the 1860s. The pioneer venture has the distinction of having been the first iron furnace in Texas.

Jefferson S. Nash, a native of Georgia, came to Texas by way of Tennessee in the 1840s. He is known to have been a settled planter in Cass County as early as 1846, and it was there that he became enthusiastic about the possibilities of smelting iron from the ores of northeast Texas. The ores in the region are mostly hematite and limonite. These mineral resources were supplemented at the time by large stands of hardwood trees that were appropriate for the production of charcoal, the favored fuel of the day for small iron-smelting works. Nash, as well as others, became convinced that great fortunes could be made by exploiting the resources at hand to produce iron, which

could compete in the marketplace with that brought into the state from other parts of the country.

Being a prudent man, Jefferson Nash set about first to test the iron resources before investing in expensive smelting equipment. He took specimens of ore from the area where he proposed erecting a furnace and fired them in a brick kiln. The resulting product was a mass of iron heavily impregnated with carbon and other impurities, but experimentation indicated that most of these substances could be removed by hammering the metal as it cooled. He showed the iron to his neighbors and friends, and they pronounced the examples to be of excellent quality. Next he took specimens of the iron to local blacksmiths for their opinions. One of these men, John W. West, a well-known smith in Clarksville, made a nail from Nash's sample, bent it into a fishhook shape, and

Looking east into the depression that marks the actual furnace site at the Nash Iron Furnace. Photograph by the author, 1975.

then straightened it. He repeated the process through twenty bends without breaking it. West considered this test to be conclusive, and he declared Nash's product as good as any he had ever seen. As a final trial, Nash sent samples of his iron to Tennessee for further analysis and tests, all of which proved to be favorable.

Convinced that he could smelt good-quality iron, in 1847 Nash commenced building a furnace a few feet above the waters of a tributary to Alley's Creek, which flowed into Big Cypress Creek about sixteen miles west of Jefferson. (This area at the time was in Cass County, but it became part of Marion County when the latter was organized in 1860.) Behind the furnace site was a higher rocky ridge, which provided a track for animal-drawn vehicles to carry both ore and fuel to the projected works.

Although no complete description of the Nash Iron Furnace is known, it is possible from information available to sketch a comparatively accurate picture of what it must have been like. Built of masonry, the furnace had a square or rectangular base fitted with a depression into which the molten iron flowed. The furnace walls were built upward from this floor, gradually tapering to form a chimney. The area between the floor and chimney, called the bosh, formed a combustion chamber. Near the base of the walls and leading into the bosh were a series of holes through which air was forced to increase the heat of the burning fuel.

In the vicinity of the furnace, Nash and his men produced their own charcoal as fuel. They cut timbers, transported them to the furnace area, and placed them in layers on the ground. After the wood was ignited they covered it with soil to smother the flames but allow combustion to take place to convert the wood into charcoal. Usually about 150 bushels of charcoal were needed to smelt one ton of iron ore, so the production of charcoal clearly must have been one of the major operations at the furnace.

It is not known whether Nash used lime in his early operations, but in time he did begin adding it to his ore before smelting. Its use eliminated the need to hammer the metal as it cooled to remove impurities. When lime was used, it was added in the ratio of one part lime to ten parts ore. Nash's favorite ore, the one he used exclusively, was a form of hematite known locally as "honeycomb." Its supply in the area seemed to be inexhaustible.

Nash's plans were not only to smelt iron but also to build a foundry where he might produce useful and saleable iron articles. For his first years, however, he was forced to be satisfied with merely producing bar iron, which he sold mainly to blacksmiths as raw material for their work. His nearest market was Jefferson, sixteen miles away over unimproved roads. Because of the cost of freight to Jefferson and then the added costs for steamboat shipment beyond there, Nash's market remained local.

Realizing that one of his problems was lack of knowledge and skill in iron production, Jefferson Nash in 1857 brought into his business enterprise one David Browder. The latter had experience in the iron industry in the eastern states, and his expertise added much to the operation of the Texas furnace. With Browder's entry into the business, it was organized as J. S. Nash and Company. For years Nash attempted to secure state support for his venture, which

he saw as an infant industry that in time could produce great wealth for the state, but it appears he never received government aid in any form.

Through the 1850s a steady if small supply of bar iron continued to leave the Nash Iron Furnace. Local users were enthusiastic about the quality of the product, but the enterprise remained hampered by lack of capital, lack of sufficient equipment, and difficulties in transportation. The firm went through several reorganizations as Nash attempted to secure more capital to invest in the operation. In 1858 it became the Nash Iron, Steel and Copper Manufacturing Company, and in 1863, the Texas Iron Company. In 1858 David Browder made a return trip to the eastern states to promote Texas iron and to seek capital for expanding the business, but he returned with only promises of support that never materialized. At least some funds must have been raised, however, for in 1859 the operation was expanded to begin at least a small level of foundry work producing cast-iron articles. By early 1860 the company boasted of producing goods ranging from stoves to wagon boxes, all of them "as neat and durable" as the same articles produced at any other foundry in the country.

The Civil War changed economic conditions in Texas almost overnight. When the conflict began, business deteriorated rapidly. Loyal to the Southern cause, Jefferson Nash and his partners offered to put their foundry at the disposal of the war effort. Even though the Confederacy had a great demand for iron, the Nash foundry was so isolated in northeast Texas that its small production could contribute little. It is known to have produced only a few cannonballs. As

Detail of the material composing a heap of slag adjacent to the site of the Nash Iron Furnace. Photograph by the author, 1975.

the war progressed and the Texas economy deteriorated even further, Nash and his backers were forced to sell their plant. Toward the end of the war, the company sold its entire holdings, which included "a large amount of pig iron," to the George A. Kelly Iron Company. The new owners dismantled the old smelting and foundry equipment and moved it by ox wagon to a new site, Kellyville, about four miles west of Jefferson. This second-hand equipment served as the real beginning for the Kelly Plow Works, which after the war grew to become the first and only full-line agricultural implement factory in Texas (see entry no. 54). The site of the abandoned Nash Iron Furnace was left to deteriorate into ruins, a grim monument of the first effort to smelt iron in Texas.

Location: The site of the Nash Iron Furnace is located a few hundred feet east of FM 729, about three-quarters of a mile southeast of the Rock Island community in western Marion County. The ruins of the furnace and foundry are on private property and not accessible to the public.

Suggested Reading:

Jones, Robert L. "The First Iron Furnace in Texas." *Southwestern Historical Quarterly* 63, no. 2 (October, 1959): 279–89.
Kennedy, W. "Iron Ores of East Texas." *Transactions of the American Institute of Mining Engineers* 24 (February, 1894): 258–88.

65. Nueces Bay Causeways

A series of four bridges erected in 1916, 1921, 1950, and 1963, the Nueces Bay Causeways for seventy-five years have provided a link between Corpus Christi across Nueces Bay and the developed agricultural area and seacoast resorts of San Patricio County. The earlier highway bridges across the entrance to the bay, though mostly forgotten, were once well-known engineering works and were instrumental in promoting the economic development of both Corpus Christi and the area above it on the Gulf Coast.

The first highway bridge spanning the entrance to Nueces Bay was a county-built structure erected between 1915 and 1916. In 1914 the voters of Nueces County authorized the sale of $165,000 in county bonds to fund the construction of this "permanent" bridge across the shallow water to San Patricio County.

The design of the 1916 Nueces Bay Causeway was striking. Although structurally the bridge consisted of twenty-five hundred feet of ordinary reinforced-concrete girder spans, it had the appearance of a concrete arch bridge because the spans on the outer sides of the bridge were designed with elliptical profiles, which made them seem to be long, graceful arches. Structurally, the spans on the 1916 bridge consisted of four reinforced-concrete girders thirty-two feet, six inches long, center to center. The piers supporting the girders were composed of creosoted timber pilings driven into the bottom of the shallow bay over which concrete caps two feet, six inches wide were poured. These caps extended to the bottom of the bay. The pilings, varying in length to a maximum of fifty-

five feet, were driven by a sixty-eight-hundred-pound gravity-drop pile-driving hammer. The forms for pouring the concrete girders were carried without the use of falsework on eight thirty-two-foot-long wooden timbers, which rested on the completed concrete-capped piers while the girders were poured. The forms for the girders were made from dressed lumber and were assembled in position on the thirty-two-foot wooden timbers. After each series of girders was poured, the timbers were simply moved to the next pier and work was begun there.

Near the Corpus Christi end of the causeway, where the water at the time was the deepest and to conform with U.S. Army Corps of Engineers requirements, the county erected a bascule draw-span. It was fabricated by the Phoenix Bridge Company of Phoenixville, Pennsylvania, and assembled on the spot. It provided a working horizontal clearance of thirty-two feet to permit the passage of barges and fishing boats through the bridge from Nueces Bay into the much larger Corpus Christi Bay.

The 1916 causeway had extensive approaches at its northeast end. From Indian Point near Portland, the county constructed a six-thousand-foot oystershell approach. The source of the dredged shell material was the bay area in the immediate vicinity of the bridge. To secure the toe of the approach from erosion, the builders placed in position both stone riprap and brush faggots made of mesquite branches. A two-hundred-foot approach of similar design was constructed at the southwest end of the bridge.

Surviving concrete-capped pilings of the 1916 causeway, seen from the area of the long-removed bascule draw-span at its west end. Photograph by the author, 1975.

The concrete causeway across Nueces Bay served the residents of Nueces and San Patricio counties for only three years. It was destroyed by a storm in the summer of 1919, only its bascule draw-span surviving in usable condition. The long oystershell approaches simply washed away, and the concrete spans were battered by debris thrown about by the storm. A temporary wooden causeway was built, but it was far from satisfactory for heavy use.

Efforts began almost immediately to raise money for the construction of a truly permanent bridge to replace the destroyed 1916 causeway. In May, 1920, the Nueces County Commissioners' Court decided that it would undertake the reconstruction and proposed that the entire structure be built from wooden timbers. While the commissioners were making their plans, the State Highway Commission entered the picture. A Highway Commission engineer suggested that the county officials investigate the possibility of

securing both state and federal assistance in their proposed effort. In time, funds from both of these sources became available, resulting in a joint effort of the three governmental entities in building the new bridge.

With some revision in plans, the new causeway design by late 1920 called for a structure 8,156 feet long. The draw span from the 1916 bridge was to be removed and reused. Delays at the U.S. Bureau of Roads postponed the initiation of construction, but in January, 1921, the bids finally were opened for the project. The Austin Brothers Bridge Company of Dallas, Texas, received the contract. The firm began work on April 1, 1921, completing the structure on September 15 of the same year. The causeway was opened to the public on October 1.

The 1921 Nueces Bay Causeway remained in use for the next thirty years, although it was heavily damaged by a tropical storm in the early 1930s and re-

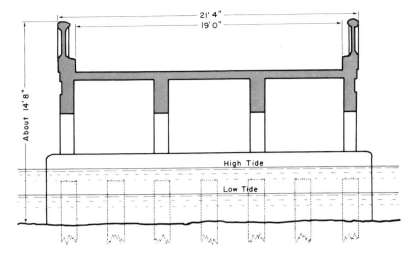

Section of the 1916 causeway showing its pilings, concrete cap, concrete girder spans, and roadway. Based on Terrell Bartlett, "Corpus Christi Causeway Contains 2300 Feet of Reinforced-Concrete Girder Spans," *Engineering Record* 73, no. 12 (March 18, 1916): 390–92. Drawing by the author.

constructed. In 1948 the state opened bids for the construction of a completely new concrete causeway to replace the older structure. This new bridge was built in 1950, and the old structure was removed. In 1963 another new concrete causeway was built parallel to the 1950 bridge, giving motorists two lanes of traffic in each direction across the bay.

Location: Although the old 1916 and 1921 Nueces Bay Causeways have been gone for many years, their remains still may be seen. The former bridges stood parallel to and just east of today's modern concrete causeways. At the northeast end of the present causeways one can see the much-eroded concrete and tops of creosoted timber pilings from the abutment of the

1916 bridge. At the other side of the entrance to the bay, more can be found. There one can examine not only the abutment for the bascule span from the 1921 bridge, but also the long line of concrete-capped pilings extending out into the water, which served as the piers for the 1916 causeway.

Suggested Reading:

Bartlett, Terrell. "Corpus Christi Causeway Contains 2300 Feet of Reinforced-Concrete Girder Spans." *Engineering Record* 73, no. 12 (March 18, 1916): 390–92.
Wolffarth, Louise. "The Transportation Problem of Corpus Christi, Texas." M.A. thesis, Texas Technological College, 1939.

66. *Oil Springs Oil Field*

The Oil Springs Oil Field, opened in 1866 by Lyne Taliaferro Barret, was the site of the first successful oil well in the state of Texas. Remarkably, oil production continues in the area, 120 years after Barret's initial discovery.

Lyne Barret, driller of the first oil well in Texas, was a native of Appomattox County, Virginia. He migrated as a child in 1842 to Texas, when it was still a republic. His home was located about 6.5 miles "as the crow flies" north of the geographical feature known as the Oil Springs, near the Melrose community in Nacogdoches County. Located on the route of the old Camino Real, the springs had been used by Spanish and later Anglo residents of the area for over half a century. These pioneer settlers trekked to Oil

Springs to gather natural petroleum from the surface of the water to use for greasing the axles on their carts and wagons, for softening leather, and for medicinal purposes. They used long poles to stir the pools of water, causing the petroleum to rise to the surface. They then skimmed it off and placed it in handmade wooden containers to carry it away.

The legends and tales of the early use of the petroleum from Oil Springs intrigued Lyne Barret, so in 1859 he leased 279 acres around the springs. He realized that the petroleum must have commercial value. His plan was to bore into the ground for oil in hopes of securing more of the valuable liquid than could be gathered just by skimming it from the top of the spring water. Fate intervened, however, with the outbreak of the Civil War, which postponed his efforts for five years.

After the close of the war, Barret returned to his home in Nacogdoches County and to his planned experiment in boring for oil. He secured a second lease on the property around the springs and formed a corporation to back his search for petroleum. On October 9, 1865, with three partners he formed the Melrose Petroleum Oil Company. While two of his partners went to New York and Pennsylvania to seek additional financial support, Barret, still in Texas, spent the winter of 1865–66 gathering equipment and supplies for the actual drilling effort.

He hired a young man, Bunch Hardeman (who later became a pioneer driller in other fields), to be his assistant in boring the projected well at Oil Springs. In drilling their well, Barret and Hardeman employed principles that today are embodied in modern rotary well drilling techniques. Over the well site they erected a large wooden tripod. It supported an eight-inch-diameter iron auger. Beside the auger and tripod they installed a steam boiler and engine, which they connected by means of a shaft to a cog-type drive mechanism clamped to the auger. With the drilling mechanism engaged, the auger bit down into the earth to excavate a hole. As the auger churned its way downward, joints of pipe were attached to it when it became necessary to extend its shank. The entire assembly was withdrawn from the ground by the following means. A rope was attached to the top joint of pipe, passed through a pulley fastened to the tripod top, and then tied to the harness of a mule. A workman then led the mule away from the well, in the process extracting the auger and joints of pipe.

Barret, Hardeman, and their men drilled over 100 feet into the ground. The work became more difficult with every foot. They may have started to wonder if they would encounter anything but East Texas soil. Then at 106 feet, as Barret himself later recalled, "the auger dropped through a vein six inches deep, when oil, water, and gas gushed to the top of the well." The men drew the auger to the surface, finding the "earth adhering to the auger perfectly saturated with oil." Within only a few minutes they saw "pure oil several inches deep" flowing from the hole they had excavated. Barret estimated the flow at ten barrels a day. The crew then cased the well and capped it to control its flow, all of them feeling that they had found the oil that would make their fortunes.

The completion of the Barret well at Oil Springs

Lyne T. Barret, driller of the first oil well in Texas. Photograph courtesy Special Collections, Ralph W. Steen Library, Stephen F. Austin State University, Nacogdoches, Texas.

occurred sometime in the late summer or early autumn of 1866. By late October Lyne Barret himself was on his way to Pennsylvania to secure financial backing for the development of the petroleum resources he had found. At Titusville he made a contract with the Brown brothers, well-established Pennsylvania oilmen, for them to develop the Oil Springs field. They agreed to send five thousand dollars' worth of equipment under the supervision of engineer John F. Carll to begin drilling in Nacogdoches County. Together Barret and Carll traveled back to Texas. They began drilling a second well, but not at Oil Springs. Instead, they worked at a site about a mile west of Melrose, over six miles away from the proved oil resources at Oil Springs. They reached a depth of about eighty feet, but found no petroleum.

By this time the Brown brothers had reconsidered their investment in Texas. At the time the state was under its Reconstruction government and was still occupied by Union troops. Barret and the other land-poor Texan backers of the Oil Springs project had only land with which to pay for operating expenses.

The remains of a cypress oil well casing still preserved at Oil Springs. Photograph by the author, 1981.

The Brown brothers in distant Pennsylvania could not have cared less about the seemingly worthless lands in faraway Texas. Furthermore, by 1866 oil production in Pennsylvania had reached three million barrels annually, glutting the market and driving the prices down to $1.35 a barrel. The oil country began suffering the effects of a regional depression. On the Brown brothers' orders, John Carll packed up his equipment and returned to the North. The disappointed Barret continued trying to convince Pennsylvania investors to take Texas land certificates in exchange for their machinery and services, but it was to no avail. No one was interested.

Ironically, Barret lived to see an oil boom in the area where he first successfully searched for petroleum. About 1886 a geologist named B. F. Hitchcock decided that it might be economically feasible to drill for oil in the area of Barret's discovery. Accordingly,

he, E. H. Farrar, and two New Orleans backers formed the Petroleum Prospecting Company. In 1886 they employed five experienced drillers from Pennsylvania and transported them and a cable-tool drilling rig to Oil Springs. There they drilled an initial well, completed at a depth of seventy feet, which came in with a reported flow of 250 to 300 barrels of oil per day. Oral tradition maintains that Hitchcock immediately left for Nacogdoches to report the discovery to the outside world. To reach the telegraph office before it closed, he rode his horse so hard that it fell exhausted just as he reached town. The drillers were totally unprepared for large flow, and they had no tanks or reservoirs to contain it. Soon these were built to store the flow from this and later wells. By 1889 over forty successful wells had been drilled in the field.

At the site of the new discoveries a boomtown called Oil City sprang to life. In its heyday it had a dozen stores, seventy-five houses, a barrel factory, a large boardinghouse, and a saloon, not to mention scores of tents and derricks everywhere. In time the field contained over a hundred producing wells, and Oil City became a very busy place that employed over 150 men. It was during this time that H. H. Sawyer, a civil engineer and graduate of Harvard, built the first pipeline in Texas. Made from three-inch pipe, it stretched a distance of about 14.5 miles from Oil Springs to a two-thousand-barrel tank located in Nacogdoches. From there the petroleum was shipped by rail. The pipeline was too small for the thick oil it was meant to transport, so during the winter months it sometimes became necessary to make pine-knot fires along the line to heat the oil enough to cause it to flow.

Another significant "first" at Oil Springs was the construction of the first steel tanks in Texas for the storage of oil. They were built in 1889 to replace some older wooden tanks, and they are still preserved at the site.

The 1880s Oil Springs boom lasted until the production of the wells began to lag. By 1890 Oil City was declining. Most of the oilmen, who had come to Texas from Pennsylvania, had moved on to more promising areas. The pipeline, less than two years old, was taken up and sections of it later used as distribution mains for the Nacogdoches water system. A decline in production in Pennsylvania in 1887 and 1888 undoubtedly contributed to the temporary boom in Texas, but with increased production in the "real" oil country of Pennsylvania and recognition of the limited resources actually available in Nacogdoches County, the new Texas field was mostly forgotten.

Location: Oil Springs is located in southern Nacogdoches County. Access to the site is via a graded county road 3.7 miles northeast of a turn-off on FM 226 between Woden and Etoile. The turning point, marked by a sign, is located 4.8 miles south of Woden and 6.5 miles northwest of the intersection with State Highway 103 in the Etoile community. At the site is a park containing the actual Oil Springs, which continue flowing crystal-clear water. There are historical markers; the two 1889 steel oil-storage tanks, the oldest in Texas; and a number of wellheads protruding from the ground, the remains of century-old oil wells. In some instances, petroleum still oozes to the surface from the wrought-iron and cypress casings.

Petroleum still oozing to the surface from a decades-old wrought-iron oil well casing at Oil Springs. Photograph by the author, 1981.

Most visitors are amazed to see continuing production from some of the old wells in the immediate Oil Springs vicinity. Here local oil producers still operate small pumps over some of the shallow wells, some of them almost a hundred years old.

Suggested Reading:

Ericson, Linda. "A History of Oil Springs: Texas' First Oil Field." *Texas Historian* 32, no. 3 (January, 1972): 2–9.
Tolbert, Frank X. *The Story of Lyne Taliaferro (Tol) Barret Who Drilled Texas' First Oil Well.* Dallas: Texas Mid-Continent Oil & Gas Association, 1966.

67. Old Alcalde Iron Furnace

Born of a belief that the state penitentiary system should pay its own operating expenses, the Old Alcalde Iron Furnace at Rusk paved the way for the development of large-scale iron production in East Texas.

During the Reconstruction period that followed the Civil War, chaos in state administration resulted in the entire state penal system's being placed in the hands of private contractors. Having no funds available to operate the prison, the legislature in 1871 passed an act that allowed the system to be leased to private individuals. These lessees agreed to provide for the material needs of the prisoners and obligated themselves to maintain control of them; in turn, the businessmen were permitted to use the prisoners as laborers. For well over a decade the lease system functioned, resulting in the most unsatisfactory period of penitentiary management in the history of the state. Because of the flagrant abuses that took place, on May 15, 1883, the legislature revoked the agreements with the lessees and resumed managing the state penal system.

As early as 1875 a prison to serve East Texas had been established at Rusk, but it was not completed until 1883. One reason for choosing the site at Rusk was the proximity of vast reserves of iron ore coupled with forest resources, which might provide charcoal as fuel for smelting the ore. At the suggestion of Gov. Oran M. Roberts, who was known popularly by the nickname "Old Alcalde," the State Penitentiary Board constructed an iron furnace at the Rusk prison. Its purpose was twofold: to demonstrate the potential for iron production in Texas and to function as a money-making venture for the penitentiary to reduce its drain on the state treasury. The new furnace, built between 1883 and 1884 under the supervision of R. A. Barrett of Saint Louis, was named the Old Alcalde in honor of Governor Roberts.

The state facility, which stood outside the prison walls, had a blast furnace with a six-foot, six-inch internal diameter, a nine-foot, six-inch bosh, a four-foot, ten-inch crucible, and a smokestack sixty-seven feet tall. Initially, private contractors operated the furnace using the local ore, but their management proved to be a disappointment. Due to their inexperience in smelting, they failed to secure the metal they expected, declaring that "to make iron from this ore is an impossibility." After the expenditure of considerable state funds, however, the assistant superintendent of penitentiaries in charge at Rusk decided to give the furnace a second try.

In June, 1885, he hired John Birkenbine, an iron

Looking east toward the site of the Old Alcalde Iron Furnace, now a shaded park area in front of the Rusk State Hospital. Photograph by the author, 1975.

authority from Philadelphia, to visit Rusk and examine the furnace. Contrary to the opinions of the unsuccessful contractors, Birkenbine reported that the Old Alcalde was "a furnace plant better equipped than a majority of the charcoal furnaces in the United States" and that "the ore supply appears to be sufficiently abundant for the requirements of the present and near future, and, as indicated by analysis made, will give you an ore richer than the average ores throughout the United States." He noted that there were good facilities for producing charcoal cheaply from the wood of nearby forests, but added that the lack of a standard-gauge railway and the relative distance of good limestone for flux could impede the development of the enterprise.

After receiving Birkenbine's favorable report, the Penitentiary Board employed R. A. Barrett, who had overseen the construction of the furnace, to supervise its operation. He ran an experimental test of the Old Alcalde from November 30, 1885, to January 10, 1886. The results suggested that the most important problem in the previous contractors' efforts had been their own inability. In a run that seldom amounted to less than twenty-five tons of pig iron a day, he produced 1,044 tons in all. From this initial test run, Barrett sent specimens of the Texas iron to a number of potential customers for their examination. A representative of the Johnson Iron Works in New Orleans sent Barrett a typical response: "The sample of pig iron sent us has been used up in the manufacture of machine castings. The iron is of excellent quality, and runs well in the mould. We would have no hesitation in using this grade of iron for any class of our work."

The fuel for the Old Alcalde was charcoal. To ensure a steady supply, the State Penitentiary Board over the next decade purchased thousands of acres of East Texas forest land within about twenty miles of Rusk. Outlying camps of convicts were established at which two hundred or more men were housed to cut timbers and then burn them in special ovens to produce charcoal. This fuel then was transported to the furnace first in wagons and after 1896 in railroad cars of the Texas State Railway. Iron ore was strip-mined a comparatively short distance from the prison and hauled to the furnace in wagons. When the roads were not muddy, six wagons, each with a driver and four mules, could transport about seventy-two tons of iron ore daily. During the 1888–90 legislature biennium, a tram railway replaced the teams and wagons for ore movement. Steel rails laid on wooden ties led from

the ore bodies to the furnace. Prisoners loaded the ore onto railway cars that then were allowed to roll downhill to the smelting works. After being unloaded, the empty cars were pulled back to the ore deposits by teams of mules.

The first major contract for the Old Alcalde Furnace was to supply iron castings needed in the construction of the new state capitol. The Penitentiary Board made a contract with the builders of the structure to provide a large amount of the ironwork required. The contract included principally columns with their pedestals, caps, and bases, as well as the castings required to support the metal dome atop the building. The board signed the contract on October 26, 1885, and the work was completed and the last castings delivered to Austin in February, 1887. This initial large job for the Old Alcalde not only provided a commercial outlet for its products, but also presented an opportunity to display its work as an advertisement both for the state and for the prison industries.

In addition to producing pig iron and providing custom foundry work, the Old Alcalde supplied the raw materials for a pipe foundry constructed adjacent to the blast furnace. In 1885 Birkenbine had recommended the addition of a pipe foundry because of a growing demand for this commodity in Texas and because the nearest foundries producing any appreciable amounts of iron pipe were located no nearer than Birmingham, Alabama, and Saint Louis, Missouri. Special equipment for the pipe foundry began arriving in Rusk in the fall of 1886, with the new facility beginning operation in early 1887. The pipe foundry was ready to begin consuming iron from the furnace as soon as the capitol contract was completed. During the next twenty months the foundry produced approximately 2,070 tons of water pipe. It operated until the furnace closed two decades later. The pipe foundry was situated so that it could use molten iron directly from the blast furnace, thus reducing the expense that otherwise would be incurred to remelt the pig iron to mold the pipe.

During the decade of the 1890s an additional foundry inside the walls of the Rusk Penitentiary utilized pig iron produced by the Old Alcalde Furnace to manufacture a wide range of iron goods. Some of these were made solely for penitentiary use, and others were sold commercially. Among these products were heating stoves, ranges, sadirons, thimble skeins and boxes for wagons, cane mills, grates, flywheels, window-sash weights, pulleys, railway car castings, and a wide variety of hollowware. Examples of these castings still may be seen in the area around Rusk.

As the years passed, the Old Alcalde Furnace faced increasingly stiff competition from furnaces in other parts of the United States because of the increasing use elsewhere of coke as fuel in iron production. This more efficient fuel lowered the cost of production for many furnaces, but the cost of smelting iron using charcoal at Rusk remained about the same. During the 1890s the least-fit convicts often were assigned to furnace duties, with the more able-bodied prisoners being used as farm laborers, employment that gave the penitentiary system greater revenues. The cumbersome bureaucratic system within which the furnace managers operated also handicapped their efforts to make the enterprise succeed. By 1902 the financial agent for the penitentiary system recommended abandoning the Old Alcalde as an unprofitable venture, but the state legislature disagreed. It appropriated $150,000 for the expansion of the furnace and for the purchase of new timber lands. As part of this program the Old Alcalde was torn down in 1904 and replaced with a more efficient furnace with a rated capacity of fifty tons of pig iron daily. This new furnace operated only until 1909. Its closing ended the state's effort in convict production of iron. Far from being a failure, the Rusk experiment had introduced large-scale iron smelting to East Texas, where it continues.

Location: The site of the Old Alcalde Furnace today is a shaded park area in front of the Rusk State Hospital on the northwest side of the town of Rusk. The Texas State Railway, begun in 1896 to haul charcoal to the furnace and later expanded to become a common carrier, now operates as a functioning historic steam railroad running between Rusk and Palestine under the management of the Texas Parks and Wildlife Department.

Suggested Reading:

Fred A. Jones Company, Dallas, Tex. "Engineers' Report on Rusk Penitentiary." Typescript. 1908. Records of the State Penitentiary (4-8/705), Texas State Archives, Austin, Tex.

Texas. Penitentiary Board. *Reports of the Superintendent and Financial Agent.* Austin, Tex.: State Printer, 1886–1905.

68. Old Lone Star Brewery

Erected in stages between 1883 and 1904, the Old Lone Star Brewery is in fact a complex of industrial buildings. The structures housed a major brewery until the advent of Prohibition in 1919, after which they were used for a variety of purposes. Today they serve as the galleries and work areas of the San Antonio Museum of Art.

The Old Lone Star Brewery had its beginnings in 1883, when two San Antonio businessmen, John Henry Kampmann and Edward Hoppe, joined forces to create a stock company to erect a brewery. Their firm, the Lone Star Brewing Company, officially began commercial beer production in September, 1884. They built their brewery on a tract located on the San Antonio River upstream from the downtown business district and conveniently near the tracks of the Southern Pacific Railway. The facility included not only the brewery itself but also coopers' shops, a bottling works, and its own ice plant.

The ties of the Lone Star Brewing Company to the brewing empire of Adolphus Busch of Saint Louis were strong. Mr. Busch was one of the major stockholders in the Texas company and for several years served as its president. The San Antonio facility was the first outside Saint Louis in which he had any large investment. Because of the link with the Busch enterprises, the brewery buildings were designed by the Saint Louis architectural firm of E. Jungenfeld and Company, with the San Antonio architects James Wahrenberger and Albert Felix Beckman employed as "superintending architects." The collaboration between the Saint Louis and San Antonio architects was successful, for the complex grew smoothly through the years, section by section, in an expansion and rehousing of the thriving business.

From the outset, the Lone Star Brewing Company seems to have been a commercial success. An article in the December, 1900, *Texas Liquor Dealer* lauded the operation, which at the time had a capacity for over 250,000 barrels annually. This made it the largest brewery in the entire state. The article reported that the Lone Star Brewery was unable to meet

The Old Lone Star Brewery complex after restoration and conversion to the San Antonio Museum of Art. Photograph courtesy San Antonio Museum Association, San Antonio, Texas.

the demand for its products, and that, consequently, the company was planning to expand its brewing capacity through a major building project.

During the summer of 1900, the expansion project began. Over the next four years many of the original wooden buildings were removed to make way for fireproof pressed-brick structures. Covering an area of ten acres, no effort was spared in making the new brewery not only efficient but also attractive.

As it operated after the completion of the major expansion in 1904, the Old Lone Star Brewery consisted of a number of brick buildings of various sizes and heights, which retained an architectural unity of form and materials. The main plant consisted of five massive brick sections, which varied from two to five stories tall, each with its own roof line. Among the structures composing the complex were the main building, an icehouse, stables, engine and boiler house, bottling works, washhouse, and general offices. Each building provided its own specific needs and was located according to the demands of brewing

technology at the turn of the century. The massive brick walls of the buildings are strengthened by interior iron structural members, and the floors of concrete, brick, and tile ensure fireproof construction. From a distance the plant appears to be a single building made up of semi-independent parts, but on closer inspection the separate buildings become apparent.

The brewery continued operating until the beginning of national Prohibition in 1919. Its owners then shifted production to a short-lived nonalcoholic drink called Tango, but it proved unsuccessful. By 1921 the Lone Star Brewing Company had become the Lone Star Cotton Mills, but entered into receivership within about a year. By 1924 the former brewery complex was occupied by the Lone Star Ice Company, which maintained operations in at least some of the structures as the Lone Star Ice Food Stores until the early 1970s.

Ownership of the brewery complex passed to the San Antonio Museum Association in 1971. Six years later a major renovation of the buildings began, converting the old industrial facility into a new San Antonio Museum of Art, which opened to the public in 1981. Comparatively few changes were needed to convert the industrial structures into an art gallery. Glass-walled elevators were installed in the two towers of the complex, and a new pedestrian walkway was built to link these two exhibit areas. Additional changes included the addition of foyer skylights and a rooftop restaurant. The exterior was changed relatively little, with the exception of the bricking up of some windows and the installation of larger panes of glass, instead of the original, smaller-pane wood-sash windows, in others. Despite these alterations, the structural integrity of the former brewery has been maintained. Today the old complex houses public exhibits of eighteenth- to twentieth-century American paintings as well as pre-Columbian and American Indian art, not to mention a fine collection of Texas decorative arts and furniture.

Location: Known today as the San Antonio Museum of Art, the Old Lone Star Brewery is open to the public daily with a small admission fee at 200 West Jones Avenue in San Antonio. It should not be confused with the present-day Lone Star Brewery at 600 Lone Star Boulevard, which is connected to the old brewery in name only.

Suggested Reading:

"Look What's Brewing in San Antonio." *Historic Preservation* 24, no. 5 (September/October, 1982): 32–35.
U.S. Department of the Interior. National Park Service. National Register of Historic Places. Nomination forms for Old Lone Star Brewery. Typescript. 1972 and 1979. Office of Archeology and Historic Preservation, National Park Service, Department of the Interior, Washington, D.C.

69. Orange–Port Arthur High Bridge

For decades a ferry provided the only vehicular crossing over the Neches River between Orange and Port Arthur. Finally, in 1936 the Texas Highway Department began erecting a major bridge twenty stories tall and 1.5 miles long to provide this needed link. Completed in 1938, the structure was acclaimed as the highest highway bridge in the entire South.

The Neches River near its mouth at Sabine Lake passes through several miles of boggy salt marsh. At one time, this area formed part of a much larger Sabine Lake, but by the twentieth century it had become a bed of soft, wet muck about thirty-five feet deep. Though the marsh was topped by a thin mat of vegetable matter about a foot or two above the level of the water in the river, it was too soft to support any appreciable load. It certainly could not hold up heavy construction equipment. This situation posed difficult problems for the engineers planning the construction of a bridge across the river and adjacent marsh, and these difficulties undoubtedly delayed any attempt until the mid-1930s.

Plans for a bridge spanning the Neches were pre-

A crane positioning steel members at one of the main spans for the Neches River high bridge in 1937. Photograph courtesy Photographic Archives, Texas Department of Highways and Public Transportation, Austin, Texas.

Men placing steel girders in position high above the Neches River on the Orange–Port Arthur Bridge in 1937 or 1938. Photograph courtesy Photographic Archives, Texas Department of Highways and Public Transportation, Austin, Texas.

pared by the Texas Highway Department about 1934. The plans had to take into consideration several important requirements: first, there was the problem of the extensive salt marshes on both sides of the river; second, there had to be high clearance over the river, since it served as the channel used by oceangoing vessels calling on the Port of Beaumont; finally, the highway structure had to be built to withstand the extreme winds of Gulf hurricanes. After the final plans were prepared, the Highway Department secured supplemental funding from Jefferson County and, more important, from the Public Works Administration of the federal government, which supplied almost half of the money for the project.

Work began at the bridge site in spring, 1936. The salt marshes surrounding the construction site forced the contractors to use unusual methods to move their equipment and supplies into position. Instead of attempting to fill in the area to build up the construction site, they dredged out channels along the west side of the projected spans and approaches for the entire length of the bridge. Then they loaded all their equipment onto barges to create a completely floating construction outfit. Cranes and pile drivers were mounted on barges, and even boilers, compressors, and workers' lounges were placed on them and then floated to wherever they were needed at the construction site.

The bridge uses two types of foundation. Supporting the heaviest steel superstructure of the seven central spans are eight pairs of reinforced-concrete caissons. Ranging from eighteen to thirty-two feet in diameter, these caissons were sunk about a hundred feet through soft muck and sand to a hard clay base. The piers for the remainder of the bridge were made from reinforced concrete poured on footings of untreated timber pilings. Because of the need to drive 1,580 of these piles, the contractors devised their own floating pile-driving rig, which with ease could drive the timbers at any desired angle.

Since the Neches River serves as the navigation channel for the Port of Beaumont, the new bridge had to provide considerable vertical clearance for the passage of ships. Thus the central span was placed 176 feet above the water, though the extreme height of the superstructure is 230 feet. The river channel at the bridge was 1,000 feet across, but the requirements of shipping demanded only a 600-foot horizontal clearance for a shipway.

The need for height combined with that for strength in determining the design chosen for the structure. As built, the Orange–Port Arthur Bridge consists of a 680-foot cantilever central span flanked by combined through-truss and deck-truss spans. Beyond these spans are long approaches on a 5 percent grade consisting of deck girder and concrete-slab spans. The total length of the structure is 7,752 feet.

The high bridge was designed for a wind load of seventy-five pounds per square foot in longitudinal, transverse, and diagonal directions. To achieve this strength, the towers supporting the high superstructure were planned integrally with the steel spans so that the wind stresses could be carried down to the foundations. The spread of the towers beneath the central span is 110 feet, although the trusses forming the span are only 34 feet apart. The caissons beneath the seven central spans were sunk sufficiently deep to support these spans during high winds, and the piers beneath the other spans depend on the batter of the wooden pilings beneath them for their stability.

Work progressed smoothly on the Orange–Port Arthur Bridge. Started in spring, 1936, by February of the next year 60 percent of the foundation work was finished and work was ready to begin on the superstructure. By the end of 1937, the superstructure had been built up on the two large towers on either side of the Neches, with the steel from one side meeting the steel from the other high above the river in January, 1938.

The Neches River project was completed in autumn. Although some structural painting still remained to be done, Gov. James V. Allred dedicated the $2,685,000 bridge in festivities held on September 7–8, 1938. The celebration included speeches by dignitaries from both Texas and Louisiana, a bathing beauty contest, and musical entertainments. The culmination came with the ribbon-cutting ceremonies on the center span of the bridge, 176 feet above the Neches. An estimated twenty-mile line of automobiles had gathered to drive across the new structure after the ribbon was cut. Since that sunny afternoon in 1938, the Orange–Port Arthur High Bridge has served the citizens of the Gulf Coast region.

Location: The Orange–Port Arthur Bridge, also known locally as the Rainbow Bridge, carries State Highway 87 across the Neches River approximately three miles southwest of Bridge City, between Orange and Port Arthur. It can be seen for miles from any direction.

Suggested Reading:

"On Texas Highways." *Texas Parade* 3, no. 5 (October, 1938): 26–28.
"Unusual Foundation Plant for Long Bridge." *Engineering News-Record* 119, no. 11 (September 9, 1937): 421–24.

The Orange–Port Arthur High Bridge as it now appears. Photograph by the author, 1981.

Looking northwest to the Paddock Viaduct from the bluff at its south end. Photograph by the author, 1975.

Erected between 1912 and 1914, the Paddock Viaduct in Fort Worth was the first concrete arch bridge erected in the United States to employ self-supporting reinforcing steel. It remains in service carrying vehicular traffic across the Trinity River.

The location of Fort Worth at the upper forks of the Trinity River meant that the central city was surrounded on three sides by watercourses. During its early days, this presented comparatively few problems except in times of flooding. Simple bridges and fords satisfactorily carried the citizens across the streams. In 1890 Fort Worth had only about twenty-three thousand people, and the number grew to only about twenty-seven thousand by 1900. With increasing industrialization, however, the city almost tripled in population in the next decade, to seventy-three thousand. Much of this growth was to the north, where many men were employed in the newly built Fort Worth Stockyards (see entry no. 35). A new link across the main channel of the Trinity River was needed to replace an old bridge, which was wholly inadequate for the traffic requirements.

The topography that called for bridges on three sides of downtown Fort Worth also dictated the conditions for bridge construction. Although the branches at the head of the river were not long, they were prone to severe flooding during heavy rains. Such floods could easily destroy the temporary falsework that

usually was employed to support bridges during their construction. This situation was coupled with soil conditions at the crossing, which led to unequal settlement of bridge piers. These two complications induced the Tarrant County commissioners to look for bridge engineers who could design a structure that would withstand the local conditions.

Tarrant County retained the firm of Brennke and Fay of Saint Louis, Missouri, as a company possessing the needed engineering expertise. This firm assigned one of its best men, S. C. Bowen, to design the large bridge as well as three smaller structures Fort Worth needed. To deal with the danger to construction from flash floods and the problem of unequal settlement of bridge piers, Bowen applied to the American situation a bridge design that had been used successfully in Europe since 1897. Because it was comparatively expensive to build, the plan had never before been attempted in the United States. This design centered on using steel reinforcement, which would support its own weight during construction.

In Bowen's Trinity River bridge the steel reinforcement for four large ribbed-concrete arches was designed so that it would support its own weight without the use of falsework. The avoidance of falsework prevented major construction delays caused by flooding. The problem of uneven settling of bridge piers was solved by the design of the reinforced-concrete

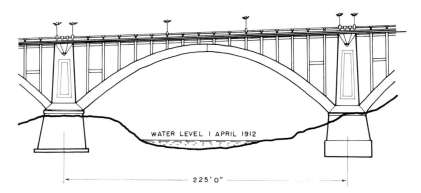

Elevation of the main span of the Paddock Viaduct over the Trinity River. Based on S. C.
Bowen, "The Design and Construction of Four
Reinforced Concrete Viaducts at Fort Worth,
Texas," *Transactions of the American Society
of Civil Engineers* 77, no. 1329 (1915), plate
20. Drawing by the author.

WATER LEVEL 1 APRIL 1912

225' 0"

arches chosen for the bridge. Each of the ribs composing these arches has three hinges, one at the center
and one at each end of the concrete piers. After the
three-hinged plan was selected, it was modified to fit
the topography at the construction site, where the
south end of the bridge was to stand several feet
higher than the north end. This gave the roadway a 4
percent grade. The north end of the bridge, unlike the
more impressive south end, was designed with a combination of ordinary reinforced-concrete girder spans
and earth fills enclosed by concrete retaining walls.

Construction on the Paddock Viaduct began in
December, 1912, and continued to completion in
March, 1914. General contractor for the project was
the Hannan-Hickey Brothers Construction Company
of Saint Louis; the Virginia Bridge and Iron Company
of Roanoke, Virginia, was subcontractor for the
structural steel. Work began first on the footings for
the piers while at the same time workmen built a temporary construction camp on the north side of the
river. After the piers were begun the subcontractors
began erecting the four series of steel reinforcing
arches. With the steel in position and anchored to the
hinges at the piers, the contractors attached wooden
forms to the self-supporting reinforcement. They
then poured concrete into the forms around the reinforcement, creating the reinforced-concrete arches.
On the completion of the arches, further concrete
was poured in forms to create the ribs and braces that
extend from the arches upward to the level of the
roadway. At this point additional concrete was poured
to make the posts and deck for the span. While this
work was progressing at the four arch spans, other
workmen were building the more ordinary north end
of the bridge, consisting of concrete girder spans and
earth-filled concrete retaining walls. The total cost
for the bridge was $386,410.28.

As completed in the spring of 1914, the Paddock
Viaduct stretched 1,752 feet across the Trinity River
and its floodplain. Its south end consisted of one large
arch span 225 feet long across the main channel of
the river, flanked by 175-foot arches on each side and
a fourth concrete arch, 150 feet long, to the north.
From this point the bridge continued on northward
in a long series of reinforced-concrete girder spans
and concrete retaining walls. The structure was provided with a 54-foot roadway and two 8-foot sidewalks. This width permitted the passage at the same
time of two streetcars on tracks down the center and
four fully loaded wagons.

The builders of the Paddock Viaduct stated that
they desired to erect a bridge that with a minimum of
maintenance would last indefinitely. They achieved
their goal even more successfully than they could
have imagined, for the Paddock Viaduct stands today
almost exactly as it was built seventy years ago. In
1965 the City of Fort Worth undertook cosmetic renovation of the roadway, giving it its superficially modern appearance, but beneath the sidewalks and pavement the viaduct is virtually unchanged.

Location: The Paddock Viaduct spans the Trinity
River at Main Street, adjacent to the Tarrant County
Courthouse on the north side of Fort Worth.

Suggested Reading:

Bowen, S. C. "The Design and Construction of Four
    Reinforced Concrete Viaducts at Fort Worth, Texas."
    *Transactions of the American Society of Civil Engi-
    neers* 77, no. 1329 (1915): 1206–62.
"Self-Supporting Concrete Arch Reinforcement of
    Structural Shapes." *Engineering Record* 70, no. 16
    (October 17, 1914): 437–38.

71. Paris Abattoir

Established in 1909, the Paris Abattoir has the distinction of having been the first significant municipally operated slaughterhouse in the United States. Through the 1910s and 1920s it was the object of much interest nationwide, and its municipal operation as a public utility was copied by cities as far away as Durham, North Carolina.

In the years before the widespread availability of mechanical refrigeration, the slaughter of livestock in rural areas and in small towns often was restricted to the winter months. Only at this time could the owners of stock be certain that their meat would not spoil after their animals were killed. With this difficulty came the associated problem of unsanitary conditions prevailing at many small-scale commercial slaughtering and butchering operations. Local leaders at Paris felt that these problems were particularly acute in their community, a market center and county seat in northeast Texas. Unwilling to permit the situation to persist, under the leadership of Mayor E. H. McCuistion they found an innovative solution to their problems.

Most of the meat sold in Paris was killed and cut at one or the other of several crudely constructed slaughtering shacks on the outskirts of the town, just beyond its jurisdiction. There they were built on low ground where the only available water came from shallow wells and pools. Little effort was made to maintain the shacks in any semblance of sanitary condition. In the offal that collected outside the shacks, flies multiplied by the millions when warm weather began.

Mayor McCuistion's first attempt to deal with the meat problem in Paris was an effort to convince the local butchers to organize themselves and to erect a decent abattoir for their joint use. Their commercial rivalries, however, prevented them from engaging in any form of voluntary collaboration. The only solution seemingly open to the city officials was the erection of their own slaughterhouse for public use so that they could enforce sanitation ordinances.

Accordingly, in 1909 Paris built a municipal abattoir on the north side of town, just west of Main Street. The complex consisted of a killing room, chill-

The Paris Abattoir as it appears today, housing the offices of the Water and Sewer departments for the City of Paris. Photograph by the author, 1975.

ing room, cold-storage chamber, reduction plant, engine room, and office, together with holding pens adjacent to the building. The original plant was built from wood and corrugated sheet steel, with concrete floors throughout. When interviewed in 1915, Mayor McCuistion stated that "we were seeking to economize so far as possible," and that he seems to have done, for the entire complex cost the taxpayers only ten thousand dollars. For this modest sum the city gained an abattoir capable of handling 50 head of cattle and about half that many smaller animals per ten-hour day. It processed a remarkably large number of animals. The statistics preserved for the year from July 1, 1913, to June 30, 1914, show the slaughter of 1,881 cattle, 305 calves, 2,053 hogs, and 110 sheep. The city operated the facility as a public utility, its first two years making a small profit and the next few years running at a slight loss subsidized by the city.

An ordinance passed by the City Council on January 4, 1910, regulated the slaughter of all animals from which meat was offered for sale within the town. It did not require that all meat for sale in the town be killed and cut in the municipal abattoir, but it did require that all animals killed for sale be slaughtered in comparable facilities and that the animals have the same inspection by an authorized city inspector. The ordinance had the effect, however, of funneling virtually all the meat sold in the city through the municipal abattoir.

Although town residents could have their private stock slaughtered in the city abattoir, its operation primarily served the local butchers. These businessmen generally had their own feeding pens, buying their cattle in carload lots and feeding them until they were ready to kill. They also purchased stock as they wanted them from local farmers. They then took their animals to the abattoir on the day they wanted them killed, each butcher having a holding pen designated for his use. From that point onward the animals were handled exclusively by municipal employees operating under very strict sanitation regulations established by city ordinance.

Each animal first was examined alive by a city inspector, himself a veterinarian. It then was led to the killing room. After each head of stock was killed, the veterinarian inspected its carcass, paying particular attention to the viscera and the lungs and liver. The rules were the same as those followed by federal inspectors in commercial packinghouses. The carcass was moved on an overhead trolley to the chilling room and finally to a cold-storage chamber. For these services customers in 1915 paid $1.25 per head for cattle and 75 cents for calves and smaller animals. The fee included up to four days of cold storage or delivery to a butcher's shop.

The operation of the Paris Abattoir proved to be so successful that Lamar County joined with the city in expanding the facility. This made the plant accessible to farmers throughout the county, not merely available to city residents and butchers. The addition, which adjoined the original 1909 building, was built of brick masonry. It remained in use for a number of years until the demand for local slaughtering decreased to such an extent that the operation of the abattoir created a financial drain on the local government, at which time the plant was converted to alternative use.

Location: The red brick building that remains today from the Paris Abattoir stands in the City of Paris service departments complex at 110 West Hickory Street, a short distance west of Main Street, on the north side of Paris. The building today houses the offices of the City of Paris Water and Sewer Department.

Suggested Reading:

Currie, Barton W. "A City That Kills Its Own Meat." *Cattleman* 2, no. 4 (September, 1915): 19–23.
McCuistion, E. H. *The Municipal Abattoir.* Texas Department of Agriculture Bulletin No. 51. Austin, Tex.: Department of Agriculture, 1916.
Paris, City of. City Ordinances, vol. A, pp. 333–42. Office of City Clerk, City Hall, Paris, Tex.

72. *Pliska Aeroplane*

The Pliska Aeroplane, today preserved in a special building at the Midland Air Terminal, was built between 1911 and 1912 by John Valentine Pliska and Gray Coggin. Built only a short time after the Wright Brothers' first successful flight, it is one of the oldest surviving Texas-made aircraft.

The principal character in the story of the Pliska Aeroplane is John Valentine Pliska, an immigrant to

John V. Pliska (standing), Gray Coggin (at the controls) and their aeroplane at the polo field on Henry Halff's ranch near Midland in 1912. Photograph courtesy Mary Beth Pliska and the Institute of Texan Cultures, San Antonio, Texas.

Texas from Czechoslovakia. Pliska's family arrived in Texas in 1897, after his brother first had located in the state and then sent reports encouraging his family to join him there. Before emigrating, John Pliska served his mandatory military service in the Austrian army, learning the rudiments of aerodynamics in army balloon and glider school. John's family settled at Flatonia, near La Grange in Fayette County, and in that area the young man worked for several years in local blacksmith shops. In 1903 he left Central Texas for Mexico, where he hoped to find his fortune. On the way his train stopped at Midland. According to oral tradition preserved by his descendants, John Pliska learned that a part had been broken at the city water well and that no one in the town had been able to repair it. The traveler successfully fixed it. His ability so impressed the local blacksmith, W. A. "Greasewood" Smith, that he offered Pliska a job. Dreams of wealth in Mexico faded away as soon as the young Czech found employment with steady pay in the dusty little West Texas town in the middle of ranch country.

Pliska remained in the Midland area for the remainder of his life. For his first two years he worked at

Greasewood Smith's shop and on the C. C. Slaughter Ranch doing ironwork and blacksmithing. In January, 1905, he made a return trip to Fayette County to marry his sweetheart, Louise Hundle. The newlyweds established their home first on the Slaughter Ranch and then after a few months, in Midland.

In 1907 Pliska and his brother-in-law bought a complete set of blacksmith and machine tools from L. C. Brunson. With the assistance of Jess Prothro, Pliska and his partner built their own blacksmith shop at the southwest corner of Baird and West Texas streets near downtown Midland in 1909. For a number of years Pliska was the only actively working blacksmith in the area, and he had a tremendous volume of business. Among his customers was Gen. John J. Pershing, who on occasion while visiting Camp Marfa brought his cavalry troops to the Midland area for training exercises and came to Pliska to have his horse shod.

The Czech blacksmith was known throughout the region as a master craftsman of branding irons. During the Texas Centennial in 1936, curators from the Texas Memorial Museum dismantled the door to his shop, on which Pliska had burned scores of brands, to exhibit it in Austin, where the door is preserved to this day. Pliska's renown in West Texas, however, did not come from his skill as a metalworker. He is remembered instead as the builder of the blacksmith's aeroplane.

Already having a basic understanding of aeronautical principles gained during his military training in balloon school for the Austrian army, John Pliska in 1908 began preparing drawings and assembling materials for the construction of his own flying machine. His activities were stimulated in 1911, when Midland was visited by an aviator flying a twin-propeller Wright Brothers biplane on a flight from Los Angeles to the East Coast. The pilot landed near Midland in November, 1911, for refueling. Schools were dismissed and most of the townspeople hurried to the landing place about a mile and a half from town to see what for most of them was their first aeroplane. Among the most interested spectators were John V. Pliska and another man who soon would join him in his aeroplane venture, Gray Coggin.

Coggin was Midland's most experienced automobile mechanic. For some time he had operated a garage for the few automobiles in the area, but he earned most of his income by driving the mail car between Midland and Carlsbad, New Mexico, a two-day run in each direction. In spring, 1911, he resigned as a mechanic and mail driver to become chauffeur for Henry M. Halff, a prominent local rancher. Coggin decided to collaborate with Pliska in building an operational flying machine. Their plan was to construct a plane and fly it to towns and cities around the country, charging enough money to pay for their expenses, the construction of the plane, and a reasonable profit. They concluded that Coggin would do most of the actual flying because of his experience handling automobiles.

The two men started to work in earnest at the Pliska blacksmith shop, spending most of their evenings there in the lamplight working on the strange contraption. Patterned after the Glenn Curtis biplanes, it was to be a pusher-style plane with the engine and propeller located behind the wings and open cockpit. It was made with a wood and steel superstructure, and its wings and control surfaces were covered with fabric. To finance the project when it ran low on funds, Pliska tried to borrow money from family members, one of whom responded that birds and angels were meant to fly—not men.

After work had progressed on the superstructure of

the plane, Pliska and Coggin needed an engine to power it. At the time the only source of such engines that they knew about was the Roberts Motor Company of Sandusky, Ohio. Coggin and Pliska traveled to Ohio to examine the company's products, to select the motor for their plane, and to learn more about actual aeroplane construction. To save money they hired on as helpers on a cattle train from Midland to Kansas City, which gave them free tickets back home from that point. Traveling on to Ohio, the two men spent about a month at Sandusky learning all they could before returning home with their new motor. It was a four-cylinder, two-cycle, internal combustion engine. Its main bearings were lubricated by grease cups, but the pistons and other internal parts were lubricated by the addition of oil to the fuel. The men bought the engine through installment payments, its total cost being fifteen hundred dollars.

Pliska and Coggin worked on their project every evening after their normal work was done. Among the more complex elements in the plane was its propeller. They made it by gluing together pieces of straight-grained wood and then shaping the curved surfaces by hand with draw knives and rasps. After a few trials on the plane, they learned that the propeller became scarred and damaged by striking mesquite and brush, so they protected its tips with improvised metal sheaths. Only a short time after this, metal-tipped propellers became standard equipment on all aircraft.

When the plane was finished and its engine installed, in the spring of 1912, the two aviators hauled it by wagon for trial runs on a large, dry lakebed on a ranch northwest of Midland. The initial tests were not overly successful and consisted only of short hops into the air for about a quarter of a mile at a time. Pliska and Coggin decided at this time to try to improve the lifting capacity of the wings by giving the canvas surfaces a coating of shellac. This lessened the air friction and reduced the leakage of air through the wings, thereby improving the plane's performance. The aviators then moved their flying machine by wagon to a polo field located on the Halff Ranch, also near Midland. There they continued their experiments through the spring and early summer of 1912. It was during this time that they had their most successful flights, one to two miles in length. They found that the best time of the day for flying was early in the morning because the more humid air at that time seemed to give the plane more capacity for lift.

186

The general public had its first and only opportunity to see the Pliska Aeroplane in operation on the Fourth of July, 1912. On that day Midland planned a large Independence Day celebration with Pliska, Coggin, and their flying machine as its featured event. City crews cleared the mesquite from both sides of a stretch of Grant Avenue in Midland to form a runway for the aeroplane. A large crowd of spectators who had paid to see the flying machine in the air gathered while one of the pilots taxied up and down the improvised landing strip. Then they attempted a sustained flight, but the hot, dry air afforded the plane only enough lift for occasional short hops off the ground. Several local cowboys who had paid admission loudly demanded that the plane either fly or that they be refunded their money. Their actions alarmed Pliska, who left the scene very upset. During the night he and Coggin quietly returned to load the aeroplane on their wagon and haul it back to the blacksmith shop.

The two experimenters blamed their lack of success on the motor powering their craft. It simply did not have enough strength to provide the service that they expected. Since they were still making monthly payments for the engine, they returned it to the factory, expecting to purchase a larger one in the near future. There being no other place to store the flying machine in the interim, they disassembled it and placed it in the rafters of the blacksmith shop. Instead of returning to the air, it rested there for half a century.

In 1962, when the blacksmith shop was torn down, the aeroplane was rescued and given to Midland by the Pliska heirs. It then was restored, fitted with a 1911 Roberts Motor Company engine, and placed inside its own building at the Midland Air Terminal, where it remains on exhibit today.

Location: The restored Pliska Aeroplane is housed in its own building adjacent to the passenger area at the Midland Air Terminal. The airport facility is located just north of U.S. 80, about ten miles southwest of downtown Midland.

Suggested Reading:

Pliska, Mary Beth. *A Blacksmith's Aeroplane.* N.p.: privately printed, 1965.

73. *Point Bolivar Lighthouse*

One of two surviving iron lighthouses on the Texas Gulf Coast, the Point Bolivar Lighthouse is one of the most prominent historical landmarks on Galveston Bay.

The first efforts toward the erection of a lighthouse on the Bolivar Peninsula, across Galveston Bay from the port of Galveston, came in 1848. In that year the U.S. Treasury Department purchased the site for an installation near the tip of the peninsula. Several years passed, however, before construction began. Finally in 1851 Congress appropriated fifteen thousand dollars for the erection of an iron lighthouse on the site.

The Point Bolivar Light Station as it now appears. Photograph by the author, 1981.

This structure served only about a decade, for during the Civil War it was dismantled and transported inland by Confederate forces to prevent its use as a lookout by Union soldiers or sailors.

After the end of the war, the Treasury Department placed a temporary light at the end of the peninsula, but it was not until 1872 that work began on the current structure. The project continued until its completion in late autumn, 1873. The lighthouse, erected on a concrete foundation placed on wooden pilings, stands 116 feet tall. It consists of one-inch-thick prefabricated malleable iron plates, which are riveted together around a brick lining. This lining varies from eighteen inches thick at the base to twelve inches thick at the top. Within the tower a spiral cast-iron stairway provides the only access to the iron and brass lantern that housed the lamp and lens. On the side of the tower are three windows fitted with quarter-inch-thick glass panes. The lantern originally also was fitted with thick curved glass, which for many years has been broken.

Light for the Point Bolivar Lighthouse initially was provided by a large kerosene lamp mounted within a rotating lens. The mechanism that turned the lens was somewhat like that of a clock fitted with large weights. The glass lens, as it rotated, gave the illusion of a flashing light.

From its return to service on November 19, 1873, until it was retired on May 29, 1933, the Bolivar Lighthouse missed only two nights as a navigational aid. These nights immediately followed the August, 1915, Galveston hurricane, during which the lighthouse is credited with saving the lives of sixty people. These local residents of the peninsula sought refuge in the tower on August 16, sitting for the night huddled in pairs on alternate steps of the cast-iron stairway within the tower. They watched with apprehension as the waters rose several feet inside the base of the tower and then with genuine fear as the wind and water burst open the heavy iron door. The lighthouse, however, stood the test. According to local tradition, the top of the tower swayed twelve inches back and forth during the greatest fury of the storm, preventing the mechanism from turning the lens, although the keepers maintained the light. Since the lens would not rotate mechanically, they turned it by hand throughout the night. The storm destroyed the oil storage house at the base of the tower, so that for the two nights after the storm, August 17 and 18, the light did not burn for lack of fuel.

The Point Bolivar Lighthouse during its heyday as a government-operated navigational aid. Photograph courtesy National Archives, Washington, D.C.

The Bolivar Lighthouse is also credited with saving a number of lives during the more famous 1900 Galveston storm. On this occasion 125 people found shelter inside the iron tower. According to an inspector's report after the hurricane, "through the keeper's efforts, the lives of 125 people were saved, and to my personal knowledge he harbored and fed a large number of them for a considerable period." He fed the refugees from his family's own supply of food, which had been intended to last them for several months, and provided them with bedding and clothing until all his were given away.

The Point Bolivar Lighthouse operated until 1933, when the Bureau of Lighthouses discontinued its service. The site of the lighthouse and the structure itself were sold and remain private property at this time. In 1977 its significance was recognized by its acceptance into the National Register of Historic Places.

Location: The Point Bolivar Lighthouse stands near the tip of the Bolivar Peninsula just across Galveston

Bay from Galveston. The tower is located just north of State Highway 87, approximately three-tenths of a mile west of its intersection with FM 2612, less than a mile south of the town of Port Bolivar. The lighthouse and preserved keepers' houses are privately owned and not accessible to the public, but they can be viewed clearly from the two paved highways.

Suggested Reading:

Baughman, J. L. "Taps for Texas Lighthouses." *Houston Chronicle* (Houston, Tex.), June 29, 1952, magazine section, pp. 6–7.

Holland, Francis Ross, Jr. *America's Lighthouses: Their Illustrated History since 1716.* Brattleboro, Vt.: Stephen Greene Press, 1972.

74. *Point Isabel Lighthouse*

Established in 1852, the Point Isabel Lighthouse provided a beacon for Gulf Coast shipping near the mouth of the Rio Grande until 1905. Today a Texas state park, it is open to the public seven days a week and is one of the most frequently visited tourist attractions in the Lower Rio Grande Valley.

The area around the present-day town of Port Isabel was a quiet backwater until 1846, when it came to the forefront of national attention after hostilities broke out between the United States and Mexico. It was into this area that Gen. Zachary Taylor moved his troops in March of that year, and it was near here that the first skirmishes in the war with Mexico took place. Brazos Santiago Pass between the south end of Padre Island and the north end of Brazos Island, about seven miles up the coast from the mouth of the Rio Grande, became the principal port of arrival for incoming military supplies to sustain the American forces in the region. Because of the tremendous increase in shipping at the pass, the U.S. Lighthouse Board realized the need for a navigational aid at that location. Consequently, in 1850 Congress appropriated fifteen thousand dollars for the construction of a lighthouse on the mainland at Point Isabel, on the site of a former military post that had been transferred by the War Department to the Treasury Department, the government agency then responsible for lighthouses.

The lighthouse at the tip of Point Isabel, completed in 1852, exhibited a light consisting of four lamps fifty-seven feet above the ground and eighty-six feet above sea level. The tower was built of red brick transported by sailing ship from Louisiana. Its walls were erected four feet thick at the base, tapering toward the top. By 1854 its lighting was increased to fifteen lamps with twenty-one reflectors, making the beacon visible for sixteen miles. Then in 1857 a third-order lens was added to the facility, giving the station a fixed light varied by flashes every sixty seconds. The lens turned through the operation of a mecha-

nism that might be likened to that of a grandfather clock, actuated by weights suspended on ropes within the tower.

The Point Isabel Lighthouse was used as an observation post by both Confederate and Union forces during the Civil War. The Lower Rio Grande Valley was first held by the Confederacy, but by 1863 it fell to Federal troops. When the first Union soldiers landed on Brazos Island, Col. John S. "Rip" Ford of the Texas Rangers removed the lens from the top of the tower to prevent its use as an aid to Federal vessels in the area. Without the light blinking from the main-

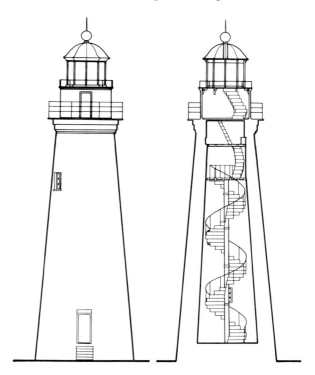

Elevation and cross-section of the Point Isabel Lighthouse. Based on measured drawings in U.S. Department of the Interior, National Park Service, Historic American Buildings Survey, Site Tex-33-Ab-1. Drawing by the author.

The Point Isabel Lighthouse as it now appears. Photograph by the author, 1981.

land, Union ship captains found navigation almost impossible at night in the unfamiliar waters and a number of them ran aground. The missing lens, which was never returned, is probably still buried somewhere in the Port Isabel–Brownsville vicinity. Visitors to the lighthouse today can see purported Civil War cannonballs recovered in the area of the light station.

The Point Isabel tower survived the war in better condition than did most of the other Texas lighthouses, as it was not subjected to intentional demolition or destruction. After minor repairs and the replacement of the lamp and lens, it returned to operation on February 22, 1866. Time, however, finally took its toll of the iron and brass lantern at the top of the tower. By 1878 it was so battered that during storms it leaked water "in every direction" and had to be replaced.

In 1887 the U.S. Lighthouse Board decided that there was no further need for the light on Point Isa-

bel. This decision was based in part on the fact that the area was also served by the Brazos Santiago Lighthouse operating nearby at the south end of Padre Island. The lamps atop the old red brick tower were extinguished. Over the subsequent few months, however, the board received numerous petitions requesting that the Point Isabel beacon be restored. This would not have been a difficult matter except that the legitimate owners of the property where the tower was located appeared to claim not only the ground but also the lighthouse and its auxiliary structures. It was discovered that the former military camp where the lighthouse had been erected in 1852 had never been federal property. Negotiations dragged on for months and then years between several government agencies on the one hand and the private owners on the other. Finally, the title to the site passed to the government in 1894. In 1889 Congress had appropriated funds for the reestablishment of the light station, but it was not until July 15, 1895, that the light was re-exhibited. The station operated for the next ten years before the Lighthouse Board discontinued it permanently.

In 1927 the federal government sold the lighthouse at auction to a private buyer. It remained in private hands until 1950, when the owners deeded the site to the state of Texas to be preserved as a historical monument. Using old plans, the state restored the structure in 1952, its centennial year, and opened it as a state park. Today it is one of the most popular tourist attractions in South Texas, visited by thousands of people annually. Almost all the visitors take the sixty-nine-step climb to the lantern at the apex of the tower to see the magnificent views of Padre Island, Laguna Madre, the Rio Grande Valley, and the Gulf of Mexico. Equipped with a modern mercury vapor lamp, the lighthouse is marked on marine charts as an unofficial private aid to navigation.

Location: The Point Isabel Lighthouse is located at the tiny Port Isabel Lighthouse State Park in the fishing village and seaside mecca of Port Isabel. It is adjacent to State Highway 100 at the northeast side of town, just southwest of the Padre Island Causeway. The white-painted tower can be seen for miles in every direction.

Suggested Reading:

Mungo, Marjie. "Beacon of the Rio Grande." *Texas Highways* 18, no. 8 (August, 1971): 16–18.

U.S. Department of the Interior. National Park Service. Historic American Buildings Survey. Site Tex-33-Ab-1. Manuscript, typescript, and photographs. Library of Congress, Washington, D.C.

U.S. Department of the Treasury. Coast Guard. *Historical Famous Lighthouses.* Washington, D.C.: Government Printing Office, 1972.

75. *Porter's Bluff Highway*

Built in 1920, the Porter's Bluff Highway in Smith County is a classic example of the early efforts to improve and pave Texas highways during the years immediately following World War I. Portions of the roadway laid over sixty years ago still remain intact on the west side of Tyler.

The paving and improvement of the Porter's Bluff Highway in 1920 was a project funded half by Smith County and half by the federal government, with

road funds distributed by the Texas Highway Department. Actual construction was undertaken by crews of the Smith County Highway Commission. The route stretched a total distance of 8.58 miles from Tyler to the Neches River, the boundary with Van Zandt County. At the time, a ferry carried traffic across the river. The pavement for the first 2.82 miles of the highway was concrete, the remainder iron ore gravel.

A stretch of concrete-paved highway in Smith County in the 1920s. Photograph courtesy Photographic Archives, Texas Department of Highways and Public Transportation, Austin, Texas.

A concrete-paved segment of the 1920 Porter's Bluff Highway as it now appears. Photograph by the author, 1975.

The design and specifications for the Porter's Bluff Highway were prepared by county engineer D. K. Caldwell, who took his job at Tyler in August, 1919. He and his assistant, A. C. Gentry, prepared the preliminary plans for the road during the late summer and fall of 1919, submitting them to the highway department late in the year. The plans and specifications were redrawn in Austin in early 1920, at which time the project was assigned designation as Texas federal highway aid project number 115, job number 212-A.

The final plans, still preserved in Tyler, called for a concrete roadway starting at the Cotton Belt Railroad tracks in Tyler. Federal aid for road construction was limited to areas where the houses averaged at least two hundred feet apart, and westward from downtown Tyler this condition began at the tracks. This is the area of Palace Avenue today. The paved roadway was projected to extend 2.82 miles in a westerly direction, beginning at the railroad crossing. From the end of the concrete pavement, the highway was planned to continue an additional 5.76 miles, with an iron ore gravel surface to the ferry crossing at the Neches.

The Porter's Bluff Highway in both its concrete and gravel portions had a sixteen-foot-wide roadway. After the embankments for the road were prepared, the surfacing material was added. For the first 2.82 miles of the route concrete was laid. To enhance drainage of moisture from the surface, it was seven inches thick at the center and tapered to five inches thick at the edge, giving the roadway a slope of one-quarter inch to the foot. The gravel surface was specified to be eight inches thick for the first 4.41 miles and then six inches thick for the last 1.35 miles to the river. The gravel surface, as thick at the edge as at the center of the roadway, had a slope of three-quarters inch per foot from the center to allow for drainage to the ditches at the sides of the road.

The concrete surface at the east end of the Porter's Bluff Highway remained in serviceable condition for many years, but the iron ore sections developed a distinctly washboardlike surface during dry weather. Even with the rough surface, however, they were far superior to the old sand and clay roads that they replaced. During the early 1920s county engineer D. K. Caldwell initiated a program of placing asphalt surfaces on gravel roads in Smith County. Sometime after summer, 1922, he had county crews place a heavy three-course inverted penetration pavement on gravel portions of the Porter's Bluff road.

With the passage of time, the route of the Porter's Bluff Highway was either covered over or skirted by newer highway construction. Much of present-day State Highway 64 rests atop the old gravel portion of the 1920 road, obliterating traces of the former construction. Several thousand feet of the concrete pavement, however, remain intact on the west side of Tyler.

Location: The portion of the 1920s Porter's Bluff Highway that is easiest to view is the concrete section that lies near State Highway 64, just west of Loop 323 at the west side of Tyler. There the old concrete roadway begins parallel with and just north of the present highway at its intersection with the loop. The concrete roadway then passes under the current highway to the south side, where it takes a gentle loop to the south before returning to be buried beneath the modern highway.

Suggested Reading:

Crutcher, I. H., Jr. "Early Highway Development in Smith County." *Chronicles of Smith County, Texas* (Tyler, Tex.) 10, no. 1 (Spring, 1971): 1–15.

Texas. State Highway Department. "Plan and Profile of Proposed State Highway Federal Aid Project[,] Smith County[,] from Tyler to Smith–Van Zandt County Line." Manuscript measured drawings. 1920. 15 lvs. Engineering Department, Texas Department of Highways and Public Transportation, Tyler, Tex.

76. Possum Kingdom Stone Arch Bridge

A seeming anachronism in mid-twentieth-century highway construction, the Possum Kingdom Stone Arch Bridge is one of the most beautiful of all the historic bridges in Texas. Erected by Works Progress Administration (WPA) laborers under Texas Highway Department supervision between 1940 and 1942, the bridge remains in use today as the State Highway 16 crossing over the Brazos River, a mile below the Morris Sheppard Dam (1935–41) in Palo Pinto County.

The Possum Kingdom Stone Arch Bridge formed part of an improvement to State Highways 16 and 254, linking the Palo Pinto County communities of Brad, Graford, and Salesville. It was planned in the late 1930s and built with federal government aid between 1940 and 1942. The bridge project, which also received heavy federal funding, was designed by highway department engineers to span the Brazos just below the Morris Sheppard Dam, which at the time was under construction. Because it was known that in the future floodwaters would be released from the dam in tremendous volumes, the bridge downstream was designed to withstand the destructive forces of completely overtopping floodwaters. For this reason, a masonry arch, low-water-type plan was chosen.

The WPA provided all the manpower to build the

stone bridge. The laborers were unemployed workers from the surrounding counties. Daily they were transported to the site from the outlying communities in converted cattle trucks. They spent their workday at the bridge and then were transported home in the same vehicles. Many of the men were former coal miners from the Thurber, Mingus, and Strawn areas. Their skill as stonecutters, learned in underground mining, equipped them perfectly for the task of shaping the limestone blocks that went into building the bridge.

Initial work on the project consisted of excavating footings for the piers and abutments. The bridge has two abutments and seventeen stone piers. Two of these piers, numbers seven and thirteen, are more heavily built as "bracing piers." The footings for all are founded on hard, gray sandstone. While work on the foundations was being conducted, stonecutters began quarrying limestone from nearby bluffs. After they removed the blocks of stone, other men trucked them to the bridge site. There skilled workers began shaping the stones and laying them in mortar to form the portions of the piers above the concrete footings that had been placed several feet down on bedrock.

When the stone piers had reached approximately

WPA employees shaping stone and laying it in position over wooden falsework to build the arches in the 1940–42 Possum Kingdom Stone Arch Bridge. Photograph courtesy Fred Burkett, Fort Worth, Texas.

Elevation showing details of construction of an abutment, a typical pier, and a bracing pier in the Possum Kingdom Stone Arch Bridge. Based on Texas, State Highway Department, "Arch Detail of Brazos River Bridge," measured drawing, 1940, in Texas, State Highway Department, "Plans of Proposed Highway Improvement, State Project LWR 362-2-2, Palo Pinto County—Highway No. 16 & 254," Engineering Department, Texas Department of Highways and Public Transportation, Fort Worth, Texas.

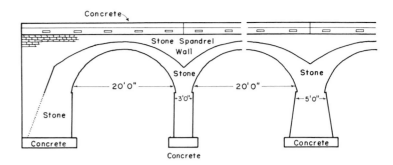

the level of the riverbed, work began on the eighteen stone arches that make up the bridge. At this point wooden falsework was assembled between selected pairs of piers. The stonemasons laid cut stones in position with mortar to form the arches. When the arches were finished, stone sides for the bridge were laid up to the level of the roadway. The area inside the stonework then was filled with layers of compacted earth fill. Finally, after the earth fill had reached the proper level for the roadway, concrete pavement was laid the length of the bridge to form its wearing surface. Concrete curbs with drains were placed at this time.

The eighteen spans of the Possum Kingdom Stone Arch Bridge measure 433 feet, 4 inches long. The spans, seemingly all the same length, actually vary from 23 to 30 feet. They all rest on stone piers that extend 9 to 10 feet down to concrete footings on sandstone bedrock. The arches themselves stand 8 feet, 6 inches above the piers, and the top of the concrete curbing on the roadway stands 13 feet, 9 inches above the piers.

The nature of the bridge project as a WPA effort during the Great Depression made it quite different from projects today. The bridge, which cost only $760,000, was built by men who tried to save money

Looking southwest along the downstream side of the Possum Kingdom Stone Arch Bridge today. Photograph by the author, 1978.

wherever possible. Not only was the limestone quarried locally, but the sand and gravel needed on the project was dug from the riverbed in the close vicinity of the construction site. Very little machinery other than ordinary trucks was used. Stones were lifted into position by the men, assisted by small, hand-powered hoists. Even the lumber used in building the falsework for the arches was scrap material salvaged from the much larger nearby Morris Sheppard Dam project. Thirty-five years later, an engineer who had been associated with the project remembered that the morale of the WPA crew had been very high and that the stonemasons were particularly proud of their effort.

The Possum Kingdom Stone Arch Bridge has stood the test of time as a credit to its designers and builders. To this day it retains its original appearance with virtually no alteration from its 1942 condition. Designed to withstand extreme floods, it has been overtopped by over eight feet of raging waters with no ill effects to either its arch structure or its approaches. The bridge still bears at each end of its roadway brass plates that state for all who will stop to read that it

was built by the unemployed coal miners hired by the Works Progress Administration.

Location: The Possum Kingdom Stone Arch Bridge carries State Highway 16 across the Brazos River directly downstream from the Morris Sheppard Dam in Palo Pinto County, about twenty-eight miles south of Graham.

Suggested Reading:

Burkett, Fred, Fort Worth, Tex., to W. C. Griggs, Texas Tech University, Lubbock, Tex., February 17, 1975. Typescript letter. "Possum Kingdom Stone Arch Bridge" file, Texas Historic Engineering Site Inventory, Center for the History of Engineering, Texas Tech University, Lubbock, Tex.

Texas. State Highway Department. Construction and Maintenance files for Project Control Number 362-2-2, Palo Pinto County. Manuscript and microfilm. Engineering Department, Texas Department of Highways and Public Transportation, Fort Worth, Tex.

77. *Post City Windmill Waterworks*

Perhaps best known among the numerous windmill waterworks that once served towns throughout the state, the Post City Windmill Waterworks is noted for its extensive water storage reservoirs and for the size and number of large-diameter windmills that pumped water into them.

Post City, now known simply as Post, was an experimental town established by Charles William Post in an effort to create an ideal community. A native of Illinois, Post became a multimillionaire through the manufacture and sale of a line of cereal products that

included Postum, Grape Nuts, and Post Toasties. He first visited Texas in 1885 during convalescence from an illness, and in that year he began investing in Texas ranches and other properties.

In 1906 Post returned to Texas with dreams of founding an agricultural and industrial colony on the virgin plains of West Texas. He purchased approximately a quarter million acres of land in Garza and Lynn counties, about forty miles south and southeast of Lubbock. Near the center of his property he founded his colony, which until his death was known

Several of the twenty-foot-diameter "Samson" windmills erected by C. W. Post about 1909 for pumping water to supply the Post City Windmill Waterworks. Photograph courtesy Panhandle-Plains Historical Museum, Canyon, Texas.

The deteriorating remains of the 1909–10 Post Waterworks reservoir. Photograph by the author, 1971.

as Post City. His crews divided the immediately surrounding ranchlands into 160-acre farms, fenced them, and erected standard-plan farmhouses complete with wallpaper and kitchen sinks. Everything was made ready for the prospective settlers, who could purchase the farms at reasonable prices with low interest.

At the same time, crews from Post's Double U Company erected the entire town of Post City. The work crews built streets, sewers, residences, a cotton gin, a fine stone hotel, and a large textile mill. Within a few years, Post City boasted not only electric lights, a sewerage system, and telephones, but also a country club, golf links, a commercial club, and a county fair.

Company employees planted trees all along the streets and then carefully watered them from tank wagons.

One of the major problems C. W. Post met in building his town was inadequate water supply. Had the community been located on the flat plains above the Cap Rock Escarpment to the west, its residents would have found an immense supply of pure water underground in the Ogallala aquifer. To place the town within five miles of the geographical center of the county, as the state required for county seats, however, it was built below the escarpment in rolling country. Here, unfortunately, the underground water supply was highly impregnated with gypsum and salt, which made it impotable.

Post's initial plan in 1907 called for the excavation of a more or less horizontal tunnel into the aquifer from the side of the escarpment. His engineers advised him that technical problems would make this an unusually expensive venture. This advice came just in time, for news of Post's plans had begun prompting citizens on the plains as far north as Amarillo to organize mass protest meetings because they feared that his proposed tunnel would drain their water supply away from beneath them.

The plan was changed from a tunnel to the boring of a series of wells above the escarpment and then the piping of water down to the town. In the meantime, Post's manager in Texas secured a temporary water supply by gathering water from a number of natural springs just below the escarpment. Their flow was carried by gravity through 4.5-inch pipe to the town, but the springs provided only about half of the water that was needed. To supplement the supply, the first few of the planned series of wells were drilled near the Cap Rock. This temporary system operated for the next few months until a permanent solution to the water problem was found.

In January, 1908, after Post City had been in existence for over a year and a half, the only water system serving the town consisted of an earthen reservoir similar to a present-day stock tank. The flow of the water from the springs and the few wells drilled above the town were not enough to keep it even half filled. Months before, C. W. Post had promised that his town would have a "system of waterworks," and in January, 1908, he set about keeping his word.

Post ordered excavation and construction of an underground reservoir just below the edge of the Cap Rock Escarpment, some three hundred feet above the town. Time passed with no visible progress, but by early September, 1908, men were at work digging the reservoir and lining it with concrete. On September 18 Post wired his manager in Texas to stop work on the project. One of his engineers in Michigan had calculated that the pressure of water from a reservoir three hundred feet above the town would be so great that it would require the use of special fixtures, heavy pipe, and other nonstandard equipment. Tales still told in the Post Water Department state that the pressure would have been so great that water would have burst out the bottom of a pail set beneath one of the turned-on faucets.

Post's men chose a new site for the reservoir about a hundred feet lower in elevation but in the same general area west of town. This structure, which still stands, was completed in May, 1909. In the meantime, Post's Double U Company employed a well driller to sink additional wells above the escarpment to provide water to the new reservoir. By September, 1909, he had finished seventeen wells for the waterworks.

Company crews erected a battery of huge "Samson" open, back-geared steel windmills on steel towers above the wells to pump water to the surface for it to flow to the reservoir. At one time Post's company had six huge twenty-foot-diameter Samson mills in use pumping for the town. These were among the largest windmills ever used in the South Plains region of Texas.

As soon as the new waterworks went into operation, the Double U Company installed water meters in Post City and began charging the town residents for their water. It set the rate at five cents per fifty-gallon barrel of water, with a monthly meter rental of twenty cents. The townspeople comlained so loudly about the rates that Post reduced the fees for both the water and the meter rental. The capitalist reputedly declared, "I have been supplying them with free water for a long while, and now the rates are low enough. A postage stamp for a barrel of water is not a heavy expenditure."

Efforts continued to expand the Post City water supply with the excavation of at least one hand-dug well. Also on the plains, this ten-foot-diameter and eighty-six-foot-deep well maintained a fourteen-foot water level. Its success prompted the expansion of the reservoir, a project begun in November, 1910, and completed in December of the next year. This expansion doubled the capacity of the original reservoir.

With the passage of years and continued growth in water demand, the windmills elevating water for the Post waterworks were replaced by power pumps. In the 1920s a new covered concrete reservoir was built near the old 1908–11 facility to replace it. Today the few visitors who brave mesquite brush and rattlesnakes at the site find the original stone-lined reservoir abandoned and deteriorating. It measures 250 feet long, 20 feet wide, and 15 feet deep, with slightly sloping walls. The upper area of the structure consists of steel trusses, which supported a now-missing corrugated sheet metal roof and a catwalk the length of the reservoir. The inlet to the reservoir is seen at its northwest end, and its outlet at the opposite end is marked by a series of valves. Portions of the stone walls have collapsed. Above the 1908–11 reservoir one finds the highly deteriorated remains of the uncompleted reservoir, which was abandoned before it was finished because of its excessive elevation. Although the pieces are fragmentary, rubbish tips in the general area of the two reservoirs contain parts that have been identified as coming from Samson windmills. These are thought to be remains of some of the mills that pumped for the windmill waterworks of Post City.

Location: The deteriorating remains of the reservoirs from the early Post City Windmill Waterworks are found below the Cap Rock Escarpment three miles west of downtown Post. The sites are owned by the City of Post but are leased to individuals and do not have general public access.

Suggested Reading:

Baker, T. Lindsay. "The Windmill Waterworks of Post City." *Water, Southwest Water Works Journal* 55, no. 12 (March, 1974): 4–6.

Eaves, Charles Dudley, and C. A. Hutchinson. *Post City Texas.* Austin: Texas State Historical Association, 1952.

78. Quitaque Railway Tunnel

One of two tunnels excavated during the construction of the Fort Worth and Denver South Plains Railway, the Quitaque Railway Tunnel is the last functioning railroad tunnel in Texas. The tunnel remains in service on the South Plains branch of the Burlington Northern Railroad, connecting its main line at Estelline with the irrigated agricultural region of the Texas South Plains.

In 1929 the Fort Worth and Denver City Railroad secured a charter from the Texas legislature for a new subsidiary company, the Fort Worth and Denver South Plains Railway, to extend into the rapidly developing, agriculturally rich South Plains region. The new company projected a line just over two hundred miles long from the Fort Worth and Denver main line at Estelline in a generally southwesterly direction through Turkey, Quitaque, South Plains, Lockney, Petersburg, and Plainview to Dimmitt with branches from Sterley north to Silverton and south to Lubbock.

Soon railway company civil engineers began surveying a route for the line, with the company acquiring right-of-way from the Red River Valley at Estelline to Quitaque and then up the drainage of Quitaque Creek to the top of the Cap Rock Escarpment. From that point the projected route crossed the level plains to its termini at Lubbock, Silverton, and Dimmitt. The climb up the escarpment posed the most difficult problems for the engineers laying out the route, for they needed to keep as slight a grade as possible to attain economy of fuel consumption as the trains climbed from 2,560 feet elevation at Quitaque to 3,200 feet elevation at the top of the escarpment. They concluded that the most efficient route would

include two tunnels passing through jutting bluffs near the escarpment edge. Both of these tunnels were located approximately ten miles southeast of Quitaque in Floyd County.

The Fort Worth and Denver South Plains Railway contracted with the firm of Peterson, Shirley and Gunther to excavate the two tunnels. Its work began months before any construction started on other phases of the effort. By July, 1927, it had completed the upper of the two tunnels and had started the second. The local press noted that since the project was so unusual in the region, "the construction of the tunnel . . . has attracted thousands of visitors from all the Plains cities." The newspaper also noted that heavy treated timbers already had been placed throughout the completed tunnel and it was ready for railroad company crews when they reached it laying rails. This occurred several months later.

While the tunnel work was being conducted south of Quitaque, miles away on the main line supplies and materials were being concentrated at Estelline for the actual laying of the two-hundred-mile rail line. By summer, 1927, most of the roadbed on the plains had been graded and prepared for track-laying crews, but some work still remained to be done in the rougher country in the Red River drainage above Estelline. With the roadbed being graded and the tunnels completed, sleepy little Estelline in summer, 1927, was transformed into a beehive of activity as trainload after trainload of materials arrived. A local reporter noted that summer that "Estelline is full to overflowing with rail equipment" and that "sufficient rails are on the yards and on the wye there to lay practically all of . . . the new South Plains line." He added that at the time three hundred carloads of creosoted ties were being unloaded.

Work on the Fort Worth and Denver South Plains Railway line continued through the next year, with the rails reaching Plainview, a major agricultural center, on May 24, 1928. By this date a rail-laying train was on its way to Dimmitt, the western terminus, while another crew was actively laying rails into Lubbock, the southern terminus. The general manager of

View to the outside from within the Quitaque Railway Tunnel. Photograph, 1976, courtesy Center for the History of Engineering, Texas Tech University, Lubbock, Texas.

the Fort Worth and Denver predicted that the line would begin service before the end of the summer. His prediction was a bit optimistic, but the new branch line did commence regular operation by October.

To celebrate the completion of the new railway line serving the South Plains, Plainview hosted a huge banquet. As part of the festivities six special trains from various parts of the state converged at Childress on November 20, 1928. These trains were sponsored by local business and civic groups and by the railway company itself. From Childress the separate trains combined to form one train for a trip over the new line from nearby Estelline to Plainview and Lubbock. On arrival in Plainview, all the guests, numbering in the hundreds, were treated to a "wild duck banquet" at which a thousand roasted ducks were served.

The South Plains line proved to be a very wise investment. For a number of years it constituted a "bread-and-butter" line for the Fort Worth and Denver City Railway as agriculture grew increasingly important in the region it served. The two tunnels at the Cap Rock Escarpment, however, were largely forgotten, and few people outside the immediate area even knew of their existence.

The tunnels became news items in 1968 when a freight train derailed inside the upper tunnel. The damage to the structure was so great that the only feasible means of freeing the trapped cars and returning the line to service was to "daylight" the tunnel. Crews using heavy earth-moving machinery cut down from above to convert the tunnel into a deep open cut. This left only the lower tunnel, 689 feet long, which then became the only functioning railway tunnel in the state.

This tunnel was threatened in 1973, when it too

was the scene of a freight train derailment. It remained closed for seventeen months and Fort Worth and Denver trains had to be diverted via the Quanah, Acme and Pacific and Santa Fe tracks to serve their territory on the South Plains. Company officials even considered abandoning the entire South Plains line due to the expense of reopening the tunnel, but in the end they decided to clear out the rubble and damaged freight cars to restore service. During this time they replaced the old rails in the tunnel with heavier rails in an effort to forestall any future derailments. With these repairs, completed, the Quitaque Railway Tunnel returned to serve the South Plains line of the Fort Worth and Denver.

Location: The Quitaque Railway Tunnel is located on the Burlington Northern Railroad approximately ten miles south-southwest of Quitaque in Floyd County. The tunnel itself is private property, is located in an area surrounded by privately owned ranches, and has no public access.

Suggested Reading:

Amarillo Daily News (Amarillo, Tex.) (May 25, 1928), p. 7; (October 27, 1928), p. 1.
Amarillo Sunday News-Globe (Amarillo, Tex.) (July 25, 1927), sec. 2, p. 1; (November 4, 1928), sec. 3, p. 1.
Fort Worth and Denver South Plains Railway Files. Manuscript. Colorado Historical Society, Denver, Colo.
Lubbock Avalanche-Journal (Lubbock, Tex.) (September 10, 1973), sec. A, pp. 1, 10.

79. Red Brick Road

One of the best-known stretches of brick-paved highway in Texas is the segment of former State Highway 1 between Weatherford and Mineral Wells. Laid between 1937 and 1938, this 16.87-mile stretch of highway remains in use as the westbound lane of U.S. 180.

The 1930s Red Brick Road between Weatherford and Mineral Wells was not the first paved road connecting the two towns. As early as 1922 the Palo Pinto County portion of the original State Highway 1 between the two towns had been paved by the Texas Highway Department. According to plans approved on September 1, 1922, the 3.99-mile stretch was paved

with brick resting on a base of crushed stone. Laid fifteen feet wide, it had an eighteen-inch-wide concrete curb on either side to help hold the paving bricks in place. This gave the total road a width of eighteen feet. At some unknown date at least some parts of the highway across the line in Parker County and on to Weatherford were paved with asphalt to provide a sixteen-foot-wide, all-weather roadway. This road remained in use as State Highway 1 into the late 1930s, when the Red Brick Road replaced it.

In 1936 and 1937 Texas Highway Department engineers prepared plans for a more direct new route for

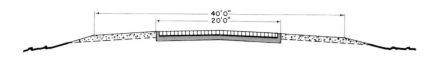

Cross-section of the 1937–38 Red Brick Road, showing its earthen embankment, reinforced-concrete base course, and brick paving. Based on Texas, State Highway Department, "Typical Section Sheet," measured drawing, 1937, in Texas, State Highway Department, "Plans of Proposed State Highway Improvement, Federal Aid Project 132-Reop. Unit IV, State Highway 1 Parker County from Palo Pinto County Line to West City Limits of Weatherford," sheet 3, Engineering Department, Texas Department of Highways and Public Transportation, Fort Worth, Texas. Drawing by the author.

State Highway 1 between Mineral Wells and Weatherford. This relocated highway stretched 16.87 miles from city limits to city limits. The section in Palo Pinto County was approved in late 1936, and the portion in Parker County was approved in the autumn of 1937.

The specifications for both sections of the highway project were basically the same. They provided for an earthen subgrade, with ditches on each side, on which a reinforced-concrete base course and curb were laid. After the concrete had cured, workmen placed a layer of dry sand on the concrete base and smoothed it to an even one-inch thickness. With the sand cushion in place, two brick setters followed. These skilled workmen laid individual bricks in position on the sand, each of them keeping an average of seven laborers busy delivering bricks for placement. The brick setters laid four courses at a time and then straightened them by striking them with 4-by-4-inch timbers. The setters were most concerned with speed,

Looking east along U.S. 180. The westbound Red Brick Road is on the left. Photograph by the author, 1975.

Detail of the hand-laid brick paving in the 1937–38 Red Brick Road. Photograph by the author, 1975.

for they were paid by the linear foot of pavement laid per day. The record on the Red Brick Road was an amazing 1,625 feet of 19-foot pavement laid by two setters in one day.

The paving material used in the road was manufactured at a brickyard in Mineral Wells, and trucked to the construction site. The individual bricks measured 2½ by 4 by 8¾ inches. They were manufactured with two quarter-inch lugs on one side so that they automatically provided space for fill material that later was placed between the bricks. The setters placed the bricks at a right angle to the centerline of the highway except on curves and at intersections. At curves they had to lay what they called "dutchmen," triangular sections of bricks laid irregularly to offset the gain on the inside of the curves.

After the setters had placed their bricks in position, other workmen completed the paving job. First a laborer on a self-propelled roller settled the brick into the sand evenly by rolling up and down a segment of newly laid pavement parallel with the centerline of the highway and then switching to roll back and forth across the pavement at a right angle to the centerline.

Rolling completed, other workers proceeded to give the surface of the bricks several coats of whitewash as a bond-breaking material for an asphalt filler that would be applied in the next step. The nozzle of the sprayer used was shaped so that it produced a fine mist of whitewash that fell nearly vertically, and coated only the tops of the bricks.

Men next placed hot liquid asphalt in the quarter-inch spaces between the bricks, leaving the excess on the roadway. After the asphalt had started cooling, other workers using sidewalk cleaners-scrapers came along and removed the excess asphalt from the upper surfaces of the bricks. The coating of whitewash

allowed them to strip the extra asphalt away in rolls. These in turn they placed back into the asphalt pots to remelt and use again. Finally, the entire surface of the roadway was covered with a thin layer of sand and given a last rolling. Three months later the sand was removed and the completed section opened to traffic.

Though mostly covered with subsequent layers of asphalt pavement, the bricks are still visible in places, proving the durability of this type of pavement and the quality of the workmanship that went into laying it almost half a century ago.

Location: The Red Brick Road comprises the westbound lane of U.S. 180 between Weatherford and Mineral Wells.

Suggested Reading:

Stone, J. R. "The Red Brick Road." *Texas Highways* 11, no. 2 (February, 1964): 3–7.

Texas. State Highway Department. "Plans of Proposed State Highway Improvement, Federal Aid Project 132-Reop. Unit IV, State Highway 1 Parker County from Palo Pinto County Line to West City Limits of Weatherford." Manuscript drawings. 1937. Project Control No. 8, Section 2, Parker County. Engineering Department, Texas Department of Highways and Public Transportation, Fort Worth, Tex.

Texas. State Highway Department. "Plans of Proposed State Highway Improvement, Federal Aid Project, Palo Pinto County from Mineral Wells City Limits to Parker County Line." Manuscript drawings. 1936. Project Control No. 8, Section 1, Palo Pinto County. Engineering Department, Texas Department of Highways and Public Transportation, Fort Worth, Tex.

80. Regency Suspension Bridge

Looking north to the 1939 Regency Suspension Bridge from the San Saba
County side of the Colorado River. Photograph by the author, 1975.

The Regency Suspension Bridge (1939) across the Colorado River is one of the most handsome surviving suspension bridges in Texas. It is a fine representative example of the type of suspension spans erected for rural use throughout the United States in the years between the two world wars.

In spring, 1939, the counties of Mills and San Saba contracted with the Austin Bridge Company of Dallas, Texas, to build a bridge across the Colorado River to connect western Mills County with northern San Saba County. The site selected by the two groups of county commissioners was the Regency Crossing, a point with a high bluff on the south side of the river that made it ideal for a suspension span that would be

safe from flood danger. A crew of a dozen men began work on the bridge in late spring, 1939, and completed it in the autumn. They used primarily hand tools, the only mechanized equipment available being a winch truck, a gasoline-fueled concrete mixer, and for a short time a steam shovel for digging foundations. One of the men who participated on the project estimated that 90 percent of the work was done by hand.

The bridge consists of a 340-foot suspension span to which is added a 57-foot girder approach span at its north end. The foundations and piers are concrete, and the four towers consist of welded angle steel topped with cast-steel saddles to support the cables.

Detail of the wire cable, hanger rods, and one of the welded steel towers of the Regency Bridge. Photograph by the author, 1975.

The cables comprise 475 individual strands of No. 9 galvanized wire with a combined diameter of 3.25 inches. The 16-foot roadway consists of wooden timbers supported on steel floor beams.

The initial work on the Regency Bridge centered on excavating anchors for the steel cables. As this work progressed, foundations were dug for the abutments and piers, and concrete was poured for these portions of the structure. Four welded-steel towers with saddle castings in their tops were erected over the piers. Then cables were strung to support a light wooden catwalk stretching 340 feet across the river valley between the towers.

Workers crossed the catwalk hundreds of times carrying the wires one at a time to form the large cables that eventually would support the roadway. The men used special belts with rollers that would allow the wire to unroll smoothly as they crossed and recrossed the narrow catwalk suspended in the air. At each tower the wire was lifted by another worker to the saddle atop the tower and then lowered either to be carried to the other side or to go to the anchor at the extreme end of the project. This operation took approximately six weeks.

The most dangerous work, wrapping the completed cables with wire and then covering them with a special treatment to resist corrosion, remained to be done. "That was about the hardest part of all because you was suspended in the air," one of the men recalled years later. "You had to ride those cables . . . sit down and scoot along those cables to get the wire wrapped around them." Two weeks were required for this portion of the job.

In the meantime, other laborers attached steel hanger rods, which connected the cables with the steel floor beams to support the wooden roadway for the bridge. Then the wooden timbers and floor decking were put in place. The final work on the project consisted of installing a steel cable and wooden handrail along the side of the roadway to protect pedestrians from accidental falls.

The Regency Suspension Bridge remains in service today in remarkably sound condition. There have been no major changes in the structure. The bridge itself is very pleasing to the eye, and the view of the Colorado River far below is most impressive. In part to ensure its preservation, the Regency Suspension Bridge was placed on the National Register of Historic Places.

Location: The Regency Suspension Bridge was built to connect rural areas of Mills and San Saba counties, and there are no large towns near the bridge even today. It may be approached from either north or south. From the north, access is by a graded county road running southward from FM574 five miles east of its intersection with State Highway 45, about 18.3 miles west of Goldthwaite. From this point, proceed 5 miles south on a graded county road past the old Regency Store to the bridge itself. This route includes the crossing over Rough Creek on a small but handsome steel pony-truss bridge, which is worth examination. The Regency Bridge may be approached from the south from FM 500. The bridge is 1 mile north of this highway via a graded county road. The turn-off on FM 500 is 8 miles northeast of its intersection with State Highway 45, or 17.5 miles northeast of San Saba on FM 500.

Suggested Reading:

Austin Bridge Company, Dallas, Tex. Measured Drawings for Contract No. 2305, Suspension Span across Colorado River near Regency, Tex. Blueprint drawings. 1939. "Regency Suspension Bridge" file, Texas Historic Engineering Site Inventory, Center for the History of Engineering, Texas Tech University, Lubbock, Tex.

Moore, Jack B., to John E. Moore and T. Lindsay Baker. Interview at Abilene, Tex., July, 1975. Tape recording in "Regency Suspension Bridge" file, Texas Historic Engineering Site Inventory, Center for the History of Engineering, Texas Tech University, Lubbock, Tex.

Detail of one of the two cables supporting the Regency Suspension Bridge. This cable consists of 475 individual No. 9 galvanized wires. Each strand was carried across the river on a light wooden catwalk to form the completed cable. It required six weeks of work to build up the two cables. Photograph by the author, 1975.

81. Republic of Texas Boundary Marker

On the Texas-Louisiana state line southeast of Deadwood in Panola County stands the last known granite international boundary marker delimiting the borders of the Republic of Texas and the United States of America. Erected in 1841, it was one of a series of markers placed by a joint United States–Republic of Texas commission that surveyed, mapped, and marked the international boundary between 1839 and 1841.

The story of the United States–Texas boundary survey actually begins much earlier, with the 1819 Adams-Onís Treaty between the United States and Spain. This agreement fixed the western boundary of the Louisiana Purchase at the Sabine River from its mouth up to the thirty-second parallel of latitude, thence due north to the Red River, and up the Red River to the hundredth meridian of longitude. The boundary then proceeded north and west to the Pacific Ocean. This international boundary continued in effect for the remainder of the Spanish period in Texas history, through the Mexican period, and for the decade of the Republic of Texas as well. Consequently, when the national governments of the United States and the Republic of Texas appointed commissioners to survey their joint border, it was the lower portion of the Adams-Onís line that they mapped and marked.

On April 25, 1838, a young engineer, W. J. Stone,

The granite international boundary marker erected by the joint United States–Republic of Texas boundary commission on April 23, 1841. Photograph by the author, 1981.

received his appointment as one of the U.S. commissioners to survey his country's boundary with the Republic of Texas. He promised at the time to complete his task "with all due speed and accuracy," but it was three years before he achieved his goal. Neither he nor the other members of the joint commission realized the magnitude of the task that they were undertaking in charting the border between the two countries.

The Boundary Commission met first in New Orleans, the outfitting point for their expedition. Assembling there on August 7, 1839, they spent several days gathering provisions and arranging for their transportation to the mouth of the Sabine River, where their work was to begin. They first landed at the mouth of the river on the coast, but "owing to the peculiar unhealthiness of the season and other obstacles," they moved their camp thirty-five miles up

206

the river to Green's Bluff. There they awaited the arrival of other U.S. commissioners, who were bringing with them the astronomical instruments needed for the mapping work. In the meantime, the first party shifted its camp upstream another twelve miles to Millspaw's Bluff. The tardy American commissioners did not reach New Orleans until December 18, and they were unable to secure transportation to the mouth of the Sabine until January 27, 1840. Three days later, they reached the other commissioners' camp.

Once the full complement of commissioners was assembled, they started charting the route of the Sabine from its mouth to the point where it intercepted the thirty-second parallel. While some members of the party drew maps and took astronomical observations to determine the longitude and latitude, others erected occasional earthen mounds as official boundary markers. They continued tracing the route up the river, often making their astronomical observations at night when the skies were clear. The dense forests and frequent driftwood rafts blocking the Sabine slowed the progress of the surveying party to a very deliberate pace. Finally, in June, 1840, after having expended all its funds from both governments, the commission disbanded for the summer season, agreeing to meet again on November 1 to continue its effort.

The Joint Commission did reassemble, but not in the fall of 1840. The Texas Congress did not appropriate funds for its half of the commission until later, so it was February 14, 1841, before the commissioners renewed their work. March rains delayed progress again for a number of days. Finally, effective work began anew on the survey as the field party started on the portion of the boundary north from the intersection of the Sabine with the thirty-second parallel. Every mile of the way they erected mounds of earth five feet high and fifteen feet wide surmounted by wooden posts eight feet high identifying the border and noting the number of miles the marker was located north of thirty second parallel. Three miles north of the Sabine, on April 23, 1841, the commissioners erected a particularly imposing carved granite monument. The stone bore the inscriptions, "U.S."

and "R.T.," referring to the United States and the Republic of Texas, as well as the words, "Meridn. Boundary Established 1840." When the marker was carved, it was expected that it would be placed in 1840, but the delays pushed the date forward one year.

By May 14, 1841, thirty-eight miles had been covered. On that day the commissioners left their work to travel to Greenwood, Louisiana, to attend a memorial service for President Benjamin Harrison, who had died in office. Four days later they reached Caddo Lake and established the forty-six-mile post on an island in the lake. Work proceeded through the early summer. With great difficulties caused by the almost overpowering forest growth, numerous streams to be crossed, illness, and lack of supplies, the commissioners at last reached the Red River and the end of the survey on June 24, 1841. As the journal of the expedition recorded, "The Meridian portion of this boundary has been achieved amid difficulties of no ordinary character, arising as well from the nature of the country through which it passed, as from the unpropitious season of the year. . . . The plans or maps of the whole extent of the boundary are determined . . . and authenticated by the signing of this journal by the joint commission."

The job of the commissioners was completed. Most of their earthen mounds are long eroded away, but the U.S. commissioners' maps and journals are still preserved in the National Archives, and the granite marker they erected on April 23, 1841, still stands where they placed it almost a century and a half ago.

Location: The granite Republic of Texas Boundary Marker stands about a hundred feet north of State Highway 31, at the Louisiana state line, about ten miles southeast of Deadwood. A footpath leads from the side of the roadway to the marker, which is protected by a welded pipe fence.

Suggested Reading:

Mungo, Marjie. "Epic Journey." *Texas Highways* 18, no. 4 (April, 1971): 18–21.

82. *Riverside Swing Bridge*

The Riverside Swing Bridge, fabricated by the Wisconsin Bridge and Iron Company between 1914 and 1915 and erected in 1916, is one of the last surviving railway structures of its type in Texas. Pivoting on a huge steel pin mounted in a central concrete pier, the bridge was designed to turn ninety degrees to

The Riverside Swing Bridge open during high water to allow the passage of driftwood in the mid-1920s. Photograph courtesy Mrs. Vernon Schuder, Riverside, Texas.

permit the passage of steamboats and barges on the Trinity River.

Building across Walker County from south to north, from Houston toward Palestine, the Houston and Great Northern Railroad erected its first bridge across the Trinity at Riverside between 1871 and 1872. Although this initial span allowed the passage of trains across the river for many years, during World War I it was replaced by a more modern structure, the present-day Riverside Swing Bridge. All that remains from the earlier bridge are the remnants of two stone piers that once supported part of the former structure.

The ownership of the rail line connecting Houston and Palestine changed several times in the forty-five years between its construction and the time when the present Riverside bridge was built. In 1873 the company merged with the International Railroad Company to become the International and Great Northern Railroad. In 1908 this firm went into receivership to emerge in 1911 as the International and Great Northern Railway, the only difference in name being the change from "Railroad" to "Railway." It was this corporate entity that built the swing bridge.

In 1910 the company prepared specifications for a new bridge across the main channel of the Trinity River at Riverside. These called for a type of bridge then popular on American railroads elsewhere in the country but one that even at the time was considered unusual by Texas standards. The specifications called for a modified Pratt through-truss steel bridge mounted on a single large concrete pier. Under these plans the entire bridge would rotate through a system of gearing to turn about on a huge steel pin mounted in the center of the

pier. This swinging would allow free clearance for potential barge and steamboat traffic on the Trinity River.

In 1912 work began at the construction site. Two of the original stone piers from the previous bridge were shortened and then recapped with fresh concrete to serve as piers for the approaches at the ends of the proposed steel span. Their role was merely to stand in position at the ends of the swing span, since the entire weight of the steel truss was to be supported on its one central pier. Work progressed on this portion of the project as well. At the center of the proposed steel truss span, a foundation was excavated for a thirty-three-foot-diameter concrete pier to support the swing span. After the foundation was dug, elm pilings were driven into the riverbed to bedrock to provide a secure footing. Then a five-sixteenths-inch steel shell made of used oil tank material was placed in the excavated area and wooden forms were placed in position above the level of the riverbed for a large concrete pouring job. With steel reinforcing rods in position, fresh concrete was poured over the pilings, filling both the steel shell and the wooden forms above. This portion of the project was completed by October, 1912, and work was suspended until other parts of the project caught up.

Bids had been opened for the fabrication of the steel superstructure for the new bridge by the time work had begun at the construction site. The Wisconsin Bridge and Iron Company of North Milwaukee, Wisconsin, received the contract for the project. Bridge company engineers drew up final plans for the structure in October, November, and December, 1914, with actual fabrication of the steel members being conducted in their plant during 1915. After their completion and inspection in Wisconsin, the elements of the prefabricated overhead truss span, together with its operating machinery for turning, were shipped by rail to Texas.

Actual erection of the bridge came in 1916. The truss members were supported on wooden falsework erected in the riverbed until the completed span supported itself on its central pier, after which time the temporary falsework was removed.

When the structure officially was turned over to the railroad, a ceremony was held to dedicate it. One longtime resident, who as a young woman attended the dedication, remembered the event this way: "Before the railroad would accept it, they had a little ceremony, and they turned that bridge. It turned very slow. It was turned by hand, not by machinery . . . they used a wheel, similar to a ship's wheel, with spokes, and it would screech, and go a little bit, and screech, and go a little bit further. The contractor told the railroad people, 'A hundred years from now this bridge will turn this good.'"

The swing bridge has a total length of 294 feet, 4 inches. It is 15 feet wide and has 21 feet, 8.5 inches of vertical clearance from the top of the rails to the underside of its overhead truss members. The span itself weighs 523,240 pounds and its turning mechanism weighs 72,700 pounds. Its open deck consists of creosoted timbers with the rails attached directly to them.

In addition to the historic swing span, the Riverside Bridge has very extensive approaches on its north side across the wide, low bottoms of the Trinity Valley. These approaches consist of a thirty-nine-panel ballast deck timber-pile trestle 507 feet long constructed in 1940, a twenty-nine-panel open-deck timber-pile trestle 375 feet long erected in 1941, a thirty-four-panel concrete trestle 996 feet long built in 1955, and a fifty-five-panel concrete trestle 612 feet long erected in 1956. At the south end of the swing span there is a single 60-foot-deck plate-girder approach span put in place in 1938. All these approach sections give the bridge a total length of 2,850 feet.

During all its history, the Riverside Swing Bridge has turned only twice, neither time for its intended

Looking east to the 1916 Riverside Swing Bridge from State Highway 19, just north of Riverside. Photograph by the author, 1981.

Detail of the gear mechanism at the base of the swing span and at the top of the concrete central pier of the 1916 Riverside Swing Bridge. Photograph by the author, 1981.

purpose of allowing the passage of barge traffic. The first time was during its dedication in 1916. The second occasion came a decade later when the bridge turned to permit the passage of a huge log jam of driftwood that had piled against it during a major flood. At the time of this high water, the bridge itself was damaged considerably. To prevent its being completely washed away by the tremendous force of the floodwater, railway employees rolled a number of heavily loaded freight cars onto the structure to increase its weight and thus protect it. Even with this precaution the north end of the truss structure was heavily damaged and had to be rebuilt.

In 1914 the International and Great Northern Railway again entered receivership, emerging in 1922 as the International–Great Northern Railroad. Under this name it operated the track crossing the Riverside Bridge until the mid-1950s, when it became part of the Missouri Pacific system. On September 12, 1955, the U.S. Corps of Engineers gave its approval for the new owners to weld the ends of the swing span to the

bridge approaches, converting it into a fixed bridge. It continues to operate in this manner today.

Location: The Riverside Swing Bridge is located on the main line of the Missouri Pacific Railroad across the Trinity River at the north side of the town of Riverside. It may be approached on foot along the railway right-of-way from town, but it should be noted that the bridge and its approaches are private railroad company property. The bridge itself is dangerous and visitors are warned not to trespass on the structure. Perhaps the best view of the bridge is from the State Highway 19 bridge just north of Riverside.

Suggested Reading:

Hale, Leon. "Laying to Rest the Sam Houston Syndrome." *Houston Post* (July 20, 1975), sec. B, p. 3.
Missouri Pacific Railroad Company, Saint Louis, Mo. Bridge record file for Bridge 71.1, Trinity River. Manuscript. 1914–56. Engineering Department, Missouri Pacific Railroad Company, Saint Louis, Mo.

83. San Antonio Acequias

Tracing their history almost to the very founding of the city, the acequias are the still-functioning Spanish colonial irrigation canals of San Antonio. "Acequia" translates literally as "ditch"—and this term describes the system perfectly. It consists of a

series of ditches that were dug from the San Antonio River or San Pedro Creek and that carried their waters, nearly at the natural elevation contours of the land, to the agricultural areas requiring irrigation.

The oldest of the acequias is the Alamo Madre,

which was excavated to serve the lands of the San Antonio de Valero Mission. It was begun in 1718 and is known to have been operating by 1727, though it was expanded until 1744, when it watered about six hundred acres east of the San Antonio River. The canal functioned until the early twentieth century, by which time the area it had formerly irrigated was occupied by urban construction.

The Alamo Madre was followed by the San José Acequia. It was begun about 1720 to provide irrigation water to the fields of the San José y San Miguel de Aguayo Mission on the west side of the river. Taking its water from the river a short distance below its juncture with San Pedro Creek, the canal meandered about five miles before returning its excess flow to the river. The repeated washing out of its loose-rock dam eventually caused its abandonment about 1860.

In 1731 three East Texas missions, Purísima Concepción de Acuña, San Francisco de la Espada, and San Juan Capistrano, were transferred from their original locations to San Antonio. These were relocated at sites downstream from the other two missions and were given the right to use waters of the San Antonio River for irrigation. Soon the mission fathers and their Indian neophytes began constructing canals to carry needed water to their fields. The Concepción Acequia, begun about 1731, took its supply from the San Antonio River at a stone diversion dam approximately in line with present-day South Presa Street in downtown San Antonio, near what today is the public library. Through the use of numerous lateral canals, it watered mission lands on the east side of

the river. It remained in use until 1869, when its dam was removed because of the danger it posed to downtown areas when it backed up floodwaters during heavy rains.

Also begun about 1731 was the San Juan Acequia, one of the two still-functioning canals. Its waters were diverted from the river at a point opposite from Mission San José and conducted on the east side of the river to irrigate the San Juan lands. During the nineteenth century this acequia served about five hundred acres. By the mid-twentieth century the canal had fallen into disuse, and its diversion dam was removed in the course of the construction of a flood control project undertaken in the 1960s. A lawsuit by the owners of the San Juan water rights late in the decade, however, forced the construction of a new concrete diversion dam, and today the San Juan again serves farmers on the south side of the city.

The best known of the San Antonio Acequias is the Espada. Its notoriety comes from its impressive original diversion dam and stone aqueduct, which hold the distinction of being the last functioning documented Spanish colonial dam and aqueduct in the United States. The Espada takes its flow from behind a dam consisting of flagstones laid in courses on a natural ledge across the river at the foot of present-day Mission Burial Park. From this point the ditch flows in a generally southerly direction three miles to the former Espada mission lands. On the way it crosses one major barrier, Piedras Creek, which it spans on a solid masonry aqueduct. Built sometime between 1731 and 1745, the aqueduct, which is 195

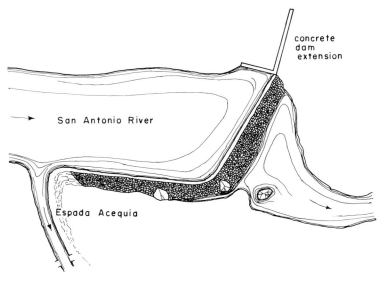

Plan view of the Espada Dam, which continues to divert San Antonio River water into the head of the eighteenth-century Espada Acequia. Based on measured drawings in U.S. Department of the Interior, National Park Service, Historic American Engineering Record, Site Tex-1. Drawing by the author.

The Espada Dam in service diverting irrigation water for over two centuries. Photograph by the author, 1975.

feet long with approaches, includes two arches, one 12 feet in length and the other 16 feet, 6 inches in length. It stands 15 feet, 6 inches high at the point where it actually crosses the creek.

The Espada Acequia remained in use until the 1880s, when it fell idle. In 1895 the owners of water rights along the canal organized themselves into a private company that cleaned, widened, and deepened the ditch, repaired the diversion dam, and made some changes in the upper courses of the canal. Today the acequia, still in active use, measures 4.5 miles long with an average bottom width of 5.5 feet. Its grade is twenty-three inches per mile, giving it a water

flow of approximately twelve cubic feet per second. The portion of the river where the acequia is diverted was bypassed by a new flood control channel during the 1960s, but the San Antonio River Authority took appropriate measures to preserve the historic Espada Dam and to maintain the proper water level behind it.

The first acequia built to serve the civilian or non-mission population at San Antonio was the San Pedro Acequia (built between 1738 and 1740). The canal headed at the San Pedro Springs and flowed along the divide between San Pedro Creek and the San Antonio River to the east. This position on the watershed freed the San Pedro from the cross-drainage problems

Plan and elevation of the Espada Aqueduct. Based on measured drawing in U.S. Department of the Interior, National Park Service, Historic American Engineering Record, Site Tex-1. Drawing by the author.

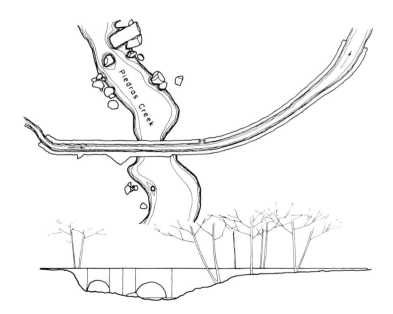

Looking downstream on Piedras Creek to the Espada Aqueduct, about 1895. From William Ferguson Hutson, *Irrigation Systems in Texas,* U.S. Department of the Interior, Geological Survey, Water-Supply and Irrigation Paper No. 13 (Washington, D.C.: Government Printing Office, 1898), opposite p. 44.

that plagued the other canals. Flowing in a generally southerly direction, the acequia watered about four hundred acres along its four-mile length. It operated until 1906, by which time the lands it had irrigated had been converted to urban use.

In 1773 Spanish authorities moved a substantial number of settlers from East Texas to San Antonio. Although most of these people eventually returned to East Texas, some of them remained at their new home and were authorized to build a ditch to serve their irrigation needs. This, the last canal dug during the Spanish period, was known as the Upper Labor Acequia. Taking its supply at a diversion point just below the head of the San Antonio River, the canal flowed in a roughly southwesterly direction to the area of the San Pedro Springs. Work began on the project in 1776 and was completed two years later, at which time the ditch irrigated about six hundred acres. It operated until the late nineteenth century.

Two additional acequias were constructed during the nineteenth century, the Alazán Ditch and the Valley Ditch. The Alazán, built between 1872 and 1876, was actually an extension of the old Upper Labor

Acequia. It took its flow from the San Pedro Springs at the head of the Upper Labor Acequia and proceeded in a roughly southerly direction to irrigate areas west of San Pedro Creek. It remained in use until 1896. The Valley Ditch also was begun in 1872. It took water from the old Alamo Madre Acequia at a point near Grand Avenue and was to convey it to the then-unused Concepción Acequia, but it was soon abandoned because of errors in its grade. No remains of either of these ditches are known to have survived.

The acequias played an essential role in the early history of San Antonio as it grew from an agricultural community in the wilderness into a prosperous trade center. When Texas passed from Mexican to Anglo-American administration, the systems of canals remained the foundation for the local agricultural economy as well as serving as a major source of domestic water for San Antonio residents. The ditches continued to be an integral part of the way of life in the city until their functions finally were assumed in the late nineteenth century by increased numbers of artesian wells and by a modern waterworks. By the twentieth century most of the canals had been abandoned, with the exception of the two farthest away from the city center, the Espada and the San Juan. These two remain in use today much as they operated when they were built two and a half centuries ago.

Location: Acequias and remains of acequias may be seen in many parts of San Antonio. Some of them have reached the status of tourist attractions.

Preserved stretches of the Alamo Madre, the oldest of the acequias, may be visited in three places. In 1966 a 94-foot-segment of the Alamo Madre was excavated in the courtyard of the San Antonio Museum of Transportation in the Hemisfair Plaza. In 1969 another segment of the ditch was partially excavated just east of downtown San Antonio, where it passes through the south side of the irregularly shaped block bounded by Bowie, Nacogdoches, Elm, and Starr streets. Averaging just over 4.5 feet in width and with its original stone lining intact, its bottom unfortunately is covered with a concrete-capped storm sewer, which prevented its complete excavation. A sluice gate on its west side gives interesting insights into the construction of such auxiliary structures, and along one side at approximately 5-foot intervals, one finds cut into the stone lining a number of notches that once supported fence posts. A third section of the canal lies behind the chapel at the Mission San Antonio de Valero. Originally a branch of the Alamo Madre that flowed through the mission compound, it was lined with concrete earlier in this century to form an elongated fishpond.

Most remains of the San José Acequia have been obliterated, although traces of the canal may be seen just outside the north wall of the San José Mission compound. There one may also examine the reconstructed San José gristmill, which was powered by water supplied by the acequia. Built about 1790 and discovered during excavations conducted in 1934, the gristmill was reconstructed over its original foundations in the mid-1930s. A stream of acequia water passing through an equalizer vat powered a horizontal waterwheel not unlike a modern turbine. This wheel drove a vertical shaft to which the millstones on the floor above were attached.

Though not impressive in appearance, the San Juan is one of the two still-functioning acequias. It draws its flow at the east end of a modern concrete diversion dam on the San Antonio River just below Padre Park east of Mission San José. The canal generally follows the contours of the land to a point about a fifth of

a mile east of Mission San Juan, where it separates into "lower" and "upper" branches. The lower branch passes westward to the old mission lands, where farmers use it for irrigation purposes, and then it flows for an additional mile and a quarter, roughly parallel to the river before returning any unused flow to the river. This segment of the canal passes within a short distance of the visitors' parking lot at the mission and is easily observed. The upper branch flows in a southerly direction from the point of separation for slightly over a mile and a half before returning to the river. Currently, the upper segment carries water only during the times of high water in the river.

The Espada Acequia presents perhaps the most interesting remains of all the San Antonio acequias. Its original eighteenth-century diversion dam may be viewed from the paved road that leads southward into Espada Park from Military Drive, immediately west of the river. The canal flows through the Mission Burial Park and private property to the aqueduct, where it passes over Piedras Creek. This area, today a park, is located on Espada Road just south of its intersection with Ashley Road southeast of Stinson Airport. The canal flows on southward to the old Espada Mission lands, where its lateral ditches are still irrigating agricultural fields.

The Upper Labor Acequia, the last of the ditches dug during the Spanish period, also has interesting remains that may be visited. At its diversion point at the head of the San Antonio River at the northern end of Brackenridge Park and just south of Hildebrand Avenue, a reconstructed fifty-yard segment of acequia carries water away from the river to a point where it meets backflow from a channel that drains part of the San Antonio zoo. Farther down the course of the former irrigation canal, its channel serves in a greatly modified state as part of the waterfowl habitat for the zoo.

Suggested Reading:

Appendices to the Brief of the Plaintiffs in State of Texas et al. vs. Valmont Plantations. Mission, Tex.: Times Publishing Co. [1962].

Glick, Thomas F. *The Old World Background of the Irrigation System of San Antonio, Texas.* Southwestern Studies No. 35. El Paso: Texas Western Press, 1972.

Holmes, William Henry. "The Acequias of San Antonio." M.A. thesis, St. Mary's University, San Antonio, Tex., 1962.

84. *San Antonio Sewerage System*

One of the oldest wastewater treatment systems in the state, the San Antonio Sewerage System is notable for its early and continued successful use of broad irrigation as a means of disposing of excess effluent. The irrigation system operated until 1981, and many of its historic structures can still easily be seen by visitors.

One of the first notices of a planned sewerage system for San Antonio appeared on July 26, 1894, when the nationally read engineering weekly, *Engineering News,* reported that San Antonio was "considering the construction of a sewerage system." Already, plans and estimated costs for the project had been drawn up by Samuel M. Gray, a civil engineer from Providence, Rhode Island. The plans were not for merely a collection system, but also for a canal to carry the wastewater to a point south of the city for disposal. There the effluent was to be distributed by irrigation over cultivated agricultural fields.

Actual construction of the system began in February, 1896. The specifications called for seventy-four miles of mains within the city as well as for a canal to carry the wastewater to the area to be irrigated. (It is interesting to note that in excavating ground for the mains at the San Antonio River in the center of the city, some Spanish coins dated 1790 and a cannonball were uncovered. It was supposed at the time that the cannonball was from the siege of the nearby Alamo in 1836.) The outfall sewer line from the city led southward to what came to be known as the "sewer farm" located near present-day Rilling Road in the area where Stinson Airport now stands. City employees applied that portion of the effluent needed to irrigate about five hundred to eight hundred acres of land, running the remainder of the raw sewage into the channel of the San Antonio River below the city. The experiment proved to be a failure for several reasons, not the least of which was the inability of the city to pay for its sewage disposal costs with the limited revenues generated by the sale of the crops raised on its sewage farm. More important, considerable pollution was created in the San Antonio River, which resulted in lawsuits against the city.

To solve the problems it had encountered in attempting to dispose of its wastewater on its own, in 1901 the city changed its approach. On September 23 of that year the City Council signed an agreement with a firm known as the Mitchell Lake Company,

which soon became the San Antonio Irrigation Company, to accept all the city's effluent and to dispose of it through broad irrigation on agricultural land. As part of the agreement, the company committed itself to building a dam across a minor tributary of the Medina River south of the city to impound all the wastewater that it was unable to use immediately for irrigation purposes. The impoundment created a reservoir, known as Mitchell Lake, covering about nine hundred acres. Strengthened and enlarged through the years, the dam structure still stands.

The San Antonio Irrigation Company within only a few years had placed approximately fifteen hundred acres under irrigation through the operation of a comparatively complex system of canals and flumes. The main canal was built 5.5 miles in a generally southerly direction toward the Mitchell Lake reservoir from the outfall of the city sewers at the old sewage farm. Its right-of-way, together with immunity from damage claims along its route, was secured by the city for the company by granting the landowners along its route water rights for their own private irrigation with wastewater provided at no cost. In addition to these private acreages, the San Antonio Irrigation Company successfully irrigated about eight hundred acres above the reservoir by gravity flow through lateral ditches originating at the main canal. Below the dam it also irrigated about four hundred acres by gravity flow, not to mention watering about three hundred acres of agricultural land above the lake through the use of pumps. The firm had approximately fifteen hundred irrigated acres by 1916. Irrigated acreage continued to expand through the years, and by 1954 forty-five hundred acres were being irrigated. During the winter, when the need for irrigation water was reduced to a minimum, the company stored excess effluent in Mitchell Lake. This wastewater for about a decade was diluted by storm runoff from the approximately seven thousand acres drained by the lake, but this situation was changed by the construction of two small dams that created freshwater ponds a short distance upstream from Mitchell Lake.

One of the striking features of the San Antonio Irrigation Company system was its extensive use of flumes to carry effluent at its proper grade of 10 feet per mile over minor drainage areas. In 1905 the system employed 1,500 feet of wooden flumes for this

BUILDING THE LONE STAR

One of the galvanized sheet-steel flumes carrying wastewater to the Mitchell Lake area about 1916. From Terrell Bartlett, "Successful Sewage Disposal by Broad Irrigation," *Engineering News* 76, no. 13 (September 28, 1916): 487.

purpose. The original sections of flumes, which varied from 4 to 6 feet wide and from 2 to 2.5 feet deep, were made from tongue-in-groove two-inch cypress lumber forming wooden troughs mounted on four-inch-square cypress posts anchored in postholes in the ground 8 feet apart and further strengthened by wooden stringers diagonally bracing the posts. By World War I the cypress flumes had been replaced with mass-produced galvanized steel sections supported on the original wooden posts. Although the flumes no longer remain in service, lengthy sections of them remain in place and are quite impressive.

Among the crops satisfactorily raised under sewage irrigation in San Antonio were various feedstuffs, sorghum, Johnson grass, alfalfa, and cotton. The cultivation of vegetables for human consumption was never permitted on the irrigation company acreage, although early in this century some excitement was created in the city when it was discovered that some

of the private land owners along the main canal were using wastewater to irrigate their truck gardens for the local market.

The irrigation company fields were rented to tenants who resided on the properties. At one time about a hundred families, or about five hundred people, lived and worked on the company lands. Then about 1915 the firm began converting some of its farms into irrigated Johnson grass pastures stocked with cattle. This reduced the number of workers on the property to about forty or fifty, although irrigation of cultivated fields continued.

The San Antonio Sewerage System operated basically as described here for several decades. In 1930 the city placed in operation its first actual sewage treatment facility, the Rilling Road Plant, located in about the same area as the initial 1897 sewage farm. This activated-sludge plant treated sewage originating in the city and then passed the treated effluent and

One of the still-standing sections of cypress post and galvanized sheet-steel flume erected by the San Antonio Irrigation Company early in this century. Photograph by the author, 1974.

waste-activated sludge down the old canal for irrigation and impoundment in Mitchell Lake. By 1937, due to increasing volume of flow, the city constructed an effluent discharge canal from the Rilling Road Treatment Plant to the San Antonio River. As the city grew, additional treatment facilities were required, with a second major installation being opened on Rilling Road in 1950 and a third expansion beginning operation in 1966. During the 1950s an additional closed conduit was laid to carry effluent to the Mitchell Lake area, and in 1973 the open canal was closed and all effluent diverted into the closed line. In 1963 ownership of Mitchell Lake itself passed from the heirs of its original builders to the city, and since that time the municipality has operated the reservoir. It was modified in the mid-1970s by the construction of a dike and lagoon at its northern inlet so that part of it might serve as a lagoon for excess activated sludge produced by the three Rilling Road plants.

Until recently a small amount of irrigation was still being conducted south of the city with treated effluent, a legacy of the decades of successful sewage disposal by broad irrigation in San Antonio. In 1981, in conformance with long-range plans for improvement and expansion of its wastewater system, which included the phasing-out of Mitchell Lake operations, the city began the evaporative drying of the lake and lake-bed land reclamation that will lead to the removal of the old earthen dam structure in the future.

Location: The area of the original 1897 San Antonio sewage farm and of the 1930, 1950, and 1966 Rilling Road Sewage Treatment Plants may be reached on Rilling Road just east of State Highway 536 (Roosevelt Avenue), on the south side of San Antonio. The Mitchell Lake area is most easily viewed by taking the old Pleasanton Road south from its interchange with Interstate 410 (Loop 410) at the Moursund Boulevard exit at the south side of the city. The most accessible remaining flumes from the old San Antonio Irrigation Company system stand parallel to and just west of U.S. 281, about two miles south of its interchange with Loop 410.

Suggested Reading:

Bartlett, Terrell. "Successful Sewage Disposal by Broad Irrigation." *Engineering News* 76, no. 13 (September 28, 1916): 486–87.

Bowie, A. J. "Irrigation in Southern Texas." In U.S. Department of Agriculture, Office of Experiment Stations. *Annual Report of Irrigation and Drainage Investigations, 1904, Separate No. 6*, pp. 347–507. Washington, D.C.: Government Printing Office, 1905.

Wells, W. N. "San Antonio Sewage Treatment Plant." *Southwest Water Works Journal* 37, no. 7 (October, 1955): 37, 40, 42.

85. San Antonio Waterworks

"We thought how easy to make San Antonio the most famed city for natural beauty on the continent. . . . Water-pipes could be laid from the head . . . of the river . . . supplying water to residences . . . and then lead to the city . . . to supply it with spring water, or to feed a thousand dancing fountains." Thus

The 1878 Lambert Beach Pumping Station as it appears today, near the San Antonio Zoological Gardens. At the bottom of the station are the openings through which water from the power canal left the building after powering the turbines. Photograph by the author, 1975.

The 1885 Brackenridge Park Pump House, better known in San Antonio as the Borglum Studio. Photograph by the author, 1975.

dreamed a San Antonio promoter during the hot summer of 1867, although a decade would pass before San Antonio would have its own waterworks.

In 1877 the time had come for the establishment of a system to provide water to the residents of the Alamo City. On April 3 the City Council gave a twenty-five-year franchise to build and operate a system to J. B. LaCoste and his associates. They issued stock in the amount of $100,000 under the name of the San Antonio Water Works Company and employed the King Iron Bridge and Manufacturing Company to construct the system for $94,000.

The contractors excavated a power canal, or raceway, across a bend in the San Antonio River near its head. This canal led to a limestone pump house near what today is known as the Lambert Beach swimming area in Brackenridge Park. The "drop" from the river level at the inlet of the raceway to the pumping plant was nine feet, and this gave the water flowing down the canal sufficient force to operate a turbine that was connected directly to the plunger of a large pump. According to tradition, the old Spanish colonial diversion dam for the Upper Labor Acequia initially diverted the river flow into the raceway. The pump house, completed in 1878, still stands in Brackenridge Park near the San Antonio Zoological Gardens.

Although at first the waterworks company had planned to excavate a stone reservoir for pumped water on upper Rock Quarry Road, this site proved to be impractical. Instead, they chose the alternate higher summit of another elevated point, today the

extreme east end of Mahncke Park. There they constructed an earthen reservoir eighteen feet deep in both excavation and embankment. With a capacity of five million gallons, it had inner slopes paved with limestone to reduce leakage. From the reservoir, which was kept filled with water by the pump on the river, water flowed through mains by gravity to consumers in various parts of the city. The Mahncke Park reservoir continued to be used into the mid-twentieth century, with its original capacity increased at the turn of the century.

The LaCoste waterworks was completed in 1878, but for a number of years its patronage was limited. Most of the citizens preferred instead to use water from flowing streams, irrigation ditches, or their own shallow wells or cisterns. Other people purchased their supply from the *aguadores,* men who carried water from the river or the acequias to stores and residences. Whereas the stockholders had expected hundreds of customers for their water system, they found that they had only a handful of actual users. The financial burdens of the company grew so great that in 1883 the owners sold the controlling interest to San Antonio capitalist George W. Brackenridge. The entrepreneur and his backers incorporated as The Water Works Company on October 9, 1883, an operating firm for the original San Antonio Water Works Company. On December 1 of the same year the two firms entered into a joint operating agreement, with Brackenridge serving as the president of both enterprises.

Seeing that the Lambert Beach pumping station

One of the large steam engines that powered pumping equipment at the Market Street Pumping Station just after the turn of the century. From Arthur Curtis Scott, *Test of a Vertical Expansion High Duty Pumping Engine in Operation at the Water Works, San Antonio, Texas,* University of Texas Bulletin No. 59 (Austin: University of Texas, 1905).

was becoming inadequate to provide for what he felt would be an increasing need for water in the city, Brackenridge purchased extensive acreage along the San Antonio River below the original facility. About 1885 the waterworks company began building a second pumping facility, which came to be known as the Brackenridge Park Station.

Employees excavated a second long power canal to the site of the new pump house. Water flowing down this raceway powered two turbines directly connected with a duplex double-acting power pump with a capacity of three million gallons daily. This station also pumped water to the reservoir in Mahncke Park, from which point it continued to flow through mains

to the customers. The Brackenridge Park Pumping Station remained in service until 1915, when most of its equipment was removed. It later was spotted by sculptor Gutzon Borglum, the noted creator of the Mount Rushmore sculpture, who used it as his studio during his residence in San Antonio in the 1930s. For this reason the building today is known locally as the Borglum Studio. After the sculptor's departure in 1937, it continued to serve as an art studio and classroom until 1961, since which time it has stood unused.

For fear that the spring-fed source of the San Antonio River might fail in the event of drought, in the late 1880s George Brackenridge attempted to drill an artesian well in Mahncke Park. The effort ended in failure because the well did not provide sufficient flow. About the same time, the capitalist increased the capacities of the two existing pumping facilities by adding auxiliary steam equipment.

Despite the initial failure, the waterworks company pursued its efforts to secure an artesian water supply for the city. In 1890 it purchased property in downtown San Antonio at the intersection of Market Street with the San Antonio River. On this site the following year the company sank another well, this time striking a strong artesian aquifer at 890 feet. When the drill struck the aquifer, the water flowed to the surface with so much pressure that it shot 15 to 20 feet into the air and blew out pieces of rock reputedly "as large as a man's head." The well flowed at the rate of three million gallons a day and demonstrated to company officials that artesian wells could provide a sufficient supply of water for decades to come. Soon seven additional wells were drilled at the Market Street location, and in 1891 a new pumping facility was erected there.

The Market Street Pump House contained three electrically powered 750,000-gallon Gould triplex pumps, each with three outside-packed plungers ten inches in diameter and with twelve-inch strokes. This equipment elevated artesian water into a new forty-five-foot standpipe and also to the old Mahncke Park reservoir three miles away. Acclaimed as "one of the earliest electric pumping plants in the country," the Market Street facility actually used electricity for

only a few years. In 1895, with increasing demand for water from the downtown plant, another building was erected at the Market Street location and equipped with two vertical tubular boilers and a 5-million-gallon Worthington triple-expansion pumping engine. In 1897 yet another building was added to connect the initial two structures, and it was fitted with a Corliss steam engine to drive the three Gould triplex pumps, which initially had been operated by electricity. (The cost of electricity from the local electric light company had grown so expensive that it was no longer economical to use this power source.) At the same time three more Gould triplex pumps were added to the plant. In 1904 and 1908 new reciprocating steam pumps with 15-million- and 20-million-gallon capacity, respectively, were installed. The Market Street plant remained the principal downtown pumping station until it was replaced by a new adjacent facility in 1958 and the old structures removed.

While artesian flow was being developed successfully at the Market Street Station, similar efforts were begun to add artesian supply to that of the river water used at the two older pumping plants. Wells were bored at each of the stations in Brackenridge Park to add to the supply already available from the river. Already by 1890 both of these plants had been equipped with auxiliary steam pumping equipment, so they were fully capable of handling the additional supply.

In both 1892 and 1902 the franchise of the San

The boiler house and pump house at the 1914 Brackenridge Park Pumping Station just after its completion. From "Turbine Pumping Station below Ground in San Antonio," *Engineering News* 75, no. 24 (June 15, 1916): 1125.

View down into the pump pit of the 1915 Brackenridge Park Station shortly after it went into operation. From "Turbine Pumping Station Below Ground in San Antonio," *Engineering News* 75, no. 24 (June 15, 1916): 1126.

Antonio Water Works Company was renewed for a ten-year period, but in 1906 the local owners sold their interests to George C. Kobusch of Saint Louis, who organized the San Antonio Water Supply Company. Soon thereafter, the Mississippi Valley Trust Company of Saint Louis, which handled Kobusch's financial affairs, began negotiating the sale of his interests in the company to a Belgian syndicate with its headquarters in Antwerp. In 1909 the Belgian investors acquired 90 percent of the stock in the company and began operating its system as the Companie des Eaux de San Antonio, with the Mississippi Valley Trust Company acting as its agent. In 1910 an engineer sent by the trust company to inspect the San Antonio water system reported that at the time only the Market Street Station was in operation and that additional pumping capacity was needed.

On the basis of the 1910 engineering report, a fourth pumping station was built. Constructed in 1914 near the site of the old 1885 pump house in Brackenridge Park, the new plant was designed to utilize underground water exclusively. Because it was located at a relatively high elevation, the designers found it necessary to place the pumps for the four wells at the station at the bottom of a pit approximately fifty feet below ground level. This gave the pumps a controlling position in relation to the hydrostatic level of the water. Adjacent to the pump pit the contractors built a rectangular brick boiler house, which contained three 250-horsepower water-type boilers to power the pumps.

In the summer of 1914, the new Brackenridge Park Pumping Station was considered one of the showplaces in the recreational area. The water company kept the building open at all hours to permit park visitors to view the pumping equipment in the bottom of the lighted pit from a high gallery designed specifically for this purpose. Shade trees, drives, and flower beds made the facility an attractive addition to the park. The pump house operated into the 1950s, but at the end of the decade its aboveground structures were razed and the pit filled, so that today the only visible remains of the once important station consist of an area of slightly uneven lawn at one side of the park.

After World War I, the Belgian stockholders who controlled the San Antonio Water Supply Company decided to liquidate their interests in Texas to use the funds in rebuilding properties in their home country. In 1920 they sold their stock to a syndicate of San Antonio businessmen. As the franchise period for the system neared the end of yet another contract period on January 1, 1924, the investors announced that water rates would have to be increased under any subsequent contracts that might be negotiated. The company did raise the rates, but the city denied the increase. The dispute went to the federal courts, which issued a temporary injunction sustaining the new rates. This situation brought public attention to the possibility of municipal acquisition of the utility. In an election held on April 18, 1925, a revenue bond for seven million dollars to purchase the system of the

San Antonio Water Supply Company passed by an overwhelming 9,917 to 2,405, and the city secured title to the entire system. Since that time the San Antonio Water Board, a self-perpetuating board, which is separate and independent from the city administration, has operated the waterworks for the citizens of San Antonio. This board has added greatly to the overall system, has purchased several smaller private water companies, and has guaranteed the San Antonio metropolitan area a dependable supply of water by securing access to new water sources.

Location: The most prominent and interesting remaining portions of the early San Antonio Waterworks may be visited in Brackenridge and Mahncke parks. The 1878 Lambert Beach Pumping Station and its power canal are located quite near the San Antonio Zoological Gardens within Brackenridge Park. The 1885 Brackenridge Park Station and its millrace are found just south of the parking lot for the Brackenridge Park golf course at Millrace Street and Avenue B. The old Mahncke Park reservoir may be examined at the extreme eastern end of Mahncke Park, east of Brackenridge Park. In addition to these historic sites, I recommend visiting the San Antonio Water Museum, located at 1000 East Commerce Street and operated by the City Water Board, where one can enjoy fascinating exhibits on the history of water resource development in the San Antonio metropolitan area.

Suggested Reading:

Baker, T. Lindsay. "An Interesting History: How San Antonio Water Planners Can Guarantee Adequate Supply for Fast-Growing City." *Water, Southwest & Texas Water Works Journal* 60, no. 4 (July, 1978): 12–15.

Hay, William Wren. "Concrete Rings, Superimposed, Sunk to Form San Antonio Pump Pit," *Engineering Record* 71, no. 24 (June 12, 1915): 741–42.

Scott, Arthur Curtis. *Test of a Vertical Expansion High Duty Pumping Engine in Operation at the Water Works, San Antonio, Texas.* University of Texas Bulletin No. 59. Austin: University of Texas, 1905.

The slightly disturbed ground that marks the site of the now-demolished 1915 Brackenridge Park Pumping Station. Photograph by the author, 1975.

86. *San Jacinto Monument*

Seldom considered by visitors as an engineering work, the construction of the San Jacinto Monument (1936–39) is one of the most impressive engineering projects ever undertaken in Texas. Erected by the state and federal governments at the site of the 1836 battle in which Texas won its independence, the reinforced-concrete shaft with limestone facing stands 570 feet tall, making it in its day the tallest masonry structure in the world. Because of the size and the unusual design of the monument (it was the only such structure of its kind ever attempted up to 1936), the contractor, the W. S. Bellows Construction Company of Houston, was forced to use new and untried methods throughout much of the project.

The San Jacinto Monument is an octagonal shaft of reinforced concrete faced with Texas Cordova shell limestone. It measures 48 feet square at its base, tapering to 19 feet square at its top. Above the tower

The temporary steel construction tower looming above the base of the San Jacinto Monument. Clearly seen are the main construction platform and the two outer swinging scaffolds used in shaft construction. Works Progress Administration photograph courtesy Houston Metropolitan Research Center, Houston Public Library, Houston, Texas.

proper rests a large structural-steel-and-concrete five-pointed star also faced with limestone, which symbolizes the Lone Star State. Around the base of the shaft is a museum and art gallery complex measuring 124 feet square and rising 45 feet above ground level.

One of the most interesting aspects of the construction of the San Jacinto Monument was its foundation work. The concrete base for the monument is 124 feet square, 15 feet thick at its center, and 5 feet thick at its edge. The plans for the project specified that the foundation had to be laid in one continuous concrete pour. Failure to make a continuous pour would have made it necessary for the contractor to remove every-

thing from the site of the foundation and to start again, a ruinous expense.

The builders went to great lengths to make contingency plans for any circumstances that might have prevented the completion of the continuous pour for the foundation. Water for mixing the concrete, for example, was pumped three thousand feet from a lake by electric pumps. A spare gasoline-powered pump was hooked into the waterline for use if needed, tanks at the construction site were filled to give a four-hour water reserve, and extra pipe and fittings were stockpiled should there be a break in the line at any point. A system of floodlights was installed for night work together with a backup system of carbide lighting should the electricity fail. As a precaution against rain, a large circus tent was erected over the excavated foundation site, and the site was provided with ditches to carry any rainwater away from the work area.

One of the most important factors in completing the big pour was the need for a satisfactory labor force. As some of the funds for the monument construction project came from the Public Works Administration, all workers had to come from unemployment rolls within twenty miles of the project. Since very little labor had been used in the project so far, with only the excavation of the foundation and placement of reinforcing steel having been done, the laborers were selected "by looks only." From 150 men employed, only about 35 had ever worked on any construction project. Several rehearsals of the big pour were made in advance of the actual job, and "to keep the men in a good humor," the contractors provided them with sandwiches and coffee at all times. During the actual pour, which took fifty-seven hours, the men consumed thirty-eight hundred sandwiches and fifty-seven hundred cups of coffee.

The big pour of six thousand cubic yards of concrete was conducted exactly as planned. The superintendent for the contracting firm later recalled, "Needless to say, the Architect, Engineer and Contractor were all much relieved when the pour was finished."

After the completion of the continuous-pour foundation, the builders followed ordinary procedures for the construction of the reinforced-concrete basement walls and museum exhibit area located directly above the foundation. The construction of the shaft portion of the monument, however, presented problems never before faced by any builders. The concrete shaft, which would stand over five hundred feet high, was designed with walls four feet thick at the base and two feet thick at the top and was to be heavily reinforced with steel rods. According to plans, all concrete was to be poured against the inside of the stone facing so it could serve as the outer form. Further reinforcement was provided by the addition of four eighteen- by thirty-six-inch intersecting reinforced-concrete beams every twenty-four feet.

To give access to various parts of the tower construction at the same time, a temporary structural steel tower was erected from the base of the shaft. Around it the actual construction took place. The steel tower was erected by means of a guy derrick, and its upper level was maintained about a hundred feet ahead of the concrete and stonework. One large working platform and four sets of scaffolds were supported from this tower. From the main working platform, fifty feet square, supported on steel cables from the construction tower, were suspended two scaffolds on the inside of the shaft and two additional scaffolds around the outside. Through the use of eight five-ton hand winches, the working platform and its attached scaffolds could be raised at a rate of one foot each five minutes. The first scaffold, on the inside of the shaft,

Workers positioning a slab of Texas Cordova shell limestone to serve as the outer form in concrete pouring on March 23, 1937. Works Progress Administration photograph courtesy Houston Metropolitan Research Center, Houston Public Library, Houston, Texas.

Workmen preparing two-foot increment of reinforcing steel for the shaft of the San Jacinto Monument in March, 1937. Works Progress Administration photograph courtesy Houston Metropolitan Research Center, Houston Public Library, Houston, Texas.

twenty-five feet below the working platform, was used for placing the inner wall forms and for pouring concrete, and the second scaffold, on the inside of the shaft and ten feet lower, was used by workmen to remove the forms after the concrete had set. The first set of swinging scaffolds on the outside of the shaft, twenty-five feet below the working platform, was used by the masons to set all the limestone facing, and the second set of outer scaffolds, ten feet lower, was used for cleaning and pointing the stone. Through the use of the working platform and its four suspended scaffolds, all the work on the shaft was completed as it grew skyward.

As work progressed on the shaft, the contractor developed the following routine. Men first placed reinforcing steel, set a course of the outside limestone facing, set the inner wooden forms, cranked the working platform and scaffolds up two feet, and then poured two feet of concrete. Three and occasionally four times a day this procedure was repeated, making possible a schedule of building twenty-four feet per week. Four days a week were devoted to wall construction, with the fifth day each week being spent on the placement of the reinforced-concrete tie beams. This procedure was maintained for fifteen consecutive weeks until the shaft was completed. After it was finished, a concrete base was poured for the star yet to be placed atop the shaft, and the temporary steel

226

construction tower, working platform, and scaffolds were removed by the guy derrick and steel cables.

One of the most difficult aspects of the San Jacinto Monument project was the final construction of the five-pointed star at its apex. To provide a new working platform for its construction, steel beams were placed on the top slab, covered with wooden planks, and allowed to cantilever out over the walls about six feet. To move materials from the inside of the shaft to the star area, a ninety-foot cantilevered structural-steel construction tower was built on one side of the top of the shaft, anchored on twenty-four-inch I-beams, which protruded from the windows of the observation deck area at a height of five hundred feet. All building materials were taken up inside the shaft to this level and then transferred to a cage within the temporary construction tower for movement to the upper level.

Before work began on the actual star, a one-inch-to-one-foot scale model was fabricated in plywood, raised in the air, and then revised several times by the architect until he was satisfied that it had the proper shape. The contractor then built a full-sized wooden model of the star and from it drew detailed plans for his men to follow in building it in masonry atop the tower. Designed like the remainder of the shaft, the star has stone facing into which the concrete was poured. With a structural-steel framework within the masonry, it has a height of 34 feet. Since it was placed on a 19-foot base, the points overhung the edge of the shaft, making the construction more difficult 536 feet in the air. Twenty days were required to set the stone and pour the concrete for the star, which was completed in 1938. Finishing work on the monument continued into 1939.

Today the San Jacinto Monument is the centerpiece

The San Jacinto Monument today. Photograph by the author, 1981.

227

of the San Jacinto Battleground State Historical Park. It houses the San Jacinto Museum of History, which is open to the public at no charge. A small fee is charged for riding the elevator to the observation deck beneath the star.

Location: The San Jacinto Monument is located at the San Jacinto Battleground State Historical Park just north of Deer Park, Texas. The most convenient

access is via Park Road 1836, which runs north to the park from an intersection with State Highway 225 in Deer Park, 10.7 miles east of Loop 610 in Houston.

Suggested Reading:

Bullen, C. A. "Construction of the San Jacinto Memorial." *Proceedings of the American Concrete Institute* 34 (March–April, 1938): 421–32.

87. San Marcos Activated Sludge Sewage Treatment Plant

The San Marcos Activated Sludge Sewage Treatment Plant, which began operation about September 1, 1916, was acclaimed as the first successful activated sludge plant serving an entire city. During the 1920s and 1930s it became almost a "celebrity" among American sewage treatment facilities.

The years just before the First World War were a time of intense interest in the artificial treatment of sewage. Cities everywhere were growing, thus placing increased pressure on their outmoded and often inefficient disposal systems. Numerous new ideas were

proposed to solve the problems, but most of them failed to produce the promised results. One of these new theories was the use of activated sludge to decompose the constituents of sewage. In this process the growth of bacteria to decompose the effluent is enhanced by bubbling compressed air through the liquid effluent. Although the system had been tested in laboratories and experiments, it had never been applied to a working municipal system.

In 1916, at a time when virtually all forms of artificial sewage treatment were still being questioned,

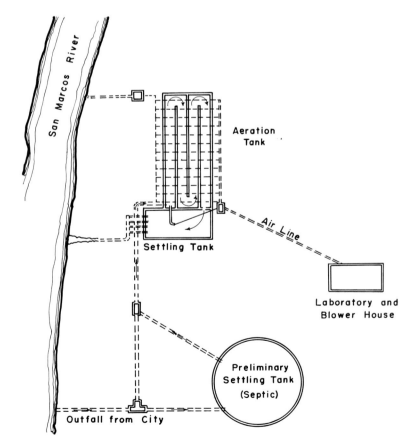

Plan of the San Marcos Activated Sewage Treatment Plant as it operated in 1916. Based on H. H. Wagenhals, E. J. Theriault, and H. B. Hommon, *Sewage Treatment in the United States: Report on the Study of Fifteen Representative Sewage Treatment Plants,* U.S. Treasury Department, Public Health Service, Public Health Bulletin No. 132 (Washington, D.C.: Government Printing Office, 1923), p. 108. Drawing by the author.

General view of the San Marcos plant in the mid-1930s, after the circular settling tank in the foreground had been converted into an additional aeration tank. The two settling tanks and the rectangular aeration tank are seen in the background beside the sludge pump shed. From E. W. Steel, "Pioneer Activated-Sludge Plant Still in Service," *Engineering News-Record* 115, no. 7 (August 15, 1935): 223.

Ashley F. Wilson, the engineer-manager of the San Marcos Utilities Company, decided that he would be the first to make a practical application of activated sludge for the treatment of sewage. He could only hope that the theory would work in practice. A decade before, in 1907, a private company had built the first sewage system for San Marcos, but the rudimentary system consisted merely of a forty-foot-diameter sump and settling tank from which effluent was pumped for disposal on nearby culivated land. This had proved to be wholly unsatisfactory, since the fa-

cility was located on the banks of the San Marcos River and only a short distance from the business district.

Wilson apparently patterned his new facility after an experimental plant then being operated in Milwaukee as a test. The central feature of the San Marcos plant was a sunken concrete aeration tank sixteen feet wide, forty feet long, and eight feet, six inches deep. The tank was divided into four channels, the bottom of each having a row of twelve-inch-square aeration plates. Compressed air was provided to these

The general area of the 1916 San Marcos Activated Sludge Sewage Treatment Plant in the present-day San Marcos City Park. Photograph by the author, 1975.

plates by an electrically powered, Boston-type Connersville blower with a rated capacity of 260 cubic feet of air per minute. Before entering the aeration tank, the raw sewage passed through the old circular sump, which served as a preliminary settling tank. From the aeration tank the treated effluent went to a second settling tank measuring ten feet wide, twenty-five feet long, and twenty-five feet deep, before passing into the San Marcos River. After only a few months of use, many of the aeration plates at the bottom of the aeration tank became clogged. Wilson replaced them through the simple and effective expedient of installing small galvanized-steel pipes with their lower ends extending down into the effluent and with their upper ends connected to a compressed air line.

In August, 1920, three U.S. Public Health Service experts visited the San Marcos plant to study its operation. They noted that connection to sanitary sewers in San Marcos at the time was not compulsory and that the system actually served about half of the total population of five thousand. They found the flow through the sewer mains to be satisfactory and somewhat diluted by groundwater entering the system through infiltration. They measured the flow and found that an average of eighty gallons of sewage entered the system for each person served. The plant operated quite smoothly, in the opinion of the visitors, and it did so with the assistance of only one part-time employee, who visited it once or twice daily mainly to oil the blower and the electric motor that powered it. In their report on the San Marcos plant, the three experts favorably stated that the treated wastewater leaving the facility "should satisfy the most exacting requirements of sewage-plant effluents."

As the population of San Marcos grew, the question of disposing of the excess activated sludge generated by the plant had to be resolved. The answer came in simply pumping the unneeded sludge from the second settling tank to an adjacent field. The land there was plowed in furrows and the sludge allowed to flow in successive rows. After a set of furrows was used, it was allowed to dry. Its surface crust then was broken by a single plowing down its center, making it ready for use again. This procedure proved satisfactory for years.

By the mid-1920s the San Marcos plant had to be expanded, but its original tanks and equipment remained in service. To increase its capacity, in 1925 the old circular settling tank was converted into a second

aeration tank through the addition of wooden partitions and the introduction of compressed air through galvanized-steel pipes. Additional final settling capacity was increased through the construction of a new settling tank measuring twenty feet square and twenty-one feet deep. Later a bar screen and grit chambers were added to cleanse the sewage further as it entered the plant from the city. As the system operated from the mid-1920s to mid-1930s, one-third of the effluent went into the old rectangular aeration tank and two-thirds went to the newly reconstructed circular aeration tank. In 1934 the facility was handling an average daily flow of 300,000 gallons with a peak flow of 435,000 gallons daily.

In 1935 the plant was substantially modified one more time. The circular tank was abandoned as an aeration tank and was replaced by the addition of an 86-foot-by-16-foot addition to the old 1916 rectangular tank, giving it a total length of 126 feet. It was divided into two channels, each 8 feet wide and with a sewage depth of 7 feet, 6 inches. A row of air diffuser plates was installed along one side of each channel, changing the original ridge-and-furrow flow pattern into a spiral flow. Otherwise the system operated basically the same as it had the decade before.

With the passage of time and the increased adoption of activated sludge for effluent treatment in the United States and overseas, the plant in out-of-the-way San Marcos became increasingly well known among the nation's sewage treatment facilities. An article in the prestigious *Engineering News-Record* in 1935, for example, noted in bold type that the "Pioneer Activated-Sludge Plant" at San Marcos was "Still in Service." Companies with their equipment in use at San Marcos wrote to officials of the city, which by that time owned the facility, asking for pictures of the plant and requesting permission to note in their advertisements that their products were in use at the famous San Marcos plant.

The old San Marcos Activated Sludge Sewage Treatment Plant remained in operation until after World War II. It then was replaced with a completely new facility located farther from the center of town. The structures at the plant were razed and the tanks filled with earth. Today the site of one of the world's pioneer activated sludge sewage treatment plants lies unmarked in the San Marcos City Park.

Location: The faint ruins of the San Marcos Activated Sludge Sewage Treatment Plant may be seen on the east bank of the San Marcos River just a few yards north of the wooden footbridge at the foot of Hutchinson Street in the San Marcos City Park.

Suggested Reading:

Elrod, Henry E. "Activated Sludge at San Marcos, Tex." *Engineering News* 77, no. 6 (February 8, 1917): 249.
Steel, E. W. "Pioneer Activated-Sludge Plant Still in Service." *Engineering News-Record* 115 no. 7 (August 15, 1935): 222–23.
Wagenhals, H. H., E. J. Theriault, and H. B. Hommon. *Sewage Treatment in the United States: Report on the Study of Fifteen Representative Sewage Treatments Plants.* U.S. Treasury Department, Public Health Service, Public Health Bulletin No. 132. Washington, D.C.: Government Printing Office, 1923.

88. *San Marcos River Covered Bridge*

One of the two known covered bridges erected in Texas and the only one of which substantial remains exist today, the San Marcos Bridge for over half a century carried travelers across the San Marcos River near Gonzales. In its day it was famed throughout the state, even though today its piers stand virtually forgotten beside the iron truss bridge that replaced it eighty years ago.

On the last day of January, 1854, John Mooney se-
cured a charter from the Texas legislature to erect a toll bridge spanning the San Marcos River in the vicinity of Benjamin Duncan's ferry, west of Gonzales. The bridge site was about two miles upstream on the San Marcos from its confluence with the Guadalupe River. Soon after receiving his charter, Mooney began work on the project, his men digging the foundations for the two large cut-stone piers that still stand. Other employees upstream began hewing the timbers

The San Marcos River Covered Bridge in service during the nineteenth century. Photograph courtesy Texas State Library, Austin, Texas.

The San Marcos River Covered Bridge on the left beside the newly completed steel truss bridge that replaced it in 1902. Photograph courtesy Texas State Library, Austin, Texas.

that would be floated downstream to become the wooden truss structure for the bridge. After the piers were built and the truss structure and the approaches put in place, the main span was covered with a protective wooden roof and sides to keep the wooden truss span from deteriorating because of the effects of the elements.

In addition to the right to erect a bridge, Mooney also received from the legislature the authority to construct a road between Gonzales and Seguin, so presumably his men also worked on road improvements in addition to building the bridge. According to oral tradition, many of the laborers on the project were slaves.

The bridge was completed in March, 1856, when it opened to the public. The news was acclaimed at least as far away as San Antonio, where, on the fifteenth of the month, the *Herald* reported that the opening of the bridge "will be very acceptable news to the public generally and the traveling community in particular, as it will prevent the many delays and dangers occasioned by rises" on the San Marcos.

According to John Mooney's original 1854 charter, he was permitted to operate his covered bridge as a money-making venture. His authorized tolls were as follows: four-horse stage, fifty cents; loaded four-horse wagon, fifty cents; six-horse wagon, sixty cents; empty wagon, forty cents; loaded wagon with one yoke of oxen, sixty cents; empty wagon with one yoke of oxen, forty cents; each extra yoke of oxen, ten cents; loaded two-horse wagon, thirty cents; two-horse carriage, forty cents; one-horse buggy, twenty-five cents; loaded cart with one yoke of oxen, thirty cents; empty cart with one yoke of oxen, twenty-five cents; man and horse, twenty-five cents; led or loose

horse, five cents; footmen, five cents; cattle, except oxen, five cents; hogs, sheep, and goats per head, one cent.

The covered bridge became one of the sights to which visitors to Texas were treated during the middle years of the nineteenth century. The fondness of Texans for the span may be seen in the following jesting description published in the July 14, 1869, issue of the *San Antonio Express:*

> Anyone who has traveled by way of Gonzales, will have a lively remembrance of the San Marcos Bridge—it was one of the sensations we treated strangers to upon their introduction to Western Texas. Imagine a long narrow frame, boarded in on the sides, roofed over head, and a floor under foot, perched upon rotten poles forty feet high over a fearful, swift, deep stream. The polite stage drivers generally requested that the gentlemen walk over, while he undertook the perilous experiment of driving over the stage with the ladies inside, if there happened to be any on board.

Though exaggerated, the above description fits the extant historic photographs and reminiscences of the San Marcos River Covered Bridge remarkably well. The entire span between the two stone piers, about a hundred feet in length, was enclosed and to travelers it seemed to be very gloomy inside. With no windows on either side, the only light entered from the two open ends, and as one man recalled in 1937, "Even when the sun was shining its brightest outside there was semi-darkness inside the old house-like bridge." The roadway was only wide enough to allow the passage of a single vehicle at a time.

Two years before the expiration of John Mooney's charter, Gonzales County purchased the San Marcos Bridge from his heirs. In a transfer of title on August 14, 1879, the heirs sold the bridge to the county for five hundred dollars. The *Gonzales Inquirer* reported favorably on the transaction, noting that public acquisition of the bridge would promote the development of the western portion of the county and stating that "we consider [it] a good investment."

For the next two decades the county maintained the covered bridge as part of its rural road system, but in 1901 it replaced it with the current steel truss bridge that stands parallel to the older structure. On November 25, 1901, the county commissioners signed a contract with E. P. Alsbury and Son of Houston, Texas, for the erection of this new bridge. It consists of a 140-foot Pratt truss span with 18-foot and 43-foot, 6-inch approaches at its ends. It has a wooden deck providing an 18-foot roadway that stands 27 feet above normal flow in the river below. The commissioners formally accepted the new bridge from the contractors on August 11, 1902.

The San Marcos Bridge was used for more than just a crossing over the river. People still living in Gonzales remember picnics under the protective canopy of the bridge's roof when rain spoiled outings at the river. Some travelers made camp beneath its roof when they were caught unprepared by wet or cold weather, and the span even became a popular meeting place for sweethearts in the horse-and-buggy days.

In time the old covered bridge deteriorated and its wooden superstructure was removed, leaving the stone piers on the downstream side of the steel bridge almost close enough to touch. An effort was made to remove the old piers and even dynamite was used, but the cut stone proved to be too strong and the piers have stood the tests of time, explosives, and floods. The site is a beautiful one to visit, and it is an ideal location for warm-weather picnics.

Location: The site of the San Marcos River Covered Bridge and of the attractive 1901–1902 overhead truss bridge that replaced it may be reached by driving west on West Cone Street and its paved county road extension 1.6 miles from Gonzales.

Suggested Reading:

"Bridge across the San Marcos." *San Antonio [Weekly] Herald* (March 15, 1856), p. 2.
Gonzales County, Tex. Commissioners' Court. Minutes, vol. 6, pp. 198–99, 271. Office of County Clerk, Gonzales County Courthouse, Gonzales, Tex.
Gonzales County, Tex. Deed Records, vol. Z, pp. 234–35. Office of County Clerk, Gonzales County Courthouse, Gonzales, Tex.
"The San Marcos Bridge." *San Antonio Express* (July 14, 1869), p. 3.

89. Santa Rita No. 1 Oil Well

The Santa Rita No. 1, drilled between 1921 and 1923, was the first producing oil well on University of Texas lands in western Texas and was the discovery well for the Big Lake Oil Field.

The story of the Santa Rita No. 1 goes back to the activities of Rupert P. Ricker, the son of a ranching family in Reagan County. He had attended the University of Texas and become a lawyer before serving as a captain in the U.S. Army during World War I. Returning home from military service, Ricker found western Texas in financial difficulties because of a protracted drought. Hoping to build his fortune, he turned from cattle to oil, considering the latter to be the most likely route to success. He studied a recent report by Prof. John Udden on the potential for mineral resources on University of Texas lands, became convinced that petroleum was to be found there, and proceeded to make arrangements to lease the mineral

rights on all of the university lands in four West Texas counties, including his home county.

Lacking the cash to pay the ten cents per acre rental, Ricker turned to Frank Pickrell, one of his former army sergeants, and Haymond Krupp, an investor from El Paso. They were in the Reagan County area to investigate the availability of oil leases, and they paid Ricker a nominal sum over the regular acreage rental fee for the rights in the area he had "blocked up." Their geologist, Dr. Hugh Tucker, then selected the site for their first well.

Pickrell managed the new business, the Texon Oil and Land Company, and served as its vice-president. It was through his clever promotion and financing that the enterprise actually began operating. Krupp became president of the firm. They were required by their agreement with the university to initiate drilling within a stipulated time. To meet the deadline, Pick-

General view of the Santa Rita No. 1 as it appears today. Photograph by the author, 1975.

rell moved a worn-out water well drilling rig by train from San Angelo to the well site in Reagan County. There on January 8, 1921, he began drilling and solved two of his most pressing problems: the initiation of a legitimate hole by the deadline and the securing of the water needed for actual oil well drilling.

The Texon firm hired Carl G. Cromwell as its driller, and he, his wife, and his daughter moved into a shack near the well site. About this time the company employed R. S. McDonald to build the eighty-foot wooden derrick that would be used in the actual oil well drilling. Its timbers were shipped by rail from Ranger, which for some time had been a major Texas oil center.

The name of the Santa Rita well had its origin in Frank Pickrell's efforts to raise financial support for the project. On one occasion he approached a group of Catholics in New York, encouraging them to invest in the Texas project. They realized that it was a speculative venture and decided to first to confer with a priest. The clergyman advised them that if they invested their funds in the project they should invoke the aid of Saint Rita, the patron saint of the impossible. Pickrell heard of the advice, and on return to Texas, he christened the well the Santa Rita by sprinkling red rose petals over the derrick and rig from atop its crown block.

Drilling at the Santa Rita No. 1 continued at a slow pace day after day, week after week, month after month. The local ranchers and their families felt sorry for driller Cromwell, his family, and helper. Mrs. Cromwell later remembered that "the ranchers were touched, in their bluff way, by the pathos of two men, a woman and a little girl in the desert country beside a rusty railroad pecking a hole in the rocks in search of oil."

The search, however, was not in vain. On Sunday afternoon, May 27, 1923, Cromwell and his tool dresser cleaned out the well with a bailer. They had reached a depth of 3,055 feet, and the material they brought up showed that they had reached an area with a showing of oil. When again they let the bailer down and then drew it back to the surface, they found it filled with oil. The two men decided to tell no one of the discovery until they could determine if there was petroleum in quantity. Thus the night passed. The next morning Mrs. Cromwell heard a hissing sound as she was preparing breakfast. She thought that it was a rattlesnake at the door of the shack, but as the family members reached the portal they saw instead a thin column of gas and oil vapor rising from the drilling rig. Cromwell cried in astonishment, "Well, I'll be damned!" Pickrell was notified and he rushed back to Texas from Arkansas to find that he had a flowing well in the center of sixty-four sections of leases.

The Santa Rita No. 1 flowed oil regularly for more than a month. At first there was nowhere to store it, so the petroleum flowed out onto the prairie

Detail of exterior working parts of the pumping equipment at the Santa Rita No. 1. Photograph by the author, 1975.

until earthen tanks could be built to contain it. The flowing well averaged about one hundred barrels a day, and after pumping was begun at the site, it produced an average of two hundred barrels daily. Although this was not an outstanding flow, it indicated great potential.

The productivity of the Big Lake Field in the years that followed the discovery at the Santa Rita No. 1 stretches the imagination. A forest of wooden and then steel derricks sprang up on the lands of the Permian Basin, which many "experts" had declared was devoid of petroleum. Complete new towns appeared and an affluence began in western Texas that in many areas remains to this day. The revenues accruing to the University of Texas, owner of much of the land, have been a tremendous force in its becoming one of the finest public educational institutions in the country.

In 1940 the original pumping rig from the Santa Rita No. 1 was disassembled and moved to Austin. There it was stored for eighteen years before being reassembled for public display on the University of Texas campus. The original well, however, remains intact in Reagan County. On the western outskirts of the town of Texon, old pumping equipment and a steel derrick of the type used in the 1920s and 1930s can be seen in place. Although it has not been in active operation pumping since 1980, the old rig can still average pumping twenty-five barrels of oil a day from the sixty-year-old Santa Rita No. 1 well when it is turned on for demonstration purposes. The only accommodation to modern times in the Santa Rita pumping equipment has been the replacement of an oil- or gas-burning engine with a large electric motor to provide power via industrial belting to the antique pumping machinery.

Location: The Santa Rita No. 1 Oil Well is located on the western edge of the town of Texon just north of the Santa Fe Railway tracks about one-half mile south of the Santa Rita historical marker on U.S. 67. The well itself is marked by a painted sign that designates it as the Santa Rita No. 1.

Suggested Reading:

Rister, Carl Coke. *Oil! Titan of the Southwest.* Norman: University of Oklahoma Press, 1949.
Schwettmann, M. W. *Santa Rita No. 1.* Austin: Texas State Historical Association, 1958.

90. Shafter Mining District

Encompassing the most intensively developed underground mining in all of Trans-Pecos Texas, the Shafter Mining District from the 1880s to the 1940s was Texas' most consistent silver-producing area. For four decades the local mines have been comparatively quiet, however, leaving the former boomtown of Shafter virtually abandoned in the scenic Chinati Mountains.

Although there had been prospecting and some minor mineral production in the Chinati Mountains, a teamster named John W. Spencer discovered the first genuinely rich deposits of silver in the area. Making his discovery in October, 1880, he secured backing from several U.S. Army officers in the area: Louis Wilhelmi, John L. Bullis, and William R. Shafter, whose name later was given to the mining district. The three officers and Spencer purchased several sections of land in the vicinity of his strike and agreed to divide their profits equally. In 1882 they signed a contract with Daniel Cook, a California mining entrepreneur, to develop the resources on the land they had purchased.

In the course of the following year, Cook's field parties found considerable resources of silver in the vicinity, mostly on the land that Bullis had purchased. With other backers, Cook organized the Presidio Mining Company of San Francisco to undertake actual mining and milling of the ores. The company offered to purchase the land from the partners for sixteen hundred dollars plus five thousand shares of stock in the company for each of the four men, and all but Bullis agreed. After a lengthy delay Bullis also consented, but only after he had lost a major court case in which he sought to maintain ownership of all the ores removed from "his" property.

Already by the spring of 1884, mining activity was moving ahead at rapid pace in the Shafter district. Men had excavated shafts and then dug tunnels outward from them, and an ore-reduction mill was erected on the banks of Cibolo Creek about a mile from the principal mine, the Shafter Mine.

The Presidio Mining Company and its Shafter Mine prospered year after year. Free-milling silver was found in paying quantities for six decades, the ore being found mainly in pockets in the surrounding limestone. Within the mine the walls stood quite well after the ore was extracted, and timbering was only occasionally required. It was not at all unusual for the miners to remove all the ore and leave underground chambers 50 to 75 feet high and 500 to 1,000 feet

long. They followed one pocket of ore a distance of 2,500 feet long, 10 to 40 feet wide, and from near the surface to 250 feet deep. Such ore bodies often were connected with each other so that the underground workings took quite irregular shapes.

To locate the ore underground, the miners excavated two major shafts at the Shafter Mine. One of these was four hundred feet deep and had four levels one hundred feet apart. The second was dug to a depth of seven hundred feet by 1930, but in the later years of production was extended to fifteen hundred feet in a futile attempt to locate new ore deposits. At one time the workings extended over a length of four thousand feet.

Initially, ore was hauled from the mine to the ore-reduction mill beside Cibolo Creek in large mule-drawn wagons. In 1913 an aerial tramway was erected to transport the ore more efficiently and thus reduce cost. In the beginning, ore reduction was accomplished through the use of a stamp mill and the pan-amalgamation method, though in later years the cyanide treatment process was used.

The Shafter Mine holds the distinction of having been the most productive of all the silver mines in Texas. During its sixty-two-year history, it produced an impressive two million tons of ore from which 30,293,606 ounces of silver were smelted together with smaller values in gold and lead. This represents about nine-tenths of the output of silver of the entire state.

By 1884 a village had begun growing along Cibolo Creek in the area of the ore-reduction mill. Taking the same name as the district, by the early years of this century it could be described as a place "where plenty of shade, good water, electric light, etc., render life in that comparatively arid region unusually pleasant." The community continued growing until it could boast a population of approximately two thousand by 1930. Because of a number of causes, among them low silver prices, labor difficulties, and increasing problems with water in the underground workings, the Shafter Mine closed in September, 1942. This sounded the death knell for the nearby town.

Within a few years virtually all the residents departed Shafter, leaving only a handful of people to give it a semblance of being an inhabited place. As houses were deserted, the remaining residents took away their roofs for the wood, allowing the adobe walls to erode back into the soil. Today the commu-

Looking over ruins of the ore-reduction mill at Shafter toward abandoned housing in the distance. Photograph by the author, 1982.

nity retains a post office, a store, and a Catholic church, but it is mostly deserted and has a population of only about two dozen or three dozen. The district has seen sporadic mining activity during the past forty years, most of it focusing on reprocessing old tailings, but silver prices have not risen sufficiently to return life to the Shafter District. Because of its historical significance, most of the area is encompassed by the Shafter Historic Mining District in the National Register of Historic Places.

Location: Shafter is located on U.S. 67 about nineteen miles north of Presidio and about forty miles southwest of Marfa. Most of the ruins and much of the mining area are readily visible from the public rights-of-way on the highway and on the town streets.

Suggested Reading:

Carlson, Paul H. "Opening of Big Bend's Chinati Silver Mine." *Greater Llano Estacado Southwest Heritage* 6, no. 1 (Spring, 1976): 19–21.

Phillips, William B. "Shafter Silver District, Presidio County, Texas." *Engineering and Mining Journal* 90, no. 27 (December 31, 1910): 1303–1305.

91. Slayden Bridge

Initially erected in 1898 and rebuilt in 1907, the Slayden Bridge is a classic example of the bridges constructed by Texas counties in the years around the turn of the century. Still in service, it is a handsome structure in a beautiful setting spanning the San Marcos River in northern Gonzales County.

Slayden, today a ghost town, was established in the 1880s as a siding on the San Antonio and Aransas Pass Railroad. The town was named for James Luther Slayden, an influential San Antonio merchant and rancher. By the mid-1890s area residents had started asking county officials to erect a bridge across the San Marcos River near their community to facilitate communication and travel in the direction of Belmont and Seguin to the west.

Accordingly, in early 1898 the Gonzales County commissioners began soliciting plans and bids for the construction of an iron truss bridge over the San Marcos near Slayden. On May 10 they opened the

bids but found all of them too high. They notified the agents of the bridge companies that all the bids had been rejected and told them that they would gather again to consider new plans and bids in two days. In this second session the commissioners accepted the bid made by E. P. Alsbury and Son, who at the time were agents for the New Jersey Steel and Iron Company of Trenton, New Jersey.

The contract between the bridge company and the county called on the former to erect a one-hundred-foot overhead truss span with timber approaches. According to the document, still preserved in the Gonzales County Courthouse, the company agreed to have the structure open for traffic by October 1, 1898, provided there were no unavoidable delays. The price agreed upon was $3,298.

Work progressed on the Slayden Bridge without undue difficulties. Crews from the New Jersey Steel and Iron Company first excavated footings for four

The main span of the 1907 Slayden Bridge seen from the west bank of the San Marcos River. Photograph by the author, 1982.

piers that in time supported the truss structure. Into the four excavated areas they placed 36-inch steel cylinders, which they then filled with concrete to form the piers. They proceeded to construct an east approach 60 feet long and a west approach 40 feet long, both of these made from 10-by-10-inch heart cypress timbers. After the truss span was put into position, a roadway was assembled from 2.5-inch lumber resting on 3-by-12-inch wooden joists. Finally, two wooden runners made from 2-by-6-inch lumber were spiked into place to protect the decking from the abrasive action of wagon and buggy wheels. The county commissioners formally accepted the completed structure on December 2, 1898.

The Slayden Bridge as originally constructed remained in service for less than a decade. Probably as a result of flood damage, in 1907 Gonzales County contracted with the Ottumwa Bridge Company, for which A. A. Alsbury was agent, to replace the former structure. By the terms of the contract, the company completely rebuilt the Slayden Bridge.

The original 100-foot span was replaced with a new 150-foot overhead truss span. Its piers also consisted of concrete-filled steel cylinders. The west approach was a 40-foot steel girder span combined with a 60-foot Warren truss span, both supported on steel piers. At the east end of the bridge the old timber approach was removed and replaced by a 75-foot Warren truss span. The 150-foot overhead span was a pin-connected Pratt truss with a 16-foot roadway and wooden decking. Its portal was decorated with ornamental ironwork and the words "Gonzales County." For their work in reconstructing the San Marcos River bridge at Slayden, the Ottumwa firm received a contract price of twenty-one hundred dollars, a modest fee for the work undertaken. Since that time the rebuilt Slayden Bridge has remained in service and is easily accessible to travelers on nearby U.S. 183.

Location: The Slayden Bridge is located 1.6 miles west of U.S. 183 on a graded county road. Visitors to the site should turn west onto the gravel road at an intersection 6.6 miles north of Gonzales and 1.9 miles south of the U.S. 183 juncture with FM 1486. Just west of the turn-off, drive through the Slayden ghost town, today marked only by a few scattered residences, the former roadbed of the San Antonio and Aransas Pass Railway, and an attractive cemetery off the road.

Suggested Reading:

Gonzales County, Tex. Commissioners' Court. Minutes, vol. 5, pp. 451–54, 524; vol. 7, pp. 15–16. Office of County Clerk, Gonzales County Courthouse, Gonzales, Tex.

92. *Somerville Tie and Timber Preserving Plant*

Built using both German and American technology, the 1906 Somerville Tie and Timber Preserving Plant became the largest and eventually the only wood treatment plant on the Santa Fe Railway system. Since railroads used and still use millions of wooden crossties annually, for decades the attention of some of the finest minds in the industry has been devoted to efforts to make ties resistant to decay and rot. The story of the Somerville plant demonstrates how inventive genius has been applied to the practical problem of preserving wood.

The first wood treatment plant at Somerville, a small town in Burleson County, was established in 1896. The Texas Tie and Lumber Preserving Company in that year purchased twenty-five acres of land with convenient access to the Santa Fe tracks and there started building a plant to treat ties and timbers under the zinc-tannin process. Beginning in 1897 the firm ran a facility with six treating cylinders, which handled an estimated two million crossties annually, selling them under contract to the Santa Fe Railway.

Realizing that it needed to expand its wood treatment capacity, in January, 1905, the Santa Fe Railway bought the timber preserving firm and in the same year began constructing a completely new plant at Somerville. The company had two additional plants, at Las Vegas, New Mexico, and Bellemont, Arizona, but these facilities were unable to keep up with the demand for ties and for bridge and other timbers. The old Somerville plant operated until November, 1905, when it was dismantled and some of its parts incorporated in the plant under construction nearby.

The new wood preserving facility, which began operating in February, 1906, consisted of five treating cylinders and two pressure cylinders housed in a large reinforced-concrete building with adjacent boilers,

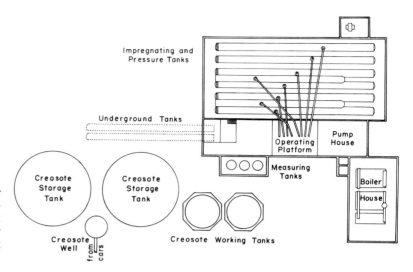

Plan of the 1906 Somerville Tie and Timber Preserving Plant. Based on "New Tie and Timber Preserving Plant of the Atchison, Topeka & Santa Fe Ry. at Somerville, Texas," *Engineering News* 55, no. 18 (May 3, 1906): 490. Drawing by the author.

mechanical equipment, and chemical storage tanks. Each cylinder was able to receive charges of six hundred 3.4-cubic-foot ties, giving the plant a capacity for about fifteen thousand ties each twenty-four hours.

The first stage in wood treatment at the 1906 Somerville plant consisted of unloading and stacking freshly cut ties and timbers so they could season. This drying process generally took several months, the length of time depending on the type of wood and on the season. The timber yard occupied an area measuring about twelve hundred feet wide and three thousand feet long. After the wooden timbers were properly seasoned, they were loaded into specially designed tramlike cars with configurations compatible with the cylinders and fitted with railway-type wheels so that they could roll completely inside the cylinders.

The chemical treatment practiced at Somerville was the German-patented Rueping process. After filling a 132-foot-long steel treating cylinder with a full charge of ties and timbers loaded on a series of tram cars, workmen closed and sealed the large airtight door at its end. The first step in the process was to increase the air pressure within the cylinder to 75 pounds per square inch, which required thirty minutes. Then heated liquid creosote was passed into the treating cylinder from the pressure cylinder above it, flowing into the chamber with the timbers until the latter was filled to the proper level. A pressure pump was applied to force additional creosote into the wood at a slowly increasing pressure, which finally reached 150 pounds per square inch; this took about an hour and a half. This maximum pressure was

maintained for about fifteen minutes to be certain that the wood was accepting all the creosote it could absorb at this highest pressure level. The operators then released the pressure in the treating cylinder and allowed the excess creosote to drain into an underground tank.

In the treated wood cells, the air, which during the process was compressed to 150 pounds per square inch, expanded when the pressure in the cylinder was released. This forced surplus creosote out of the wood cells, causing the ties and timbers to become coated with extra creosote which might be lost or wasted. To recover this valuable residue, a twenty-two-inch vacuum was created within the cylinder for a few minutes to remove the excess creosote, which then was permitted to drain into the underground tank for reuse. This last operation completed the entire treatment cycle, which required a little over four hours. Workers then opened the large circular door at the end of the cylinder and removed the string of timber-laden cars. The only work remaining was for men to load the ties and timbers on railway cars for shipment to wherever they might be needed on the Santa Fe system.

A surprising number of links connected the Somerville plant with Europe. The details for the design of the equipment in the plant, for instance, were prepared at Charlottenburg, Germany, by B. Kuckuck, an engineer for the German patentees of the Rueping treatment process. Kuckuck traveled from Europe to Texas to supervise the fabrication and installation of the equipment and to oversee the start of plant operations. During the early years, the creosote used in the

Somerville facility came to Texas from either Germany or England through a contract the railway company negotiated with the firm of C. Lembecke and Company in New York to supply five million gallons annually. It was delivered by special "tank steamers" to an unloading dock at Galveston, from which point it was transported by rail to Somerville.

The Somerville Tie and Timber Preserving Plant operated in roughly the manner described until 1954, when the Santa Fe introduced an improvement into its wood treatment operations. In this year it began using a special vapor drying process, which allowed it to treat unseasoned "green" timbers. This innovation greatly lessened the problems, expense, and labor involved in maintaining a huge timber yard of seasoning material. In this new process petroleum naphtha, the drying agent, flowed into the bottom of a charged cylinder and was heated into vapor form. The hot vapors drove out an average of 1.5 gallons of sap water per cubic foot of timber being dried, or about 5 gallons per crosstie. The mixed naphtha and water vapors left the treatment cylinder through lines leading to a cooling condenser, where they were returned to liquid

form and separated, the naphtha to be reused and the water to be conveyed to a waste pond where it was evaporated. Then the ties were impregnated with the preservatives under a pressure of 175 pounds per square inch. By the 1940s the operation of the facility had become so refined that the preservative mixture had changed to 30 percent creosote and 70 percent oil for ties, a 50-50 mixture for bridge and other timbers, and straight creosote for communication poles.

Using the vapor drying technique combined with creosote treatment, the Somerville plant continued treating timbers until 1975. At this time it was replaced by a completely new wood treatment plant, also at Somerville. The old plant continued operation while the new buildings, cylinders, tanks, and other structures and equipment were being built and installed, but as soon as the new plant began treating timbers in the summer of 1975, the 1906 plant was closed, its old equipment removed, and its buildings razed. Today only the 1975 plant remains, although it has the distinction of treating all the ties and timbers used on the entire Santa Fe system.

Trams loaded with ties being placed into cylinders for creosote treatment at Somerville in November, 1927. Photograph courtesy Atchison, Topeka and Santa Fe Railway Centralized Tie Plant, Somerville, Texas.

Elevation of typical treating and pressure cylinders and their supports within the reinforced-concrete treatment building constructed at Somerville in 1905–1906. Based on "New Tie and Timber Preserving Plant of the Atchison, Topeka & Santa Fe Ry. at Somerville, Texas," *Engineering News* 55, no. 18 (May 3, 1906): 491. Drawing by the author.

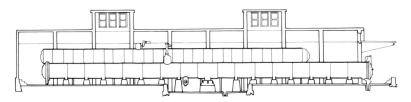

Location: The Somerville Tie and Timber Preserving Plant is located along the main line of the Atchison, Topeka and Santa Fe Railway on the north side of Somerville, Texas. Although the industrial facility is not open to the public, many of its operations may be observed from State Highway 36, which parallels the plant, and from FM 1361, which crosses the railway tracks just southeast of the plant.

Suggested Reading:

"At Somerville, Tex.[,] New Tie Treating Plant Is Operating." *Santa Fe Magazine* 68, no. 10 (September, 1975): 4–5.

"New Tie and Timber Preserving Plant of the Atchison, Topeka & Santa Fe Ry. at Somerville, Texas." *Engineering News* 55, no. 18 (May 3, 1906): 490–93.

"Santa Fe RR's Somerville Tie Plant." *Brenham Banner-Press* (Brenham, Tex.) (October 9, 1963), p. 3.

93. *Terlingua Mining District*

The Terlingua Mining District for almost six decades served as a major source of mercury for the United States. The most important of the mines in the district belonged to the Chisos Mining Company, but there seemingly were always other smaller mines being worked or prospects being investigated. A number of the operations were quite substantial. Since World War II the district has seen little activity, and today the abandoned Terlingua mining camp is one of the state's best-known ghost towns.

Cinnabar is a bright red ore from which mercury is refined. When this ore is heated, mercury is given off as a vapor, which may be trapped and condensed into a liquid state. This is the only metal that takes a liquid form at normal temperatures, and its uses in industry are manifold. Usually the term "mercury" designates the substance as used by chemists and pharmacists, and "quicksilver" refers to it as an item of commerce. The general public uses the two terms interchangeably.

The first documented production of quicksilver in commercial quantities in the Terlingua area took place in the 1880s. Through the 1890s local extraction and refining were conducted in a very primitive manner at various mining claims. Anglo-American supervisors oversaw work by Mexican laborers who removed the ore from the surface or near the surface and hauled it in burro-drawn carts to collecting areas. Here men hand-sorted the ore prior to further processing.

The relatively high metal content of the Terlingua

A "poor-boy" cinnabar furnace in the Big Bend country in 1936. Photograph courtesy Allen Richards and the Institute of Texan Cultures, San Antonio, Texas.

N

The headframe from an abandoned quicksilver mine near the Terlingua mining camp. Photograph by the author, 1975.

cinnabar during the initial years allowed its refining by one of the simplest of all methods of metal recovery, the use of retorts. The small operators needed only a crude furnace to transform the cinnabar into quicksilver ready for marketing.

As the surface deposits were depleted, the Mexican laborers were forced to excavate deeper and deeper to find more ore. They first found "stringers," tiny veins of cinnabar, which they followed in hopes of locating deposits in commercially recoverable quantities. Even by the turn of the century, the mining methods had advanced only slightly. The principal tools of the miners were still picks, shovels, sledges, and hand drills. One observer noted that the efforts to follow the "stringers" to ore bodies resulted in "an amazing series of passages resembling the burrows of a rabbit warren." By 1902 the deepest shafts had been sunk only about eighty feet. Some of the shafts were equipped with hand-operated winches to lift ore from the underground workings, but elsewhere it was common practice for the laborers to bring the cinnabar to the surface on their backs in rawhide buckets. Access

to these shafts was by notched wooden poles that served the miners as ladders.

Interest in the Terlingua district widened during the early years of this century, especially after accounts of the quicksilver deposits were published in national mining magazines. By 1903 a "rush" had begun into the Big Bend country to locate and mine cinnabar. Before the end of that year an estimated two million dollars had been invested in Brewster County quicksilver mines.

The individual most responsible for the eventual development of the minerals in the Terlingua Mining District was Ohio-born Howard E. Perry, an entrepreneur and investor. By the late 1880s he had come into the possession of extensive acreage in the Big Bend country that by his good fortune contained some of the richest cinnabar-producing areas in the mining district. Several years passed before Perry began developing his underground resources, but on May 8, 1903, he organized the Chisos Mining Company to do so.

Over the next four decades Perry built the Chisos

243

The Terlingua mining camp as it now appears. Photograph by the author, 1975.

Mine at Terlingua into one of the largest quicksilver operations in the country. During the early 1920s it held the distinction of being the largest producer of the precious metal in the entire United States. Other mines operated in the vicinity of the Chisos Mining Company, but their efforts were almost always smaller.

The name "Chisos" became almost synonymous with "Terlingua." In addition to operating the mines and refinery, the mining company also ran the Chisos Store, "the biggest store between Del Rio and El Paso"; the Chisos Hotel; a primitive water system; and the Terlingua post office. In time the company built a school building, which it rented to the local school district for the education of the miners' children, and even added a motion picture theater and a confectionery.

Perry paid his miners at Terlingua exceedingly low wages. His goal was to secure the highest productivity at the least possible cost. Since most of his men crossed the Rio Grande from Mexico, he paid them daily in Mexican pesos, most of which ended up back in his hands through sales at the company store. In 1934 Perry was paying his common laborers only seventy-five cents to a dollar per nine-hour day. They were permitted, however, to live with their families in simple stone and adobe "company housing" at no cost as long as they were employed. The low wages, however, were still double what the workers could expect back home in Mexico.

The Chisos Mine operated until 1942, when it closed because of exhaustion of its ore bodies. Since that time there has been sporadic mining activity in the Terlingua area but none on a sustained basis. Today Terlingua is known to most Texans as the site of an annual chili cook-off competition during which thousands of people converge on the old town from all parts of the United States, many of them only superficially aware of its mining heritage.

Location: The Terlingua mining camp is located on the north side of FM 170, approximately 3.8 miles west of its intersection with State Highway 118 in Brewster County. The mining district encompasses the entire area from the intersection and nearby Study Butte westward for several miles beyond the Terlingua ghost town. The areas off the road are privately owned and generally not accessible to the public, although many structures are visible from the public rights-of-way. Extreme care should be taken by anyone viewing the ruins at the mines due to the presence of many open and unprotected vertical shafts, some of them hundreds of feet deep.

Suggested Reading:

Day, James M. "The Chisos Quicksilver Bonanza in the Big Bend of Texas." *Southwestern Historical Quarterly* 64, no. 4 (April, 1961): 427–53.

Ragsdale, Kenneth Baxter. *Quicksilver: Terlingua and the Chisos Mining Company.* College Station: Texas A&M University Press, 1976.

94. *Texas Gulf Intracoastal Waterway*

Promoted by the Gulf Intracoastal Canal Association and built by the U.S. Army Corps of Engineers, the Texas Gulf Intracoastal Waterway was the concept of C. S. E. Holland, a young Victoria, Texas, banker. Today it carries millions of tons of shipping in a protected channel that stretches the length of the Texas Gulf Coast, from Orange to Brownsville.

During the hot summer of 1905, Holland conceived the idea of a canal all along the Texas coast. He knew that much of this length would be in protected natural lagoons behind the coastal islands. He called a meeting at Victoria for August 8 to organize an association to promote the construction of such a waterway, but many locals laughed at his plans, calling

Two large dredges meeting each other to complete the last section of the Texas Gulf Intracoastal Waterway between Corpus Christi and Brownsville on the afternoon of June 18, 1949. Photograph courtesy U.S. Army Engineer District, Galveston, Texas.

them the result of dementia induced by the heat of the South Texas summer. The meeting was held, however, and the Gulf Inland Waterway League was formed. Later known as the Gulf Intracoastal Canal Association, its purpose was to promote U.S. government construction of a waterway to carry protected shipping along the Gulf Coast.

The early efforts of the waterway league produced quite visible results. The U.S. Army Corps of Engineers, which had investigated the potential for a coastal canal as early as 1873, surveyed much of the proposed route and by 1913 actually had dredged a two-hundred-mile segment southwestward from Galveston. This stretch of canal was dug forty feet wide and five feet deep.

With this success behind them, the waterway promoters continued their efforts to stimulate government enlargement of the fledgling canal system. Thanks mostly to their efforts, Congress passed bills in 1925 and 1927 authorizing the construction of an integrated canal system connecting New Orleans with Corpus Christi. Additions to the system were made under the River and Harbor Act of 1942, which authorized construction of the last portion of the canal from Corpus Christi to Brownsville. This act also increased the overall dimensions of the system to 125 feet wide and 12 feet deep.

While this work was being undertaken in Texas, other areas of the Gulf Coast were being tied into the system. Consequently, when the last segment of the canal south of Corpus Christi was opened on June 18, 1949, it became part of a main channel that extended over a thousand miles from the west coast of Florida to the border of Mexico. Since that time much work has been done to improve barge access to cities and towns along the entire coast.

The major vessels using the Texas Gulf Intracoastal Waterway are freight-hauling barges, although the canal provides numerous opportunities for recreational use as well. The principal commodities transported on the system are petroleum and petroleum products, along with basic chemicals, iron and steel products, coal, concrete, plastics, wheat, and other agricultural products. It is also used by the federal government as an artery for the movement of missiles and defense materials being transported to and from the state. Today the Gulf Intracoastal Waterway system handles more than 100 million tons of freight annually.

Location: The Texas Gulf Intracoastal Waterway stretches about 421 miles along the Gulf Coast from Orange to Brownsville. It is crossed by state and federal highways at numerous points along its length and is easily observed from any of these places.

Suggested Reading:

Clark, Joseph L., and Elton M. Scott. *The Texas Gulf Coast: Its History and Development.* 4 vols. New York: Lewis Historical Publishing Company, 1955.
Perry, George Sessions. "Now You Can Sail through Texas." *Saturday Evening Post* 223, no. 3 (July 15, 1950): 26–27, 131–34.

95. *Thurber Mining District*

The Thurber Mining District, located at the only significant bituminous coal deposits in lignite-rich Texas, produced coal for fueling steam locomotives from the mid-1880s into the 1920s. The district represents the epitome of company towns, for it had a population of ten thousand living in a community where all real estate and businesses were built and owned by the mining company.

Coal extraction at Thurber, originally known as Johnson's Mine, was begun by William Whipple Johnson. An engineer who worked for the Texas and Pacific Railway, in the course of his professional work he discovered the rich bituminous coal deposits around Thurber. He and his brother purchased several thousand acres in the vicinity, and he resigned his position with the railroad and commenced mining in 1886. Johnson continued to mine coal until his laborers, encouraged by the Knights of Labor, struck in 1888. The capitalist decided to close down his mines rather than operate at a loss. The miners consequently moved to temporary shacks just outside company land to await the reopening of the mines, but events took an unexpected turn.

In November, 1888, three Eastern capitalists, Col. R. D. Hunter, Edgar E. Marston, and M. K. Thurber, organized the Texas and Pacific Coal Company specifically to buy out Johnson's interests in Texas mining. They named their enterprise after the railroad not because of any corporate connections but rather to flatter their principal customer, for the railway had

The brick manufacturing plant at Thurber, about 1910. Photograph courtesy Joe Martin and the Institute of Texan Cultures, San Antonio, Texas.

agreed to purchase 100 percent of the coal extracted.

The town at the mines was named after Thurber, but the driving force there was Colonel Hunter, who for years ruled the district with an iron hand. Hunter offered the unemployed miners wages lower than those formerly paid by Johnson, and they balked at his offer. The disgruntled workers declared themselves "on strike" against the Texas and Pacific Coal Company, even though they had never been its employees. Hunter saw no role for organized labor in "his" town, once reputedly announcing, "I'll run my business, and I'll run my town, or I'll run it to Hell."

Colonel Hunter was responsible for building Thurber into a town at a time when it had virtually no inhabitants. He employed crews to erect a four-strand barbed-wire fence around nine hundred acres, including the town site and mines, and then used armed guards to keep out any "union agitators." He then proceeded to construct a complete town, which he expected to be inhabited by workers once the labor unrest subsided. The Texas and Pacific Coal Company spent over fifty-six thousand dollars building over two hundred residences as well as mercantile stores, offices, churches, schools, and stables. Thus, even before it had more than a handful of miners, Thurber existed as a town. Hunter sought nonunion labor various places in the country, but the only men who would cross the union picket lines were black miners whom he brought from distant areas. The capitalist reached an agreement with the local miners in July, 1889, and the town that had already been built was occupied.

Mining in the Thurber District, which at one time had fifteen different shafts, was conducted by the "long-wall advancing" method. Miners first excavated a vertical shaft from the surface to the coal-bearing strata. Then they dug four or more tunnels radiating from the base of the shaft to extract the coal from its comparatively narrow twenty-seven-inch seams. They hauled the coal back from low tunnels into larger tunnels, where they dumped it into carts pulled by mules. The animals drew the coal back to the shaft, from which point it was hoisted to the surface. Within seven years of the reopening of the Thurber mines, the Texas and Pacific Coal Company employed between one thousand and fifteen hundred miners who produced fifteen hundred to two thousand tons of coal daily.

In 1897 another economic activity began at Thurber. In this year the Texas and Pacific Coal Company erected a huge brickyard there to exploit reserves of high-quality brick clay found on nearby company lands. Specializing in paving brick, but also producing building brick, the plant operated until 1933 and provided brick for use in Texas as well as in surrounding states. Maroon-red Thurber brick went into such impressive projects as paving Seawall Boulevard behind the Galveston Seawall, the construction of the meatpacking plants at the Fort Worth Stockyards, and the paving of Congress Avenue in Austin. All the bricks are plainly marked THURBER. The facility consisted of at least seventeen kilns in one large complex. The bricks were made primarily by the so-called stiff-mud process, in which moist clay is forced under pressure into a continuous column, sliced into individual bricks, dried, and finally fired in the kilns. With the addition of the brickyard in 1897, the future of Thurber seemed secure.

Because of Thurber's location in western Texas, hundreds of miles from the major coal-mining areas of the United States, the managers of the Texas and Pacific Coal Company tried to make it a desirable place to live to maintain a dependable labor force. During its early years the company added a seventeen-ton ice plant, an electric-generating plant, a meatpacking plant for fresh meats, a dairy for milk and dairy products, a drugstore, the only public library in the county, a high school with fifteen teachers, a two-hundred-room hotel, and even two saloons, the Snake and the Lizard. Thurber even boasted a 655-seat opera house, lighted by electricity and heated by steam, which hosted many of the top road shows in the country. In 1903 the management conceded to worker demands for recognition of labor unions, and Thurber became "the only 100% union town in America."

In 1917 W. K. Gordon, who had assumed supervision of the Thurber operations on the retirement of Colonel Hunter, discovered oil nearby at what was to become the great Ranger Oil Field. At this time the company had twenty-five hundred men employed in mining alone. The discovery of petroleum on company lands ensured the prosperity of the company, which became the Texas and Pacific Oil Company, but at the same time it indirectly sealed the fate of Thurber. By this time steam locomotives were already being converted from coal to oil, and the market for coal was declining. For a short time the oil boom at Ranger brought affluence to Thurber as the company expanded housing for oil field workers. The population rose to an all-time high of approximately ten thousand.

By 1920, however, most of the railroad customers that formerly had purchased 90 percent of the Thurber coal had switched to oil as fuel. In that year the miners' union contract with the company came up for renewal, but neither side could agree on terms, negotiations ceased, and the mines closed in 1921. Many of the workers lingered in the area, expecting the mines to reopen, but they were disappointed as they watched company crews systematically sell and dismantle the hundreds of vacant houses in Thurber. Everything of value at the residences was either sold to the highest bidder or scrapped. All of the above-

The chimney from the former ice and electricity plant erected at Thurber in 1908. Photograph by the author, 1975.

ground mining equipment was sold, but only two of the shafts were stripped. The others were left intact together with an estimated 137 million tons of coal still underground.

Another change in transportation sounded the death knell for Thurber. Its other principal industry, the brickyard, had specialized in the production of paving brick. By the 1930s asphalt and concrete had supplanted brick as paving material in most areas, a situation coupled with a general slump in the brick market. Consequently, in 1933 the Texas and Pacific Oil Company closed the brick plant as well as the remaining mercantile store, and in the same year it moved all its corporate offices to Fort Worth. The razing and scrapping of structures continued, with the removal of the brick plant in 1937. Thurber, once the largest town between Fort Worth and El Paso, in a matter of a few years became a ghost town.

Today visitors to Thurber see the handful of buildings that were not removed in the 1930s, a blanket of foundations, sidewalks, and rubble from the former structures, and a beautiful 150-foot brick chimney, which remains from the former ice and electric plant. The townsite is bisected by Interstate 20, and its remains lie on both sides of the thoroughfare. The principal surviving structures include a brick mercantile store, a wood-frame firehouse, a brick water-treatment plant, and a two-story brick drugstore that now houses a restaurant. Three residences remain, one the former home of town manager W. K. Gordon, the second a former guest house, and the third a current ranch worker's home made by joining two remaining miners' houses. Historical interpretation is

found both in the area around the old smokestack and inside the privately owned restaurant.

Location: The Thurber Mining District is located in extreme northwestern Erath County, seventy miles west of Fort Worth on Interstate 20.

Suggested Reading:

Floyd, Willie M. "Thurber, Texas: An Abandoned Coal Field Town." M.A. thesis, Southern Methodist University, 1939.

Gentry, Mary Jane. "Thurber, Texas: The Life and Death of a Texas Coal Town." M.A. thesis, University of Texas, 1947.

Spoede, Robert William. "William Whipple Johnson: An Enterprising Man." M.A. thesis, Hardin-Simmons University, 1968.

Mine entrance and small powered hoist at a coal mine near Thurber. Photograph by the author, 1975.

96. *Trinity and Brazos Valley Railway Depot and Office Building*

The two-story red-brick depot and office building of the Trinity and Brazos Valley Railway, erected in the autumn of 1903, in Cleburne, is one of the last prominent structures remaining of those built by the company. Ornamented with decorative gables and multiple arched windows and doors, it is among the most attractive of the smaller early twentieth-century railway stations in Texas.

The Trinity and Brazos Valley Railway (T&BV), chartered in 1902, was built between 1903 and 1907. Its purpose was to serve an agricultural region between the Brazos and Trinity rivers in Central Texas and to provide an alternate short-line connection between Fort Worth and Dallas on the north and Houston and Galveston on the south. Using leased track rights between Fort Worth and Cleburne, the line ran

Part of the east front of the 1903 Trinity and Brazos Valley Railway Depot and Offices in Cleburne, as the structure appeared before the initiation of major restoration efforts. Photograph by the author, 1973.

via Teague and Mexia to Houston. A branch line led north from Teague to Waxahachie, from which point the company used leased Missouri, Kansas and Texas Railroad track to carry its traffic into Dallas. It also leased Santa Fe track rights to continue on from Houston to Galveston.

Construction crews linked Cleburne to Hillsboro and the T&BV system in late 1903 or early 1904, with the first commercial trains traveling between the towns on January 26, 1904. The first T&BV through passenger train from Fort Worth to Houston passed through Cleburne on January 28, 1907, and it was met by a group of local dignitaries and officials who assembled to welcome the train. The T&BV existed as a company until 1930, when it was acquired by the

newly organized Burlington–Rock Island Railroad. This firm continued to serve Cleburne until it abandoned the line between there and Hillsboro on September 16, 1932.

The construction of the Trinity and Brazos Valley Railway building was a significant event in the history of Cleburne. Local boosters predicted that the arrival of the T&BV and the location of its station in the town portended great things for the community. To encourage the company to place its offices and proposed future railway shops in Cleburne, local businessmen in 1903 provided the site for the depot building at no cost and subscribed twenty-five thousand dollars as an inducement. These efforts resulted in the construction of the present depot building, but the projected extensive railway shops never materialized. Although it took the company three years to accomplish the move, it did transfer its general offices from Hillsboro to Cleburne in January, 1906, keeping them there until September of the same year, when they moved to Fort Worth.

The Cleburne depot and office building is indeed a handsome structure. Standing two stories tall and built of red brick with white limestone trim, it originally had four large rooms in a row on its ground floor. From south to north these were the waiting room for whites, a ticket office with agent's bay window, a waiting room for blacks, and a freight and baggage room. The last of these was equipped with a still-intact walk-in vault for which the original embossed T&BV key has survived. The location for the structure was secured on June 20, 1903, from Mrs. Constanza A. Lucey, but before construction could begin, the two-story Mansion Hotel on the site had to be razed. As the building progressed, the local press reported that Cleburne citizens regularly came by to view the progress and to admire the new ornament to the city.

A man who served as a helper to the masons on the project recollected that two brickmasons were in charge of laying the bricks in the building. One was right-handed and the other left-handed, and neither could work very well with the other. The two men agreed, however, that the left-handed mason would lay the bricks for the corners. They also were in accord in their complaints about the numerous structural arches for the doors and windows, which slowed their progress. Their efforts, however, have stood the test of time, and the three- and four-course brick walls are solid to this day.

After abandonment of the T&BV track between Cleburne and Hillsboro, in 1932, the Cleburne station building stood vacant for several years before it passed into private hands. It subsequently was used to house a wholesale grocer, offices and warehouse space for the Civilian Conservation Corps, a veterans' meeting hall, and a steam laundry. In 1972 it was purchased by the present owners, who have restored the structure and employ it in their ceiling fan and antique business. Today the depot is in probably its best structural condition since it was built. Located just off U.S. 67, it often is viewed by travelers whose attention is attracted by the original white banner-shaped sign at the gable, "T&BV Ry."

Location: The 1903 Trinity and Brazos Valley Railway depot and office building is located one-half block south of U.S. 67, just west of the Santa Fe Railway tracks and Amtrak rail passenger station in Cleburne. Standing at 428 East Chambers Street, it is four blocks east of the Johnson County Courthouse.

Suggested Reading:

Allhands, J. L. *Boll Weevil: Recollections of the Trinity & Brazos Valley Railway.* Houston: Anson Jones Press, 1946.

Research and clipping file on the Cleburne depot of the Trinity and Brazos Valley Railway. In the possession of Dan Leach, The Fan and Antique Depot, Cleburne, Tex.

Detail of the decorative gable and its railway company sign at the south side of the Trinity and Brazos Valley Railway Depot and Offices in Cleburne. Photograph by the author, 1973.

97. Tyler Hydraulic Fill Dam

Serving the citizens of Tyler for ninety years, the earthen structure creating Lake Bellwood is probably the most significant hydraulic fill dam erected in the history of engineering in Texas. It represents a type of dam construction that enjoyed considerable popularity in the late nineteenth century but that today is comparatively rare. Hydraulic fill methods allowed engineers in the age of steam to move large amounts of earth in the years before the availability of modern earth-moving machines. All an engineer needed was a supply of earth fill, a source of water, and a comparatively small and portable steam boiler and pump.

Hydraulic fill technology was born in the goldfields of California during the latter years of the nineteenth century. Miners used large sprays of water under high pressure to wash away banks of earth along rivers and streams to expose gold deposits that had been eroded from higher elevations. To produce the strong jets of

water, the mine operators used either flumes carrying water from higher areas or boiler-driven steam pumps. Although initially the unwanted materials were simply allowed to flow as watery mud into the streams beside which they were produced, engineers soon realized that such materials in other settings might be put to worthwhile use, particularly in the construction of dams, levees, and approaches to bridges. By the 1890s the hydraulic fill method of building dams had achieved a short-lived popularity among civil engineers.

The most famous of the hydraulic fill dams in Texas is the one erected in 1894 just west of Tyler in Smith County. As early as 1883 the community had a waterworks, which had been built by the city and then sold to private owners, who formed the Tyler Water Company. The initial source of supply for the system was a small body of water located southeast of the court-

Looking southward across the Tyler Hydraulic Fill Dam while under construction in 1894. Note the sand ridges on each side used to contain the combined mud and water; note also the jet of water being directed against the hillside in the distance. From James Dix Schuyler, *Reservoirs for Irrigation, Water-Power and Domestic Water-Supply,* 2nd rev. ed. (New York: John Wiley & Sons, 1909), p. 91.

Workmen using water under high pressure to sluice away earth from the hill at the south end of the Tyler damsite for use as hydraulic fill material in 1894. From James Dix Schuyler, *Reservoirs for Irrigation, Water-Power and Domestic Water-Supply,* 2nd rev. ed. (New York: John Wiley & Sons, 1909), p. 92.

house, but by 1891 the owners of the system realized that a greater supply was needed. Accordingly, they purchased from T. J. Adams eighty-five acres on Indian Creek, about four miles west of town. There Adams had operated a gristmill known as the Star Mill, and his millpond became the new source of water for Tyler. In 1893 the water company purchased additional acreage along Indian Creek with a view toward building an entirely new dam to create a reservoir with much greater capacity. About this time the company laid a new thirteen-inch water line from a pump house built at the old mill site into town. Oral tradition states that this pipe had been used on the grounds of the 1893 World's Columbian Exposition in Chicago and was purchased by the water company after the fair closed.

With the property on Indian Creek where a reservoir was planned safely in the possession of the water company, its engineer, J. M. Howells, conceived the idea of building the dam through the use of hydraulic fill techniques. Using an old Worthington steam pump with 750,000-gallon daily capacity, which he borrowed from the waterworks pump house, Howells set up a fire hydrant about halfway up a 150-foot hill at the south end of the proposed dam site. To complete his hydraulic jetting outfit, the engineer connected a 2.5-inch fire hose to the hydrant and placed at its end a 1.5-inch nozzle.

To provide a footing for the dam, crews excavated a trench four feet wide and several feet deep through the surface soil down to clay subsoil. This trench was then refilled with carefully selected puddle clay to build up an impervious core. In the meantime, an outline of the dam was made by throwing up low sand ridges at the slope lines on upstream and downstream faces. Men using hoes and wheelbarrows maintained these ridges as the dam rose in height.

At the hillside that was to provide the earth fill, other men were hard at work. They directed a jet of water from the fire hose against the surface of the hill at a 3 percent grade. This soon gave them a working face about ten feet high, which gradually increased to thirty-six feet high. By maintaining the jet of water against the base of the "cliff," they easily undermined the earth, which was carried away with the flow. This mixed earth and water in turn was transported to the construction site through a series of connected thirteen-inch sheet-iron pipes assembled with loose joints like stovepipe. The muck gradually filled the areas between the sand ridges, where the men with hoes allowed the water to drain away while leaving the earth behind. As work progressed, the sand ridges were raised until they reached the correct level for the full height of the dam. The south end, nearest the source of supply, reached the proper grade level first. Analysis showed that the earth forming the structure was 65 percent sand and 35 percent clay.

When the structure approached completion, the pipes had to be placed on temporary wooden trestles to give them the necessary grade to transport the

Looking south across the length of the 1894 Tyler Hydraulic Fill Dam as it appears today. Photograph by the author, 1975.

muck to the far end. With the dam almost finished, the hose and nozzle were shifted to the north end, where they were used to jet away an opening through the dam to serve as its spillway. The earth moved in this process was put back into other parts of the structure.

The expense for the construction of the Tyler waterworks dam was remarkably small. The entire project, including not only the earthen dam but also its auxiliary structures, cost a mere $1,140. Even in 1894 engineers declared that it "must be regarded as a marvel of cheapness for a structure of the size . . . and one performing the function of an impounding dam of its magnitude." Standing 32 feet high and 575 feet long, the earthen dam created a reservoir containing 1,170 acre-feet of water at an amazingly inexpensive sixty-five cents per acre foot. While the dam was being built, the water company also erected a new brick pump house at the east side of the new reservoir. It was so much nearer to the town than the old pump house that the shortening of the principal influent main saved enough money to pay for the construction of the dam.

For ninety years the Tyler Hydraulic Fill Dam has served Tyler. The only substantial change was the raising of its height five to seven feet and the reconstruction of its spillway in 1936. It continues to be used and remains a beautiful legacy of engineering history in East Texas.

Location: The Tyler Hydraulic Fill Dam, known locally as the Lake Bellwood Dam, is located about 4 miles west of downtown Tyler. The most convenient access is via Lake Bellwood Road, a paved local road that runs south from State Highway 31 about 1.5 miles west of its intersection with Loop 323 on the west side of Tyler. Turn south from the state highway at the sign for Lake Bellwood, follow Lake Bellwood Road southward four-tenths of a mile under the St. Louis Southwestern Railway tracks, and then to the first unpaved road to the right. Follow this unpaved road an additional one-half mile to the north end of the dam itself. The hill from which the earth fill was jetted may be viewed at the opposite end of the dam.

Suggested Reading:

"History of Water Distribution and Water Plant of the City of Tyler." Typescript. May 19, 1936. Office of City Water Department, City Hall, Tyler, Tex.

Schuyler, James Dix. *Reservoirs for Irrigation, Water-Power and Domestic Water-Supply.* 2nd rev. ed. New York: John Wiley & Sons, 1909.

98. Vaughn Brothers Irrigation Plant

One of the last surviving examples of the pioneer irrigation plants installed on the High Plains between 1910 and 1916, the Vaughn Brothers Irrigation Plant remains stand beside a plowed field just south of Tulia in Swisher County.

Irrigation, which in the 1940s and 1950s converted the Texas High Plains into a veritable garden on the semiarid southern Great Plains, had its beginnings thirty years before. In 1910 D. L. McDonald of Hereford drilled the first successful irrigation well in the region, inaugurating a flurry of activity that spread over the next half dozen years.

Starting in 1910 numerous land promoters contracted with McDonald, with Layne and Bowler Company of Houston, or with other individuals or firms to drill large-volume irrigation wells and to fit them with pumping equipment. Most of these wells were located in Hale, Floyd, Deaf Smith, and Bailey counties, although others were drilled in adjoining counties like Swisher. The principal motivation for

The Vaughn Brothers Irrigation Plant as it appeared in 1968, with the derrick still standing and the engine house collapsed onto the Primm engine. Photograph courtesy Donald E. Green; negative in Panhandle-Plains Historical Museum, Canyon, Texas.

255

the speculators in boring these wells was to enhance the value of the agricultural land that they were selling to farmers. Most of the buyers came to Texas from the Midwest, lured by comparatively low land prices on the plains. The promoters believed that the visible success of irrigated agriculture would permit them to raise the prices they were charging for the lands that they hoped to sell. One company at Plainview, the Texas Land and Development Company, even provided its customers with operational irrigation wells. A small minority of the irrigation wells were drilled for specific farmers; the Vaughn brothers' well was one of these.

It is estimated that between 1910 and 1916 more than two hundred irrigation plants were installed on the High Plains. The effort to develop the underground water resources, however, was generally unsuccessful. The idea of irrigating crops was a concept introduced by land promoters from the towns and not one that originated among the farmers themselves. In essence, the plan put the cart before the horse.

Additional factors hindered the success of the early irrigation movement. Drilling an irrigation well and installing pumping equipment cost several thousand dollars, placing these plants far beyond the financial reach of average High Plains farmers. America's entry into World War I increased the prices for raw materials, further raising the prices for pumps, engines, and auxiliary equipment. During the 1910s, farmers in the region had not yet developed major cash crops that were suitable to the uncertain climate of the plains. In addition, most farmers were unfamiliar with the operation of heavy machinery, and consequently, many of them encountered problems running the large oil-burning engines that powered their pumps.

An exception to the general rule of land promoters dominating the installation of irrigation pumping plants was a plant near Tulia made for Joe D. and John W. Vaughn. Among the most wealthy and influential men in Swisher County, they were estimated to be worth sixty thousand dollars in 1909. After viewing some of D. L. McDonald's early irrigation plants, they decided in 1913 that it would be advantageous for them to have one placed on their property south of Tulia. Accordingly, they contracted with Layne and Bowler Company for a complete installation at their farm.

The Vaughn Brothers Irrigation Plant consisted of a 140-foot well, a 22-inch Layne and Bowler three-stage "pit-less" pump, and an eighty-horsepower Primm single-cylinder oil-burning engine. Over the well stood a wooden derrick about 35 feet tall, and the engine and leather belts that linked it with the drive shaft for the pump were protected from the elements beneath a wooden shed.

The Layne and Bowler crew arrived on the site in January, 1914, and completed the well in May of the same year. The men used a portable rotary drilling rig powered by two small oil-burning engines, one fifteen horsepower and the other ten horsepower. To the Vaughn family the work seemed to progress very slowly.

The large Primm engine arrived in Tulia on a railway flatcar sharing space with another Primm engine that had been ordered for a well drilled for Lewis Klous a few months earlier. August A. Vaughn, son of Joe D. Vaughn, was on hand when it arrived, and he remembered that the big engine was unloaded onto a wagon for the short trip to the well site. Along the way the wagon crossed some rough ground, and this coupled with the weight of the load broke one of the wagon axles. The men had to transfer the heavy engine to a second wagon.

By May, 1914, the engine had been placed on its permanent concrete footings a few feet south of the well. Connected to the drive shaft of the pump by six-ply leather belts fourteen inches wide and a quarter inch thick, the engine powered the Layne and Bowler pump in its first season of active use during the summer of 1914. The pump, located in the well, elevated water to the surface through a ten-inch discharge pipe for irrigation use.

The engine, like most of the low-compression oil-burning engines of its day, had no electrical system whatever. Instead it was a so-called hot plate engine, which, once started, generated the heat in its own combustion chamber to continue igniting additional fuel and thus maintain operation. The Vaughn brothers' Primm engine was made by the Power Manufacturing Company of Marion, Ohio.

Starting the engine was by no means a simple matter. First the operator "spotted" the piston in the proper position within the combustion chamber by turning the big sixty-inch flywheels on both sides of the engine with iron levers that were wedged into openings in the wheels. Once the piston was moved to the correct position, the operator used a blowtorch to heat a special "hot pin" about ten to twelve inches long until it turned red hot. Quickly he placed the pin into a hole leading inside the combustion chamber

The Primm engine from the Vaughn Brothers Irrigation Plant as it appears today. Photograph by the author, 1983.

and locked it into place. Without wasting any time he primed the engine by pouring some gasoline into a special valve on the backside of the piston that would permit the fuel to be sucked into the combustion chamber when the piston next was moved.

With all these preparations made, the operator opened a valve on a line leading from a compressed-air tank into the combustion chamber. This compressed air began moving the parts of the engine by forcing the cylinder away from the chamber while at the same time the gasoline prime was drawn into the chamber, where it ignited from the heat of the "hot pin." If everything worked as it should, this ignition would start the big engine running, as the movement of the cylinder automatically drew fuel oil into the combustion chamber. Once the engine began firing, it generated its own heat concentrated on a "hot plate" inside the combustion chamber to continue igniting fuel.

Unlike most of their contemporaries on the High Plains, the Vaughn brothers often ran their irrigation plant day and night. Most farmers used their engines to irrigate only during daylight hours. August A. Vaughn remembered that on one occasion during the irrigation season they operated their plant day and night for an entire month without ever stopping the engine. He was impressed with the reliability of the Primm engine, remarking that "we never had to buy any parts for it." Once the initial expense was paid, it was comparatively inexpensive to run the engine with fuel oil, which cost only 4 to 4.5 cents a gallon at Tulia. The plant itself, however, was not cheap. The Primm engine alone cost twenty-one hundred dollars, with the entire installation costing the brothers approximately six thousand dollars.

The Vaughn brothers irrigated approximately 160 acres from the 1914 well, but only part of it was watered at once. The well could provide enough water conveyed through open ditches to irrigate about 50 to 60 acres at a time, generally dividing the irrigated acreage into about 50 acres of wheat, with the remainder devoted to kaffir corn or other grain sorghums. An attendant had to stay with the engine all the time it was running, and another person had to remain in the fields to tend the ditches and see that the water flowed to the proper areas.

The 1914 irrigation plant continued in use with its original power and pumping equipment into the 1940s. After the Primm engine ceased to be used, the old pump was operated through belt connection with the power take-off on a farm tractor. Finally, both it and the well were abandoned. By the mid-1960s the wooden shed that had protected the engine and belts had collapsed, and a few years later it and the derrick were removed.

Today the irrigation plant site is marked most prominently by the well-preserved Primm oil-burning engine. It stands on its original concrete footings with a new growth of small elm trees coming up around it.

Location: The Vaughn Brothers Irrigation Plant is located six-tenths of a mile south of Tulia, just beyond the end of the pavement on a county road that leads to the Rose Hill Cemetery. The site is approximately two-tenths of a mile east of U.S. 87.

Suggested Reading:

Green, Donald E. *Land of the Underground Rain: Irrigation on the Texas High Plains, 1910–1970.* Austin: University of Texas Press, 1973.
Vaughn, August A., to T. Lindsay Baker. Interview at August A. Vaughn Farm, Swisher County, Tex., November 28, 1983. Typescript. Research Center, Panhandle-Plains Historical Museum, Canyon, Tex.

99. Victoria "Dutch" Windmill

The Victoria "Dutch" Windmill, erected in 1870 by two German immigrants, is the last surviving nineteenth-century European-style windmill in Texas. It stands today as a historical monument in Victoria.

The story of the Victoria "Dutch" Windmill goes back to the middle of the nineteenth century. Fred Meiss, Sr., and Otto Fiek erected the mill in 1870. Meiss purchased an older windmill that F. G. Witte had built about two miles east of Goliad well before the Civil War. Witte had ordered his grindstones from Norway, and they arrived by sea at the Texas port of Indianola, from which point they were shipped inland by oxcart to Goliad County. According to family tradition, Witte's windmill was the first in the area, and farmers brought their grain from miles around

for him to grind. The capacity of his mill, however, was limited, for he could process only about five hundred pounds of grain a week, "if the wind was blowing." After several years Witte sold his mill and grindstones to Louis Albrecht, who lived on Coleto Creek near Fannin, also in Goliad County. It was from Albrecht that Fred Meiss purchased the mill.

When Meiss bought the grindstones and remains of the windmill, they were in far from operable condition. He moved the pieces by wagon to his farm near Spring Creek, north of Victoria in Victoria County, and set to work. On the farm Meiss and Fiek reconstructed the tower that supports the mill, giving it an additional fifteen feet of height. They built the superstructure entirely of heavy timbers held together with

The exterior of the 1870 Victoria "Dutch" Windmill. Photograph by the author, 1982.

Wooden teeth in the brake wheel just in front of the wallower gear atop the main shaft inside the Victoria "Dutch" Windmill. Photograph by the author, 1973.

wooden pegs. They planned it in the style of the Dutch windmills in Europe, with a cap at the top designed to rotate so that the blades could be directed into the wind.

Inside the mill Meiss and Fiek replaced all the worn or missing parts with equivalents that they fashioned from wood. The four-bladed windwheel initially was mounted on a wind shaft hewn from a tree trunk that was carefully shaped and then fitted with a cogged brake wheel inside the mill. The teeth protruding from this wheel fit notches in a smaller wallower gear attached to the top of the main vertical shaft, which reached all the way down through the tower to ground level. It, too, was cut from a single tree trunk fifteen inches in diameter and twenty feet long. Additional gearing connected the shaft with the grindstones, which were mounted on the second-floor level of the mill. Grain to "feed" the mill, poured through an opening in the upper stone, was ground between this stone and the one beneath. The blades of the windwheel, mounted on four arms, were made so that woven fabric could be stretched over all or part of them to catch the wind. Attaching and removing this fabric covering quite obviously could be a dangerous task.

After operating for a number of years, the "Dutch" windmill fell into disuse on the Meiss farm. Few people thought about its potential historical significance until field representatives from Henry Ford's

Greenfield Village attempted in 1935 to purchase the structure for restoration at the Michigan museum. Family members realized that they possessed a structure of unusual value, but they lacked the means and expertise to care for it properly. To ensure its preservation for the future, they deeded the structure to the Victoria Morning Study Club, a ladies' organization. The study club, in collaboration with the City of Victoria and with the assistance of numerous local business leaders, moved the windmill from the Meiss farm to a new site in Victoria. There it was restored to near operable condition, and now for almost half a century it has been one of the most prominent tourist attractions in the city.

Location: The Victoria "Dutch" Windmill stands at the center of Memorial Square, bounded by Power Avenue and DeLeon, Commercial, and Wheeler streets in Victoria. It is open only by appointment through the office of the director of Parks and Recreation for the City of Victoria.

Suggested Reading:

"The Old Windpower Grist Mill, Memorial Square, Victoria, Texas." *Old Mill News* 8, no. 3 (July, 1980): 4.
"Owners of Old Mill Refused Henry Ford's Bid for Relic." *Victoria Advocate* (Victoria, Tex.), historical edition 1968, sec. 8, p. 12.

100. Waco Suspension Bridge

Built between 1868 and 1869 and used by vehicular traffic for over a century, the Waco Suspension Bridge was the first bridge ever to span the Brazos River and was the first major suspension bridge erected in the state. It stands to this day as one of the most spectacular of all the historic engineering works in Texas.

In the 1860s Waco was a small but pushing community of about fifteen hundred on the west bank of the Brazos River. The town lay on the site of an ancient Waco Indian village, from which it took its name when it was first occupied by white settlers in 1849. Fortunately located on the Chisholm Trail, the town began to prosper in the years after the Civil War both from the cattle trade and from increasing economic activity in the Brazos Valley. Through these years the only way to cross the Brazos was by ferry or by fording the waters when the level was low. High water prevented all but the foolhardy from attempting to cross.

By the mid-1860s the residents of Waco and its surrounding area had begun to clamor for the construction of a bridge across the Brazos, but neither the municipal nor the county governments could afford it. These were the days of Reconstruction, when cash was scarce and interest rates were high. In 1866 a group of local business leaders petitioned the state legislature for a charter as a private company to erect a toll bridge across the Brazos at Waco and to operate

it for a term of twenty-five years. On November 1 of that year the legislature formally issued the charter for the Waco Bridge Company.

Several months passed before the company founders took further steps toward the actual construction of a bridge. They finally called an organizational meeting on May 8, 1868, and at that meeting the officers opened subscriptions for stock in the corporation. After all the stock was purchased, the stockholders met and formally elected officers. The president of the company then journeyed to New York City to confer with several bridge companies on the size and type of structure needed at Waco. His choice was between an iron truss bridge and one of the interesting new suspension-type bridges, which had been developed by John A. Roebling and Son of Trenton, New Jersey. On August 9 he wrote to the board of directors to report that he had decided on a suspension span as "the cheapest and best" for the Brazos and to state that he planned to go the next day to the Roebling offices in Trenton to order the steel cables, hydraulic cement, and other specialized building materials that would be required to build it. In the same letter he stated that he had employed Thomas M. Griffith, an experienced civil engineer who had worked on other such structures, to draw the plans for the Waco Bridge and to supervise its construction. By early September both the company

The Waco Suspension Bridge in near original appearance before its reconstruction in 1913–14. Photograph courtesy Texas Collection, Baylor University, Waco, Texas.

Looking southwestward along the Waco Suspension Bridge across the Brazos River. Photograph by the author, 1975.

president and engineer Griffith were back in Waco overseeing preliminary work.

The construction of the bridge began with the excavation of footings for the two large double towers that would support the steel cables for the span. Although Griffith wanted to use stone, locally manufactured brick was employed throughout for the towers. After the footings were prepared, erection of the towers began. They required an incredible 2.7 million bricks. The original design of the towers included ornamentation reminiscent of medieval castles, which at the time seemed to suit perfectly the tastes of Waco residents.

After the towers were completed, workmen began carrying the wires across the river, creating the cables that would in time support a wooden roadway. Progress on the bridge was slower and more expensive than company officials had expected. Nevertheless,

with repeated calls for support from the stockholders combined with a last-minute loan, the bridge was completed in the last days of December, 1869. The first tolls were collected on January 1, 1870, and the structure was dedicated on the sixth of the month with a huge celebration. The achievement of the local entrepreneurs was widely lauded through the state, with the *San Antonio Express* proclaiming, "All honor to Waco! She is leading all the inland cities in enterprise and prosperity."

The Waco Suspension Bridge was indeed a spectacular engineering feat. Built at a time when most of Texas was still reeling from the effects of the Civil War, it is impressive to visitors even in this day of modern technology. The main span stretches 475 feet over the waters of the Brazos. The roadway was so wide that two stagecoaches could pass each other going in opposite directions. No other bridge in the state for years could compare with it in either scale or beauty.

The suspension span operated as a toll crossing under the ownership of the Waco Bridge Company from 1870 to 1889, at which time it was purchased by McLennan County. The county then turned the structure over to Waco for its operation and maintenance as a free public bridge. In 1913–14 the municipal government had the bridge reconstructed by the Missouri Valley Bridge and Iron Company of Leavenworth, Kansas. City engineer G. E. Byars and county engineer R. J. Windrow cooperated with the bridge company engineers in redesigning much of the old structure. The original decorative brickwork, for instance, was modified to have a much plainer appearance, and the 1868 Roebling steel cables were removed and replaced with newer and stronger steel cables. The suspension span and the east approach span were completely rebuilt. A truss approach initially had been added to the east end of the bridge in 1885. The new spans, designed to carry much heavier loads, employed steel trusses on both sides of the roadway and in addition provided for walkways.

After the fabrication and installation of the new cables and spans, wooden decking was laid for both the roadway and the walkways. Opening again in 1914, the Waco Suspension Bridge remained in use for vehicular traffic until 1971. In that year the City Council retired the bridge to be preserved as a historical monument. Since that time it has been open to pedestrians in a park area just east of downtown Waco. In 1976 the city undertook major renovation of the old bridge, helping to ensure that it will stand for another century spanning the waters of the Brazos for the use and enjoyment of future generations.

Location: The Waco Suspension Bridge crosses the Brazos River at the foot of Bridge Street, just east of the Waco central business district. It is located in a park area near the site of the original Waco Spring, and it is interpreted by several historical markers.

Suggested Reading:

Conger, Roger N. "The Waco Suspension Bridge." *Texana* 1, no. 3 (Summer, 1963): 181–224.

101. *Waxahachie Creek Bridge*

Built in 1889, the Waxahachie Creek overhead truss bridge is a classic example of the type of iron bridges purchased by Texas counties a century ago to span smaller rivers and streams. In remarkably sound condition, it remains in daily service carrying South Rogers Street traffic across Waxahachie Creek on the south side of downtown Waxahachie.

Ellis County was organized in December, 1849, and Waxahachie was chosen as county seat the following year. The town was built along Waxahachie Creek on sixty acres of rising ground donated for the purpose by Maj. Emory Rogers. The town grew slowly, having about twenty-five hundred people in 1870, forty-seven hundred in 1880, and eighty-five hundred in 1890. Transportation became an increasingly important concern as the population increased. Accordingly, between 1888 and 1890, the county commissioners of Ellis County awarded thirteen contracts for the construction of bridges in various parts of the county. Most of these were described in the early 1890s as "substantial iron-truss bridges, built to withstand the wear and tear of many years." All were built by one firm, the Wrought Iron Bridge Company

of Canton, Ohio. Its local agent, who negotiated the contracts with county officials, was T. R. Anderson. The prices paid by the county ranged from $1,240 to $2,658.

On June 1, 1888, the Ellis County Commissioners' Court met to consider the construction of a bridge across Waxahachie Creek on South Rogers Street, only a few blocks from the courthouse where they were meeting. At this time they signed a contract that T. R. Anderson had prepared. According to this legal instrument, the bridge company agreed to erect a one hundred-foot, two-lane overhead truss bridge complete with approaches across the said stream. In return the county commissioners agreed to pay the contractor a total of twenty-five hundred dollars divided as follows: two thousand on January 1, 1889, and five hundred at the completion of the project. Soon crews appeared in Waxahachie from Canton, Ohio, to begin work on the piers for the prefabricated iron structure.

Today the Waxahachie Creek Bridge stands basically as the Wrought Iron Bridge Company erected it in 1889. The one-hundred-foot-long Pratt through-

Full view of the Pratt through truss forming the main span of the 1889 Waxahachie Creek Bridge. Photograph by the author, 1982.

truss span rests on four concrete piers poured into large riveted-steel cylinders. Driving from downtown across the bridge, one first comes to a forty-five-foot approach span with a wooden decking before passing onto the timber roadway of the overhead-truss span. Then one proceeds on across to the south approach, which also is decked with a wooden roadway forty-three feet long. The roadway itself is eighteen feet wide and is equipped with guardrails. On the east side of the bridge pedestrians cross with safety on a five-foot cantilevered walkway. From the bridge, visitors can look down twenty-three feet to the clear water of Waxahachie Creek.

The Waxahachie Creek Bridge remained the principal route of southbound vehicular traffic from the town until 1931. In that year the State Highway Department erected a new concrete bridge across Waxahachie Creek two blocks to the west. Today this newer structure, itself half a century old, carries most of the traffic of U.S. 77 through the town, and the old iron bridge is used only by local motorists. Although city

and county officials from time to time have discussed replacing the old iron bridge, local residents and historic preservationists have realized the significance of the structure as a valuable surviving example of a once common but today increasingly rare form of nineteenth-century engineering. The bridge is within the area of the Waxahachie Downtown Historic District in the National Register of Historic Places and is registered as an official Texas Historic Site with a marker designating it as such and sketching its history.

Location: The Waxahachie Creek Bridge spans Waxahachie Creek on South Rogers Street, about half a dozen blocks south of the Ellis County Courthouse in Waxahachie. It is known locally as the South Rogers Street Bridge.

Suggested Reading:

Ellis County, Tex. Commissioners' Court. Minutes, vol. H, p. 257. Office of County Clerk, Ellis County Courthouse, Waxahachie, Tex.

102. Williamson Dam

On its completion in 1924, the Williamson Dam had the distinction of being the largest hollow concrete dam in the world. Built across Sandy Creek about three miles north of Cisco, it impounds the storage reservoir for the local waterworks.

By 1920 the town of Cisco in Eastland County had grown to such an extent that its civic leaders decided that it required a larger and more dependable water supply. Up to that time its source had been a small reservoir known as Lake Bernie. The Cisco City Council employed the Henry Exall Elrod Engineering Company of Dallas to prepare plans for a concrete dam across Sandy Creek at a point where it flowed between two large hills. About the same time the city sold bonds in the amount of $1 million to fund the proposed project. After the plans were drawn, the city aldermen awarded the contract for the project to the H. F. Freisted Construction Company of Chicago and Houston.

Work began on September 15, 1920. The initial effort was directed toward the erection of a construction camp and the building of a railway spur from the Missouri, Kansas and Texas Railroad in town. Most of the supplies and equipment for the project were moved to the construction site via the 2.25-mile spur

by a pair of steam locomotives. The construction camp consisted of cottages for the foremen and their families, several bunkhouses for laborers and mechanics, warehouses, field offices, a recreational club, and a kitchen. By January 1, 1921, the camp and railway spur were completed, and work was ready to begin on the footings for the dam.

As built, the Williamson Dam was 1,060 feet long, 133 feet, 6 inches high, 154 feet wide at its base, and 6 feet wide at its top. Later, a highway was added across the top of the structure. The project required fifty thousand cubic yards of concrete, 1.5 million board feet of lumber for the fabrication of the forms into which the concrete was poured, and 2 million pounds of reinforcing steel. The project, exceeding the estimates, cost the taxpayers $1.5 million.

According to the original contract between Cisco and the contractor, the Williamson Dam was to be completed in 285 working days. The contractor employed about four hundred men, working both day and night, and for a few months the effort progressed rapidly. Then everything stopped because of a lawsuit between the city and its contractor. After the dispute was settled, a huge barbecue, held at the damsite, was attended by an estimated twenty thousand visitors.

The Williamson Dam during the construction of the giant swimming pool at its downstream side in 1927. Photograph courtesy Texas State Library, Austin, Texas.

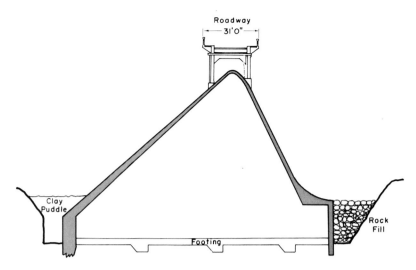

Cross-section of the spillway area of the Williamson Dam, near its center. Based on City of Cisco, Texas, "Williamson Dam and Lake Cisco," measured drawing number 12/09.0/B, n.d., Office of City Manager, Cisco, Texas. Drawing by the author.

Work progressed on the structure until the final concrete portion was completed on November 1, 1923. The floodgates did not arrive at the construction site until January of the next year, so it was February, 1924, before the dam actually could go into service. On its dedication it was named in honor of J. M. Williamson, the Cisco mayor who conceived the idea of its construction.

The Williamson Dam is known to many Texans because of the huge outdoor swimming pool that was built at the base of its downstream face. This great open-air recreational facility was constructed in 1927, three years after the dam was finished. Measuring 300 by 700 feet and costing $118,000 to build, the pool was owned and managed by the Lake Cisco Amusement Company, which operated other concessions in the lake area. The giant pool was divided by an island into shallow and deep areas and was served by a variety of diving towers, slides, and roller coasters for bathers. Nearby stood a 55-by-120-foot bathhouse fitted with showers, booths, lockers, and the like on its ground floor and a roller rink/ballroom on its upper floor. The pool attracted thousands of visitors to the Cisco area for half a century, but closed in the mid-1970s.

Location: The Williamson Dam, which still impounds Lake Cisco, is located just west of State Highway 6, three miles north of Cisco. It is easily accessible to the public.

Suggested Reading:

Roberts, Bill M. *Where the Rails Crossed.* Burnet, Tex.: Eakin Publications, 1981.

103. Yellowhouse Canyon Bridge

Erected in 1913 by the Austin Brothers Bridge Company under contract to Lubbock County, the Yellowhouse Canyon Bridge is perhaps the oldest surviving engineered wagon bridge on the Texas South Plains. Today it is beautifully restored as a footbridge in the Canyon Lakes park area, which encompasses several miles of the Yellowhouse Canyon as it passes through much of the city of Lubbock.

The original wagon road from Lubbock northward toward Abernathy, Plainview, and eventually to Amarillo crossed the Yellowhouse Draw, a tributary of the North Fork of the Double Mountain Fork of the Brazos River, in the area of the present-day North University Avenue crossing in Lubbock. Early in this century, before the drastic lowering of the water table through power-pump irrigation, the Yellowhouse Draw was a constantly flowing stream in the bottom of the Yellowhouse Canyon. Whenever drivers of buggies, wagons, or early automobiles needed to cross the stream, they were forced to ford the water. In times of heavy rains, the travelers had no choice except to go around the head of the draw, several miles out of their way, or to wait for the waters to recede. Even then the crossing was muddy.

Early in this century residents of the northern part of the county began requesting that the county build

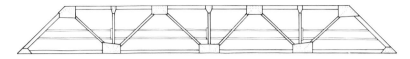

Elevation of one of the truss spans used in the construction of the 1913 Yellowhouse Canyon Bridge. Based on Austin Brothers Bridge Company, Dallas, Texas, "60-Ft. Standard Span," measured drawing, December 25, 1914, Engineering Department, Austin Bridge Company, Dallas, Texas, and field photographs. Drawing by the author.

a bridge across the draw to facilitate their travel to the county seat to transact business. In time their requests produced action, for on February 15, 1913, the commissioners of Lubbock County decided that they should fund the construction of "a bridge . . . over the Canyon on the Lubbock and Abernathy Road." They instructed the county judge to advertise for bids from contractors and furthermore stated that all the bids received by the deadline of the second Monday in March, 1913, would be opened on that date. Bids came from the Austin Brothers Bridge

Company of Dallas, Texas, and from the Midland Bridge Company of Kansas City, Missouri.

Time passed after the opening of the bids before the county commissioners made any further decisions concerning the proposed bridge. Then on April 14, 1913, they met again to consider the matter of the Yellowhouse Canyon bridge. They found that "the Bid of Austin Brothers, is the lowest and best bid for such work" and they awarded the Dallas firm the contract for $1,138.

According to the specifications stipulated in the

The Yellowhouse Canyon Bridge restored for use as a footbridge in the Canyon Lakes Park. Photograph by the author, 1984.

266

contract, the Austin Brothers Bridge Company agreed to erect on suitable abutments a single-span low Warren truss bridge sixty feet long with a twelve-foot wooden roadway. This prefabricated steel structure was the firm's standard sixty-foot bridge number 60-A. It already had erected dozens of similar spans throughout the state. The Lubbock County bridge was to be completed by July 14, 1913, and as far as surviving records indicate, it was completed on or before schedule.

The Yellowhouse Canyon Bridge remained in service as the principal crossing over the Yellowhouse Draw for many years. With the passage of time, however, its ten-ton capacity and twelve-foot roadway grew inadequate for the heavy and wide loads that needed to cross it, so county maintenance crews altered the structure considerably. Removing the two Warren trusses, they poured a heavy twenty-two-foot-wide concrete culvert in the place of the bridge and then mounted the former structural truss members as guardrails. The bridge continued to be used in this manner for many years. It was finally replaced entirely with a new crossing just to the east.

The "Cinderella story" for the Yellowhouse Canyon Bridge began in the early 1970s. At this time Lubbock undertook the construction of five small dams on Yellowhouse Draw, creating a huge new park in the Yellowhouse Canyon. Initially, planners and officials considered simply removing the abandoned culvert with its ugly old "guardrails," but then they asked for advice from the engineers and historians from the History of Engineering Program at Texas Tech University. These staff members went to work determining exactly what remains had survived, how old they were, and how they might be reused.

The historians began by examining the minutes of the County Commissioners' Court meetings to find out when the bridge was erected and what company did the work. Fortunately, the contracting firm, now the Austin Bridge Company, was still in business. The historians immediately got in touch with its officials, who were delighted to cooperate. The company still had the original sixty-year-old construction drawings for their standard sixty-foot bridge and sent copies to Texas Tech. While this investigation was being undertaken by the historians, the engineers associated with the History of Engineering Program examined the actual remains of the bridge. They recommended replacing the lower chords of the trusses, which had deteriorated during their years of encasement in concrete during the bridge's "culvert" stage, and they suggested other minor repairs. Local government crews undertook the repairs, sandblasting, and repainting that had been recommended by the university engineers.

After the steel truss spans of the bridge had been rehabilitated, they were placed on new abutments, new floor beams were put in position, and a light timber deck was built across the old steel members. Today it looks almost new. No longer a vehicular bridge, the Yellowhouse Canyon Bridge now carries hikers across the Yellowhouse Draw near the upper reservoir of the Canyon Lakes park only a few feet away from its original 1913 location.

Location: The Yellowhouse Canyon Bridge, now refurbished as a footbridge, spans the Yellowhouse Draw in the park area just west of the present-day FM 1264 (North University Avenue) bridge across the draw. This location is only about one-half mile south of Loop 289, on the extreme northwest side of Lubbock.

Suggested Reading:

Lubbock County, Tex. Commissioners' Court. Minutes, vol. 2, pp. 477, 494–95. Office of County Clerk, Lubbock County Courthouse, Lubbock, Tex. "Old Yellowhouse Bridge Reclaimed for Hikers." *Lubbock Avalanche-Journal* (Lubbock, Tex.), July 24, 1974, morning edition, sec. A, p. 2.

Appendix

LIST OF HISTORIC ENGINEERING SITES

This appendix presents a selected list of over a thousand historic engineering sites in Texas. Each entry provides the name of the site, the county where located, and abbreviated historical and descriptive data. The enumeration is based in part on the Texas Historic Engineering Site Inventory prepared by me and others at the Center for the History of Engineering at Texas Tech University and in part on files compiled exclusively by me in the years since my departure from Texas Tech in 1979. The information on which the listing is based varies in both quantity and quality; files for some of the sites have multiple pages of data, whereas others contain only sufficient data for positive identification. Many of the engineering works listed remain intact and even in use, but many others have been modified or obliterated. No effort has been made here to give more than brief informa-

tion due to the restraints of space placed on an appendix of this nature. In preparing the listing, I have included the sites that are discussed in detail in this book and have marked them with asterisks. This inclusion was made to place these projects in their proper perspective as representatives of the hundreds of sites making up the Texas engineering heritage.

This listing should be considered neither comprehensive nor complete. It does, however, give a starting point for additional research on the history of engineering in Texas. Many of these projects themselves are sufficiently important to merit research leading to the preparation of individual articles, masters' theses, monographs, and even books. I hope the appendix will stimulate others to investigate these sites more deeply than I have done in this basic guide.

Abilene and Northern Railway. Jones and Taylor counties. Railway line built in 1907 from Stamford to Abilene; taken over in that year by Colorado Southern Railway and later leased to Wichita Valley Railway.

Abilene and Southern Railway. Jones, Runnels, and Taylor counties. Railway chartered in 1909 and built from Ballinger to Hamlin; acquired by Texas and Pacific Railway in 1926.

Abilene Dam. Taylor County. Earthen dam constructed on Elm Creek, six miles northwest of Tuscola between 1919 and 1921 to impound water for Abilene waterworks.

Abilene Water Tower. Taylor County. Site of a

major water tower failure at State Epileptic Colony in 1904; received wide attention in national engineering journals.

Abilene Waterworks. Taylor County. Water system for Abilene built between 1885 and 1886; supplied with water both from wells and from Lytle Creek.

Acme Gypsum Works. Hardeman County. Gypsum mining and processing operations begun at Acme in the late nineteenth century and continuing today.

Acme Tap Railroad. Hardeman County. Shortest common carrier in Texas; chartered in 1909 to serve a gypsum plant at Acme.

Alamito Creek Irrigation Project. Presidio County. Corporate irrigation project on Alamito Creek south of Marfa; included storage reservoir and two main canals built in 1911.

Alamocitos Irrigation System. Oldham County. Irrigation system constructed on Matador Ranch about 1910; included pumping plant elevating water from Canadian River.

* *Alamo Portland and Roman Cement Works.* Bexar County. Factory built in 1880 as the second portland cement works in United States and first west of the Mississippi; listed on National Register of Historic Places.

Aldrette Acequia. El Paso County. Community irrigation ditch in El Paso valley excavated about 1850; in 1914, 1.6 miles long, 6 feet wide, and carrying ten cubic feet of water per second; sold to U.S. government in 1917.

Alibates Flint Quarries. Potter County. Flint quarries exploited thousands of years ago by prehistoric Indians to provide stone for knives, scrapers, spear points, and other tools; listed on National Register of Historic Places.

Allamoore Railway Water System. Hudspeth County. Water supply system consisting of wells and overhead storage tank built by Southern Pacific Railroad at Allamoore in 1880s.

Amarillo Army Airfield. Potter County. Training camp for air crews and ground mechanics in U.S. Army Air Corps during World War II; continued as air force base into 1950s.

* *Amicable Building.* McLennan County. Steel-frame skyscraper twenty-two stories high in Waco; built between 1910 and 1911; acclaimed in its day as "tallest building in the South."

Anderson's Mill. Travis County. Water-powered mill erected by Thomas Anderson in 1863 and used as powder mill during Civil War.

Angelina and Neches River Railroad. Angelina County. One of oldest short-line railroads in Texas; begun in nineteenth century but not chartered until 1900; served lumber industry.

Aransas Harbor Terminal Company Railway. Nueces and San Patricio counties. Seven-mile railway line connecting Aransas Pass with Port Aransas.

Aransas Pass Harbor Improvements. Nueces and Aransas counties. Harbor improvements at Aransas Pass beginning in mid-nineteenth century, including channel dredging, jetties, and dock construction.

* *Aransas Pass Lighthouse.* Aransas County. Brick lighthouse erected at Aransas Pass by U.S. Treasury Department in 1857 and operated until 1952; listed

on National Register of Historic Places.

Aransas Pass Plank Causeway. San Patricio County. Wooden causeway constructed in 1931; for thirty years served as traffic route from town of Aransas Pass to the landing for Port Aransas ferry.

Archer City Waterworks. Archer County. Municipal waterworks constructed between 1927 and 1928 to serve Archer City; secured supply of water from a river-fed reservoir near the town.

Archer County Copper Mines. Archer County. Site of efforts to locate commercial quantities of copper in Archer County during the 1870s.

Arcola Windmill Water System. Fort Bend County. System at Arcola that as early as 1860 used a Mitchell Patent Self-Regulating Windmill to elevate well water for use by steam locomotives on Houston Tap and Brazoria Railroad.

Arledge Field. Jones County. Airfield established near Stamford in 1941 to give primary flight training to Army Air Corps cadets.

Artesian Belt Railroad. Atascosa and Bexar counties. Railway chartered in 1908 and built thirty-eight miles from Kirk to Christine; purchased by Missouri Pacific Railroad in 1926.

Arthur Cotton Gin. Tom Green County. Water-powered cotton gin built on Dove Creek in 1885 by Stephen Dexter Arthur; some stone remains still exist.

Asphalt Belt Railway. Uvalde County. Railway line built eighteen miles to serve bitumen mines in Uvalde County; successor to Kinney and Uvalde Railroad, chartered in 1921.

Austin and Northwestern Railroad. Burnet, Llano, and Travis counties. Railroad chartered in 1881 and built from Austin to Burnet; later extended to Llano.

Austin and Oatmanville Railway. Travis County. Railway incorporated in 1880s by builders of state capitol to haul stone to Austin for the project; railway line built, but stone proved inferior and track was abandoned.

* *Austin Artesian Well.* Travis County. In 1857 one of the earliest artesian well drilling experiments conducted in the state; located on grounds of the state capitol.

* *Austin Dam.* Travis County. Erected between 1890 and 1893 and destroyed by flood in 1900; first major dam and hydroelectric plant constructed in Texas; now site of the Tom Miller Dam.

Austin Dam and Suburban Railway. Travis County. Railway chartered by local residents in 1895 to link Austin with Austin Dam; purchased by International—

Great Northern Railroad in 1923.

Austin "Moonlight" Tower Street Lighting System. Travis County. System established in 1895 using electric lamps mounted atop a series of 165-foot wrought-iron towers to illuminate streets of Austin; listed on National Register of Historic Places.

Austin Waterworks. Travis County. One of oldest waterworks in the state; founded by a private company in 1875 to pump water directly from Colorado River.

Austwell Waterworks. Refugio County. Waterworks built about 1911 at Austwell; reputedly employed mains made from hollowed trunks of cypress trees.

Ballinger Waterworks. Runnels County. Well-preserved late nineteenth-century waterworks including stone pump house and masonry dam.

Balmorhea Irrigation Project. Reeves County. Dating from 1860s, one of the few large spring-fed irrigation systems in Texas and one of the handful of projects in the state aided by U.S. Bureau of Reclamation.

Bankhead Highway. Howard, Martin, Midland, and Mitchell counties. In 1920s a pioneer highway route westward from Colorado City to Midland.

Barber's Hill Oil Field. Chambers County. Oil field opened to production in 1918 but not reaching its peak until lower horizons were reached in 1933.

Barker Dam. Harris County. Rolled earth dam on Buffalo Bayou near Addicks; constructed by U.S. Army Corps of Engineers in 1945 to protect downstream areas from flooding.

Barron Air Corps Training Field. Tarrant County. Military facility opened at Everman in 1917 for training Canadian pilots during World War I.

Bartlett and Western Railway. Williamson County. Short-line railway chartered in 1909 and built from Bartlett to Florence.

Bastrop Cotton Mill. Bastrop County. Cotton textile mill at Bastrop; had eleven hundred spindles in operation by 1867.

Batson Oil Field. Hardin County. Oil field opened in 1903 in wake of major discoveries in geologically similar formations at Spindletop two years earlier.

Battleship Texas. Harris County. Launched in 1914 and served in two world wars; today the last surviving American battleship of the dreadnought class; listed in National Register of Historic Places.

Baze Irrigation System. Tom Green County. Irrigation system built in 1870s by diverting water from Dove Creek near Knickerbocker through use of a brush and earth dam; carried water in a ditch about four miles to fields.

Beaumont and Great Northern Railroad. Houston, Polk, Trinity, and Walker counties. Railway chartered in 1905 and built from Trinity to Livingston and from Trinity to Weldon.

Beaumont and Saratoga Transportation Company Railway. Jefferson County. Logging tram railway; became a common carrier in 1905; built twelve miles from Voth into the Kirby Lumber Company timber area near the town.

Beaumont Harbor Improvements. Jefferson County. Late nineteenth- and early twentieth-century harbor and dock improvements undertaken to make Beaumont a deep-water port.

Beaumont, Sour Lake and Western Railway. Hardin and Jefferson counties. Railway chartered in 1904 as successor to 1903 Beaumont, Sour Lake and Port Arthur Traction Company; built an electric interurban line from Port Arthur to Sour Lake.

Beaumont Waterworks. Jefferson County. Waterworks established to provide water to residents and commercial businesses in Beaumont as early as 1888.

Beaumont Wharf and Terminal Company. Jefferson County. Wharf and terminal company chartered in 1899 to build docks and railway facilities at Port of Beaumont.

Beaumont Wood Preserving Plant. Jefferson County. Tie and timber preserving plant begun at Beaumont in 1897 by International Creosote and Construction Company.

Beefhead Ditch Stone Arch Bridge. Fayette County. Stone arch bridge built at La Grange from cut sandstone blocks set in mortar about 1850; still intact.

Belmont Cotton Gin. Gonzales County. Well-preserved but nonfunctioning steam-power cotton gin; retains most of its historic equipment and machinery at Belmont.

Belo Telephone Line. Galveston County. The first telephone line installed in Texas; placed in 1878 between the offices of the *Galveston News* and the home of its publisher, A. H. Belo, in Galveston.

Belton Dam. Bell County. A rolled-earth dam across the Leon River; built by the U.S. Army Corps of Engineers between 1949 and 1954.

Belton Waterworks. Bell County. Water system built for Belton by the municipal government in 1884 and leased to private company for its operation; took initial supply from Leon River and pumped it into a standpipe.

Benbrook Dam. Tarrant County. Dam on the Clear Fork of the Trinity River built from compacted earth with a concrete spillway by U.S. Army Corps of Engineers between 1947 and 1950.

Bend Suspension Bridge. Lampasas and San Saba counties. Suspension highway bridge across Colorado River near Bend; erected in 1939 and dismantled in 1972.

Ben Ficklin Dam. Tom Green County. Dam built across South Concho River at Ben Ficklin in 1870s; rebuilt with concrete about 1900.

Bergstrom Field. Travis County. Military aircraft flight training facility established in 1942; later became a permanent installation as Bergstrom Air Force Base.

Bexar County Roads. Bexar County. System of county roads noted as very modern in early twentieth-century engineering circles.

Biggers Irrigation Well. Lubbock County. Pioneer irrigation well in Lubbock County drilled by Don C. Biggers about 1912 in effort to introduce irrigated agriculture to area.

Biggs Field Balloon Hangar. El Paso County. Large hangar built in 1920s to house nonrigid military observation balloons.

Big Hill Dome Sulfur Mine. Matagorda County. Major sulfur mine opened in 1919 by Texas Gulf Sulphur Company through use of Frasch liquid extraction process.

Big Inch Pipeline. Cass, Gregg, Harrison, and Marion counties. Laid in 1942, first major oil pipeline from Texas to eastern United States.

Big Lake and Central West Texas Oil Fields. Crane, Glasscock, Howard, Reagan, and Upton counties. Discovered in 1923 at Santa Rita No. 1 Oil Well;* one of major producing oil fields in western Texas up to present.

Big Rocky Creek Iron Truss Bridge. Lavaca County. Iron truss bridge erected across Big Rocky Creek 1.5 miles east of Novohrad in 1904.

Big Sandy Iron Truss Bridge. Smith and Upshur counties. Iron truss bridge erected across Sabine River about 1910 between Big Sandy and Winona.

Big Spring Army Air Force Bombardier School. Howard County. Airfield and training school for military bombardiers; operated just southwest of Big Spring from 1942 to 1945.

Bivins Dam. Randall County. Earthen dam across Prairie Dog Town Fork of Red River, eight miles northwest of Canyon; constructed between 1926 and 1927 to impound water used to recharge a series of wells pumped to supply Amarillo waterworks.

Blackland Army Airfield. McLennan County. Airfield established in 1942 as glider training school until it became an advanced two-engine pilot training facility; now a civilian airport.

Blackwell, Enid and Texas Railway. Wilbarger County. Railway chartered in 1901, and within a year built from Blackwell, Oklahoma, to Vernon.

Bluff Dale Public Well. Erath County. Well dug by employees of Fort Worth and Rio Grande Railroad at Bluff Dale about 1887; since that time has served entire community.

* *Bluff Dale Suspension Bridge.* Erath County. Suspension bridge erected by Erath County over Paluxy River in 1890; in 1934 moved to present location spanning the Paluxy 1.5 miles upstream; listed on National Register of Historic Places.

Blumenthal Stationary Cotton Gin Boiler and Steam Engine. Gillespie County. Late nineteenth-century-style stationary steam boiler and engine, which powered a cotton gin at Blumenthal well into twentieth century.

Boca Chica Floating Bridge. Cameron County. Floating bridge built across Boca Chica Inlet in 1846 by U.S. Army troops under command of Gen. Zachary Taylor during war with Mexico.

Boca Chica Railway Trestle. Cameron County. Wooden railroad trestle constructed by Union army troops between 1864 and 1865 across Boca Chica Inlet to transport military supplies inland to Brownsville after Lower Rio Grande Valley occupied by Federal troops during Civil War.

Bodan Lumber Mill. Angelina County. Sawmill established by Harris-Lipsitz Lumber Company at present-day Pollok in early 1880s.

Boggy Creek Iron Truss Bridge. Lavaca County. Iron truss bridge erected across Boggy Creek in Shiner in 1890s.

Bois d'Arc and Southern Railway. Dallas County. Railway chartered in 1934 and built specifically to ship gravel from deposits along its seven miles of track.

Boling Dome Sulfur Mine. Wharton County. Major sulfur mine opened in 1928 by the Texas Gulf Sulphur Company through the use of the Frasch liquid extraction process.

Bon Ami Sawmill. Jasper County. Sawmill established at Bon Ami by Lee-Irvine Lumber Company in 1901; sold to Bean Lumber Company in 1902 and operated until abandonment in 1929.

Bonham Cotton Mill. Fannin County. Textile mill built at Bonham about the turn of the century; operated until about 1970.

Bonham Foundry. Fannin County. Foundry in Bonham owned by John Dickey; during World War II manufactured bomb noses under contract to War Department.

Bonham Steam Street Railway. Fannin County. Steam-powered street railways constructed at Bonham in the 1890s; operated until about 1915.

Bonham Waterworks. Fannin County. Waterworks begun at Bonham about 1894; deep wells added in 1910.

Bonner Mill and Shoe Factory. Freestone County. Gristmill and shoe factory established by William Bonner at Stewards Mill in second half of nineteenth century.

Bonner's Saltworks. Anderson County. Saltworks begun at present-day Salt City by Tom Bonner before 1860; in 1903 came to be known as Palestine Salt Works.

Boquillas Mining Camp. Brewster County. Mining camp in Boquillas Canyon; grew in the 1890s with establishment of Del Carmen lead and silver mine, which operated until abandonment in 1906.

Brackenridge Park Lenticular Arch Bridge. Bexar County. Perhaps last surviving lenticular arch bridge in Texas; constructed in 1890 by Berlin Iron Bridge Company of East Berlin, Connecticut, and now spanning San Antonio River in Brackenridge Park in San Antonio.

Brady Waterworks. McCulloch County. Water system for Brady started about 1908; secured supply from both wells and surface sources initially pumped through mains by gasoline-fueled pumps.

Brannon's Crossing Suspension Bridge. Parker County. Suspension bridge erected by firm of Mitchell and Pigg for Parker County across Brazos River at Brannon's Crossing in 1905.

Brazos River Harbor Improvements. Brazoria County. Harbor improvements at mouth of Brazos River on Gulf of Mexico; begun in late nineteenth century to provide deep-water port facilities.

Brazos River Lighthouse. Brazoria County. Iron skeleton tower lighthouse erected on north side of mouth of Brazos River in 1896.

* Brazos Santiago Lighthouse. Cameron County. Southernmost lighthouse on Texas Gulf Coast; established in 1852 or 1853 and today marked by screw

piles of a later (1877–78) light station.

Breckenridge Oil Field. Stephens County. Oil field opened in 1918 in wake of discoveries the year before in Ranger Oil Field just to the south.

Brenham Waterworks. Washington County. Waterworks established to provide domestic water to citizens of Brenham as early as 1885.

Bridgeport Dam. Wise County. Rolled-earth dam with concrete spillway constructed across West Fork of Trinity River four miles west of Bridgeport between 1930 and 1931 to provide flood protection and to impound water for Fort Worth waterworks.

Bronte Waterworks. Coke County. Water system built at Bronte in 1922; took supply from a man-made reservoir on a nearby stream

Brooks Field. Bexar County. Today Brooks Air Force Base, established in 1917 as army flight training camp; for decades remained an active aviation training center.

Brownsville and Matamoros Bridge. Cameron County. Railway bridge built across Rio Grande by Brownsville and Matamoros Bridge Company between 1909 and 1911.

Brownsville Waterworks. Cameron County. In 1931 first waterworks in United States to use porous tubes or plates for air-diffusion water purification.

Brownwood Cotton Compress. Brown County. Cotton compress begun at Brownwood in 1880s; much of the nineteenth-century equipment remains.

Brownwood Dam. Brown County. Earthen dam constructed on Pecan Bayou near Brownwood between 1930 and 1933 for municipal, industrial, and limited agricultural use.

Brownwood North and South Railway. Brown County. Railway chartered by local individuals in 1910; by 1912 had built from Brownwood to May.

Brownwood Waterworks. Brown County. Water system for Brownwood built between 1886 and 1887; secured original supply from natural reservoir on Pecan Bayou and pumped it to a standpipe.

Bruce Field. Runnels County. Army Air Corps training field established at Ballinger in 1941 for primary flight training; operated until abandonment in 1944.

Bryan and Central Texas Interurban Railway. Brazos County. Interurban railway that ran from Bryan to Brazos River between 1918 and 1923.

Bryan and College Interurban Railway. Brazos County. Electric interurban railway built seven miles from Bryan to Texas Agricultural and Mechanical

College in 1910; operated until 1923.

Bryan Army Airfield. Brazos County. World War II military training facility used principally as air corps instructors' school.

Bryan Mount Sulfur Mine. Brazoria County. First major sulfur mine opened on Texas Gulf Coast (1912); used Frasch liquid extraction method.

Bryan Waterworks. Brazos County. Water system begun to serve citizens of Bryan about 1890; took water from local wells to a standpipe for distribution to consumers by gravity through mains.

* *Buchanan Dam.* Burnet and Llano counties. Major concrete dam across Colorado River erected between 1931 and 1938 to impound water for irrigation, municipal, recreation, flood control, and hydro-electric-generation purposes.

Buckners Creek Bridge. Fayette County. Modified Pratt pony truss bridge with unusual vertical and end posts erected across Cummins Creek in 1883; moved to present location ten miles north of Flatonia in 1890.

Buffalo Bayou, Brazos and Colorado Railway. Fort Bend and Harris counties. First railway in Texas; chartered in 1850 and built from Harrisburg to Alleyton before Civil War.

* *Buffalo Gap Railway Water System.* Taylor County. Steam locomotive water system built by Santa Fe Railway at Buffalo Gap between 1910 and 1911; consisted of two hand-dug wells, a steam pumping plant, and a large steel standpipe; now leased by town of Buffalo Gap for municipal supply.

Buffington Mining Cabin. Culberson County. Last surviving miners' cabin in the Guadalupe Mountains National Park; built of box-and-strip wooden construction in 1930s by a man who worked in Texas Calumet Copper Mines.

Burkburnett Oil Field. Wichita County. Site of one of the most colorful of all Texas oil booms; field brought into major production in 1918 and reached its peak in 1919.

Burlington–Rock Island Railroad. Freestone, Grimes, Harris, Leon, Madison, and Montgomery counties. Originally part of Trinity and Brazos Valley Railway, a line known from 1905 onward as Burlington–Rock Island, connecting Teague with Houston.

Burnam's Ferry. Fayette County. Ferry across Colorado River near present-day La Grange established by Jesse Burnam about 1824.

Burr's Ferry, Browndell and Chester Railroad. Jas-

per County. Eleven-mile railway built to serve lumber and turpentine camps around Aldridge in 1906.

Burt Oil Refinery. Jefferson County. Pioneer Texas oil refinery established by group of businessmen at Beaumont in 1902 during Spindletop oil boom.

Bushy Creek Iron Truss Bridge. Ellis County. Iron truss bridge erected across Bushy Creek in 1890s, about five miles northwest of Palmer.

Cairo Springs Logging Camp. Jasper County. Logging camp begun by Texas Tram and Lumber Company in 1876; noted as first commercial lumber camp in Jasper County.

Caldwell Waterworks. Burleson County. Municipal waterworks begun at Caldwell in 1905; elevated supply with electric pumps from drilled wells.

Call Field. Wichita County. Army flight training field operated south of Wichita Falls from 1917 to 1919.

Calvert Ice, Water and Electric Plant. Robertson County. Combined ice, water, and electric plant erected in 1880s to serve Calvert.

Calvert Sewerage System. Robertson County. Unusually complete small sewage treatment plant constructed for Calvert between 1912 and 1913.

Cameron County Concrete Highway. Cameron County. Pioneer highway in South Texas paved with concrete in 1920 to connect Harlingen and San Benito.

Cameron Waterworks. Milam County. Waterworks serving Cameron begun about 1895, with water pumped to a standpipe from Little River.

Camilla-Swartwout Ferry. Polk and San Jacinto counties. Ferry across Trinity River on Camilla-Swartwout Road near Swartwout; established as early as mid-1830s; remained ferry crossing until 1930; now general area of Lake Livingston Dam.

Camp Barkeley. Taylor County. Site of one of largest army camps in Texas during World War II; occupied from 1940 to 1945.

Canadian River Highway Bridge at Electric City. Hutchinson County. Two-lane reinforced-concrete highway bridge constructed across Canadian River at Electric City about 1950.

* *Canadian River Wagon Bridge.* Hemphill County. Overhead truss steel wagon bridge spanning Canadian River at north side of Canadian; erected by Hemphill County between 1915 and 1916.

Cane Belt Railroad. Austin, Colorado, Matagorda, and Wharton counties. Railroad chartered in 1893; by 1903 built from Eagle Lake southward to Matagorda; acquired by Santa Fe Railway in 1903.

Canon Ranch Eclipse Windmill. Pecos County. Erected about 1906, today largest remaining operational wooden-wheel, turbine-type windmill in United States; listed on National Register of Historic Places.

Capitol Hotel PBX Board. Harris County. Generally accepted as first private branch exchange telephone switchboard in United States; installed at Capitol Hotel in Houston in 1882.

Carmona Sawmills. Polk County. Site of large sawmills built early in this century by William Cameron and Company and by Saner-Ragley Lumber Company.

Caro Northern Railway. Nacogdoches and Rusk counties. Logging tram railway chartered in 1894 and constructed from Caro to Mount Enterprise.

Carpenters Bluff Railroad Bridge. Grayson County. Railway bridge built across Red River in 1910; later converted to carry highway traffic.

Castolon Portable Steam Engine. Brewster County. Portable steam boiler and engine purchased from Brownell Company, Dayton, Ohio, in 1915, to irrigate fields with Rio Grande water and to power equipment at Castolon cotton gin.

Castroville Waterworks. Medina County. Waterworks for Castroville begun about 1890; secured initial supply of water from a stream from which it was pumped to a storage tank.

Central and Montgomery Railway. Burleson and Grimes counties. Railway chartered in 1877 and built to connect Navasota with Somerville; purchased by Santa Fe Railway in 1887.

Central National Road of the Republic of Texas. Collin, Dallas, Fannin, Hunt, Lamar, Red River, and Rockwall counties. Road authorized by Congress of Texas on February 5, 1844, and surveyed to create a highway from Trinity River near present-day Dallas to Red River opposite mouth of Kiamanchi River in Red River County.

Champion Paper Mill. Harris County. Paper mill established in 1939 at Pasadena on Houston Ship Channel to produce bleached sulfate pulps; in 1940 began manufacturing high-quality paper products.

Chicago, Burlington and Quincy Steam Locomotive No. 4994. Lubbock County. Coal-burning railway locomotive built in 1923 by the Baldwin Locomotive Works for use in main-line freight service; now preserved in Lubbock.

Chicago, Rock Island and Gulf Railway. Dallas and Tarrant counties. Railway chartered in 1892; by 1903 built between Fort Worth and Dallas.

Chicago, Rock Island and Texas Railway. Dallas, Montague, Tarrant, and Wise counties. Railway chartered in 1892; by the next year built from Terral, Oklahoma, to Fort Worth; in next decade extended to Dallas.

Chicago, Texas and Mexican Central Railway. Dallas, Ellis, and Johnson counties. Railway chartered in 1876; by 1882 built from Dallas to Cleburne, after which time it was acquired by Santa Fe Railway.

Childress Army Airfield. Childress County. Army Air Corps bombardier training facility opened near Childress in 1942 and operated until 1945.

Childress Waterworks. Childress County. Water system built to serve the town of Childress in 1927; took supply from reservoir on nearby stream and from local wells.

Choctow, Oklahoma and Texas Railroad. Carson, Deaf Smith, Gray, Oldham, Potter, and Wheeler counties. Railroad chartered in 1901 and built from Oklahoma state line via Amarillo to New Mexico state line entirely across Texas Panhandle by 1910; consolidated with Chicago, Rock Island and Pacific Railroad in 1939.

Cisco and Northeastern Railway. Eastland, Stephens, and Throckmorton counties. Railway chartered in 1918 and built from Cisco to Breckenridge by 1920; purchased by Texas and Pacific Railway in 1926 and extended to Throckmorton.

Clear Creek Iron Truss Bridge. De Witt County. Iron truss bridge erected by De Witt County in 1912 across Clear Creek, about 2.5 miles east of Mustang Mott community.

Clear Fork of the Brazos Iron Truss Bridge. Scurry County. Single-lane through-truss bridge erected across Clear Fork of the Brazos River at Willingham Land and Cattle Company about 1916.

Clear Fork of the Brazos Single Chord Iron Bridge. Scurry County. One-lane single-chord iron bridge built across Clear Fork of the Brazos at Willingham Land and Cattle Company about 1916.

Clear Fork of the Brazos Suspension Bridge. Shackelford County. Suspension bridge erected by Shackelford County in 1896 across Clear Fork of the Brazos River, about seventeen miles north of Albany.

Cleburne Automatic Telephone Exchange. Johnson County. First automatic telephone exchange in Texas; built in 1903 and operated by Cleburne Automatic Telephone Company.

Cleburne Waterworks. Johnson County. Small-town waterworks established in late nineteenth century; numerous turn-of-the-century structures remain.

Clemens Dam. Comal County. Masonry dam across Comal River in New Braunfels; originally built in 1882 to provide water power to pump for New Braunfels waterworks and to operate machinery at a nearby flour mill.

Cliffside Helium Plant. Potter County. Natural gas field containing helium purchased by U.S. government in 1927; began operation as helium-producing facility in 1929.

Clifton Mill. Bosque County. Gristmill established at Clifton shortly after Civil War; later converted to small hydroelectric-generating station.

Clint Ditch. El Paso County. Irrigation ditch securing supply of water from Rio Grande; first dug during Civil War to supply water to fields around Clint; in 1914 nine miles long, ten feet wide, and carrying forty cubic feet of water per second.

Clinton-Oklahoma Western Railway of Texas. Gray, Hemphill, and Wheeler counties. Railway chartered in 1927 by Santa Fe Railway subsidiary and built from Cheyenne, Oklahoma, to Clinton, Texas; in 1929 extended to Pampa.

Close Iron Foundry. Galveston County. Iron foundry established by Hiram Close in Galveston in the 1840s; produced farm equipment and tools until diversion to military goods during Civil War.

Clyde Waterworks. Callahan County. Water system begun for Clyde in 1927; secured supply from local wells.

Coffee Mill Creek Dam. Fannin County. Earth fill dam across Coffee Mill Creek, twelve miles northwest of Honey Grove; constructed by U.S. Forest Service for recreational use in 1938.

Coleman Field. Coleman County. Army Air Corps training field established in August, 1941, for primary flight training and operated until 1944.

Coleman Waterworks. Coleman County. Water system built to serve town of Coleman about 1906; secured supply by pumping through a pipeline from reservoir on nearby river.

Colorado City Ice Plant. Mitchell County. Facility for the mechanical manufacture of ice; established at Colorado City about 1925.

Colorado City Sewage Treatment Plant. Mitchell County. Sewage treatment plant at Colorado City; in 1925 thought to have been first facility in Texas to use mechanical aeration.

Colorado City Waterworks. Mitchell County. Waterworks begun about 1885 to serve Colorado City; secured water from wells and had about seven miles of mains in its early years.

Col-Tex Oil Refinery. Mitchell County. Refinery reconstructed by Anderson-Prichard Corporation in 1924 near Colorado City from an older facility; operated until 1969.

Columbus Waterworks. Colorado County. Waterworks to serve Columbus begun in 1883; took supply directly from Colorado River by pumping to a still-existing brick standpipe and directly into mains.

Comyn Tank Farm. Comanche County. Oil tank farm constructed by the Humble Pipeline Company at Comyn in 1918.

Concho, San Saba and Llano Valley Railway. Coke, Concho, Runnels, Sterling, and Tom Green counties. Railway chartered in 1909 to build from Concho County to Lubbock County, but only constructed from Miles to Paint Rock and from Sterling City to San Angelo.

Congress Avenue Bridge. Travis County. Completed in 1910 across Colorado River at foot of Congress Avenue in Austin; one of most graceful of all reinforced-concrete bridges in Texas.

Copano Bay Causeway. Aransas County. Timber causeway over Copano Bay erected by Texas Highway Department between 1930 and 1931; preserved as fishing pier by Texas Parks and Wildlife Department.

Cordes Cotton Gin. Fayette County. Steam-powered cotton gin with separate stone boilerhouse and enginehouse; constructed at Freyburg in 1880s.

Corpus Christi Harbor Improvements. Nueces County. Varied efforts from mid-nineteenth century to present to make Corpus Christi a deep-water port.

Corpus Christi Seawall. Nueces County. Reinforced-concrete seawall erected by Corpus Christi between 1939 and 1940 to protect against damage from tropical storms.

Corsicana Oil Field Discovery Well. Navarro County. Discovery well for first large oil field west of Mississippi (1894); listed on National Register of Historic Places.

Corsicana Waterworks. Navarro County. Waterworks for Corsicana; established in 1884; water well drilled for this system in 1894 became discovery well for Corsicana Oil Field.*

Cotulla Railway Water System. La Salle County. Steam locomotive water supply system constructed by International and Great Northern Railway about

1891; secured supply from a drilled well.

Courtney Bridge. Grimes and Washington counties. Iron truss bridge across Brazos River at Courtney erected by King Iron Bridge Company in 1877; fell twice during construction because of flood damage.

Crain Mill. Comal County. Gristmill built by J. B. Crain about 1855 on Guadalupe River, about seventeen miles above New Braunfels.

Crazy Well. Palo Pinto County. Drilled in 1885, one of most famous of many mineral water wells in Mineral Wells because of its water's reputed ability to cure hysterical manias and other maladies.

Crockett Telephone Exchange. Houston County. Telephone exchange installed at Crockett by John Crook about 1900; later acquired by Continental Telephone Company of Texas.

Crockett Waterworks. Houston County. Municipal water system established about 1916 to serve Crockett; secured supply from local wells from which water was carried to the town in a concrete pipeline.

Crook Dam. Lamar County. Earthen dam across Pine Creek constructed in 1923 to impound water for Paris waterworks.

Crosbyton Cotton Gin. Crosby County. Wooden building housing two-stand Murray cotton gin equipment; erected at Crosbyton in 1902.

Crosbyton Sewage Treatment Plant. Crosby County. Sewage treatment plant constructed for Crosbyton about 1928.

Crosbyton–South Plains and Santa Fe Railroad. Crosby and Lubbock counties. Railroad built in 1910 from Lubbock to Crosbyton, where Corley and Bassett Live Stock Company was promoting sale of a large tract of land to farmers.

Crowell Waterworks. Foard County. Municipal waterworks initially established for Crowell about 1931; secured supply from local wells and later from surface sources.

Cuero Field. De Witt County. Military airfield established as Army Air Corps flight training facility near Cuero in 1941 and inactivated in 1944.

* *Cuero Hydroelectric Plant.* De Witt County. One of pioneer hydroelectric plants in Texas; begun in 1896 and operated until 1965.

Cuero Waterworks. De Witt County. Waterworks to serve Cuero; placed in operation about 1890; took original supply directly from Guadalupe River and pumped to a standpipe.

* *Cullinan Oil Refinery.* Navarro County. Opened in 1898 as first major oil refinery in southwestern

United States.

Cummings Mill. Austin County. Gristmill erected on Mill Creek by James, John, and William Cummings in 1826; one of first Anglo-American-built water-powered mills in Texas.

Cummins Creek Iron Truss Bridge. Fayette County. Single-span Pratt through-truss bridge erected by King Iron Bridge and Manufacturing Company across Cummins Creek, about two miles northwest of Round Top in 1890; listed in National Register of Historic Places.

Cunningham Paper Mill. Harris County. Pioneer Texas paper mill; about 1890 began producing paper with bagasse, a sugarcane waste product.

Curtis Field. McCulloch County. Airfield at Brady begun as Army Air Corps flight training field in 1940; deactivated in 1945.

Curtis Windmill Irrigation System. Midland County. Windmill irrigation system six miles north of Midland; built at turn of the century by J. C. Curtis; provided eighty-six hundred gallons of water for vineyard irrigation per six hours of pumping.

* *Daisy Bradford No. 3 Oil Well.* Rusk County. Discovery well for East Texas Oil Field (1930); largest oil field in contiguous United States.

Dalhart Army Airfield. Dallam County. Airfield activated in 1942 as U.S. Army glider training facility; later used additionally for bomber and fighter training.

Dallas and Greenville Railway. Dallas, Hunt, and Rockwall counties. Railway chartered in 1886 as Missouri, Kansas and Texas Railroad subsidiary and built from Dallas to Greenville.

Dallas and Waco Railway. Dallas, Ellis, and Hill counties. Subsidiary of Missouri, Kansas and Texas Railroad; chartered in 1886, and by 1890 completed from Dallas to Hillsboro.

Dallas and Wichita Railway. Dallas and Denton counties. Railway chartered by Dallas citizens in 1871 to reach from Dallas to Wichita County, but by 1878 built only twenty miles; purchased by Texas and Pacific Railway in 1880 and extended to Denton.

Dallas, Cleburne and Southwestern Railway. Johnson County. Subsidiary of Missouri, Kansas and Texas Railroad; chartered in 1902 and built ten miles from Egan to Cleburne.

Dallas Concrete Pipe Factory. Dallas County. Facility for manufacture of concrete pipe established by Lock-Joint Pipe Company at Dallas during World War I.

Dallas–Oak Cliff Viaduct. Dallas County. Completed in 1912 across Trinity River and its floodplain; in its day one of longest reinforced-concrete arch bridges in America.

Dallas, Palestine and Southeast Railroad. Dallas and Kaufman counties. Railroad chartered in 1878 and by 1883 built from Dallas to Gossett; purchased by Southern Pacific Railroad in 1895.

Dallas Terminal Railway. Dallas County. Terminal railway company chartered in 1884 to serve Dallas industrial districts.

Dallas Union Terminal. Dallas County. Built between 1914 and 1916 as one of the handful of truly magnificent railway stations in Texas.

Dallas Union Terminal Electrical Power Plant. Dallas County. Early twentieth-century electricity-generating station constructed to supply power for Dallas Union Terminal.*

Dallas Waterworks. Dallas County. Waterworks established to serve residents and businesses of Dallas as early as 1876.

Dayton–Goose Creek Railroad. Chambers, Harris, and Liberty counties. Railroad chartered in 1917 and built in 1918 to connect Goose Creek Oil Field with Humble Oil and Refinery Company facilities.

Decatur Waterworks. Wise County. Water system built in 1883 to serve Decatur residents; took water from well pumped by a Cook deep-well pump.

Decross Point Lighthouses. Matagorda County. Two lighthouses erected in 1872 and destroyed in 1875 by a hurricane, with loss of four lives.

DeKalb and Red River Railroad. Bowie County. Timber tram railroad connecting DeKalb, Lennox, and Marysville; in 1891 became a common carrier.

DeLeon Waterworks. Comanche County. Water system established in 1918 to serve DeLeon; took supply from local wells.

Del Rio Waterworks. Val Verde County. Waterworks founded at Del Rio in 1883; took initial supply from springs.

Denison and Pacific Railway. Cooke and Grayson counties. Railway chartered in 1878 and by 1880 built from Denison to Gainesville.

Denison and Pacific Suburban Railway. Grayson County. Railway chartered in 1895 by interests representing Texas and Pacific Railway and by 1896 built seven miles to connect Denison with Texas and Pacific tracks in Sherman.

Denison and Southeastern Railway. Fannin, Grayson, and Hunt counties. Railway chartered in 1877 by citizens of Denison and Greenville and by 1879 constructed between the two towns.

Denison and Washita Valley Railway. Grayson County. Railway line chartered in 1886 and built from Ray to Warner Junction in Texas and from Atoka to Coalgate in Oklahoma.

Denison, Bonham and New Orleans Railroad. Fannin, Grayson, and Hunt counties. Railroad chartered in 1887 and by 1901 built from Denison to Wolfe City.

Denison Dam. Grayson County. Rolled-earth dam on Red River that created Lake Texoma; begun in 1939 and completed in 1943.

Denison Waterworks. Grayson County. Waterworks established in 1886 by a private company to provide domestic water to residents of Denison.

Denning Steel Truss Bridge. San Augustine County. Steel truss bridge built south of Denning about 1922.

Denton Field. Denton County. World War II military installation for training of glider pilots; closed at end of conflict.

Deport Steel Truss Bridge. Lamar County. Single-lane, turn-of-the-century-style Warren truss steel bridge spanning Deport Creek in Deport.

Desdemona Oil Field. Eastland County. Oil field discovered at Desdemona in 1918 after spectacular developments nearby in Ranger Oil Field.

Devils Lake Dam and Hydroelectric Plant. Val Verde County. Limestone masonry gravity dam with hydroelectric plant on Devils River, sixteen miles northwest of Del Rio; constructed by Central Power and Light Company between 1927 and 1928 for generation of electricity; covered by waters of Amistad Reservoir.

Devine Waterworks. Medina County. Municipal waterworks begun for Devine about 1928; used water pumped from wells into an elevated tank and directly into mains.

Diamond F Ranch Water Well. Carson County. Bored in 1887, one of earliest drilled wells in Carson County.

Diboll Domestic Water Distillation Plant. Angelina County. One of three systems in East Texas where in the 1930s the domestic water supply for residents of a town was distilled from water taken from log ponds.

Dickson Gun Plant. Harris County. Factory operated from 1942 to 1945 by Hughes Tool Company; produced gun tubes of various calibers for war effort.

Dixie Ranch Windmill Water System. Lubbock

County. Early windmill system for livestock watering; put into service on Dixie Ranch by Maj. W. V. Johnson about 1884.

Don Patricio Causeway. Nueces County. First causeway connecting Padre Island with Texas mainland; privately owned timber bridge of unusual design built in 1927.

Droemer Brick Yard. Lee County. Brick-manufacturing facility established about 1870; operated near Giddings until 1940; listed in National Register of Historic Places.

Dryenforth Rainmaking Experiments. Andrews County. Rainmaking experiments conducted for U.S. Department of Agriculture by R. G. Dryenforth on an Andrews County ranch in 1890s.

Dublin Mill and Elevator Complex. Erath County. Large wooden flour mill built at Dublin around turn of the century; now used only for feed-storage purposes.

Duncan Field. Bexar County. Airfield built as repair depot for aircraft after World War I; in 1942 joined to Kelly Field.

Durrum's Ferry. Marion County. Ferry established by Berry Durrum about 1836 across Big Cypress Bayou at present-day Jefferson.

Eagle Coal Mine. Hudspeth County. Coal mine developed in 1880s with a 230-foot shaft; produced reputedly good-quality coking coals.

Eagle Lake Irrigation System. Colorado County. System begun in 1899 to provide water for rice irrigation on lower Colorado River.

Eagle Lake Waterworks. Colorado County. Municipal waterworks established for town of Eagle Lake between 1927 and 1930; some of original mains remain in service.

Eagle Mountain Dam. Tarrant County. Earthen dam across West Fork of Trinity River; erected between 1930 and 1932 to impound water for municipal supply in Fort Worth, to provide recreational facilities, and to supply limited amount of irrigation water.

Eagle Pass Army Airfield. Maverick County. Airfield constructed in 1942 to serve as single-engine advanced training field; converted into basic air corps flying school in 1944; closed in 1945.

Eagle Pass Hydroelectric Plant. Maverick County. Hydroelectric plant constructed ten miles upstream on Rio Grande from Eagle Pass by Central Power and Light Company between 1931 and 1932; used water from main irrigation canal of Maverick County Water Control and Improvement District No. 1 to turn its turbines.

Eagle Pass Waterworks. Maverick County. Waterworks begun to serve citizens of Eagle Pass about 1885; secured initial supply from Rio Grande.

Eagle Spring Stage Stand. Hudspeth County. Stagecoach station on Butterfield Overland Mail route built in 1850s between Fort Davis and Fort Quitman; some adobe and stone remains exist.

Earhart Irrigation Well. Lubbock County. One of the pioneer irrigation wells in Lubbock County; drilled in 1911.

Eastern Texas Railroad. Jefferson County. Railroad chartered first in 1852 under a different name and built between 1859 and 1861 from Sabine Pass to Beaumont.

East Fork of Double Bayou Iron Bridge. Chambers County. Late nineteenth-century iron bridge spanning East Fork of Double Bayou at J. C. Jackson store.

Eastland, Wichita Falls and Gulf Railroad. Eastland County. Railroad built between 1918 and 1919 by Richard T. Ringling, better known as a circus owner, from Mangum to Breckwalker.

East Line and Red River Railroad. Camp, Cass, Collin, Franklin, Hunt, Marion, Morris, and Titus counties. Railroad chartered in 1871 by citizens of Jefferson and built from there to McKinney by 1881.

East Navidad River Bridge. Iron bridge consisting of eighty-foot Pratt through-truss span with girder approaches; erected by King Iron Bridge Company near Dubina in 1885.

East Texas and Gulf Railway. Tyler County. Four-mile timber tram railway from Hyatt to Hicksbaugh; became a common carrier in 1917.

East Texas Oil Field. Cherokee, Gregg, Rusk, Smith, and Upshur counties. Discovered in 1930; largest oil field opened in America before World War II.

Ector County Oil Field. Ector County. Oil field discovered in 1926 as result of successes nearby in Big Lake Field; grew to become second in importance only to East Texas Oil Field in overall Texas petroleum production.

Eddleman Dam. Young County. Earth fill dam built across Flint Creek two miles northwest of Graham between 1928 and 1929 to impound water for the Graham waterworks; enlarged and raised between 1957 and 1958.

Electra Oil Field. Wichita County. Oil field first discovered in 1904, but not reaching prominence until oil flowing naturally to surface was struck by drilling in 1911; peak of production in 1914.

Ellison Creek Dam. Morris County. Four-thousand-foot-long rolled-earth dam across Cypress Creek; constructed between 1942 and 1943 by Defense Plant Corporation for Lone Star Steel iron furnace at Lone Star.

*Elissa. Galveston County. Launched in 1877 in Scotland and today preserved in Galveston; oldest seaworthy square-rigged iron sailing ship in the world; listed on National Register of Historic Places.

El Paso and Northeastern Railroad. El Paso County. Railroad chartered in 1896; by 1899 had purchased or built track from El Paso to New Mexico state line.

El Paso and Southwestern Railroad. El Paso County. Railroad chartered in 1902 to link El Paso and El Paso Smelter* with the major open-pit copper mines of New Mexico and Arizona.

* El Paso and Southwestern Railroad Rio Grande Bridge. El Paso County. Large five-span, parallel chord, steel deck girder bridge erected across Rio Grande by El Paso and Southwestern Railroad in 1902.

El Paso Bicycle Racetrack. El Paso County. Bicycle racing track built at El Paso in August–September, 1894, by El Paso Cycle Track Association.

El Paso Bridge. El Paso County. Spanish colonial bridge once spanning Rio Grande; five hundred feet long, seventeen feet wide and built of pine logs resting on timber caissons.

El Paso Highway Bridge. El Paso County. Lightweight highway bridge built across Rio Grande about 1913; innovative methods used to sink pilings into quicksand.

* El Paso Smelter. El Paso County. Established in 1887, today one of best-known general smelting works in Texas.

El Paso Southern Railway. El Paso County. Railway incorporated in 1897 to build from international bridge to Mount Franklin; actually built as terminal railway connecting Mexican railways with three American lines in El Paso.

El Paso Terminal Railroad. El Paso County. Railroad chartered in 1901 and built between 1902 and 1903 to serve industrial districts in El Paso.

El Paso Valley Irrigation. El Paso County. Systems of ditch irrigation in El Paso valley that date as early as late seventeenth century.

* El Paso Waterworks. El Paso County. Waterworks established for city of El Paso by a private company in

1882; purchased by city in 1910.

Ennis Railway Shops and Locomotive Roundhouse. Ellis County. Railway repair shops constructed by Southern Pacific Railroad at Ennis in 1891.

Ennis Sewage System. Ellis County. Sewage treatment plant built about 1916 to serve Ennis.

Epperson's Ferry. Bowie County. Ferry constructed across Sulphur River in southern Bowie County in 1837; later supplanted by a wooden bridge and then in 1924 by a modern span.

Eubank Cotton Card Factory. Williamson County. Cotton-card manufacturing plant built by Joseph Eubank, Jr., in 1862 to produce cotton cards needed for cotton fabric production during Civil War.

Eureka Mill. Williamson County. Gristmill on San Gabriel River constructed about 1857 near present-day Jonah by Joseph T. Mileham and James P. Warnock.

Ezzell Iron Truss Bridge. Lavaca County. Iron truss bridge erected over Lavaca River two miles northeast of Ezzell by King Iron Bridge Company in 1889.

Falfurrias Gypsum Mine. Brooks County. Gypsum mine begun near Falfurrias by Wilson and Wilson Company about 1931.

Ferris Brick Yard. Ellis County. Brickyard established at Ferris about 1907; produced red brick used in virtually every part of Texas.

Fisher's Mill. Fannin County. One of first steam-powered mills in northeast Texas; built in 1855 on Bois d'Arc Creek south of Bonham by Thomas Williams; also known as Bonham Roller Mill.

Flat Iron Building. Tarrant County. Seven-story steel-frame office building with triangular shape erected in Fort Worth in 1906; at the time one of tallest buildings in North Texas.

Foard County Copper Mines. Foard County. Copper mining conducted by a private company in Foard County in years after Civil War.

Fort Belknap Military Water System. Young County. Water system begun at Fort Belknap at its founding in 1851; secured supply, hauled in water wagons, from Clear Fork of Brazos and later from a large hand-dug well that still exists.

Fort Bliss Military Water System. El Paso County. Waterworks-type system built to serve Fort Bliss about 1890; took original supply from five Southern Pacific Railroad wells.

* Fort Davis Military Water System. Jeff Davis County. U.S. Army water system that from 1854 to 1891 used several different means to provide water for men and livestock at a frontier military post.

Fort Griffin Iron Truss Bridge. Shackelford County. Iron truss bridge erected across Clear Fork of Brazos at Fort Griffin community in 1885; listed on National Register of Historic Places.

Fort Hancock Railway Water System. Hudspeth County. Steam locomotive water supply system securing supply from one well that at turn of the century provided an average of eighty thousand gallons daily.

Fort Phantom Hill Dam. Jones County. Rolled-earth dam across Elm Creek five miles south of Nugent constructed between 1937 and 1938 to impound water for Abilene waterworks.

Fort Stockton Field. Pecos County. Airfield established in 1942 by Defense Plant Corporation and operated until 1944 as civilian school for teaching primary flying.

Fort Worth and Denver City Railway. Clay, Montague, Tarrant, Wichita, and Wise counties. Railway chartered in 1873 to build from Fort Worth to Denver, Colorado; actually built from Fort Worth to Wichita Falls, where it met a line being built southeastward from Colorado; now part of Burlington Northern system.

Fort Worth and Denver City Railway Bowie Passenger Station. Montague County. Turn-of-the-century railroad passenger depot built as a late Victorian-style frame structure surrounded by cantilevered porch and bearing three-story tower on north end.

Fort Worth and Denver Northern Railway. Childress, Collingsworth, Donley, and Gray counties. Branch line of Fort Worth and Denver built from Childress to Pampa between 1929 and 1932.

Fort Worth and Denver South Plains Railway. Briscoe, Castro, Hale, Hall, Floyd, and Lubbock counties. Branch line of Fort Worth and Denver built to serve irrigated agricultural area of Texas South Plains, including on route the Quitaque Railway Tunnel.*

Fort Worth and Denver Terminal Railway. Tarrant County. Railway chartered in 1890 to provide belt line and terminal facilities for Fort Worth and Denver City Railway in Fort Worth.

Fort Worth and New Orleans Railway. Ellis and Tarrant counties. Railway chartered in 1885 and the next year built from Fort Worth to Waxahachie to connect Fort Worth with Houston and Texas Central Railroad.

Fort Worth and Rio Grande Railway. Brown, Comanche, Erath, Hood, McCulloch, Menard, and Tarrant counties. Railway chartered in the 1880s to build from Fort Worth to Brownwood, which point it

reached in 1890; extended to Menard in 1911; purchased by Santa Fe Railway in 1937.

Fort Worth–Cleburne Interurban Railway. Johnson and Tarrant counties. Branch of Northern Texas Traction Company lines connecting Fort Worth and Cleburne ca. 1912–31.

Fort Worth Quartermaster Depot. Tarrant County. Depot activated in 1942 as army troop supply facility during World War II.

Fort Worth Salt Company Saltworks. Mitchell County. Saltworks near Colorado City in the 1880s; secured supply from underground brine pumped to surface by windmills and then evaporated to produce salt.

* *Fort Worth Stockyards.* Tarrant County. Operating for nine decades, largest and most important livestock market in American Southwest for many years.

Fort Worth Stockyards Belt Railway. Tarrant County. Railway chartered in 1895; built as line serving the packing, grain, and produce plants in North Fort Worth, particularly Fort Worth Stockyards.*

Fort Worth Waterworks. Tarrant County. Waterworks serving the city of Fort Worth; established by private company in 1882.

Foster Army Airfield. Victoria County. Army Air Corps facility for advanced single-engine training; established at Victoria in 1941 and operated until 1945.

Four-Mile Irrigation System. Kimble County. Irrigation system built near Junction about 1902; consisted of timber diversion dam and ditches.

* *Franklin Canal.* El Paso County. Late nineteenth-century Anglo-American irrigation system renovated by U.S. Reclamation Service between 1912 and 1916; continues to supply irrigation water to El Paso valley.

Frazier Pottery. Marion County. Pottery works begun near Jefferson by Milligan Frazier and his son Sam in 1865.

Fredericksburg and Northern Railway. Gillespie and Kerr counties. Railway built in 1912 from Kerrville to Fredericksburg.

Fredericksburg and Northern Railway Tunnel. Gillespie County. Tunnel excavated along route of Fredericksburg and Northern Railway about 1912; abandoned in 1944.

Friend Lime Plant. Coryell County. Lime kilns constructed in 1880s by Ben Friend around which Lime City grew and prospered for a few years before declining.

Frio Draw Irrigation Well. Deaf Smith County. First successful irrigation well on Texas High Plains;

drilled by D. L. McDonald near Hereford in 1910.

Fuchs Mill. Blanco County. Gristmill established on Cypress Creek in Blanco County in 1867.

Fulton Refrigerated Packing house. Aransas County. Commercial meat packinghouse built at Fulton in 1871; used Carre and Vander Weyde systems of ice manufacture; thought to have been first use of mechanical refrigeration in meatpacking business in Texas.

Gaines Ferry. Sabine County. Ferry across Sabine River at Old San Antonio Road; crossing established in 1830s and operated until river was bridged many years later.

Gainesville, Henrietta and Western Railway. Clay, Cooke, and Montague counties. Railway chartered in 1886 and the next year built from Gainesville to Henrietta.

Gainesville Waterworks. Cooke County. Water system to serve citizens of Gainesville; built by Gainesville Water Company between 1883 and 1884; secured water from Elm Fork of Trinity River and pumped it into a storage reservoir.

Galveston and Brazos Navigation Company Canal. Brazoria County. Canal excavated between 1850 and 1855 to connect West Galveston Bay with area at mouth of Brazos River.

Galveston and Western Railroad. Galveston County. Narrow-gauge railway line built for thirteen miles along Galveston Island in 1884; abandoned by owners in 1922, except for four miles of industrial track sold to Santa Fe Railway.

Galveston Bay Railway Bridges. Galveston County. Series of wooden pile railway trestles constructed between 1860 and 1909 to connect Galveston Island with Texas mainland.

Galveston, Brazos and Colorado Railroad. Galveston County. Narrow-gauge railway constructed on Galveston Island in 1876; operated until 1880.

* *Galveston Causeway.* Galveston County. Erected between 1909 and 1912; first bridge connecting Galveston Island with Texas mainland to withstand the forces of tropical storms; listed on National Register of Historic Places.

* *Galveston Grade Raising.* Galveston County. Major effort from 1903 to 1911 to raise elevation (by means of hydraulic fill) of City of Galveston to protect it from flooding by tropical storms.

Galveston, Harrisburg and San Antonio Railway. Harris County westward to Val Verde County. Successor in 1870 to Buffalo Bayou, Brazos and Colo-

rado Railroad; line built from Alleyton westward to beyond Pecos River by 1883; later enlarged through consolidation with other lines; in 1905 became part of Southern Pacific system.

* *Galveston Highway Bridge.* Galveston County. Built in 1893 to link Galveston Island with Texas mainland; acclaimed in its day as longest highway bridge in world.

Galveston, Houston and Henderson Railroad. Galveston and Harris counties. Railway chartered in 1853 and built between Galveston and Houston; operated under original charter name longer than any other railroad in Texas.

Galveston, Houston and Northern Railway. Galveston and Harris counties. Railway chartered in 1899 and built between Galveston and Houston, with branches serving nearby bayshore areas.

Galveston-Houston Interurban. Galveston and Harris counties. Electric interurban railway that operated between Galveston and Houston from 1911 to 1936; noted in 1926 as fastest interurban in United States.

Galveston-Houston Long-Distance Telephone Line. Galveston and Harris counties. First long-distance telephone line in Texas; built by Southwestern Telegraph and Telephone Company between Galveston and Houston in 1883.

* *Galveston Jetties.* Galveston County. Engineering efforts from the mid-nineteenth century to present to ensure accessibility of Galveston Harbor to deepwater vessels.

* *Galveston Military Fortifications.* Galveston County. Military fortifications dating from early nineteenth century to mid-twentieth century built to protect Galveston Harbor.

Galveston, Sabine and St. Louis Railway. Polk County. Railway chartered in 1882 to build from Galveston to Saint Louis, but only eleven miles constructed, from Camden to Martin's Creek.

* *Galveston Seawall.* Galveston County. Reinforced-concrete structure begun in 1902 and expanded in segments into 1950s to protect Galveston from hurricane storm tides and waves; listed on National Register of Historic Places.

Galveston Street Railways. Galveston County. Mule-drawn and later electrically powered street railways serving city of Galveston from mid-nineteenth to mid-twentieth centuries.

Galveston Telephone Exchange. Galveston County. Built in 1879 by Western Union Telegraph Company;

first telephone exchange in Texas.

Galveston Terminal Railway. Galveston County. Railway chartered in 1905 to provide terminal facilities for Chicago, Rock Island and Pacific and Colorado and Southern railways serving Galveston.

* *Galveston Waterworks.* Galveston County. Well-preserved waterworks system dating from late nineteenth century; operates essentially as it did when renovated in 1895.

Galveston Wood Preserving Plant. Galveston County. Wood preserving plant built by Ricker, Lee and Company at Galveston in 1896 to manufacture treated wooden paving blocks.

Garner Army Airfield. Uvalde County. Airfield for primary flight training established at Uvalde in 1942 for Army Air Corps; facility abandoned in 1946.

Garrett Bridge. San Augustine County. Wooden bridge erected during nineteenth century across Attoyac Bayou; pilings remain about five hundred feet downstream from current State Highway 21 crossing.

Garrison Coal Mines. Nacogdoches County. Lignite mines operated by E. G. Douglas at Garrison from about 1890 to about 1915.

Garza Dam. Denton County. Earthen dam across Elm Fork of Trinity River; constructed between 1924 and 1927 to impound water for Dallas waterworks; now covered by waters of much larger Garza–Little Elm Reservoir.

Gasoline Cotton Gin. Briscoe County. Gasoline-fueled cotton gin established about 1915 at present-day community of Gasoline.

Gentry's Mill. Hamilton County. Gristmill on Warren Creek built by Frederick Gentry shortly after Civil War; ruins survived to mid-twentieth century.

Georgetown and Granger Railroad. Williamson County. Railroad chartered in 1890, and by 1904 built from Georgetown to Granger.

Georgetown Brick Yard. Williamson County. Brick manufacturing operation that produced brick on south bank of San Gabriel River near Georgetown in late nineteenth century.

Georgetown Railroad. Williamson County. Railroad chartered in 1878 and built from Georgetown to connect with International and Great Northern at Round Rock.

Georgetown Waterworks. Williamson County. Waterworks built for Georgetown in 1884; took supply from San Gabriel River, from which water pumped to standpipe and directly into mains.

Glasscock Windmill Irrigation System. Midland County. Turn-of-the-century irrigation system built near Midland; used windmill to pump water from twenty-foot-deep hand-dug well to irrigate twenty acres.

Glenmore Dam. Tom Green County. Concrete dam constructed about 1912 across South Concho River near San Angelo to replace earlier brush and earth dam diverting water to Glenmore farm.

Goldthwaite Railway Water System. Mills County. Steam locomotive boiler water supply system built by Santa Fe Railway at Goldthwaite about 1885; secured supply from large hand-dug well.

Goliad Water and Light Company. Goliad County. Waterworks constructed at Goliad by J. A. Antrim about 1895; electric-generation station added about 1912.

Gonzales Branch Railroad. Gonzales County. Railway chartered in 1881; built twelve miles between Gonzales and Harwood to connect with Southern Pacific lines.

Gonzales Highway Bridge. Gonzales County. Collapse of new steel truss bridge over Guadalupe River at Gonzales occurred August 1, 1902, caused by structural failure.

* *Gonzales Hydroelectric Plant.* Gonzales County. One of the pioneer hydroelectric facilities in Texas; established in 1891 and operated until 1965, when abandoned; returned to service in 1983.

Gonzales Waterworks. Gonzales County. Waterworks serving town of Gonzales; built by private company in 1884 and later expanded.

Gooch and Owen Gristmill. Williamson County. Gristmill built in 1853 by Benjamin Gooch and John W. Owen on North Fork of San Gabriel River, northwest of Georgetown.

Goodfellow Field. Tom Green County. Airfield for advanced pilot training established in 1940; became Goodfellow Air Force Base.

Goose Creek Oil Field. Harris County. Oil field opened at Goose Creek in 1908; became boom field with discovery of eight-thousand-barrel producing well in August, 1916.

Gorman Waterworks. Eastland County. Waterworks begun for Gorman about 1919; initially secured supply from local wells.

Graham Waterworks. Young County. Municipal water system serving Graham begun about 1908; took supply from man-made reservoir on nearby stream.

Grand Saline Saltworks. Van Zandt County. Saltworks operating in Grand Saline area since the industry initiated by Cherokee Indians in 1834.

Granger, Georgetown, Austin and San Antonio Railway. Williamson County. Railway chartered in 1902 in effort to seek entrance to Austin and San Antonio, but built only fifteen miles between Georgetown and Granger.

Granite Mountain and Marble Falls City Railroad. Burnet County. Extension of Austin and Northwestern Railroad built 16.5 miles from Burnet to Marble Falls in 1889.

* Granite Mountain Quarry. Burnet County. Huge natural dome of pink granite; site of major quarry activity since it provided stone for the construction of state capitol in 1880s.

Grayburg Sawmill. Hardin County. Sawmill established in 1905 at present-day Grayburg by Thompson-Ford Lumber Company; operated until dismantled in 1928 because of depletion of timber resources.

Greenville and Northwestern Railway. Collin County. Railroad chartered in 1912 and built twelve miles from Anna to Blue Ridge; abandoned in 1920.

Greenville Tie and Timber Preserving Plant. Hunt County. Tie and timber preserving plant erected in 1901 by Missouri, Kansas and Texas Railway at Greenville.

Greenville Waterworks. Hunt County. Waterworks serving Greenville; begun about 1889; secured initial supply from Cowleach Fork of Sabine River.

Groveton, Lufkin and Northern Railway. Trinity County. Railway chartered in 1908; originally operated as tram road for Trinity County Lumber Company, twenty-one miles from Groveton to Vair.

Guadalupe River Iron Truss Bridge. Comal County. Iron truss bridge erected across Guadalupe River at New Braunfels in 1887.

Guffey Oil Refinery. Jefferson County. One of pioneer oil refineries in Texas; established at Port Arthur by Guffey Oil Company in 1901.

Gulf and Interstate Railway. Chambers, Galveston, and Jefferson counties. Railway line constructed in the 1890s to connect Port Bolivar with Beaumont; acquired by Santa Fe Railway in 1908.

Gulf and Northern Railroad. Newton County. Railroad chartered in 1917 and built fifteen miles, from Newton to Wiergate, as logging line; operated until 1944.

Gulf, Beaumont and Great Northern Railway. Jasper, San Augustine, and Shelby counties. Railway chartered in 1898 and by 1903 built from Roganville to Center.

Gulf, Beaumont and Kansas City Railway. Jasper, Jefferson, and Orange counties. Railway chartered by John Henry Kirby in 1883 and built from Beaumont northward to Roganville for shipment of timber.

Gulf, Colorado and Santa Fe Railway. Galveston County northwestward to Cooke County. Railway line constructed in the 1870s and 1880s to connect Galveston with Atchison, Topeka and Santa Fe Railway in Indian Territory.

Gulf, Colorado and Santa Fe Railway Fort Worth Passenger Station. Tarrant County. Two-story rectangular brick and limestone turn-of-the-century railway passenger depot in its day considered monument to transportation progress.

Gulf Sulfur Mine. Matagorda County. Sulfur mine operated by Gulf Sulphur Company, which in 1919 was reputedly second largest in United States.

Gulf, Texas and Western Railroad. Archer, Baylor, Jack, Palo Pinto, and Young counties. Railroad chartered in 1908 and by 1913 constructed from Salesville to Seymour; sold to Frisco system in 1930; abandoned in 1940.

Gum Spring Sawmill. Comal County. Sawmill built about 1850 to cut cypress lumber from trees growing on Guadalupe River.

Halbert Dam. Navarro County. Earthen dam across Elm Creek; constructed between 1920 and 1921 to impound water for Corsicana waterworks.

Halpin's Wool-Scouring Mill. Mitchell County. Wool-scouring mill constructed at Colorado City about 1893; reputedly first such facility in Southwest.

Hamilton Field. Hamilton County. Army Air Corps training field moved to Texas from Iowa in 1942; provided preliminary glider training until abandonment in 1943.

Hamlin and Northwestern Railway. Jones and Stonewall counties. Railway chartered in 1929 and built ten miles from Flattop to Hamlin, where it joined Santa Fe and Missouri-Kansas-Texas lines.

* Hangar Nine. Bexar County. Built in 1918 as temporary building; today oldest surviving military aircraft storage and repair structure in United States; listed on National Register of Historic Places.

Hankamer-Stowell Canal. Chambers County. Early twentieth-century canal constructed to provide water for rice irrigation in Hankamer vicinity.

Harlingen Army Airfield. Cameron County. Army Air Corps facility that included Harlingen Army Gunnery School from 1941 until closing in 1946;

now site of Harlingen municipal airport and Confederate Air Force Museum.

Harris County Dome Stadium. Harris County. Built between 1962 and 1965, world's first large domed sports stadium.

Harris Sawmill. Harris County. Earliest known steam sawmill in Texas; erected by John R. Harris and others between 1829 and 1830 at Harrisburg.

Hastings Oil Field. Brazoria County. Oil field opened in 1934; reached peak production in 1944.

Hazel Mine. Culberson County. Began producing copper and silver about 1885; continued sporadic mineral production until 1940s.

Hearne and Brazos Railway. Burleson, Lee, and Robertson counties. Railway chartered by local promoters in 1891 and built from Hearne southward; purchased by Southern Pacific Railroad in 1913 and extended to Giddings.

Henderson and Overton Branch Railroad. Rusk County. Railroad chartered in 1874 and built sixteen miles from Henderson to Overton; acquired in 1880 by International and Great Northern Railroad.

Henrietta Waterworks. Clay County. Early twentieth-century system providing water to consumers at Henrietta; pumped from both Little Wichita River and surface wells.

Hensley Field. Dallas County. Airfield established by City of Dallas in 1929 and leased to Army Air Corps as training facility; now Dallas Naval Air Station.

Herald Bank Lightship. Galveston County. Lightship stationed in Gulf of Mexico twenty-eight miles southeast of entrance to Galveston Bay in 1905.

H-5 Dam and Hydroelectric Plant. Gonzales County. Run-of-the-river-type hydroelectric plant located on Guadalupe River four miles southwest of Gonzales; constructed between 1929 and 1930 by Texas Hydroelectric Corporation.

H-4 Dam and Hydroelectric Plant. Gonzales County. Earth fill dam with sheet-steel core and concrete spillway section and adjacent power plant; built between 1929 and 1930 on Guadalupe River four miles southeast of Belmont by Texas Hydroelectric Corporation for generation of electricity.

Hicks Field. Tarrant County. Airfield established north of Fort Worth in World War I and reestablished for primary flight training during World War II.

High Bridge over the Pecos. Val Verde County. On its completion in 1893, third-highest bridge in the world; carried rails of Galveston, Harrisburg and San Antonio Railway across the canyon of Pecos River.

High Hill Cottonseed Oil Mill. Fayette County. Begun as small enterprise at High Hill in 1867; today recognized as first cottonseed oil mill in Texas.

High Island Swing Bridge. Chambers and Galveston counties. Erected in 1936 at Texas Gulf Intracoastal Waterway* and removed recently; last swing bridge on Texas state highway system.

Highlands Dam. Harris County. Earth fill levee creating off-channel storage reservoir; constructed by U.S. Federal Works Administration between 1942 and 1943 to impound water pumped from San Jacinto River for use in critical defense industries at Houston during World War II.

Hondo Army Airfield. Medina County. Army flight navigation school established in 1942 at Hondo and operated until 1945.

Honey Island Sawmill. Hardin County. Sawmill established by Texas Lumber Company in 1905; remained in operation into mid-twentieth century.

Hooks Switch Sawmill (Mill K). Hardin County. Sawmill begun in 1886 by Hooks Brothers Lumber Company on Sabine and East Texas Railroad at present-day Sharon; operated until 1907.

Hoskins Mound Sulfur Mine. Brazoria County. Major sulfur mine opened in 1922 by Texas Freeport Sulphur Company; used Frasch liquid extraction process.

Hot Sulphur Wells. Bexar County. Spa created by development of warm sulfur springs south of San Antonio around turn of the century.

Hot Wells Reservoir. El Paso County. Bowl-shaped, hand-excavated reservoir for storage of water for domestic and irrigation use; built by prehistoric Mogollon Indians about A.D. 1350–1400; within a site listed on National Register of Historic Places.

Houston and Brazos Valley Railway. Brazoria County. Railway line operated under ownership of a number of companies; built twenty miles in 1890s from Velasco to Chenango Junction.

Houston and Great Northern Railroad. Anderson, Harris, Houston, Montgomery, and Walker counties. Railroad chartered in 1866 and built between 1870 and 1873 from Houston to Palestine; became part of International and Great Northern Railroad.

Houston and Texas Central Railway. Harris County westward to Shackelford County. One of major nineteenth-century Texas railroads; origins in 1840s and existing as separate firm until 1893, when acquired by Southern Pacific Railroad.

Houston and Texas Central Railway Waxahachie Station. Ellis County. Red brick and limestone passenger station erected for Houston and Texas Central Railway at Waxahachie about 1881.

Houston Belt and Terminal Railway. Harris County. Railway chartered in 1905 to provide terminal and switching facilities for downtown Houston warehouse and industrial areas.

Houston Central Power Station. Harris County. Oil-fueled electric-generation station erected by Houston Lighting and Power Company between 1900 and 1906.

Houston County Coal Company Lignite Fields. Houston County. Lignite mining conducted by Houston County Coal Company as early as 1910 about ten miles south of Crockett.

* *Houston 1879 Waterworks.* Harris County. Water system for Houston begun by private company in 1879; retains original pumpwell; listed on National Register of Historic Places.

Houston, North Shore Railway. Harris County. Electric railway line constructed in 1925 to connect Houston with Goose Creek Oil Field near Baytown.

Houston, Oaklawn and Magnolia Park Railway. Harris County. Successor to Houston Belt and Magnolia Park Railway and chartered in 1889; built primarily to serve industrial areas along Buffalo Bayou, later the Houston Ship Channel.*

Houston Railway. Harris County. Short-line railway built by O. M. Carter in 1892 to serve suburb he was developing; in time came to serve industrial and warehouse areas.

* *Houston Ship Channel.* Harris County. Man-made navigation channel along Buffalo Bayou and San Jacinto River connecting Houston with Gulf of Mexico; opened to deep-water vessels in 1914.

Houston Tap and Brazoria Railroad. Brazoria and Harris counties. Railroad built from Houston to East Columbia between 1856 and 1859; one of eleven railroads constructed in Texas before Civil War.

Houston Tie and Timber Preserving Plant. Harris County. Tie and timber preserving plant erected by Southern Pacific Railroad at Houston in 1891.

Howard's Switch Sawmill. Newton County. Sawmill established in 1906 by Thad Howard and Charles A. Mixson at Howard's Switch on Orange and Northwestern Railroad; operated until abandonment in 1911.

Hughes Iron Furnace. Cass County. Iron furnace started by Reese Hughes at Hughes Springs in 1859;

did not begin actual production until 1861.

Hull Oil Field. Liberty County. Oil field opened in 1918; reached peak of production in 1921.

Humble Oil Field. Harris County. One of early large oil fields developed in Texas; produced total of two million barrels of petroleum during single three-month period in 1905.

* *Humphrey Direct Action Pumping Plant.* Kinney County. In 1915, first large installation in United States of a Humphrey Explosion Pump.

Huntsville Branch Railway. Walker County. Short-line railway built seven miles from Huntsville to meet main line of International and Great Northern Railway east of city in 1870s.

Huntsville Public Spring. Walker County. Natural spring that provided Huntsville residents with first water supply; supplanted when waterworks was established about the turn of the century.

Huntsville State Penitentiary Waterworks. Walker County. Waterworks system built in 1884 to serve Huntsville State Penitentiary; consisted of 630-foot-deep artesian well pumped by Worthington pump into a standpipe and directly into mains.

Hye Cotton Gin. Blanco County. Nonfunctioning late nineteenth-century cotton gin that retains much of its old machinery and equipment.

Imperial Dam. Crane and Pecos counties. Dam on Pecos River constructed about 1917 to divert irrigation water for use in Imperial vicinity.

Imperial Sugar Mill. Fort Bend County. Sugar mill established in 1840s at present-day Sugar Land; today only large sugar refinery in Texas.

Imperial Valley Railroad. Fort Bend County. Railway chartered in 1907 and built seven miles from Sugar Land to Cabell; in 1912 sold to Sugar Land Railroad.

Indianola Cistern Water Systems. Calhoun County. Individual water supply systems at residences and businesses at port of Indianola from 1830s to 1880s; collected rainwater from roofs for domestic use.

Indianola Harbor Improvements. Calhoun County. Nineteenth-century wharves and related improvements constructed to facilitate landing of passengers and property from oceangoing vessels at port of Indianola.

Indio Ranch Irrigation System. Maverick County. Early twentieth-century ranch irrigation system that used mesquite-fired boilers to power steam pumps elevating water from Rio Grande.

Inks Dam. Burnet and Llano counties. Concrete

gravity dam across Colorado River constructed between 1936 and 1939 for hydroelectric generation.

International and Great Northern Railroad. Much of Texas within triangle bounded by Beaumont, Fort Worth, and San Antonio. Railway created by merger of Houston and Great Northern with International Railroad in 1873; considerable mileage added before acquisition of line by Missouri Pacific in 1924.

* *International and Great Northern Railroad Station.* Bexar County. Passenger depot erected at San Antonio by International and Great Northern Railroad between 1906 and 1907; one of finest Mission Revival buildings in Texas; listed on National Register of Historic Places.

Iowa Park Waterworks. Wichita County. Waterworks built in 1920 to serve Iowa Park; used electric pumps to elevate water from local wells.

Isla Acequia. El Paso County. Community irrigation ditch excavated about 1850 but abandoned for a number of years until 1898, when it began drawing water from Franklin Canal.*

Jacksonville Sewage Treatment Plant. Cherokee County. Sewage treatment plant at Jacksonville thought in 1927 to have been first in United States to install submerged brushwood aerators.

James, DeMontell, and Herndon Mill. Bandera County. Saw- and gristmill built on Medina River near Bandera about 1853–55; destroyed by floodwaters in 1900.

Jasper and Eastern Railway. Jasper and Newton counties. Railway chartered in 1904 and built from Kirbyville eastward into Louisiana principally to carry lumber products.

Jefferson and Northwestern Railroad. Cass, Marion, and Morris counties. Originally lumber tram railroad; chartered as common carrier in 1899 and serving Jefferson, Linden, and Naples; abandoned in 1942.

Jefferson City Mills. Marion County. Milling complex established at Jefferson by G. B. McDonald in 1874; was noted for fine-quality flour and meal.

Jefferson Foundry and Machine Works. Marion County. Foundry and machine shops begun at Jefferson by Charles McKeoun in 1870.

Jefferson Gas Light System. Marion County. System of street lighting at Jefferson (1867) employing artificial gas produced by burning pine knots in iron retorts; first street lighting system in Texas.

Jefferson Ice Plant. Marion County. Production of ice by mechanical refrigeration machinery as early as 1868.

Jefferson Turning Basin. Marion County. Enlarged turning basin excavated in Big Cypress Bayou at Jefferson in years before Civil War to permit steamboats to turn around more easily at port of Jefferson.

Johnson Cotton Gin. Van Zandt County. Cotton gin established by E. L. Johnson at Tundra community in early 1900s.

Jones Cotton Gin and Gristmill. Bastrop County. Cotton gin and gristmill established in 1890 by G. W. Jones at terminus of Taylor, Bastrop and Houston Railroad in Smithville.

Jones Field. Fannin County. World War II primary flight training facility established at Bonham in 1941 and operated until 1944.

Jordana Acequia. El Paso County. Community irrigation ditch in El Paso valley southwest of Ysleta excavated about 1814; a century later, 2.3 miles long, 10 feet wide, and carrying sixty cubic feet of water per second.

Jordan and McGee Saltworks. Kaufman County. Production of salt at Jordan's Saline starting in 1845, when John Jordan and A. T. McGee began boiling brine in large kettles to produce salt for commercial sale.

Joy Sawmill. Cass County. Sawmill built by Will Grogan in 1933 and named in honor of one of his grandchildren.

Julia Pens. Victoria County. Cattle shipping pens built on Galveston, Harrisburg and San Antonio Railroad in 1887 from which thousands of Texas cattle were shipped until pens' closing in 1946.

Junction City Milling Company Waterpower System. Kimble County. Diversion dam on South Llano River; flumes, canal, and millrace constructed about 1895 to power turbines at Junction City Milling Company plant in Junction.

* *Justiceburg Railway Water System.* Garza County. Railway water system constructed between 1911 and 1912; included five-hundred-foot-long earthen dam, water pipeline, and cylindrical steel standpipe to provide boiler water to Santa Fe Railway steam locomotives at Justiceburg.

Kansas and Gulf Short Line Railroad. Angelina, Cherokee, and Smith counties. Railway chartered in 1880 and by end of decade built from Tyler via Rusk to Lufkin; in 1891 became Tyler Southeastern Railway.

Kansas City, Mexico and Orient Railway of Texas. From Kingola (on Red River) via Vernon, Sweetwater,

San Angelo, and Fort Stockton to Alpine. Railroad chartered in 1900 to build Texas section of line from Kansas City to Topolobampo, Mexico; constructed across much of Texas between 1908 and 1913; acquired by Santa Fe Railway in 1928.

Kansas City Southern Railway. Bowie, Jefferson, and Orange counties. Railway planned in 1880s and built by 1897; connected Texarkana with Port Arthur, passing principally through Arkansas and Louisiana.

Kansas, Oklahoma and Gulf Railway of Texas. Grayson County. Railway chartered in 1921 and built nine miles from Denison to Oklahoma state line to connect with a line from Baxter Springs, Kansas.

* Kelly Plow Works. Marion County. Tracing origins to 1843, first full-line agricultural implement manufacturer in Southwest.

Kemp Dam. Baylor County. Hydraulic fill earthen dam across Wichita River erected between 1922 and 1923 to impound water for municipal and irrigation use downstream at and near Wichita Falls.

Kenedy Waterworks. Karnes County. Municipal waterworks for Kenedy begun about 1916 using water pumped from local wells ranging from 431 to 650 feet deep.

Kerrville Waterworks. Kerr County. Waterworks serving Kerrville begun about 1890 with water pumped directly from Guadalupe River; later supplemented by flow from artesian wells.

Ketchum Bluff Swinging Bridge. Montague County. Suspension bridge erected across Red River about 1924 to connect oil fields on two sides of river; later destroyed by fire.

Kickapoo Dam. Archer County. Rolled-earth dam across North Fork of Little Wichita River constructed in 1945 to impound water for Wichita Falls waterworks.

Kildare and Linden Railway. Cass County. Railway constructed from Kildare to Linden; operated between 1891 and 1901.

Killebrew Homemade "Battle Axe" Windmill. Comanche County. Homemade windmill constructed in 1928 using discarded automobile parts to pump water from a well to a private residence outside DeLeon.

Kirby Dam. Taylor County. Earthen dam across Cedar Creek about five miles south of Abilene; constructed between 1927 and 1928 to impound water for Abilene waterworks.

Kirbyville Confederate Military Depot. Smith County. Headquarters for transportation department of Confederate Army Trans-Mississippi Department, where wagons, caissons, and other vehicles were manufactured and repaired.

Kyle Waterworks. Hays County. Waterworks system serving Kyle begun about 1888; took supply of water from Blanco River.

Lake Creek Railway. Montgomery County. Short-line railway constructed from Montgomery to Hawthicket in 1894 and abandoned two years later.

Lake Plainview. Hale County. Reservoir created by Texas Land and Development Company at Plainview using pumped groundwater in 1913 to demonstrate to prospective land buyers the tremendous amount of water available underground in the area for irrigation use.

Lake Walk Dam and Hydroelectric Plant. Val Verde County. Slab and buttress-type reinforced concrete dam with adjacent hydroelectric plant across Devils River, eleven miles northwest of Del Rio; built by Central Power and Light Company between 1928 and 1929 for generation of electric power; covered by waters of Amistad Reservoir.

* Lake Wichita Dam. Wichita County. Earthen dam built between 1900 and 1901; in its day created largest body of surface water in state of Texas.

Lake Worth Dam. Tarrant County. Dam on West Fork of Trinity River consisting of earthen embankment and concrete spillway; erected between 1912 and 1914 to impound water for Fort Worth waterworks.

Lampasas Waterworks. Lampasas County. Waterworks established by City of Lampasas in 1885; pumped water directly from Sulphur Creek into a standpipe for distribution by gravity flow to consumers.

* Landa Rock Mill. Comal County. Stone flour mill erected first by William W. Meriwether on Comal River in New Braunfels in 1840s and rebuilt by new owner, Joseph Landa, in 1875.

Lange's Mill. Gillespie County. Gristmill erected on Threadgill Creek northwest of Fredericksburg in 1849.

La Porte, Houston and Northern Railroad. Harris County. Railroad chartered in 1892 to build between Houston and Galveston; only fourteen miles completed by 1894, when consolidated with North Galveston, Houston and Kansas City Railroad.

Laredo Army Airfield. Webb County. Site of Laredo's municipal airport; originally Army Air Corps gunnery school, which operated from 1942 to 1946.

Laredo Waterworks. Webb County. Waterworks established by private company in 1883 to provide water to residents of Laredo.

Lasca Railway Water System. Hudspeth County. Southern Pacific Railroad steam locomotive water system constructed about 1900; secured supply from a hand-dug well 12 feet square and 150 feet deep.

Laughlin Army Airfield. Val Verde County. World War II aviation training field established in 1942 and operated until 1945.

* *Lavaca Bay Causeway.* Calhoun County. Timber causeway constructed by Texas Highway Department across Lavaca Bay from Port Lavaca to Point Comfort between 1930 and 1931; typifies such wooden structures on Texas Gulf Coast.

Lavaca Bay Harbor Improvements. Calhoun County. Efforts to enhance navigation in Lavaca Bay from mid-nineteenth century to present.

Lavaca River Iron Truss Bridge. Lavaca County. Iron truss bridge constructed across Lavaca River 3.5 miles southeast of Ezzell by Pittsburgh Bridge Company in 1890.

Leakey Kaolin Pits. Edwards County. Kaolin pits about four miles from Leakey; intermittently operated commercially since early 1890s.

Ledbetter Saltworks. Shackelford County. Saltworks on Salt Fork of Hubbard Creek established in 1860s to produce salt from brine by evaporation.

Lee's Mill. Newton County. Saw- and gristmill established by Windam Brothers in 1871; purchased by James R. Lee in 1879.

Lemonville Sawmill. Orange County. Sawmill built at Lemonville by Lemonville Lumber Company in 1900; changed ownership several times before closing in 1928 because of depleted timber resources.

Levelland Oil Refinery. Hockley County. Oil refinery built to distill petroleum products at Levelland about 1937; abandoned and sold as scrap about 1954.

Llano Estacado Railroad. Floyd and Hale counties. Railroad chartered in 1909 by citizens of Floydada to connect their town with Panhandle and Santa Fe in Plainview; roadbed graded and then sold to Santa Fe Railway for completion in 1910.

Llano Waterworks. Llano County. Waterworks begun at Llano about 1886; secured supply by use of W. W. Knowles and Son pumps to elevate water from Llano River.

Lockhart Waterworks. Caldwell County. Waterworks begun at Lockhart in 1887; took supply from

well pumped by windmill until 1889, when a steam pump was added.

Lockney Waterworks. Floyd County. Waterworks for Lockney begun about 1915; supply secured from local wells.

Lometa Locomotive Roundhouse. Lampasas County. Four-bay steam locomotive roundhouse originally with a turntable; erected by Santa Fe Railway in Lometa railway yards about 1940.

Lone Oak Marsh Road Fill. Chambers County. Earth fill for road across Lone Oak Marsh constructed by Ed Jackson about 1915 using homemade dragline mounted on railway rails.

Lone Star Canal. Chambers County. Early twentieth-century canal constructed to transport water for rice irrigation in Anahuac vicinity.

Lone Star Iron Furnace. Marion County. Late nineteenth-century iron furnace established at Jefferson after successful operation of Old Alcalde Iron Furnace* had been demonstrated at Rusk in mid-1880s.

Lone Star Ordnance Plant. Bowie County. Ordnance works established west of Texarkana on Red River during World War II for manufacture of artillery shells, bombs, fuses, and other munitions.

Lone Star Saltworks. Hudspeth County. Saltworks employing steam pipes in evaporating pans; built by Maj. Byron Parsons in 1891.

Lone Star Saltworks. Mitchell County. Saltworks near Colorado City in 1880s obtaining salt from a forty-foot-thick horizon of brine twelve hundred feet beneath surface through use of steam pumps; brine evaporated in vats to produce salt for commercial sale.

Lone Star Steel Furnace. Morris County. Iron and steel furnace constructed in 1943 at Lone Star by Defense Plant Corporation with Lone Star Steel Company as chief contractor; converted to private ownership and production after World War II.

Longfellow Railway Water System. Pecos County. Railway water system on Texas and New Orleans Railroad established in 1880s; consisted of wells two thousand feet deep, which reputedly passed through layer of silver ore during drilling; freight and telegraph office retired from service in 1944, and water system abandoned in 1954.

Longhorn Cavern Gunpowder Factory. Burnet County. Site of gunpowder manufacture underground in caverns for use by Confederate army during Civil War.

Longhorn Ordnance Works. Harrison County. World War II ordnance plant built for manufacture of explosives near Karnack in 1942.

Longhorn Tin Smelter. Galveston County. Smelter constructed between 1941 and 1942 at Texas City to smelt tin for war effort.

Longview and Sabine Valley Railway. Gregg and Harrison counties. Railway fostered by Longview citizens to build to Gulf of Mexico but actually constructed only from Longview to Tallys in 1878; acquired by Santa Fe Railway in 1897.

Los Ebanos Ferry. Hidalgo County. Last ferry operating on Rio Grande and only hand-pulled ferry on borders of United States.

Louisiana and Arkansas Railway. Cass, Collin, Franklin, Harrison, Hopkins, Hunt, Marion, Morris, and Titus counties. Railway originally chartered in 1881 primarily to link Texarkana with Port Arthur through Arkansas and Louisiana, but also built from Waskom westward to McKinney; merged with Kansas City Southern in 1939.

Louisiana Western Extension Railroad. Orange County. Railway chartered in 1879 and built from Orange to Sabine River by 1881; acquired by Texas and New Orleans Railroad in 1900.

Love Field. Dallas County. Airfield established in 1914 by U.S. Army as airport and aviation training center; today one of the civilian airports serving Dallas.

Lower Rio Grande Boundary Survey. Cameron, Hidalgo and Starr counties. Survey of U.S.-Mexican boundary by International Boundary Commission during winter of 1910–11.

Lubbock Army Air School. Lubbock County. Twin-engine flight training facility opened in 1941 and operated until 1945; in 1949 reopened as Reese Air Force Base.

Lubbock Brick Street Paving. Lubbock County. Street paving program in Lubbock utilizing brick; began in the 1920s and continued through 1930s.

Lubbock-Coleman Cut-off Route of the Santa Fe Railway. Lubbock to Coleman. Railway line 203 miles long constructed between 1909 and 1911 to tie Santa Fe lines in Panhandle and South Plains regions with those serving Texas Gulf Coast.

Lubbock Waterworks. Lubbock County. Waterworks established to serve City of Lubbock as early as 1911.

Lucas Gusher. Jefferson County. Discovery well for Spindletop Oil Field in 1901; known as birthplace of modern petroleum industry; listed in National Register of Historic Places.

Luckenbach Cotton Gin. Gillespie County. Well-preserved but nonfunctioning steam cotton gin at Luckenbach; retains most of its historic machinery and equipment.

Lueders Limestone Company Quarry. Jones County. Commercial limestone quarry begun at Lueders about 1908; reputedly one of first such concerns in West Texas.

Lufkin Foundry and Machine Company (Lufkin Industries). Angelina County. Established in 1902, this factory in 1920s produced some pioneer back-geared counterbalanced oil well pumping units in America, a style now used universally by the petroleum industry.

Lufkin, Hemphill and Gulf Railway. Sabine County. Railway chartered in 1912 and built between Bronson and Hemphill primarily to haul timber products; abandoned in 1938.

Luling Oil Field. Caldwell County. Significant Texas oil field discovered in 1922 by Edgar B. Davis; continues in production today.

Lutcher Moore Lumber Mill. Orange County. In 1957 first fully automated lumber mill operated in Texas.

Lynch's Ferry (Lynchburg Ferry). Harris County. Ferry across Buffalo Bayou established by Nathaniel Lynch in 1822; remains ferry crossing, today, across Houston Ship Channel; * operated by Texas Department of Highways and Public Transportation.

Lyndon B. Johnson Boyhood Home Eclipse Windmill. Blanco County. Eclipse wooden windmill (ca. 1900) restored and in operation at Lyndon B. Johnson Boyhood Home National Historic Site in Johnson City.

McBrayer Irrigation Well. Carson County. In 1952 reputedly first successful deep irrigation well drilled in Carson County.

McCamey Million-Barrel Oil Storage Tank. Upton County. Huge concrete-lined underground oil storage reservoir constructed at McCamey about 1928; never successfully served original purpose because of leakage.

McCauley Coal Mine. Montague County. Coal mine developed in mid-1880s by J. H. McCauley and others approximately six miles west of Bowie.

McClean Waterworks. Gray County. Waterworks begun at McClean about 1918; secured supply from local wells.

McDonald Observatory. Jeff Davis County. On completion in 1939, with its eighty-two-inch reflector, second-largest telescope in world.

McGeehee Homemade Windmill. Armstrong County. Thirty-two-foot-diameter homemade windmill for pumping water; built by Curtis McGeehee at Wayside community in 1920s.

McRae Church Iron Bridge. San Augustine County. Iron truss bridge erected across Venado Creek at McRae Church west of San Augustine in 1917.

McWhorter Irrigation Well. Lubbock County. Irrigation well drilled about 1911 in effort to introduce irrigated agriculture to Lubbock County.

Majors Field. Hunt County. Airfield established five miles from Greenville in 1942 for basic flight training during World War II; operated until 1945.

Malakoff Lignite Mine. Henderson County. Lignite mine begun near Malakoff in 1926 as source of fuel for nearby power plants.

Manchester Portland Cement Plant. Harris County. Portland cement plant established by Texas Portland Cement Company at Manchester in 1915; noted for early use of shell deposits as source of lime in cement manufacture.

Manning Domestic Water Distillation System. Angelina County. One of three systems in East Texas where in the 1930s domestic water supply for residents of a town was distilled from water taken from log ponds.

Manning Sawmill. Angelina County. Sawmill established by W. W. Manning in 1867, around which a community grew until mill burned in 1936.

Mansfield Dam. Travis County. Dam on the Colorado River constructed between 1937 and 1942 for flood protection and the generation of hydroelectric power.

Marble Falls Dam and Hydroelectric Plant. Burnet County. Reinforced-concrete dam and hydroelectric plant built by private company on Colorado River between 1909 and 1911.

Marfa Army Airfield. Presidio County. Airfield established near Marfa in 1942 to train pilots to fly two-engine aircraft during World War II.

Marienfeld Windmill Irrigation. Martin County. Extensive windmill irrigation by both individuals and private companies near present-day Stanton during 1890s.

Marion Steamboat Landing. Angelina County. Steamboat landing on Angelina River as early as 1830s; at one time a center of trade and commerce,

with over two hundred buildings; served as first seat of Angelina County.

Marshall and East Texas Railway. Harrison, Upshur, and Wood counties. Railway, originally chartered in 1880s and taking this name in 1908; connected Elysian Fields with Winnsboro.

Marshall Powder Mill. Harrison County. Munitions plant established to produce arms and ammunition for use by Confederate army during Civil War.

Marshall Railway Shops. Harrison County. Extensive late nineteenth- and early twentieth-century railway shops constructed at Marshall by Texas and Pacific Railway.

Marshall Telegraph Office. Harrison County. Opened by Texas and Red River Telegraph Company on February 14, 1854; first commercial telegraph office in Texas.

Marshall, Timpson and Sabine Pass Railroad. Panola and Shelby counties. Railroad chartered in 1896 to build from Carthage to Sabine Pass, but actually built only from Carthage to Timpson; purchased by Santa Fe Railway in 1897.

Marshall Waterworks. Harrison County. Waterworks started for Marshall about 1889; derived supply from a series of wells.

Martin Wagon Company Works. Angelina County. Factory in Lufkin that was the site for development in 1920s of special heavy-duty wagons used in lumbering.

Matador Ranch Headquarters Water System. Motley County. Water system at headquarters of Matador Ranch in early twentieth century; consisted of small spring-fed reservoir from which water was pumped to elevated storage tank for distribution by pipes.

Matagorda Lighthouse. Calhoun County. Cast-iron lighthouse first erected in 1852 and rebuilt twenty years later; remains in service at north end of Matagorda Island.

Mathis Dam. Jim Wells and San Patricio counties. Earth fill and concrete dam across Nueces River about four miles southwest of Mathis; constructed in 1929 and rebuilt in 1934 to impound water for Corpus Christi waterworks; inundated by waters of new Lake Corpus Christi in 1958.

Mayo Paper Mill. Orange County. Paper mill begun in 1911 by Edward H. Mayo, where he first successfully made pulp and kraft paper by sulfate pulp process.

Meacham Field. Tarrant County. Civilian airport serving Fort Worth; established in 1914 and moved to present site in 1925, where it continues to operate.

* *Medina Dam.* Medina County. Concrete gravity dam built between 1911 and 1912 as major storage facility for Medina Irrigation Project; formed in its day the fourth-largest reservoir in United States; listed on National Register of Historic Places.

Medina River Southern Pacific Railroad Bridge. Bexar County. Late nineteenth-century railway bridge over Medina River west of San Antonio; employed innovative concrete piers.

Memphis, El Paso and Pacific Railroad. Bowie County westward to Dallas County. Railway chartered in 1853 to run from Bowie County to Pacific Ocean via El Paso; actually constructed from Texarkana westward to Dallas and southward to Caddo Lake by 1873.

Mercedes Irrigation Pumping Plant. Hidalgo County. Early twentieth-century irrigation pumping plant on Rio Grande near Mercedes; initially used electricity and later steam to power pumps.

Meridian Artesian Water System. Bosque County. Waterworks system established at Meridian by private individual who drilled an artesian well about 1884 and furnished water to consumers for six dollars per year.

Mexia Oil Field. Limestone County. Oil and gas field opened initially for gas production in 1912; became site of oil boom, with major discoveries in 1921.

Mexia Waterworks. Limestone County. Waterworks begun by Mexia Water, Ice and Light Company about 1888; secured supply by pumping from man-made reservoir.

Middle Yegua Creek Iron Bridge. Lee County. Late nineteenth-century iron bridge spanning Middle Yegua Creek about four miles south of Lexington on old Highway 44.

Mid-Kansas Oil Camp. Stephens County. Oil camp established by Mid-Kansas Oil Company in northern Stephens County in 1916 and operated until 1925.

Midland and Northwestern Railway. Andrews, Gaines, and Midland counties. Railway chartered in 1916 to extend from Midland to New Mexico; actually constructed from Midland to Seminole; operated until 1925.

Midland Army Airfield. Midland County. World War II bombardier training field established in 1941 at site of a former airfield; operated until 1947.

Midland Waterworks. Midland County. Waterworks established to serve Midland about 1912; se-

cured supply from drilled wells.

Mills Building. El Paso County. Pioneer multistory, monolithic concrete office building erected in downtown El Paso about 1912.

Mills Cotton Gin. Freestone County. Cotton gin erected by Dr. J. S. Mills at present-day Cotton Gin community in 1848.

Mineral Wells Dam. Parker County. Earthen dam with concrete spillway constructed on Rock Creek, four miles east of Mineral Wells between 1918 and 1920 to impound water for Mineral Wells waterworks; improved and crest raised between 1943 and 1944.

Mineral Wells Waterworks. Palo Pinto County. Water system established for Mineral Wells about the turn of the century.

Mission Espíritu Santo Irrigation System. Victoria County. Irrigation system constructed by Indian neophytes in 1720s; consisted of diversion dam and acequias.

Mission Nuestra Señora del Rosario Irrigation System. Goliad County. Planned irrigation system, which included stone dam fifty *vara*s long; built in 1750s; canal projected but never completed.

Missouri, Kansas and Texas Extension Railway. Cooke, Fannin, Grayson, and Hunt counties. Railway chartered in 1880 by Missouri, Kansas and Texas Railroad to begin development of company lines in Texas.

Missouri, Kansas and Texas Railroad Fort Worth Roundhouse. Tarrant County. Turn-of-the-century turntable and red brick locomotive roundhouse erected at Fort Worth.

Missouri, Kansas and Texas Railroad of Texas. Network covering much of Texas from Houston and San Antonio on the south to Red River on the north and from Austin and Wichita Falls on the west to Sabine River on the east. Railway chartered in 1865 to build from Kansas southward to Rio Grande; by 1945 operated more than twelve hundred miles of track in Texas.

Missouri Pacific Railroad of Texas. Network covering Texas from Sabine River on the east to Trans-Pecos region on the west. Railroad that entered Texas in the 1870s and through actual construction and acquisition of other lines controlled approximately one-third of track in the state by 1880s.

Monahans Oil Storage Tank. Ward county. Huge underground concrete-lined oil storage tank built near Monahans in 1929; proved unsuccessful because

Monte Alto Irrigation System. Hidalgo County. Irrigation system constructed between 1936 and 1939; consisted of earthen dike twelve miles long about four miles north of Monte Alto; created off-channel storage reservoir for Rio Grande waters combined with canal system for distribution to fields.

Mont Iron Truss Bridge. Lavaca County. Iron truss bridge erected across Rocky Creek 2.5 miles southeast of Mont by King Iron Bridge Company in 1889.

Moody Windmill Irrigation System. Midland County. Irrigation system built by J. M. Moody at Midland about the turn of the century; used windmill to pump eight hundred gallons of water per hour for vineyard and orchard use.

Moore Field. Hidalgo County. World War II military airfield established near Mission in 1941 for training advanced single-engine pilots; graduated approximately six thousand cadets.

Moore Irrigation System. Kinney County. Large privately owned irrigation system begun about 1904 on G. Bedell Moore Estate; included Humphrey Direct-Action Pumping Plant* in 1914.

**Moore's Crossing Bridge.* Travis County. Iron truss bridge since 1915 spanning waters of Onion Creek south of Austin that originally carried traffic across Colorado River at the foot of Congress Avenue in Austin from 1883 until it was replaced by the present bridge in 1910.

Moore Water Well. Fort Bend County. Hand-dug well thirty-five feet deep and lined with handmade bricks; excavated at Richmond about 1885.

Morgan Waterworks. Bosque County. Waterworks established in 1889; secured initial supply from artesian well from which water flowed to a storage tank.

Mormon Mill. Burnet County. Gristmill on Hamilton Creek built in 1851 by Mormons led by Lyman Wight; remained in operation until 1901.

Morris Ferry Turpentine Camp and Distillery. Jasper County. Turpentine camp and distillery established in 1916 by Western Naval Stores Company; operated until 1920.

Morris Sheppard Dam. Palo Pinto County. Concrete and earthen dam erected on Brazos River between 1935 and 1941 for flood control, hydroelectric generation, and municipal water supply.

Morton Kleer Salt Mine. Van Zandt County. Salt mine begun by Morton Salt Company in 1929; remains in production.

Moscow, Camden and San Augustine Railroad.

Polk County. Short-line railway built in 1898 to connect Moscow and Camden, principally to carry lumber products.

Motley County Railroad. Motley County. Railroad chartered by citizens of Matador in 1919 to build spur line from Matador to connect with Quanah, Acme and Pacific near Roaring Springs; operated until 1936.

Mountain Creek Dam. Dallas County. Rolled-earth dam across Mountain Creek four miles southeast of Grand Prairie; constructed by Dallas Power and Light Company between 1929 and 1936 to impound water to cool nearby steam-electric generation station that went into service in 1938.

Mulberry Creek Iron Truss Bridge. Fayette County. Modified Pratt pony truss bridge erected in 1888 by A. J. Tullock and Company of Leavenworth, Kansas, for Fayette County across Mulberry Creek, about 2.5 miles southwest of Schulenburg; listed on National Register of Historic Places.

Nacogdoches and Southeastern Railroad. Nacogdoches and San Augustine counties. Railway chartered in 1909 and built just over forty-two miles from Nacogdoches to Calgary.

Nacogdoches Waterworks. Nacogdoches County. Water system to serve Nacogdoches, established about 1890; water originally supplied by gravity from spring-fed reservoir; five wells later added.

Nails Creek Iron Bridge. Lee County. Late nineteenth-century iron truss bridge built across Nails Creek near Giddings.

Nance's Mill. Hays County. Gristmill and cotton gin built by Ezekiel Nance about 1850 in present-day Mountain City area.

Nancy Sawmill. Angelina County. Sawmill and company town established by Angelina County Lumber Company in 1923.

**Nash Iron Furnace.* Marion County. First iron furnace operated in Texas; built by Jefferson S. Nash in 1847 and produced iron into Civil War years.

Nasworthy Dam. Tom Green County. Earth fill and concrete dam constructed across South Concho River near San Angelo between 1929 and 1930 to impound water for San Angelo waterworks.

Navarro Mill. Navarro County. Sawmill established on Richland Creek in 1850s and around which community of Navarro Mills grew.

Navasota Waterworks. Grimes County. Water system begun at Navasota about 1890; secured original supply from artesian well from which water was

293

pumped to a standpipe.

New Blox Lumber Camp. Jasper County. Lumber camp established in 1924 by Kirby Lumber Company on tram line leading from Blox community; abandoned by late 1940s.

New Braunfels Waterworks. Comal County. Waterworks started at New Braunfels in 1886; used water pumped from Comal River.

New Camp Ruby Sawmill. Polk County. Sawmill established by W. T. Carter and Brothers of Camden in 1925 at present-day New Camp Ruby community.

New Willard Sawmill. Polk County. Sawmill established in 1886 by James R. Freeman at present-day New Willard.

New York, Texas and Mexican Railway. Fort Bend, Jackson, Victoria, and Wharton counties. Railway chartered in 1880 to build across Texas into Mexico, but actually constructed from Rosenberg to Victoria by 1882; purchased by Southern Pacific Railroad in 1885.

Neyland Oil Pump. Goliad County. Prototype oil pump designed and fabricated by W. R. Neyland at Goliad in 1916; inventor hoped it would pump oil in same manner as gas.

Nickols Railway Yard. Colorado County. Railway yards and turntable built by Missouri, Kansas and Texas Railroad about 1896 in present-day Pisek community.

Nix Cotton Gin, Gristmill, and Sawmill. Edwards County. Combined gristmill, cotton gin, and sawmill established by J. L. Nix at Barksdale in 1883 and powered by boiler and steam engine.

Nocona Suspension Bridge. Montague County. Suspension bridge erected across the Red River north of Nocona in 1924; approaches still remain.

Nolte Hydroelectric Plant. Guadalupe County. Run-of-the-river-type hydroelectric plant located 2.5 miles below TP-5 Dam on Guadalupe River, about three miles southeast of Seguin; constructed by Texas Power Corporation in 1927.

North Concho River Iron Truss Bridge. Sterling County. Iron truss bridge across North Concho River near Sterling City; erected by El Paso Bridge and Iron Company about 1913.

North Concho River Stream Gaging Station. Sterling County. U.S. Geological Survey stream gaging station constructed on North Concho River just south of Sterling City in 1939.

North Fork Lavaca River Iron Truss Bridge. Lavaca County. Iron truss bridge erected in 1889 across North Fork of Lavaca River 2.5 miles west of Novohrad by King Iron Bridge Company.

North Galveston, Houston and Kansas City Railroad. Galveston County. Railroad chartered in 1892 by Minneapolis capitalists to build from Galveston to Kansas City; actually built only sixteen miles northward from Galveston; merged with La Porte, Houston and Northern Railroad, and later purchased by Southern Pacific Railroad.

North Nocona Oil Field. Montague County. Comparatively small oil field brought into production in Montague County about 1922; still retains much of its old pumping equipment.

North Side Belt Railway. Harris County. Railway chartered in 1925 and built to serve north side of Houston Ship Channel.*

North Side Sewage Treatment Plant. Harris County. Pioneer activated-sludge sewage treatment plant of conventional continuous-flow, diffused-air type first placed in service in Houston in 1917.

North Texas and Santa Fe Railway. Hansford, Lipscomb, and Ochiltree counties. Railway line chartered in 1916 and built from Shattuck, Oklahoma, to Spearman, Texas; extended to Morse in 1931.

* *Nueces Bay Causeways.* Nueces and San Patricio counties. Series of four bridges across Nueces Bay built in 1916, 1921, 1950, and 1963 to link Corpus Christi with San Patricio County.

Nueces Valley, Rio Grande and Mexico Railway. Dimmit and La Salle counties. Railway chartered in 1905 to serve some fruit- and vegetable-producing areas of Lower Rio Grande Valley, with Asherton as northern terminus.

Oakhurst Sawmill. San Jacinto County. Sawmill built at Oakhurst by Columbia Lumber Company in 1899 or 1900; in 1911 moved to Walker County.

* *Oil Springs Oil Field.* Nacogdoches County. In 1866 site of first successful oil well in Texas and still a producing oil field; listed on National Register of Historic Places.

Oklahoma City and Texas Railroad. Hardeman County. Railroad chartered in 1901 to build from Quanah northward nine miles to connect with Frisco lines across Red River in Oklahoma.

* *Old Alcalde Iron Furnace.* Cherokee County. Iron furnace that operated at Rusk State Penitentiary from 1884 until replacement in 1904.

Old Donnell Mill. Young County. Gristmill erected by James D. Donnell and sons on Clear Fork of Brazos in 1876; operated for almost half a century.

* *Old Lone Star Brewery.* Bexar County. Built on banks of San Antonio River in San Antonio in 1883 and expanded until 1904; largest brewery in Texas in its day; operated until beginning of Prohibition in 1919; today the San Antonio Museum of Art; listed on National Register of Historic Places.

Old Pecos River Highway Bridge. Val Verde County. Steel truss highway bridge across Pecos River at bottom of Pecos River Canyon; erected in 1923 and destroyed by floods in 1950s.

Old Texaco Gasoline Refinery. Foard County. Petroleum refinery established in western Foard County in 1934 and designed to produce primarily gasoline.

Old Waco Dam. McLennan County. Earth fill dam across Bosque River two miles west of Waco constructed between 1928 and 1929 to impound water for Waco waterworks; inundated by waters of new Waco Reservoir in 1965.

Olive Sawmill. Hardin County. Sawmill established by Olive-Sternenberg Lumber Company between 1879 and 1880; operated until 1911.

Olmos Dam. Bexar County. Concrete gravity dam on Olmos Creek built by San Antonio between 1925 and 1926 to provide flood protection to downtown business district.

Olney Waterworks. Young County. Water system built in 1909 to serve Olney; took its original supply from twenty-foot-diameter well with gasoline-fueled pumps.

Onalaska Sawmill. Polk County. Sawmill established by William Carlisle in 1902; named for town in Arkansas where builder also owned a sawmill.

Orange and Northwestern Railway. Orange County. Railway originally constructed as logging tram to haul timber into Orange; in 1901 chartered as common carrier.

Orange Paper and Pulp Company Mill. Orange County. Turn-of-the-century paper mill that successfully produced paper using yellow pine refuse from other plants.

* *Orange–Port Arthur High Bridge.* Jefferson and Orange counties. Major bridge over Neches River between Orange and Port Arthur; erected by Texas Highway Department between 1936 and 1938.

Orchard Sulfur Mines. Fort Bend County. Sulfur production initiated with tests in 1920s followed by successful mining through use of steam injected under pressure, beginning in 1938.

Orsak Cotton Gin. Lavaca County. Cotton gin built by Joe Orsak in 1882 at site of Worthing.

Ostrander and Loomis Ranch Telephone System. Tom Green County. Pioneer telephone system used about 1890 for communication on large ranch in western Texas.

Overland Freight Station. Sherman County. Stone structure built in 1880s on old freighting road on Bivins Ranch, southeast of Stratford.

* *Paddock Viaduct.* Tarrant County. Bridge built between 1912 and 1914 as first large self-supporting reinforcement concrete arch bridge in United States; listed on National Register of Historic Places.

Padre Island Wells and Windmills. Cameron, Kenedy, Kleberg, Nueces, and Willacy counties. Numerous shallow hand-dug and drilled wells sunk on Padre Island during past century, many of them pumped by windmills, for stock watering and domestic use.

Paducah Waterworks. Cottle County. Waterworks started at Paducah about 1912; secured initial supply from hand-dug wells outside the city from which flow was pumped to municipal system.

Palestine Waterworks. Anderson County. Water system built between 1881 and 1882 to serve Palestine took supply from series of springs from which water was piped to collection well for pumping to brick reservoir and standpipe.

Palmetto Lumber Company Sawmill. San Jacinto County. Sawmill built near present-day Oakhurst in late nineteenth century; some brick remains still exist.

Pampa Army Airfield. Gray County. World War II Army Air Corps facility established in 1942 to provide advanced twin-engine aircraft training.

Pan American Oil Camp. Willacy County. Camp established in 1943 as center for offices and residences used by employees of the Pan American Oil Company in the Willacy County area.

Panhandle and Santa Fe Railway. Network covering Texas Panhandle and South Plains regions and extending southeast to Brownwood. Rail system begun in 1886 and built up through both construction and acquisition of other lines to create a total of over 1,850 miles of track in operation by 1945.

Panhandle Oil and Gas Field. Carson, Gray, Hutchinson, Moore, Potter, and Wheeler counties. Oil and gas field discovered in 1920; reached peak of production later in decade, and in its day became largest single producing gas field in world.

Panhandle Railway Company. Armstrong and Carson counties. Railway chartered in 1887 and built 14.5 miles from Panhandle to Washburn; purchased by Santa Fe Railway in 1900 and abandoned in 1908.

Panhandle Waterworks. Carson County. Water system begun to supply the Panhandle community in 1889; secured water from local wells.

Pantex Ordnance Plant. Carson and Potter counties. Munitions plant established in 1942; today the central assembly point for American nuclear warheads.

* *Paris Abattoir.* Lamar County. Opened in 1909 as first significant municipally owned slaughterhouse in United States.

Paris and Great Northern Railroad. Lamar County. Railroad chartered in 1881 and in 1886 built seventeen miles from Paris to Red River to connect with St. Louis and San Francisco Railroad.

Paris and Mount Pleasant Railway. Franklin, Lamar, Red River, and Titus counties. Railway chartered in 1909 by Paris citizens and built to connect with Cotton Belt Railway at Mount Pleasant.

Paris, Choctaw and Little Rock Railroad. Lamar County. Railway chartered in 1888 and built ten miles from Paris before being abandoned.

Paris Sewerage System. Lamar County. Sewage disposal system serving Paris; first constructed by private individual in 1894; reconstructed after acquisition by municipality in 1897.

Paris Waterworks. Lamar County. Waterworks serving citizens of Paris; established jointly by municipal government and private company in 1888, and later expanded.

Parris Mill. Collin County. Ox-powered gristmill built by Thaddeus Parris in 1859 on Trinity Creek at present-day Parris.

Peach Creek Iron Truss Bridge. Gonzales County. Iron truss bridge with sixty-four-foot main span and two twenty-three-foot approaches; erected by Gonzales County across Peach Creek about two miles east of Dilworth in 1899.

Pease River Iron Bridge. Foard County. Iron bridge constructed across Pease River between Crowell and Quanah between 1890 and 1891; destroyed by flooding in June, 1891.

Pecos and Northern Texas Railway. Castro, Deaf Smith, Parmer, Potter, and Randall counties. Railway chartered in 1898, and by 1899 built from Amarillo southwestward to Texas–New Mexico state line; later extended through New Mexico to Belen to give a shorter route from Oklahoma and Texas Panhandle to California.

Pecos Army Airfield. Reeves County. Army Air Corps field established in 1942 and operated first for basic flight training and later for twin-engine advanced training; closed in 1945, and became a civilian airport.

Pecos Artesian Wells. Reeves County. Numerous artesian wells drilled as early as 1890s in Pecos vicinity for domestic supply and irrigation use.

Pecos Railway Water System. Reeves County. Water supply system built by Texas and Pacific Railway in 1886 for steam locomotives; consisted of a 241-foot drilled well with daily capacity of eighty-five thousand gallons.

Pecos River Railroad. Reeves County. Railroad chartered in 1890 and built from Pecos to Carlsbad, New Mexico, as outlet for agricultural products grown in Pecos Valley around Carlsbad; later extended northward to Clovis, New Mexico.

Pecos Valley Southern Railway. Reeves County. Railway chartered in 1909, and within a year built southward to connect Pecos with Toyahvale.

Pecos Waterworks. Reeves County. Waterworks begun to serve Pecos in 1880s; secured supply from artesian wells.

Peña Acequia. El Paso County. Community acequia dug in 1830s in El Paso valley; in 1914, 4.8 miles long, 12 feet wide, and carried forty cubic feet of water per second.

Penn Field. Travis County. Army airfield established near Austin for training use during World War I; sold to private owners after abandonment in 1919.

Perrin Field. Grayson County. Airfield established at Sherman in 1941 as training base for single-engine pilots during World War II; military facility until 1970.

Petrician Spring Irrigation System. Reeves County. Irrigation system developed by the turn of the century to employ waters flowing naturally from a spring about nine miles northwest of Toyah.

Petrolia Oil and Gas Field. Clay County. Oil and gas field discovered in 1904; provided natural gas to Fort Worth, Dallas, and twenty-one other cities and towns by 1913.

Peyton Creek Dam. Matagorda County. Earthen levee across a natural lake on Peyton Creek; constructed in 1912 to increase original storage capacity for rice irrigation; severely damaged by 1930 and 1932 hurricanes and never rebuilt.

Pickering Sawmill. Shelby County. Major sawmill complex erected at Haslam in 1913 and operated until 1927; site now marked by large abandoned concrete buildings and other surface remains.

Pierce Rice Irrigation Pumping Plant. Wharton County. Large steam-powered rice irrigation pumping plant erected at A. H. Pierce estate on Colorado River about 1908.

Pineland Sawmill. Sabine County. In its day the largest integrated sawmill in Sabine County; enlarged in 1902 with coming of Gulf, Beaumont and Great Northern Railroad.

Pine Springs Stage Stand. Culberson County. Stage station (now in ruins) built in 1858 as stop on Butterfield Overland Mail on northeast side of Guadalupe Pass.

Pioneer Irrigation Company Eastside Irrigation System. Reeves and Ward counties. Irrigation system constructed on Pecos River in 1890s; included thirty-five-mile canal and flume across Pecos to irrigate about seventy thousand acres.

Pioneer Irrigation Company Westside Irrigation System. Reeves and Ward counties. Irrigation system built on west side of Pecos River in the 1890s; included a seventeen-mile canal and a diversion dam that irrigated about thirteen thousand acres.

Plainview Field. Hale County. Army airfield established in 1942 as a training station for the Fourth Army Air Force Glider Training Detchment, which operated until training detachment's removal to Lamesa in 1943.

Plainview Irrigation District. Hale County. Area of early use of underground waters for irrigation before World War I; promotion of sale of irrigated farmland by Texas Land and Development Company.

Plank Sawmill. Hardin County. Sawmill established in 1882 at present-day Plank by Noble and Sheldon Lumber Company; abandoned in 1890 with depletion of timber resources in area.

Plant X Electric Generation Station. Lamb County. Large steam electric-generating station using natural gas and oil as fuels; began operation in early 1950s.

* *Pliska Aeroplane.* Midland County. Homemade airplane built at a Midland blacksmith shop by John V. Pliska and Gray Coggin between 1911 and 1912; one of oldest surviving Texas-made aircraft.

Pluck Sawmill. Polk County. Sawmill established in 1884 at present-day Pluck (Stryker) by Eagle and Stryker Lumber Company.

* *Point Bolivar Lighthouse.* Galveston County. Lighthouse erected at Point Bolivar in 1873 and operated as navigational aid until 1933; listed on National Register of Historic Places.

* *Point Isabel Lighthouse.* Cameron County. Erected in 1852 as a navigational aid; remained in service into twentieth century; listed on National Register of Historic Places.

Ponton Creek Iron Truss Bridge. Lavaca County. Iron truss bridge erected across Ponton Creek west of Worthing in 1890s.

Port Arthur Harbor Improvements. Jefferson County. Harbor improvements undertaken at Port Arthur from 1890s into mid-twentieth century that resulted in city's becoming second-largest port in tonnage in United States by 1941.

Port Bolivar Iron Ore Railroad. Gregg and Upshur counties. Railway built in 1911 to connect iron ore–producing areas of northeast Texas with other railroads and to transport ore to Port Bolivar for shipment to other parts of country for smelting.

* *Porter's Bluff Highway.* Smith County. Pioneer paved highway in Smith County from Tyler to Van Zandt county line; constructed in 1920.

Port Harlingen Ship Channel and Harbor Development. Cameron County. Harbor facilities at Port Harlingen, six miles east of Harlingen on Arroyo Colorado; made possible in 1952 by dredging of a channel twenty-five miles to Laguna Madre and Texas Gulf Intracoastal Waterway.*

Port Isabel and Rio Grande Valley Railway. Cameron County. Railway chartered in 1909 to reconstruct abandoned nonstandard-gauge Rio Grande Railway between Port Isabel and Brownsville; purchased by Missouri Pacific Railroad in 1941.

Port Isabel Harbor Improvements. Cameron County. Dredging to deepen harbor at Port Isabel at least as early as 1930s in effort to make port a shipping point for oil and cotton.

* *Possum Kingdom Stone Arch Bridge.* Palo Pinto County. Stone arch bridge spanning Brazos River; erected by Texas Highway Department between 1940 and 1942 just downstream from Morris Sheppard Dam.

* *Post City Windmill Waterworks.* Garza County. Waterworks system built between 1908 and 1909 and employing battery of windmills pumping water at Cap Rock Escarpment above Post.

Powell Oil Field. Navarro County. Oil field east of Corsicana; opened with shallow production in 1900, and with deeper wells reaching new horizons in 1923.

Pumpville Railway Water System. Val Verde County. Railway water supply system established on Southern Pacific Railroad about 1887; secured water from local wells; railway station abandoned in 1952 and wells retired from service in 1955.

Pyote Army Airfield. Ward County. Airfield established at Pyote in 1943 for training of crews for B-17 and later B-29 bombers during World War II; remained active military installation until 1963.

Quanah, Acme and Pacific Railroad. Cottle, Hardeman, and Motley counties. Railroad chartered in 1902 and eventually built from Quanah to Floydada.

* *Quitaque Railway Tunnel.* Floyd County. Excavated in 1927 by the Fort Worth and Denver South Plains Railway; last functioning railway tunnel in Texas; listed on National Register of Historic Places.

Ragley Sawmill. Panola County. Sawmill constructed in 1903 at present-day Ragley; operated until 1923.

Ragsdale Cotton Gin. Dallas County. Cotton gin erected in 1900 by W. S. Ragsdale; gave rise to community of Tripp.

Ragsdill Irrigation System. Kimble County. Irrigation system constructed in 1890s on South Llano River near Junction; employed wooden inverted siphon to carry water beneath river to its north side.

Ralph Switch Elevator. Randall County. Wooden grain elevator erected at Ralph Switch on Santa Fe Railway in southern Randall County about the turn of the century; demolished in 1983.

Randall Dam. Grayson County. Earthen dam constructed in 1909 to impound water on Shawnee Creek for Denison waterworks.

Randolph Field. Bexar County. Military airfield activated in 1930 as consolidated flight training school for Army Air Corps; still an Air Force training facility.

Ranger Oil Field. Eastland County. Discovered in 1917, a major Texas oil field through 1920s.

Reagan Wells Spa. Uvalde County. Wells producing mineral water containing calcic and magnesic sulfate water developed as spa for health seekers before the turn of the century.

Red Bluff Dam and Hydroelectric Plant. Reeves and Loving counties. Earth fill dam with concrete spillway and adjacent hydroelectric plant constructed across Pecos River five miles north of Orla by Red Bluff Water Improvement District between 1934 and 1936 to impound waters for irrigation downstream and to generate electricity.

* *Red Brick Road.* Palo Pinto and Parker counties. Red brick–paved westbound lane of U.S. 180 between Weatherford and Mineral Wells; laid between 1937 and 1938 and still in service.

Red River Bridge of the St. Louis and San Francisco Railway. Lamar County. Iron truss railway bridge on concrete piers erected across Red River by St. Louis and San Francisco Railway about 1888.

Red River Bridge of the Santa Fe Railway. Cooke County. Railway bridge erected in 1880s across Red River by Santa Fe Railway.

Red River Ordnance Depot. Bowie County. Facility for storage, issue, and repair of military combat equipment; established in 1941 and still in service as military depot.

Red River, Texas and Southern Railway. Collin, Dallas, Denton, and Grayson counties. Railway chartered in 1901 and built fifty-one miles from Sherman to Carrollton, where it connected with other lines to Dallas and Fort Worth.

Red River Toll Bridge. Cooke County. Steel truss bridge consisting of seven two-hundred-foot spans erected across Red River north of Gainesville and operated as toll crossing until about 1934.

* *Regency Suspension Bridge.* Mills and San Saba counties. Suspension bridge erected across Colorado River between Mills and San Saba counties by Austin Bridge Company in 1939; listed on National Register of Historic Places.

* *Republic of Texas Boundary Marker.* Panola County. Granite international boundary marker between United States and Republic of Texas set by a joint commission in 1841; listed on National Register of Historic Places.

Rhea Mill. Collin County. Mill established in 1857 by W. A. and J. C. Rhea to grind grain raised by local farmers; by Civil War also manufactured carding machinery.

Rhodessa Oil Field. Cass and Marion counties. Oil field discovered in western Louisiana; in 1936 extended into Texas to reach production peak in 1937.

Rhome Mill. Wise County. Three-story stone mill erected at Rhome in 1898 for production of flour and meal.

Richmond Railway Bridge. Fort Bend County. Fink triangle truss bridge 499 feet long; erected for railway use across Brazos River at Richmond in 1869 to replace earlier structure.

Rio Grande and Eagle Pass Railroad. Webb County. Railroad projected as early as 1882 and built in 1895 from Laredo up Rio Grande Valley to Minera to serve local coal mines and produce-raising areas.

Rio Grande City Railway. Hidalgo and Starr counties. Railway line planned as early as 1916 and finally built in 1924 from Samfordyce up Rio Grande Valley to Rio Grande City.

Rio Grande, El Paso and Santa Fe Railroad. El Paso County. Railroad chartered by Santa Fe Railway interests in 1914 to take over twenty-two-mile line of former Rio Grande and El Paso Railroad (built between 1880 and 1881 from El Paso to La Tuna), where it connected with another branch line that reached main Santa Fe line at Deming, New Mexico, thus giving the Santa Fe access to El Paso.

Rio Grande Northern Railroad. Jeff Davis and Presidio counties. Railroad chartered in 1893 and built six miles to serve San Carlos coal mine near Rio Grande; abandoned in 1899.

Rio Grande Railroad. Cameron County. Railroad constructed in 1871 with a forty-two-inch gauge connecting Port Isabel and Brownsville; severely damaged by tropical storms in 1873 and 1875; purchased by Port Isabel and Rio Grande Valley Railway in 1909 and rebuilt in standard gauge.

Rita Blanca Dam. Hartley County. Rolled-earth dam with concrete spillway constructed across Rita Blanca Creek three miles south of Dalhart by U.S. Soil Conservation Service between 1938 and 1939 for recreational use.

* Riverside Swing Bridge. Walker County. Bridge erected by International and Great Northern Railway over Trinity River in 1916; designed to turn on a central pier to allow passage of barge and steamboat traffic on river; listed on National Register of Historic Places.

Riviera Beach and Western Railway. Kleberg County. Railway line constructed ten miles by T. F. Koch in 1912 to serve seashore resort he was developing at Riviera Beach; abandoned in 1917.

Roberts Sawmill. Smith County. Sawmill at present-day Swan established by W. L. Roberts in 1880s on International and Great Northern Railroad; processed lumber until 1915.

Robinson Branch Iron Bridge. Johnson County. Single-lane iron bridge erected across Robinson Branch of Nolan River at Bono community in late nineteenth or early twentieth century.

Roby and Northern Railway. Fisher County. Railway chartered in 1923 and built five miles from Roby to connection with Missouri, Kansas and Texas Railroad.

Rockdale, Sandow and Southern Railroad. Milam County. Railroad chartered in 1923 and constructed from Marjorie to Sandow to haul lignite.

Rocky Creek Iron Bridge. Fayette County. Iron bridge built across Rocky Creek near Round Top in 1904.

Rocky Creek Iron Truss Bridge. Lavaca County. Iron truss bridge erected across Rocky Creek one mile south of Mossy Grove in 1890s.

Roscoe, Snyder and Pacific Railway. Mitchell, Nolan, and Scurry counties. Railway chartered in 1908 and built from Roscoe via Snyder to Fluvanna; became one of the most profitable short-line railroads in United States.

Rosenberg Waterworks. Fort Bend County. Waterworks at Rosenberg begun in 1914; secured supply from local wells.

Rotan Waterworks. Fisher County. Waterworks at Rotan established about 1928; originally provided water from local wells pumped by gasoline-fueled pumps.

Rural Shade Steam Gristmill. Navarro County. Steam gristmill built in 1870 to grind grain raised by local farmers; said to have been first steam gristmill in area.

Rush Irrigation System. Chambers County. Series of rice irrigation ditches constructed early in twentieth century by C. C. Rush with a large cable-drawn plow.

Rusk Transportation Company Tram Line. Cherokee County. Primitive donkey-drawn tram railway line constructed in mid-1870s to connect Rusk with Jacksonville.

Ruthvan Gristmill and Cotton Gin. Hidalgo County. Gristmill and cotton gin erected by Ed Ruthvan at Run community in 1901.

Sabinal Waterworks. Uvalde County. Water system for Sabinal built in 1906; took original supply from wells equipped with steam pumps and used wire-wrapped wooden mains.

Sabine and Neches Valley Railway. Jefferson, Newton, and Orange counties. Railway chartered in 1921 and built from Beaumont to Deweyville primarily to carry lumber products.

Sabine Bank Lighthouse. Jefferson County. Lighthouse fourteen miles off Sabine Pass in Gulf of Mexico erected in 1906 as only lighthouse in United States supported by caisson sunk in open sea.

Sabine-Neches Waterway and the Sabine Pass Ship Channel. Jefferson and Orange counties. Deepwater vessel waterway dredged from mouth of Sabine River at Sabine Pass up the Sabine to Port Arthur and Orange and up the Neches to Beaumont; first opened in 1890s and later expanded, deepened, and widened.

Sabine Pass Harbor Improvements. Jefferson County. Efforts beginning in 1890s to remove sandbar at mouth of Sabine River on Gulf of Mexico to permit entrance of oceangoing vessels.

St. Louis, Brownsville and Mexico Railway. Along Gulf Coastal Plain from Lower Rio Grande Valley via Corpus Christi to Houston. Railway chartered in 1903 and by 1905 linked Lower Rio Grande Valley with remainder of the state; eventually reached Houston.

St. Louis, San Francisco and Texas Railway. Grayson County. Railway chartered in 1900 to build short distance from Denison to Red River to link with Frisco system; after 1903 all Frisco properties in Texas operated under this company's name.

St. Louis Southwestern Railway of Texas. Network covering much of north-central and East Texas. Entered Texas in 1871 and became known under present name in 1891; over six hundred miles of track in Texas by 1945.

St. Mary's of Aransas Harbor Improvements. Refugio County. Wharves and other dock facilities constructed at St. Mary's of Aransas from 1850s to 1880s.

Salatral Acequia. El Paso County. Community irrigation ditch in El Paso valley dug prior to 1850; in 1914 almost five miles long, twelve feet wide, and carrying seventy cubic feet of water per second.

Salt Creek Gristmill. Young County. Gristmill constructed west of Graham on Salt Creek in 1870s; grinding stone remains intact.

Salt Fork of the Red River Highway Bridge. Collingsworth County. Wooden highway bridge at the current U.S. 83 crossing of the Salt Fork of the Red River; site of a June 11, 1933, automobile accident involving the Clyde Barrow gang of bank robbers.

San Angelo Army Airfield. Tom Green County. Airfield established in 1942 as Army Air Corps bombardier school specializing in use of Norden bombsights and in dead-reckoning navigation.

San Angelo Ice Plant. Tom Green County. Ice factory begun at San Angelo by J. L. Millspaugh in 1884.

San Angelo Sewage Treatment Plant. Tom Green County. Sewage treatment plant for San Angelo at which Henry E. Elrod in 1919 innovatively converted septic tank into aeration tank for activated-sludge treatment of 250,000 gallons of sewage daily.

San Angelo Street Railways. Tom Green County. Electric street railway system constructed about 1905 to serve San Angelo; some tracks remain in place.

San Angelo Waterworks. Tom Green County. Water system built in 1884 to serve San Angelo; pumped supply directly from North Concho River.

* *San Antonio Acequias.* Bexar County. Spanish colonial ditch irrigation systems, which have served San Antonio since eighteenth century; listed on National Register of Historic Places.

San Antonio and Aransas Pass Railway. Lines from San Antonio south to Lower Rio Grande Valley, north to Kerrville and Waco, and east to Houston. Railway chartered in 1884; built first from San Antonio to Corpus Christi, and later extended to the Lower Rio Grande Valley, Kerrville, Waco, and Houston.

San Antonio and Gulf Shore Railway. Bexar, De Witt, Gonzales, and Wilson counties. Railway chartered in 1893 to build from San Antonio to Velasco, but only built to LaVernia; purchased by Southern Pacific in 1897, and later extended to Cuero.

San Antonio and Mexican Gulf Railway. Bee, Calhoun, De Witt, Goliad, and Victoria counties. Railway chartered in 1850 and by 1861 built from Port Lavaca to Victoria; extended to Cuero in 1871 before purchase by Southern Pacific about 1880; extended from Victoria to Beeville in 1889.

San Antonio Arsenal. Bexar County. Arsenal established in 1858 to furnish arms and ammunition to U.S. Army troops; still in operation.

San Antonio Belt and Terminal Railway. Bexar County. Railway chartered in 1912 to construct terminal and industrial tracks to serve San Antonio.

San Antonio Drilled Pier Foundations. Bexar County. Sites where modern methods of drilled pier foundation construction developed in 1920s.

San Antonio Gasworks. Bexar County. Mid-nineteenth-century gas system that manufactured and distributed artificially produced gas for home use and street lighting within San Antonio.

San Antonio Lime Kilns. Bexar County. Stone lime kilns constructed near San Antonio about 1880; consist of one large chamber with dome and one small chamber.

* *San Antonio Sewerage System.* Bexar County. One of oldest wastewater treatment sytems in Texas; notable for early and continued successful use of broad irrigation as means of disposing of excess effluent.

San Antonio Street Railways. Bexar County. System of animal- and later electric-powered street railways beginning operation in 1878 to provide urban transportation in San Antonio.

San Antonio, Uvalde and Gulf Railroad. Atascosa, Bexar, La Salle, Live Oak, McMullen, Nueces, San Patricio, Uvalde, and Zavala counties. Railroad chartered in 1909 and built first from Uvalde to Crystal City, with later extensions from Crystal City to Bexar County and thence southeastward to Corpus Christi; purchased by Missouri Pacific Railroad in 1925.

* *San Antonio Waterworks.* Bexar County. Waterworks established in 1877 to serve San Antonio; retains many fine nineteenth-century structures.

San Augustine Electric Power Plant. San Augustine County. Electric power plant built to serve town of San Augustine about 1910.

San Benito and Rio Grande Valley Railway. Cameron, Hidalgo, and Starr counties. Railway initially chartered in 1912 to build street railways in Brownsville; given additional charter later to construct railroad lines through much of Lower Rio Grande Valley.

San Benito Water and Electric Plant. Cameron County. Combined waterworks and electric power plant built to serve San Benito in 1910; capacity for serving at least fifty-eight hundred consumers.

San Diego and Gulf Railway. Duval County. Railway chartered in 1929 and built three miles from sulfur deposit at Palangana to Texas Mexican Railway at Byram.

Sandies Creek Iron Truss Bridge. Gonzales County. Iron truss bridge with timber approaches erected in 1897 across Sandies Creek, about nine miles east of Nixon.

Sandusky Survey of the City of Austin. Travis County. Initial survey for Austin, ordered by President Mirabeau B. Lamar of the Republic of Texas and prepared in 1839 by William Sandusky.

San Elizario Acequia. El Paso County. Largest community irrigation ditch system in El Paso valley; built originally about 1790 and purchased by U.S. Reclamation Service in 1917 to become part of Rio Grande Project.

San Esteban Dam. Presidio County. Pioneer Ambursen-type concrete dam four hundred feet long and sixty-eight feet high; erected between 1910 and 1911 to impound irrigation water on Alamito Creek, ten miles south of Marfa, for St. Stephens Land and Irrigation Company.

Sanford and Northern Railroad. Hutchinson County. Short-line railroad from Sanford to nearby gravel pits; recognized as common carrier in 1931 so it could participate in revenues on gravel it hauled.

San Gabriel River Iron Truss Bridge. Williamson County. Iron truss bridge erected in 1890 across San Gabriel River near Circleville by Berlin Iron Bridge Company, on present-day County Road 366.

* *San Jacinto Monument.* Harris County. Rarely considered an engineering work, one of most impressive construction projects ever undertaken in Texas.

San Jacinto Ordnance Depot. Harris County. Military ordnance depot established on Houston Ship Channel* in 1941 to receive, store, and inspect munitions; remained in operation until 1959.

San José Acequia. El Paso County. One of smallest community irrigation systems in El Paso valley; built prior to 1845; in 1914 eight-tenths of a mile long, four feet wide, and carrying six cubic feet of water per second.

* *San Marcos Activated Sludge Sewage Treatment Plant.* Hays County. In 1916, world's first activated sludge-type sewage treatment plant to serve an entire city.

* *San Marcos River Covered Bridge.* Gonzales County. Erected as toll bridge between 1854 and 1856; only covered wooden bridge in Texas from which substantial remains exist today.

San Marcos River Iron Truss Bridge near Gonzales. Gonzales County. Iron truss bridge erected in 1902 by E. P. Alsbury and Son for Gonzales County across San Marcos River near Gonzales to replace 1850s San Marcos River Covered Bridge.*

San Marcos Waterworks. Hays County. Waterworks constructed initially by private company in 1883 to pump water directly from San Marcos River for use by consumers in San Marcos.

San Saba Mission Irrigation System. Menard County. Irrigation system employing acequias built by Indian neophytes at San Saba Mission in 1760s; some remains still may be seen.

Santa Fe Dock and Channel Company Wharves. Galveston County. Extensive railway sidings and docks established at Port Bolivar in 1890s; removed in 1944.

Santa Fe Railway Colorado River Bridge. Mills and San Saba counties. Bridge erected about 1910 by Santa Fe Railway across Colorado River on its line between Lometa and San Saba.

Santa Fe Railway Gainesville Depot. Cooke County. Red brick railway passenger station erected by Santa Fe Railway at Gainesville about 1906.

Santa Fe Railway Trinity River Bridge. Garvin County, Oklahoma. Through truss iron bridge originally erected by Santa Fe Railway over Trinity River at Fort Worth in 1880s; disassembled and moved to Garvin County in 1902.

Santa Rita No. 1 Oil Well. Reagan County. Discovery well (1923) that opened production on University of Texas lands in western Texas as well as in the important Big Lake Oil Field.

Santa Rosa Dam. Wilbarger County. Earth fill dam across Beaver Creek fifteen miles south of Vernon; constructed in 1929 to impound water for irrigation, domestic use, and oil field operations.

San Xavier Missions Irrigation Systems. Milam County. Systems of acequias that in 1750s carried water from diversion dam on San Gabriel River to fields at three Spanish colonial missions.

Saratoga Oil Field. Hardin County. Oil field discovered in Hardin County in 1901, after success at Spindletop prompted drilling in similar salt dome formations.

Schulenburg Cotton Compress. Fayette County. Cotton compress established at Schulenburg in 1887; operated until after World War II; now used to house factory that manufactures oil field equipment.

Seguin Hydroelectric Plant. Guadalupe County. Earth fill dam with concrete spillway and hydro-electric-generation station; constructed on Guadalupe River near Seguin by Texas Power Corporation between 1930 and 1932.

Seguin Waterworks. Guadalupe County. Waterworks serving Seguin; initially built by private company between 1886 and 1887 to supply consumers with water pumped directly from Guadalupe River.

* Shafter Mining District. Presidio County. Mining district (discovered 1880) providing most consistent silver production in Texas history; listed on National Register of Historic Places.

Sharon Ridge and Ira Oil Field Air Pumps. Scurry County. Unusual pneumatic oil well pumping units, which operated using natural nontoxic underground gas from 1920s to 1960s.

Sheldon Dam. Harris County. Series of earthen embankments with concrete spillway; constructed between 1942 and 1943, about two miles southwest of Sheldon on Carpenters Bayou, as off-channel storage reservoir for excess waters from San Jacinto River to provide water to essential industries at Houston during World War II.

Sheppard Field. Wichita County. Airfield opened in 1941 as basic training center and technical school for Army Air Corps; became Sheppard Air Force Base.

Sherman Activated Sludge Sewage Treatment Plant. Grayson County. Activated sludge sewage treatment plant completed at Sherman in 1920; noted as one of pioneer activated sludge facilities in United States.

Sherman, Denison and Dallas Railway. Grayson County. Railway chartered in 1890 as subsidiary of Missouri, Kansas and Texas Railroad and built from Sherman to Denison.

Sherman Waterworks. Grayson County. Waterworks for Sherman begun about 1888, secured water from gang wells pumped by Worthington pump into a standpipe and directly into mains.

Shiner Iron Truss Bridge. Lavaca County. Iron truss bridge erected across Rocky Creek on southwest side of Shiner in 1914.

Shreveport, Houston and Gulf Railroad. Angelina County. Logging railroad chartered in 1906 and built six miles to connect Manning with Prestidge.

Slaton Irrigation Well. Hale County. One of pioneer irrigation wells in Hale County; drilled in 1911 about four miles west of Plainview.

* Slayden Bridge. Gonzales County. Iron truss bridge spanning the San Marcos River near Slayden; first erected in 1898 and then rebuilt in 1907; remains in service.

Slayden-Kirksey Woolen Mill. McLennan County. Established at Waco about 1885, most successful Texas textile mill from years before the turn of the century.

Smith's Landing. Marion County. Steamboat port on Big Cypress Bayou 6.5 miles below present-day Jefferson; operated at least at early as 1832, and at one time considered the head of steam navigation on bayou.

Smothers Creek Iron Truss Bridge. Lavaca County. Iron truss bridge erected across Smothers Creek about two miles north of Worthing in 1890s.

Snyder Railway Water System. Scurry County. System for providing water to steam locomotives; constructed by Santa Fe Railway at Snyder about 1910; consisted of well, steam pump, boiler, pump house, and cylindrical steel standpipe.

Socorro Acequia. El Paso County. Built prior to 1790; one of the oldest community irrigation ditch systems in the El Paso valley; in 1914 6.5 miles long, 12 feet wide, and carrying eighty cubic feet of water per second.

* Somerville Tie and Timber Preserving Plant. Burleson County. Facilities for treatment of wooden timbers with preservatives for Santa Fe Railway; use dat-

ing from 1890s and continuing in operation.

Sour Lake Oil Field. Hardin County. Site of significant oil discoveries in 1901 and 1902, after successes in similar salt dome geological structures at Spindletop.

Southern Pacific Grain Elevator. Galveston County. Massive grain elevator complex erected at Galveston by Southern Pacific Company between 1900 and 1903; noted both for size and use of innovative machinery.

Southern Pacific Railroad. Network covering Texas from Sabine River to El Paso. Railway system starting with Buffalo Bayou, Brazos and Colorado Railway, the first railroad in Texas; by 1945 contained over thirty-two hundred miles of main line track.

Southern Pacific Railroad Horseshoe Curve. Hudspeth County. Horseshoe curve on Southern Pacific Railroad laid out and built during initial construction of route across Texas in 1881.

Southern Pacific Terminal Railway. Galveston County. Railway chartered in 1901 to construct sidings and railway loading facilities to serve docks at Galveston.

South Galveston and Gulf Shore Railroad. Galveston County. Railroad chartered in 1891 to build from Galveston to west end of Galveston Island; actually constructed only about four miles before being abandoned in 1896.

Southland Paper Mill. Angelina County. Paper mill established at Lufkin in 1939 to produce newsprint from loblolly and short-leaf southern pines.

South Plains Army Airfield. Lubbock County. World War II glider pilot training facility that operated from 1941 to 1945; now site of Lubbock Regional Airport.

Southwestern Railway. Archer and Clay counties. Railway chartered in 1907 and built thirty miles from Henrietta to Archer City; operated until 1921.

Southwest Pump Factory. Fannin County. Site of gasoline service station pump manufacture since establishment of factory in 1916.

Spindletop Oil Field. Jefferson County. Opened in 1901 with discovery at Lucas Gusher;* first major oil field west of Mississippi River and site of first large oil boom in Texas.

Squaw Creek Highway Bridge. Somervell County. Steel truss highway bridge erected across Squaw Creek east of Glen Rose in 1922.

Stamford and Northwestern Railway. Dickens, Haskell, Jones, Kent, and Stonewall counties. Railway chartered in 1909 and built from Stamford to Spur.

Stamford Cottonseed Oil Mill. Jones County. One of first cottonseed oil mills in West Texas; erected in 1905 and still containing much of its early twentieth-century equipment.

Standard Mine. Uvalde County. Bitumen mine founded near Cline by Standard Mining Company in 1889; intermittent operation since that time.

Stant-Rhea Stage Stand. Hale County. Stagecoach station on Amarillo-Estacado stage line between Lubbock and Plainview; operated from 1901 to 1907.

Star and Crescent Iron Furnace. Cherokee County. One of two iron furnaces begun at New Birmingham in late 1880s and operated into early 1890s.

Star Mill. Williamson County. Gristmill constructed by Christopher Gillett and David McFadin about 1857 on south bank of San Gabriel River near present-day Circleville.

Steen Saltworks. Smith County. Saltworks at present-day Lindale where substantial quantities of salt were produced from 1850 to 1865 from brine secured from wells and evaporated in open vats.

Stephens County Carbon Black Plants. Stephens County. Three installations erected in Stephens County in 1923 to burn residue gas from petroleum refineries to produce carbon black; noted as earliest carbon black plants in Texas.

Stephenson's Ferry. Bowie County. Ferry begun at Sulphur River by Joseph A. Stephenson about 1888; in use until about 1910.

Stephenville North and South Texas Railway. Erath and Hamilton counties. Railway chartered in 1907 to connect Stephenville with St. Louis Southwestern Railway and built from Stephenville to Hamilton.

Sterling Creek Iron Truss Bridge. Sterling County. Iron truss bridge across Sterling Creek near Sterling City erected by El Paso Bridge and Iron Company for Sterling County about 1913.

Steward's Mill. Freestone County. Gristmill established at present-day Stewards Mill by J. T. Steward in 1850s.

Straugh Homemade Windmill. Refugio County. Homemade windmill erected by George Straugh at Refugio about 1911 for decorative purposes on lawn of his residence.

Straw Bridge of the Red River. Hardeman County. Straw and sand "causeway" across Red River built by local settlers in 1890s and operated as toll bridge.

Straw's Mill. Coryell County. Flour mill and cotton gin established by Fenno Straw and sons in 1870; destroyed by flood in 1906.

Study Butte Mines. Brewster County. Mines established by Big Bend Cinnabar Mining Company about the turn of the century; produced quicksilver into 1940s.

Sublime Iron Truss Bridge. Lavaca County. Iron truss bridge erected across Honey Creek about two miles north of Sublime by King Iron Bridge Company for Lavaca County in 1889.

Sugar Land Railroad. Fort Bend County. Railroad chartered in 1893 and built to serve sugar plantations in Sugar Land vicinity.

Summers Mill. Bell County. Gristmill built on Salado Creek in 1860s; much-altered dam and mill building have survived.

Sun Petroleum Shipping Facilities. Jefferson County. Property at Sun, Texas, acquired by Sun Oil Company in 1917 and made into a terminal for railway tank cars, pipelines, and barges.

Sutton Sawmill. Nacogdoches County. Sawmill operated at Chireno between 1935 and 1955; considerable remains exist.

Swash Lighthouse. Matagorda County. Lighthouse constructed on Matagorda Bay in 1858 but destroyed during Civil War.

Sweetwater Army Airfield. Nolan County. Primary, secondary, and multi-engine flight training facility operated by Army Air Corps at Sweetwater from 1941 to 1945.

Sweetwater Dam. Nolan County. Rolled-earth dam across Bitter and Cottonwood creeks, six miles southeast of Sweetwater; constructed between 1928 and 1930 to impound water for Sweetwater waterworks.

Syrup Pan Water Control System. Dickens County. Collection system for surface runoff constructed near Spur about 1930 to store excess water for irrigation purposes.

Tarrant Field. Tarrant County. Military airfield established in 1942 for training bomber crews during World War II; in 1948 became Carswell Air Force Base.

Tassie Belle Iron Furnace. Cherokee County. One of two iron furnaces established at New Birmingham in late 1880s; operated into early 1890s.

Taylor, Bastrop and Houston Railway. Austin, Bastrop, Fayette, Harris, Waller, and Williamson counties. Railway begun in 1886 and by 1887 built from Taylor via Bastrop and La Grange to Boggy Tank near Houston; became part of Missouri, Kansas and Texas Railroad system.

Taylor Cotton Compress. Williamson County. Cotton compress built at Taylor in 1892; used steam-power equipment to compress cotton bales to smaller sizes for economy in shipment.

Taylor Waterworks. Williamson County. Waterworks begun at Taylor in 1882; supplied consumers with water pumped from San Gabriel River.

Telegraph Road. Harris, Montgomery, and Walker counties. Wagon road from Huntsville to Houston blazed at least as early as 1850s; name due to placement of Texas and Red River Telegraph Company lines on trees growing along route.

Temple-Northwestern Railway. Bell County. Railway planned in 1910 to connect Temple with Gatesville and Comanche, but only built five miles from Temple.

Temple Plywood Factory. Angelina County. Constructed in 1960s at Diboll; first plant in Texas to manufacture plywood from Texas trees.

Temple Waterworks. Bell County. Waterworks serving Temple; established by private company in 1884, and in 1890 site of dramatic standpipe failure.

* *Terlingua Mining District.* Brewster County. Several mines and refineries that made up one of the major quicksilver producing districts in United States from 1880s to 1940s.

Terrell Waterworks. Kaufman County. Waterworks for Terrell begun about 1889; secured initial supply from two large-diameter wells from which water pumped into a standpipe and directly into mains.

Texarkana Interlocking Railway Signal System. Bowie County. Interlocking railway signal system installed by Pneumatic Signal Company for Texas and Pacific Railway at Texarkana about 1903.

Texarkana Waterworks. Bowie County. Water system to serve Texarkana; established about 1890; used Worthington pump to elevate water into a standpipe.

Texas and Louisiana Railroad. Angelina County. Lumber tram railroad built from Lufkin into Angelina County timber lands; chartered in 1900 and built twenty miles by 1907.

Texas and New Orleans Railroad. Network serving much of Texas from Sabine River to extreme West Texas. Railway first chartered in 1856; as Southern Pacific subsidiary in 1934, purchased all railroads in Texas in which Southern Pacific Railroad owned controlling interest.

Texas and Pacific Railway. System stretching from Texarkana west to Sierra Blanca, just east of El Paso. Railway chartered in 1871, and by 1881 completed from Texarkana almost entirely across state to Sierra Blanca.

Texas and Sabine Valley Railway. Panola County. Railway chartered in 1892 and built just over two miles, from Carthage to Boren; acquired by Santa Fe Railway in 1897.

Texas, Arkansas and Louisiana Railway. Cass County. Railway built in 1897 to connect Atlanta with Kansas City Southern at Bloomburg.

Texas Calumet Copper Mines. Culberson County. Copper mines that operated in Guadalupe Mountains area in early 1930s; reportedly sent ores for refining at El Paso Smelter.*

Texas Central Railroad. Bosque, Callahan, Comanche, Eastland, Erath, Hill, Jones, McLennan, and Shackelford counties. Railway chartered in 1879 by owners of Houston and Texas Central Railway to build from Waco westward to Albany; later extended from Albany to Rotan and from DeLeon to Cross Plains.

Texas City Terminal Railway. Galveston County. Railway built in 1890s to serve docks and industrial districts at Texas City.

Texas Electric Railway. Collin, Dallas, Ellis, Grayson, Hill, McLennan, and Navarro counties. Electric interurban railway created by merger of Southern Traction Company with Texas Traction Company; by 1912 had built lines from Denison southward via Dallas and Fort Worth to Waco and Corsicana.

Texas Engineering Experiment Station. Brazos County. Research program established in 1914 at Texas A&M to foster industrial development in Texas through study of engineering problems.

* *Texas Gulf Intracoastal Waterway.* All Texas coastal counties from Jefferson on the northeast to Cameron on the south. Protected intracoastal waterway begun in 1913 and finally completed length of Texas coast in 1949.

Texas, Louisiana and Eastern Railroad. Hardin, Liberty, and Montgomery counties. Railway chartered in 1891 by Gulf, Colorado and Santa Fe Railway and built to connect Conroe with East Texas forests as far east as Silsbee, thus giving the Santa Fe a link from Beaumont to its main line at Somerville.

Texas-Mexican Railway. Duval, Jim Hogg, Jim Wells, Nueces, and Webb counties. Railway chartered originally in 1875, with new charter issued in 1881, and built from Corpus Christi via San Diego to Laredo.

Texas-Midland Railroad. Delta, Ellis, Hunt, Kaufman, and Lamar counties. Railroad initially built by Houston and Texas Central Railroad between 1882 and 1885; sold in 1893 to become Texas-Midland Railroad, which completed the line between Paris and Ennis.

Texas–New Mexico Railway. Ward and Winkler counties. Railway chartered in 1927, and by 1929 constructed from Monahans to Lovington, New Mexico.

Texas Power and Light Company Waco–Fort Worth High Tension Line. Hill, Johnson, McLennan, and Tarrant counties. Erected in 1913, pioneer long-distance, high-tension electric transmission line in Texas.

Texas Power and Light Company Waco Generating Station. McLennan County. Electricity generating station built in 1914 to replace earlier facility; produced electricity until 1974.

Texas, Sabine Valley and Northwestern Railway. Panola County. Railway chartered in 1892 and built fifteen miles from Carthage to Martin's Creek; acquired by Santa Fe Railway in 1897.

Texas Short Line Railway. Van Zandt and Wood counties. Railway chartered in 1901, and in 1902 built ten miles from Grand Saline to Alba to serve coal mines; sold to Texas and Pacific Railway in 1929 and extended ten miles to reach developing oil fields.

Texas Southeastern Railroad. Angelina and Trinity counties. Railroad chartered in 1900 and built to connect Blix with Diboll and later with Lufkin and Vair; just over twenty miles of track.

Texas State Fairgrounds Livestock Building. Dallas County. Livestock pavilion with innovative arched roof; erected in 1911 at Texas State Fairgrounds in Dallas.

Texas State Railroad. Anderson and Cherokee counties. Railroad initially built in 1896 to serve only Old Alcalde Iron Furnace* at Rusk State Penitentiary; later extended as a common carrier to connect Rusk and Palestine; now operated as historic steam railway by Texas Parks and Wildlife Department.

Texas Transportation Company Railroad. Harris County. Railroad initially chartered in 1866 but not built until 1876, when rails laid from Houston to Clinton; purchased by Texas and New Orleans Railroad in 1896.

Texas Western Narrow-Gauge Railroad. Harris and Waller counties. Narrow-gauge railroad chartered in 1875 and by 1877 built from Houston to Pattison; abandoned in 1899.

Texas Western Railroad. Harrison County. Railroad chartered in 1852; by start of Civil War, built twenty miles east from Marshall.

Thermo Brick Plant. Hopkins County. Brickyard established in 1910 on Louisiana, Arkansas and Texas Railroad at present-day Thermo.

Thicket Sawmill. Hardin County. Sawmill built at present-day Thicket by Brown-Williams Lumber Company in 1909; operated until 1920.

Thompson's Ferry. Fort Bend County. Ferry across Brazos River three miles northwest of Richmond; operated by Jesse Thompson from 1830 to 1847.

Thorp Spring Cotton Gin. Hood County. Cotton gin established at present-day Thorp Spring by Capt. Sam Millikin in 1871.

*Thurber Mining District. Erath County. Site of underground coal mining from 1880s to 1920s; today a ghost town; listed on National Register of Historic Places.

Tilmon's Mill. Caldwell County. Mill established on tributary of the San Marcos River before Civil War at present-day Tilmon; made molasses from cane grown along creek bottoms.

Tin Top Suspension Bridge. Parker County. Suspension bridge spanning Brazos River; erected by Parker County in 1906 and destroyed during a winter storm in 1982.

Tivoli Waterworks. Refugio County. Waterworks constructed in 1913 by Preston R. Austin; secured water from cotton gin well and later from two additional artesian wells.

Tomball Cotton Gin and Press. Harris County. Cotton gin and screw press that received motive power from horses; constructed in 1840s.

Torbert Railway Water System. Hudspeth County. Turn-of-the-century steam locomotive water system for Southern Pacific Railroad at Torbert; drew water from a well 1,165 feet deep.

Torres Irrigation Works. Pecos County. Mid-nineteenth-century ditch irrigation system along Pecos River constructed and operated by Torres Irrigation and Manufacturing Company.

Towash Dam. Hill County. Stone dam built in 1855 by Simpson C. Dyer to operate gristmill at Towash; reputedly first dam across Brazos River.

Towns' Mill. Williamson County. Gristmill erected by Jim Towns in 1870s, about seven miles northeast of Georgetown.

Toyah Artesian Wells. Reeves County. Numerous artesian wells, some of them drilled as early as 1890s,

which provided water to residents in the Toyah area.

Toyah Railway Water System. Reeves County. Artesian well sunk 832 feet in 1882 by Texas and Pacific Railway which provided water that was unsatisfactory for use in steam locomotives but that could be used for station supply.

Toyah Waterworks. Reeves County. Municipal waterworks serving Toyah since 1934; supply obtained from drilled wells.

TP-1 Dam and Dunlap Hydroelectric Plant. Comal County. Earth fill dam with a concrete core built by Texas Power Corporation between 1927 and 1928 on Guadalupe River for generation of electricity in adjacent Dunlap power plant.

TP-3 Dam and McQueeney Hydroelectric Plant. Guadalupe County. Earth fill dam with concrete core and spillway constructed on Guadalupe River five miles west of Seguin by Texas Power Corporation between 1927 and 1928 for generation of electricity at adjacent McQueeney power plant.

Trinidad Dam. Henderson County. Earthen dam or embankment twelve thousand feet long on an unnamed slough off Trinity River, two miles south of Trinidad; built in 1925 to impound water for cooling electric power-generating station.

Trinity and Brazos Valley Railway. Ellis, Freestone, Grimes, Harris, Hill, Johnson, Leon, Limestone, Madison, Montgomery, and Navarro counties. Railway chartered in 1902 to build from Fort Worth to Houston; actually constructed from Cleburne to Houston, with branch from Teague to Waxahachie; became Burlington–Rock Island Railroad in 1930.

*Trinity and Brazos Valley Railway Depot and Office Building. Johnson County. Erected in 1903 as offices and depot for Trinity and Brazos Valley Railway in Cleburne; today one of last structures remaining from this railroad.

Trinity and Sabine Railway. Polk, Trinity, and Tyler counties. Railway chartered in 1881 and within a year built thirty-eight miles eastward from Trinity; purchased by Missouri, Kansas and Texas Railroad and eventually extended to Colmesneil.

Trinity River Irrigation District Levee. Chambers County. Earthen levee constructed about 1914 to convert portion of Turtle Bay into reservoir for storing rice irrigation water near Anahuac; destroyed in 1951.

Trinity River Locks. Houston County. One of several sets of locks constructed on Trinity River about 1910 in the effort to develop it for barge traffic.

Trinity River Navigation Projects. From Fort Worth

and Dallas down the Trinity River to its mouth. Efforts from mid-nineteenth century to the present to make river navigable for barges.

Trinity Valley and Northern Railway. Liberty County. Railway chartered in 1906 by Dayton Lumber Company and built ten miles, from Dayton to Lumm.

Trinity Valley Southern Railroad. San Jacinto and Walker counties. Railroad chartered in 1899 and constructed six miles from Oakhurst to Dodge; abandoned in 1936.

Trotti Logging Camp. Newton County. Lumber camp established near Newton in 1898; noted for successful use of steam locomotives for hauling timber.

Trueheart Ditch. Bexar County. Late nineteenth- and early twentieth-century ditch irrigation system constructed on south side of San Antonio.

Tulia Waterworks. Swisher County. Waterworks started at Tulia early in this century; took supply from local drilled wells.

Turpentine Camp and Distillery. Jasper County. Turpentine camp and distillery established by Western Naval Stores Company at Turpentine in 1907; operated until 1918.

Tyler Gun Factory. Smith County. Factory built in Tyler to manufacture percussion firearms prior to Civil War; purchased by Confederate government in 1863 to make firearms of British and Austrian design.

* Tyler Hydraulic Fill Dam. Smith County. Built in 1894; probably the most significant hydraulic fill dam erected in Texas; listed on National Register of Historic Places.

Tyler Waterworks. Smith County. Waterworks established for Tyler by private company in 1883; site in 1894 of Tyler Hydraulic Fill Dam.*

Tyron Sawmill. Hardin County. Sawmill built on Sabine and East Texas Railroad in Olive vicinity by Joseph M. Tyron in 1881.

Uden Brewery. Marion County. Founded near Jefferson by U. B. Uden about 1870; one of pioneer breweries in Texas.

Umbarger Dam. Randall County. Rolled-earth dam with concrete ogee spillway constructed by U.S. Farm Security Administration in 1938 on Tierra Blanca Creek, about two miles south of Umbarger, for recreation and wildlife conservation.

Underwriters Production and Refining Company T. and P.-Abrams No. 1 Oil Well. Mitchell County. Discovery well (July 16, 1920) for Permian Basin Oil Field of West Texas.

U.S.S. Cavalla. Galveston County. Submarine constructed for U.S. Navy by the Electric Boat Company of Groton, Connecticut, in 1943; decommissioned in 1963; now preserved in Galveston.

Upper Pine Springs Pump Station. Culberson County. Historic ranch water system constructed in present-day Guadalupe Mountains National Park; pumped water for livestock to considerable elevations into mountains.

Upper Ponton Creek Iron Truss Bridge. Lavaca County. Iron truss bridge erected in 1889 across Ponton Creek, about five miles north of Shiner, by King Iron Bridge Company, under contract to Lavaca County.

Uvalde and Northern Railroad. Real and Uvalde counties. Chartered in 1914 and built thirty-seven miles between Uvalde and Camp Wood; abandoned in 1942.

Uvalde Waterworks. Uvalde County. Water system established late in nineteenth century to serve Uvalde; took original supply from wells pumped by wood-fired boiler and steam pump; pump pit remains today.

Valentine Railway Water System. Jeff Davis County. Division point on Texas and New Orleans Railway where in 1882 a deep well was drilled to provide steam locomotive boiler water.

Valley Mills Railroad Cut. Bosque County. Excavated "cut" made in 1880s through a hill on route of Gulf, Colorado and Santa Fe Railway near Valley Mills; said to have been deepest such excavation in Texas in its day.

Van Horn Railway Water Wells. Culberson County. Group of four wells, each six hundred feet deep, drilled by Texas and Pacific Railway at Van Horn in 1886 to provide water for its steam locomotives.

Van Oil Field. Van Zandt County. Oil field opened in 1929 by several major petroleum companies working together to maintain underground oil pressure for natural flow of wells.

Varner Sugar Mill. Brazoria County. Remains of sugar mill operated at Varner Plantation north of West Columbia; erected in 1846 and severely damaged in 1900.

* Vaughn Brothers Irrigation Plant. Swisher County. Irrigation well drilled just south of Tulia in 1914 and equipped with Layne and Bowler pump and Primm oil-burning engine.

Vernon Waterworks. Wilbarger County. Water system built for Vernon in 1909; took supply from

307

springs and wells.

Victoria "Dutch" Windmill. Victoria County. Erected in 1870 by two German immigrants; last surviving nineteenth-century European-style windmill in Texas; listed on National Register of Historic Places.

Victoria Waterworks. Victoria County. Waterworks begun by municipal government in 1885 to serve citizens of Victoria.

Victory Field. Wilbarger County. Army Air Corps primary flight training facility established at Vernon in 1941 and operated until 1944.

Vidor Logging Camp. Orange County. Lumber camp established at present-day Vidor by Miller-Vidor Company in 1907; operated until facility was moved to Lakeview in 1920.

Vidor Plant of the Beaumont Brick Works. Orange County. Brickyard belonging to Beaumont Brick Works, which manufactured brick at Vidor from 1918 to 1929.

Vienna Iron Truss Bridge. Lavaca County. Iron truss bridge erected across Navidad River one mile east of Vienna in 1890s.

Village Mills Sawmill. Hardin County. Sawmill established at present-day Village Mills by Village Mills Company in 1882; sold to Kirby Lumber Company in 1902 and operated by them until abandonment in 1931.

Vince's Bridge. Harris County. Timber bridge across Vince's Bayou destroyed on April 21, 1836, by Erastus "Deaf" Smith to prevent orderly retreat of Mexican soldiers in Battle of San Jacinto.

Vogel Lignite Mine. Milam County. Lignite coal mine established by William Vogel near Rockdale in 1888 and served by spur of International and Great Northern Railroad until 1920s, when abandoned.

Voth Sawmills. Jefferson County. Sawmill built by Keith Lumber Company in 1902 at Voth for soft wood; second mill for hardwood varieties added in 1924.

Waco and Northwestern Railroad. Falls, McLennan, and Robertson counties. Railroad chartered in 1866 but not constructed until 1872, when built from Bremond via Waco to Ross; acquired by Houston and Texas Central Railway in 1898.

Waco Army Airfield. McLennan County. Army Air Corps flight training school opened on May 5, 1942; became flight instructors' school in 1945; later became Connally Air Force Base.

Waco Gas System. McLennan County. System to manufacture and distribute gas to consumers in Waco

begun in late nineteenth century; about 1916, included innovative welded gas pipeline beneath Brazos River.

Waco Ice Plant. McLennan County. Facility for manufacture of ice started in Waco by S. A. Owens, J. E. Sears, George T. Coats, and A. Muhl in 1869.

Waco Suspension Bridge. McLennan County. Erected between 1868 and 1869 and used by vehicular traffic for over a century; first bridge to span Brazos River and first major suspension bridge in Texas; listed on National Register of Historic Places.

Waco Waterworks. McLennan County. Waterworks established by private company in 1878 to serve citizens of Waco; purchased by city administration in 1904.

Walling Gin. Cottle County. Cotton gin established about 1900 around which community of Ginsite grew.

Warren and Corsicana Pacific Railroad. Tyler County. Railroad chartered in 1899 and built from Warren to Camp Wood; abandoned in 1908.

Warren Central Railroad. Harris County. Railway constructed in 1930 from Missouri, Kansas and Texas Railroad near Houston twelve miles to serve a salt mine; abandoned in 1935.

Washburn Elevator. Armstrong County. Wooden grain elevator erected at Washburn about the turn of the century.

Washington County Railroad. Washington County. Railroad chartered in 1856 by Washington County residents, and built from Hempstead to Brenham by 1860; purchased by Houston and Texas Central Railway in 1869.

Waxahachie Creek Bridge. Ellis County. Built across Waxahachie Creek on South Rogers Street in Waxahachie in 1889; classic example of iron bridges purchased by Texas counties a century ago; located in a district listed on the National Register of Historic Places.

Waxahachie Tap Railroad. Ellis County. Railroad chartered in 1876 to build from Waxahachie to main line of Houston and Texas Central Railway near Ennis.

Weatherford, Mineral Wells and Northwestern Railway. Palo Pinto and Parker counties. Railway chartered in 1899 and by 1901 built from Weatherford to Mineral Wells; purchased by Texas and Pacific Railway in 1902, and in 1909 extended to Graford.

Weatherford Waterworks. Parker County. Waterworks founded to serve Weatherford about 1888;

took original supply from large well with radiating tunnels at its base.

Weldon Irrigation System. Kimble County. Irrigation system built by I. O. Weldon near Roosevelt about the turn of the century; included small diversion dam, ditches, and several flumes.

Wellington Waterworks. Collingsworth County. Water system built to serve Wellington in 1916; used water secured from local wells.

Wenasco Turpentine Camp. Jasper County. Turpentine camp established in 1915 by Western Naval Stores Company and operated until 1919.

Wesley Chapel Steel Truss Highway Bridge. Erath County. Steel truss highway bridge erected across South Paluxy River at Wesley Chapel community in 1921.

West Columbia Oil Field. Brazoria County. Oil field opened in 1918 with discovery at Tyndall-Hogg No. 2 Hogg Oil Well; peak production in 1921 and 1938.

West of the Pecos Railroad Construction Camps Historic District. Val Verde County. Eleven construction camps from which archeological remains exist from building of Southern Pacific Railroad line west of the Pecos between 1880 and 1883.

West Willingham Street Bridge. Johnson County. Steel and concrete bridge spanning West Buffalo Creek at West Willingham Street in Cleburne; erected by Missouri Valley Bridge and Iron Company in 1916.

White Rock Creek Interurban Bridge. Dallas County. Innovative reinforced-concrete girder bridge built about 1914 to carry interurban railway traffic across White Rock Creek in Dallas.

White Rock Dam. Dallas County. Earthen dam across White Rock Creek constructed between 1910 and 1911 to impound water for Dallas waterworks.

Whitesmine Asphalt Mine. Uvalde County. Bitumen mine opened by Lathe Carbon Company in 1888; closed in 1900, only to be reopened in 1913 and operated until 1930.

Whitney Dam. Bosque and Hill counties. Reinforced-concrete dam flanked by compacted earth embankments; constructed across Brazos River by U.S. Army Corps of Engineers between 1947 and 1950.

Whitney Waterworks. Hill County. Waterworks serving Whitney begun about 1912 with installation of pumps to elevate water from drilled wells.

Wichita Falls and Northwestern Railway. Wichita County. Railway chartered in 1906 and within a year

built to Red River and on to Forgan, Oklahoma.

Wichita Falls and Oklahoma Railway. Clay and Wichita counties. Railway chartered in 1903 and built from Wichita Falls to Byers and then across Red River to Waurika, Oklahoma.

Wichita Falls and Southern Railway. Archer, Stephens, Wichita, and Young counties. Railway chartered in 1907, and by 1911 built from Wichita Falls to Newcastle; extended to Jimkurn in 1920.

Wichita Falls and Wellington Railway. Collingsworth County. Railway built in 1910 from Oklahoma to Wellington in Collingsworth County.

Wichita Falls Railway. Clay and Wichita counties. Railway chartered in 1894 by Wichita Falls investors and built to connect with Missouri, Kansas and Texas Railroad at Henrietta.

Wichita Falls, Ranger and Fort Worth Railroad. Comanche, Eastland, Erath, and Stephens counties. Railroad chartered in 1919 and within a year built from Dublin to Breckenridge to give through service between Wichita Falls and Dublin.

Wichita Falls Waterworks. Wichita County. Waterworks begun in 1889 to serve Wichita Falls; took supply from man-made reservoir on a stream.

Wichita Valley Railroad. Baylor, Haskell, Jones and Knox counties. Railroad chartered in 1905, and by 1908 built from Seymour to Stamford.

Wichita Valley Railway. Archer, Baylor, and Wichita counties. Railway chartered in 1890, and in that year built from Wichita Falls to Seymour.

Wiergate Domestic Water Distillation System. Newton County. One of three systems in East Texas where in 1930s domestic water supply for residents of a town was distilled from water taken from log ponds.

Wiergate Sawmill. Newton County. Sawmill built in 1917 by Wier Long Leaf Lumber Company; served as a terminus for Gulf and Northern Railroad until abandonment of the mill in 1942.

William Harris Dam. Brazoria County. Rectangular earthen dam constructed by Dow Chemical Company eight miles southwest of Angleton between 1943 and 1947 to store pumped Brazos River water for industrial use.

*Williamson Dam. Eastland County. Built between 1920 and 1924; on completion, largest hollow concrete dam in world.

Wilson Utility Pottery Kilns. Guadalupe County. Pottery works operated from 1856 to 1903 about nine miles east of Seguin on present-day State Highway 466; listed on National Register of Historic Places.

Winters Sawmill and Gristmill. Hays County. Sawmill and gristmill built by William Winters on Blanco River in 1848, at present-day Wimberley.

Winters Waterworks. Runnels County. Waterworks begun in 1912 for Winters; took supply from both wells and man-made reservoir.

Witt's Steam Mill. Dallas County. Steam-powered gristmill established on Trinity River in 1853; gave rise to community of Trinity Mills.

Woodmyer Logging Camp. Newton County. Logging camp established at Woodmyer in 1911 by Kirby Lumber Company; produced approximately five million board feet of lumber monthly until its closing in 1918.

Woodsboro Waterworks. Refugio County. Waterworks to serve Woodsboro begun by a commercial club; in 1930 turned over to city for operation.

Wooten Wells Spa. Robertson County. Spa opened to public at Wooten Wells, site of a mineral water well drilled in 1883; within a decade included three hotels, bathhouses, cottages, and stores.

Worley Lignite Mine. Milam County. Lignite mine southeast of Rockdale operated by Alden I. Worley and served by spur of International and Great Northern Railroad until it closed in 1930.

Worley Windmill Irrigation System. Midland County. Water system installed by N. S. Worley on his property at Midland about 1900; used windmill to pump water from fifty-five-foot-deep well into earthen reservoir for storage until needed for vineyard irrigation.

XIT Ranch Barbed Wire Fence Telephone System. Oldham County. Telephone system using barbed wire fencing to convey messages as early as 1888.

X-Ray Natural Gas Field. Erath County. Natural gas field discovered near the X-Ray community in 1920.

Yankee Branch Iron Bridge. Williamson County. Small iron bridge with wooden decking spanning Yankee Branch west of Granger.

Yates Oil Field. Pecos County. One of the most spectacular oil fields in West Texas; discovered in 1926 and peaked in production in 1929.

* Yellowhouse Canyon Bridge. Lubbock County. Single span Warren truss bridge erected in 1913; perhaps oldest surviving engineered wagon bridge on Texas South Plains.

Yellowhouse Division Headquarters Windmill Tower. Hockley County. Erected in late nineteenth century; 126-foot-tall wooden tower that supported a windmill at Yellowhouse Division Headquarters of XIT Ranch until 1929.

Ysleta Acequia. El Paso County. Begun about 1681 by mission Indians from New Mexico; probably first European-style irrigation system built in Texas.

Zero Stone. Pecos County. Survey monument set in 1859 at Fort Stockton; beginning point for many surveys in Pecos County area.

Zodiac Mill. Gillespie County. Gristmill erected by members of a Mormon colony on Pedernales River near Fredericksburg in 1847; destroyed by flood in 1850.

Index

Sites listed alphabetically in the main entries and in the appendix are not included in the index unless they are mentioned in the description of another site.

Hoppe, Edward, 176
horses, 36, 62, 87, 89, 126, 163–64, 172, 232, 306
hospitals, 159, 174, 176
hotels, 49, 63, 196, 244, 248, 251, 275, 310
Houston, Tex., 61, 84, 121–24, 127–32, 135, 137, 145,
    147, 208, 223, 228, 233, 249–50, 255, 264, 274–75,
    282, 285–86, 288, 292, 294, 300, 302, 304–306, 308
Houston and Great Northern Railroad, 135, 208, 285,
    287
Houston and Texas Central Railway, 54–56, 62, 281,
    285–86, 305, 308
Houston Belt and Magnolia Park Railway, 286
Houston County, Tex., 271, 277, 285, 306
Houston Lighting and Power Company, 286
Houston Ship Channel, 130–32, 275, 286, 290, 294, 301
Houston Sports Center, 122
Houston Tap and Brazoria Railroad, 270, 286
Houston Water Works Company, 128–29
Howard, Thad, 286
Howard County, Tex., 271–72
Howard's Switch, Tex., 286
Howells, J. M., 253
Hoxie, J. R., 87
Hubbard Creek, 289
Hudspeth County, Tex., 270, 279, 281, 289, 303, 306
Hughes, Reese, 286
Hughes Springs, Tex., 286
Hughes Tool Company, 278
Humble Oil and Refining Company, 278
Humphrey Direct Action Pumping Plant, 133–35, 286,
    293
Humphrey Gas Pump Company, 133
Hundle, Louise, 185
Hunt, Jarvis, 64
Hunt County, Tex., 275–77, 279, 284, 290–92, 305
Hunter, R. D., 246–48
Huntsville, Tex., 5, 286, 304
hurricanes, 9, 43, 47, 92, 97–98, 122, 132, 157, 179,
    276, 278, 282, 296, 299; Carla in 1961, 146; at Corpus
    Christi in 1919, 44–45, 169; at Galveston in 1900,
    92–93, 97, 101–102, 107–108, 114, 188; at Gal-
    veston in 1915, 96, 110, 188; at Lavaca Bay, 146; and
    Padre Island beacon, 22–23
Hutchins, Robert M., 153
Hutchinson County, Tex., 274, 295, 301
Hyatt, Tex., 279
hydraulic-fill construction, 46–47, 95, 97–101, 147,
    252–55, 282, 288, 307
hydroelectric generation, 11–15, 24–26, 50–53, 115–
    16, 270, 274, 276, 277, 278, 279, 283, 285, 286–87,
    288, 291, 293, 294, 298, 302, 306
Hye, Tex., 286

ice manufacture, 176–77, 248–49, 274, 276, 282, 287,
    300, 308
Imperial, Tex., 286
independent oilmen, 59
Indian Creek, 253
Indianola, Tex., 157, 258, 286
Indian Point, 168
Indians: 17, 32, 69, 84, 136, 141, 178, 260, 270, 284,
    285, 293, 310

injuries, 126
Insull, Samuel, 24
insurance, 5–6, 79
International and Great Northern Railway, 208, 210,
    270–71, 276, 283, 285, 286, 287, 299, 308, 310
International Association of Granite Cutters, 118
International Boundary Commission, 290
International Creosote and Construction Company, 271
International Railroad, 135, 208, 287
International Steel and Iron Company, 43
International Water Company, 82
interurban railways, 40, 95, 271, 273, 281–82, 305, 309
Iowa Park, Tex., 287
iron. See cast iron; mining; smelting; wrought iron
iron pyrites, 117
irrigation systems, 17–20, 69–71, 80, 158–61, 215–18,
    255–57, 269–70, 271, 275, 276, 279, 280, 286, 288,
    292, 293, 297–99, 300, 304, 306, 307, 309; acequias,
    80, 210–14, 270, 287, 296, 300, 301, 302, 310; arte-
    sian, 296; canals, 90–92, 281, 284, 289; dams for,
    24–25, 273, 274, 286, 288, 296, 298, 301, 302; pumps
    for, 133–35, 286, 292, 293, 297; reservoirs for, 141,
    143, 285; for sewage, 215–18, 300; wells for, 272,
    281–82, 290, 291, 302; windmills for, 277, 283, 291,
    293, 310

Jack County, Tex., 284
jacks, 100, 107
Jackson, Ed, 289
Jackson, J. C., 279
Jackson County, Tex., 294
Jacksonville, Tex., 287, 299
Japanese Sunken Garden (Brackenridge Park), 4
Jasper County, Tex., 272, 274, 284, 287, 293–94, 307,
    309
Jeff Davis County, Tex., 83–85, 152–56, 280, 291, 299,
    307
Jefferson, Tex., 139, 151, 166–68, 279, 281, 287, 289,
    302, 307
Jefferson County, Tex., 149–52, 178–80, 271, 274, 279,
    284, 288, 290, 295, 297, 299–300, 303–305, 308
jetties, 102–105, 118, 131, 270, 282
Jim Hogg County, Tex., 45, 305
Jimkurn, Tex., 309
Jim Wells County, Tex., 45, 291, 305
Johnson, E. L., 287
Johnson, Horace G., 48, 50
Jonson, Lyndon B., 44, 121, 290
Johnson, William G., 13–14
Johnson, William Whipple, 246
Johnson, W. V., 279
Johnson City, Tex., 290
Johnson County, Tex., 36–39, 249–51, 275–77, 281,
    299, 305–306, 309
Johnson Iron Works, 175
Johnson's Mine, 246
Joiner, Columbus Marvin "Dad," 56–58
Joinerville, Tex., 59
Jonah, Tex., 280
Jones, G. W., 287
Jones County, Tex., 269–70, 281, 284, 290, 303, 305, 309
Jordan, John, 287